Air Force Officer's Guide

35th Edition

Col. Jeffrey C. Benton, USAF (Ret.)

STACKPOLE
BOOKS

0 11557 03452 3

Published by
STACKPOLE BOOKS
5067 Ritter Road
Mechanicsburg, PA 17055-6921
www.stackpolebooks.com

Continuously published and copyrighted since 1948 by The Military Service Publishing Company, Harrisburg, Pa. (1948–57), and Stackpole Books, Harrisburg, Pa. (1959–93), and Mechanicsburg, Pa. (1993–).
Thirty-fifth Edition.

Cover design by Wendy A. Reynolds

Printed in the U.S.A.

10 9 8 7 6 5 4 3 2

Library of Congress has cataloged this serial publication as follows:

Air Force officer's guide / by Jeffrey C. Benton
[Mechanicsburg, Pa.] Stackpole Books

     v.:ill.;23 cm.
     Began with: 23rd ed.
     Description based on: 26th ed.
     Continues: Air Force officer's guide.
  ISSN 0739-635X=Air Force officer's guide.

1. United States. Air Force—Officer's handbooks.

UG633.A1A49   358.4'00973—dc19   83-644873
                                   AACR2 MARC-S

35th Edition
ISBN: 978-0-8117-3452-3
ISBN: 0-8117-3452-8

Air Force Officer's Guide *is designed to help Air Force officers in their professional careers. The guide dates back to 1948, after the U.S. Air Force became independent of the U.S. Army. Its genesis, however, lies in the parent* Officer's Guide *(now* Army Officer's Guide, *in its 50th edition), which first appeared in 1930, and which since then has been an indispensable source of reference for hundreds of thousands of officers. Our hope is that this 35th edition of* Air Force Officer's Guide *will be an equally indispensable reference for you.*

Contents

The United States Air Force is an instrument available to the people of this republic for our common defense and for the advancement of the interests of the United States throughout the world. Insofar as the Air Force is strong, sharp, and ready, its existence tends to deter the potential aggressor, giving warning of swift punishment for the lawless. A great and historic interest of the American people lies in our desire for a world of peace and justice. The U.S. Air Force, through prompt and efficient completion of its assigned missions, can help ensure the arrival of that long-hoped-for day when all human beings may walk in freedom and in fear of none save God . . . or, by slipshod and indifferent performance on its part, the Air Force can cause the American people to lose what Abraham Lincoln called the last, best hope of earth. The issue is in the balance. You, as an officer of the U.S. Air Force, may tip the scales for better or for worse.

The U.S. Air Force seal bears the American bald eagle with wings elevated and displayed in front of a cloud.

The striking power of the Air Force is from above the clouds and is represented by the winged thunderbolt taken from the shield of Mars, which is placed above the cloudlike base represented by the nebular partition line and white background.

Thirteen stars surround the seal, and the Roman numerals MCMXLVII (1947) indicate the year of the Air Force's founding as a separate service.

The eagle is looking to the right, the field of honor.

A new U.S. Air Force symbol, developed and released in 2000 on a trial basis, was made official in 2004. The symbol is composed of common elements of Air Force identity. It is intended to bind airmen together, to capture the Air Force heritage, and to signify the service's aspirations for the future.

U.S. AIR FORCE

The Air Force symbol has two main parts.

In the upper half, the stylized wings represent the stripes of the Air Force's strength—the enlisted men and women of the force. The stripes are drawn with great angularity to emphasize swiftness and power, and they are divided into six sections which represent the Air Force's core competencies—aerospace superiority, global attack, rapid global mobility, precision engagement, information superiority, and agile combat support.

In the lower half, the sphere within the star represents the globe, which reminds us of our challenges as a worldwide expeditionary force. The star's five points represent the components of our force—our active duty, civilians, guard, reserve, and retirees. The star is framed with a diamond and two trapezoids, which represent the Air Force's Core Values—integrity first, service before self, and excellence in all we do.

The two elements come together to form one symbol that presents two powerful images—at once it is an eagle, the emblem of our nation, and a medal, representing valor in service to our nation.

Airmen may use the Air Force symbol on personal items. Although it will be used as a trademark on a variety of official marketing goods, it may not be used for unauthorized endorsements, retail sales, or advertisement without Air Force approval.

PART I

The Profession of Arms

1

The Professional Officer

OATH OF OFFICE

I, _____(name)_____, having been
appointed a _____(grade)_____, United States Air
Force, do solemnly swear (or affirm) that I will support and defend
the Constitution of the United States against all enemies, foreign
and domestic; that I will bear true faith and allegiance to the same;
that I take this obligation freely, without any mental reservation or
purpose of evasion; and that I will well and faithfully discharge
the duties of the office upon which I am about to enter, SO HELP
ME GOD.

The Air Force oath is essentially the same as that taken by American officers since George Washington. On taking the oath, young officers join a long
line of dedicated and talented officers in khaki, olive drab, and blue who have
gone before in upholding our nation's security. Their watchwords—Duty,
Honor, Country—do not belong to West Point alone.

Service as an Air Force officer is much more than a job. Officers are professionals whose duties are of great importance for the government and people
of the United States. If they accept their calling as professionals, the nation will
be well served.

THE LEARNED PROFESSIONS

There are several ways to think about the traditional learned professions: theology, the law, the various academic disciplines, and medicine. To one degree or
another, the learned professions govern themselves. In the United States, the
clergy is almost totally self-regulating; university-level teachers, physicians,
and attorneys are less so. The professions also can be thought of as service
organizations—the clergy to serve individuals' and society's spiritual needs,
teachers to help individuals develop their intellectual potential, attorneys to
help ensure justice for individuals and for society as a whole, and physicians to
cure physical injuries and disease. Professions are also defined by a specialized

expertise: the clergy by theology; attorneys by the law; teachers by various academic disciplines; and physicians by medicine. The degree of self-regulation—controlling admissions to the profession, defining professional expertise, and maintaining professional ethics—gives each of the learned professions a sense of corporate identity.

THE PROFESSION OF ARMS

Although serving as an officer was generally a prerogative of Europe's aristocracy during the Old Regime, the officer corps was not really professionalized until the Napoleonic Wars, when the requirements of mass armies, logistics, and artillery demanded professional expertise in addition to leadership skills. Only then did soldiering become one of the learned professions—joining theology, the law, teaching, and medicine.

The officer corps is fairly self-regulating internally, but it has significant external controls and governmental oversight. After all, the armed forces of many countries are the major threat to liberty and government by law. The armed forces of the United States have been constituted to serve the republic; they exist for no other purpose. Regulation of the armed forces, the corporate nature of the institution, and its overriding mission are well understood, and need not be belabored here. The expertise of the officer corps, however, is somewhat confusing and does require explanation.

MILITARY EXPERTISE

Each Air Force officer serves in two roles. One is as a technical specialist, and the other is as a military professional. Most young officers understand their roles as technical specialists—as pilots, engineers, and maintenance, logistics, or personnel officers, for example. Perhaps their academic majors have some connections with their Air Force specialties. Certainly each officer's initial training is directly related to the first job in the Air Force. Some officers identify with their specialties exclusively, never coming to understand that they are first and primarily Air Force officers, professionals, and only then specialists. This is rather difficult to understand because most, if not all, of the duty time of junior officers is devoted to their specialties. Many officers complete their careers as specialists, never having served as generalists. But even this does not change the fact that all Air Force officers are professionals first and specialists second. Why?

The armed forces exist to serve the United States by providing the military wherewithal to deter war and, should that fail, to fight and conclude war to the advantage of the United States. The armed forces do not exist for themselves, as a source of employment, as a market for American industry, or as a social welfare tool for social engineering. Nor do they exist as an internal police agency. Planning, equipping, and training to employ military force, what has been called managing violence, is an extremely complicated and demanding task. Unlike the other learned professions, the officer corps requires a very broad spectrum of specialties. And each one of these specialties exists, not independently in its own right, but to contribute to the armed forces' warfighting capabilities. This professional role demands that each Air Force officer understand the purpose of war, the capabilities of air and space power, the roles of air and space forces in warfare, and how the officer's specialty contributes to unit mission accomplishment. With understanding of the ultimate objectives of armed force and how organizations and functional specialties interact, units, specialties, and officers can maximize their potential contributions to mission accomplishment. Each Air Force officer's duty is to acquire and maintain professional expertise. Professional military education (PME) aids in achieving this responsibility, but because the breadth and depth of professional military expertise is so great, no officer can depend on PME alone. Career-long self-study is required to attain real professionalism. The place to begin is with AFDD1, *Air Force Basic Doctrine* and, if you can obtain a copy, with volume one of AFM 1-1, *Basic Aerospace Doctrine of the United States Air Force,* 1992.

ETHICS
Each learned profession is bound by a code of ethics. Some are written; others are expressed only in traditions and customs. The profession of arms is bound by both. Traditional military virtues include integrity, initiative, loyalty, physical and moral courage, and self-sacrifice. These virtues may be honored by American society as a whole; some of them—integrity, moral courage, and especially self-sacrifice—have strong religious sanctions. Few would deny that these personal characteristics are worthy of honor. But, frankly, the ultimate interest of the armed forces in these virtues is not that they are honorable and not that they are morally right; rather, the interest of the armed forces is that these virtues are practical. The nature of the everyday work of the armed forces, and especially the nature of wartime duty and mission, demands that each individual have integrity, initiative, loyalty, and physical and moral courage, and maintain the interest of service before self. The profession of arms is, ultimately, a profession of service. There is not only an ethical demand on individuals in the armed forces, but also ethical restraint on how military violence is employed. Without individual and institutional ethics, servicemembers and the armed services would be without honor.

RESTRAINTS ON THE USE OF MILITARY FORCE
Although war is violent by its very nature, its violence should be restrained for two reasons. One is obviously practical: War is an instrument of political policy, and unrestrained violence can work against achieving the political ends sought. The other is also practical, but many would say it is "merely" moral. The United States cannot use unrestrained violence without altering the very essence of our national being. The United States represents justice and right; to act to the contrary would repudiate what we are as a nation. This is not to say,

of course, that the United States cannot morally use violence at all. Ultimately, our government exists to protect the citizens of the United States. Not to do so would be immoral, and also impractical. The United States, being a sovereign power, has not been forced to bind itself to when and how it uses its military power. Rather, it has chosen to restrict its use of military force for practical reasons, and because to do so is morally right.

The basis of the restriction, customary international law and the Charter of the United Nations, is legally binding on the United States. Although the United States is a sovereign, secular state, these restrictions and historic Christian just-war theories exert a strong influence on states whose moral and philosophical foundations rest on the Western tradition. Christian just-war theory is concerned with both when to enter or engage in war and how war is waged. War must be pursued only for a just cause, such as self-defense or to defeat evil. It must be declared and directed by a competent authority; that is, war is conducted by states, not by substate players. War comes only after peaceable means have failed; that is, war is a last resort. Furthermore, war must have a probability of success; if there is no probability of success, there is no purpose in suffering the inevitable horrors of military violence. The good to be achieved must outweigh the damage done; war must be proportional. Finally, war must discriminate between combatants and noncombatants, avoiding harming noncombatants where possible. President George Bush did not cite just-war theory before the United States employed military force violently in the Gulf War, but he did explain the need to go to war in just-war terms, and much scholarly debate in the United States centered on whether liberation of Kuwait was a "just cause."

Although not legally bound by Christian just-war theory, the United States is bound by the Law of Armed Conflict (LOAC), which is composed of customs and international laws, treaties, and conventions. The purposes of the LOAC are to diminish the adverse effects of conflict, to protect people from unnecessary suffering, to safeguard fundamental rights, to prevent degeneration of organized conflict into savagery and brutality, and to facilitate restoration of peace. Military operations are affected by the principle of military necessity that requires the amount or level of force to correspond to objectives. The principle of humanity requires that targeting be as accurate as possible so that collateral damage can be avoided to the greatest extent possible. Force should be concentrated so as to end the conflict faster and to reduce lives lost. Maximization of military advantage can also end the conflict faster.

The United States Air Force is bound to the LOAC by national law and Department of Defense and Air Force directives (DOD Directive 5100.77, *DOD Law of War Program*, AFI 51–401, *Training and Reporting to Ensure Compliance with the Law of Armed Conflict*, and AFPAM 169-10, *Law of Armed Conflict, Geneva Conventions and Code of Conduct*). Adhering to the LOAC reduces potential for breakdown in discipline, it reduces the likelihood that American servicemembers will commit war crimes, and it helps avoid worldwide outrage, congressional investigations, and adverse media attention. Adherence to the LOAC is practical in the politico-military sense, and it ensures that the Air Force maintains the moral high ground.

THE BOTTOM LINE
The United States will go to war in the future. Our nation's success will rest in great part on the strength of its officer corps. If the officer corps is professional—that is, if individual officers have prepared themselves to use their specialties to contribute to the overall military capabilities of the armed forces and if they hold fast to the military virtues—the nation can count on victory. However, if individual officers define their duties too narrowly and if they think only of serving themselves, the nation should be prepared for defeat.

Professionalism is the bottom line of each officer's and airman's service in the Air Force and the way we accomplish the Air Force mission. This is well summarized by former Air Force Chief of Staff General Ronald R. Fogelman, who said:

> The Air Force is not a social actions agency. The Air Force exists to fight and win wars. That's our core expertise; it is what allows us to be called professionals. We are entrusted with the security of our nation. The tools of our trade are lethal, and we engage in operations that involve much national treasure and risk to human life. Because of what we do, our standards must be higher than those of society at large. The American public expects it of us and properly so. In the end, we earn the respect and trust of the American people because of the professionalism and integrity we demonstrate.

2

The Code of Air Force Service

This chapter sets down principles to which all officers aspire, both in their official duties and in their personal concerns, in actions seen and known by the world and in the privacy of the mind. Until 1997, these ideals did not receive official sanctions. In that year, *The Little Blue Book* set down the Air Force Core Values. This chapter presents extracts from that official publication, as well as an older, but unofficial, compilation of ideals: *Principles of the Air Force Code.*

THE AIRMAN'S CREED
I am an American Airman.
I am a Warrior.
I have answered my Nation's call.

I am an American Airman.
My mission is to Fly, Fight, and Win.
I am faithful to a Proud Heritage,
A Tradition of Honor,
And a Legacy of Valor.

I am an American Airman.
Guardian of Freedom and Justice.
My Nation's Sword and Shield,
Its Sentry and Avenger.
I defend my Country with my Life.

I am an American Airman.
Wingman, Leader, Warrior.
I will never leave an Airman behind,
I will never falter,
And I will not fail.

AIR FORCE CORE VALUES

Whoever you are and wherever you fit on the Air Force team, this is your basic guide to the Air Force Core Values. The Core Values exist for all members of the Air Force family: officer, enlisted, and civilian; active, reserve, and retired; senior, junior, and middle management; civil servants; uniformed personnel; and contractors. They are for all of us to read, to understand, to live by, and to cherish.

The Core Values are much more than minimum standards. They remind us what it takes to get the mission done. They inspire us to do our very best at all times. They are the common bond among all comrades in arms, and they are the glue that unifies the force and ties us to the great warriors and public servants of the past. *Integrity first, Service before self,* and *Excellence in all we do.* These are the Air Force Core Values. Study them, understand them, follow them, and encourage others to do the same.

Integrity First. Integrity is a character trait. It is the willingness to do what is right, even when no one is looking. It is the "moral compass," the inner voice; the voice of self-control; the basis for the trust imperative in today's military. Integrity is the ability to hold together and properly regulate all the elements of a personality. A person of integrity, for example, is capable of acting on conviction. A person of integrity can control impulses and appetites. But integrity also covers several other moral traits indispensable to national service. *Courage.* A person of integrity possesses moral courage and does what is right even if the personal cost is high. *Honesty.* This is the hallmark of the military professional, because in the military, our word must be our bond. We don't pencil-whip training reports, we don't cover up tech data violations, we don't falsify documents, and we don't write misleading operational readiness messages. The bottom line is, we don't lie, and we can't justify any deviation. *Responsibility.* No person of integrity is irresponsible; a person of true integrity acknowledges his or her duties and acts accordingly. *Accountability.* No person of integrity tries to shift the blame to others or take credit for the work of others; "the buck stops here" says it best. *Justice.* A person of integrity practices justice. Those who do similar things must get similar rewards or similar punishments. *Openness.* Professionals of integrity encourage a free flow of information within the organization. They seek feedback from all directions to ensure they are fulfilling key responsibilities, and they are never afraid to allow anyone at any time to examine how they do business. *Self-respect.* To have integrity also is to respect oneself as a professional and a human being. A person of integrity does not behave in ways that would bring discredit upon himself or herself or the organization to which he or she belongs. *Humility.* A person of integrity grasps and is sobered by the awesome task of defending the Constitution of the United States of America.

Service Before Self. Service before self tells us that professional duties take precedence over personal desires. At the very least, it includes the following behaviors. *Rule following.* To serve is to do one's duty, and our duties are most commonly expressed through rules. While it may be the case that professionals are expected to exercise judgment in the performance of their duties, good professionals understand that rules have a reason for being, and the default position must be to follow those rules unless there is a clear, operational reason for refusing to do so. *Respect for others.* Service before self tells us also that a good leader places the troops ahead of his or her personal comfort. We must always act in the certain knowledge that all people possess a fundamental worth as human beings. *Discipline and self-control.* Professionals cannot indulge in self-pity, discouragement, anger, frustration, or defeatism. They have a fundamental moral obligation to the persons they lead to strike a tone of confidence and forward-looking optimism. More specifically, they are expected to exercise control in the following areas. *Anger.* Military professionals and especially commanders at all echelons are expected to refrain from displays of anger that would bring discredit upon themselves and/or the Air Force. *Appetites.* Those who allow their appetites to drive them to make sexual overtures to subordinates are unfit for military service. Likewise, the excessive consumption of alcohol casts doubt on an individual's fitness, and if an officer is found to be drunk and disorderly, all doubts are removed. *Religious toleration.* Military professionals must remember that religious beliefs are a matter of individual choice. Professionals, and especially commanders, must not try to change or coercively influence the religious views of subordinates. *Faith in the system.* To lose faith in the system is to adopt the view that you know better than those above you in the chain of command what should or should not be done. In other words, to lose faith in the system is to place self before service. Leaders can be very influential in this regard. If a leader resists the temptation to doubt the system, then subordinates may follow suit.

Excellence in All We Do. Excellence in all we do directs us to develop a sustained passion for continual improvement and innovation that will propel the Air Force into a long-term, upward spiral of accomplishment and performance. *Product and service excellence.* We must focus on providing services and generating products that fully respond to customer wants and anticipate customer needs, and we must do so within the boundaries established by the taxpaying public. *Personal excellence.* Military professionals must seek out and complete professional military education, stay in physical and mental shape, and continue to refresh their general educational backgrounds. *Community excellence.* This is achieved when the members of an organization can work together to successfully reach a common goal in an atmosphere free of fear that preserves individual self-worth. Several factors influence interpersonal excellence. *Mutual respect.* Genuine respect involves viewing another person as an individual of fundamental worth. This means never judging a person on the basis of his or her possession of an attribute that places him or her in some racial, ethnic, economic, or gender-based category. *Benefit of the doubt.* Avoid making snap judgments about a person or his or her behavior; it is important to get the whole story. All coworkers should be considered innocent until proven guilty. *Resources excellence.* It is important to aggressively implement policies to ensure the best possible cradle-to-grave management of resources. *Material resources excellence.* Military professionals have an obligation to ensure that all of the equipment and property they ask for is mission essential. This means that residual funds at the end of the year should not be used to purchase "nice to have" add-ons. *Human resources excellence.* We should recruit, train, promote, and retain those who can do the best job for us. *Operations excellence.* There are two kinds of operations excellence: internal and external. Internal operations excellence pertains to the way we do business internal to the Air Force, from the unit level to Headquarters Air Force. It involves respect on the unit level and a total commitment to maximizing the Air Force team effort. External operations excellence pertains to the way we treat the world around us as we conduct our operations. In peacetime we must be sensitive to the rules governing environmental pollution, for example, and in wartime we are required to obey the laws of war.

Why These Core Values?

> Core Values make the military what it is; without them, we cannot succeed. They are the values that instill confidence, earn lasting respect, and create willing followers. They are the values that anchor resolve in the most difficult situations. They are the values that buttress mental and physical courage when we enter combat. In essence, they are the three pillars of professionalism that provide the foundation for military leadership at every level. With the incredible diversity of our organization and the myriad of functions necessary to make it work efficiently and effectively, Core Values remain unifying elements for all our members. They provide a common ground and compass by which we can all measure our ideals and actions.
>
> —Secretary Widnall

There are four reasons why we recognize the Core Values and have developed a strategy to implement them. First, the Core Values tell us the price of admission to the Air Force itself. Air Force personnel—whether officer, enlisted, civil servant, or contractor—must display honesty, courage, responsibility, openness, self-respect, and humility in the face of the mission. All of us must accept accountability and practice justice, which means that all Air Force personnel must possess *integrity first.* At the same time, the individual's desires must take a back seat to Air Force service: Rules must be acknowledged and followed faithfully; other personnel must be respected as persons of fundamental worth; discipline and self-control must be in effect always; and there must be faith in the system. In other words, the price of admission to the Air Force demands that each of us place *service before self.* And it is imperative that we all seek *excellence in all we do,* whether it be product and service, resources, community, or operations excellence.

Second, the Core Values point to what is universal and unchanging in the profession of arms. Some are bothered by the fact that different branches of the service recognize different values; other people are bothered by the fact that the Air Force once recognized six values and has now reduced them to three. But they need not worry. It is impossible for three or six or nine Core Values to capture the richness that is at the heart of the profession of arms. The values are road signs inviting us to consider key features of the requirements of professional service, but they cannot hope to point out everything. By examining integrity, service, and excellence, we also eventually discover the importance of duty, honor, country, dedication, fidelity, competence, and a host of other professional requirements and attributes. The important thing is not the three road signs our leaders choose; what is important is that they have selected road signs, and it is our obligation to understand the ethical demands these road signs pick out.

Third, the Core Values help us get a fix on the ethical climate of the organization. How successful are we in trying to live by the Core Values? Our answer to this question may not be the one we'd like to give. All of us have heard about the sensational scandals—senior officers and NCOs engaged in adulterous fraternization; the tragic and senseless crashes of the Ramstein CT-43 and the Fairchild B-52; contractor fraud and cost overruns; and the shootdown of the two Blackhawk helicopters over Iraq. We all have read about these incidents and experienced the shame associated with them. But these big-ticket scandals don't just happen in a vacuum, and they aren't always caused by evil people acting on impulse. The people involved knew the difference between right and wrong, and they knew what professionalism demanded in these situations. These scandals grew out of a climate of ethical erosion. Because we believe our operating procedures or the requirements levied upon us from above are absurd, we tend to cut corners, skate by, and get over. As time goes by, these actions become easier and even habitual, until one day we can no longer distinguish between the important taskings or rules and the stupid ones. Lying on official forms becomes second nature. Placing personal interests ahead of the mission seems sensible. And we develop a "good enough for government work" mentality.

In such a climate of corrosion, the Core Values are like a slap in the face. How far have you strayed from integrity, service, and excellence? What about the folks with whom you work?

Fortunately, there is a fourth reason for recognizing the Core Values. Just as they help us evaluate the climate of our organization, they also serve as beacons to keep us on the path of correct professional conduct. The Core Values allow us to transform a climate of ethical erosion into one of ethical commitment. That is why we have developed the Core Values Strategy.

The Core Values Strategy

1. The Core Values Strategy exists independently of and does not compete with chapel programs. The Core Values Strategy attempts no explanation of the origin of the Values except to say that all of us, regardless of our religious views, must recognize their functional importance and accept them for that reason. Infusing the Core Values is necessary for successful mission accomplishment.

2. You don't need to be a commander in order to be a leader.

3. The leader of an organization is the key to its moral climate. As does the commander, so does the organization. But a commander must enlist and insist upon the help of all organizational supervisors and all assigned personnel in the effort to ensure a culture of conscience for the organization.

4. Leaders cannot just be good; they also must be sensitive to their status as role models for their people and thus avoid the appearance of improper behavior.

5. Leadership from below is at least as important as leadership from above in implementing the Core Values.

6. A culture of conscience is impossible unless civilians, officers, and enlisted personnel understand, accept, internalize, and are free to follow the Core Values.

7. To understand, accept, and internalize the Core Values, our people must be allowed and encouraged to engage in an extended dialogue about them and to explore the role of the Values at all levels of the Air Force.

8. Our first task is to fix organizations; individual character development is possible, but it is not a goal. If a culture of compromise exists in the Air Force, it is more likely to be the result of bad policies and programs than to be symptomatic of any character flaws in our people. Therefore, long before we seek to implement a character development program, we must thoroughly evaluate and, where necessary, fix our policies, processes, and procedures.

The U.S. Air Force's Core Values website contains a copy of *The Little Blue Book* as well as a series of readings about the Core Values and their place in the Air Force. In addition, you will find a series of easy-to-use implementation guides, and you may submit questions about the Core Values to the website mailbox.

REQUIREMENT FOR EXEMPLARY CONDUCT

All commanding officers and others in authority in the Air Force are required by §10 USC 8583 of the U.S. Code

- to show in themselves a good example of virtue, honor, patriotism, and subordination;
- to be vigilant in inspecting the conduct of all persons who are placed under their command;

- to guard against and suppress all dissolute and immoral practices, and to correct, according to the laws and regulations of the Air Force, all persons who are guilty of them; and
- to take all necessary and proper measures, under the laws, regulations, and customs of the Air Force, to promote and safeguard the morale, the physical well-being, and the general welfare of the officers and enlisted persons under their command or charge.

PRINCIPLES OF THE AIR FORCE CODE

In addition to the official Air Force Core Values and the Requirements for Exemplary Conduct, there are other principles of the Air Force code; although unofficial, they have withstood the test of time. They express an attitude of the spirit, rarely arrived at consciously, but strongly governing the reactions of Air Force officers to all the many aspects of Air Force life.

The printed word cannot capture the code of the Air Force in its entirety, for this code is a living reality that an officer must experience to fully understand. Yet we can identify some of the deep foundations upon which our code rests. These are criteria by which we have lived and fought and many have died; these are values we have sought to uphold, the true hallmarks of the U.S. Air Force.

Patriotism. Patriotism as practiced in the Air Force is an intelligent devotion to the interests of the United States. It rests upon the conviction that preservation of the American way of life, with its noble traditions, free institutions, and infinite promise, is both practical morality and enlightened self-interest. American patriotism is not jingoism, blindly unaware of faults of our system. Rather, our patriotism works to remove faults that exist, while remaining confident that here in America the hands and minds of humans have done their best work, that ours is a most promising road toward a goal of maximum human welfare, toward freedom, dignity, and justice for each individual, and peace for the world.

Not only in the high drama of war does patriotism invoke a readiness to make personal sacrifices, but also in routine duties, during off-duty hours, in the thousands of small choices which confront us in daily life. Patriotism in the Air Force is intelligent devotion to the interests of the United States day by day, at work and at leisure, in war and in peace, in life and, if need be, in death.

Honor. Honor is the highest form of self-respect. You must live with yourself alone for a very substantial part of your life. It is imperative to peace of mind and soul that you respect your own character. Thus, honor is that code of conduct that springs not only from a "do unto others as you would have them do unto you" philosophy but also from a determination to do only those things about which your conscience is clear. A person of honor does not lie, steal, cheat, or take advantage of another. The question here is not whether you would be seriously hurt if someone did such things to you, but whether you could be proud of such practices. Service in the U.S. Air Force is honorable duty, and Air Force personnel seek to be counted as such.

Courage. Courage is ascendancy over fear. Note that where there is courage, there must be fear. The Air Force wants no officers who are unafraid. The perils that threaten the United States are such that a person who is without fear is either foolish or ignorant. The Air Force *does* want officers who can conquer their fears, suppress them in the interests of the nation, and courageously carry on despite fear. We need officers whose courage is steady and long-enduring, and who can steel themselves for the long pull over the years.

Loyalty. Loyalty is the quality of sincere confidence in and support for the purposes, methods, and capabilities of one's superiors, peers, and subordinates. Loyalty is a quality that precludes sneering comment on the faults of your commander or complaints about the errors of your fellow airmen. It is basically an attitude of warm friendship toward your comrades. If you look carefully, you will find that most of your associates well deserve your loyalty.

Discipline. Discipline is the cement that binds together any military force. Without it, the Air Force would be a mob. Obeying orders to the letter—and, more important, the spirit—is the heart of discipline. Air Force officers who grudgingly, complainingly, or unenthusiastically obey orders are poorly disciplined officers who encourage poor discipline in the airmen they are supposed to lead. Such officers do not build and maintain an effective fighting force. Almost everyone agrees that discipline is a fine thing—for everyone else. Too many of us are tempted to believe that orders and regulations were meant for the masses, but not for the Great Me. Yet we all should be aware that unless we practice discipline in our routine conduct, the stress of combat, of emergency, and of violent uncertainties can easily force us from the iron path of obedience to orders, with results disastrous to our cause and to ourselves. One thing seems certain: We will have disciplined officers of our Air Force, or we will one day have no Air Force, no nation, and no freedom.

Readiness. One of the most striking qualities of Air Force officers is their relative readiness to meet whatever tasks arise. The Far East Air Forces transformed themselves overnight from a slow-paced occupation force to the combat arm of the United Nations over Korea. Yet two days before the entry of U.S. air forces into combat in Korea, not an officer of the Far East Air Forces had an inkling such a task would arise. Eight days later, they had destroyed the North Korean air force of more than 300 aircraft. Once again, the nation called upon the Air Force for a quick reaction to the combat situation in Vietnam. Thousands of Air Force members deployed into battle in Southeast Asia to fight a bitter, difficult war. Our officers can be ready, as they were in the Gulf War. They can be well-trained, well-informed, clear-headed, and physically fit masters of their duties. We must maintain such readiness, for someday a bigger warning than Korea, Vietnam, the Gulf War, the Balkans, Afghanistan, or Iraq may suddenly ring out a dreaded alarm, calling Air Force officers to a greater trial. For this possibility, each of us must stand prepared.

Frugality. The Air Force represents a large expenditure in the U.S. budget. We are an expensive force, using extremely costly equipment and supplies. In fairness to all American taxpayers, we ought to hold this expense to the minimum consistent with national safety. This quality of frugality involves more than just these measures, however. Air Force units have sometimes found to their sorrow that the cost of wastefulness was ineffectiveness and that the price of ineffectiveness was a longer war with more lives lost. One of the dark hopes of our enemies is that the United States will bankrupt itself through its far-flung national security programs. Let us not contribute to that enemy hope.

Caution. Caution has a proper place in the code of the Air Force. The great strength we hold poised is the chief defense of the United States. Although there is no one massive national power that threatens our survival as did the Soviet Union during the Cold War, the situation is still dangerous and explosive. A mistake can still lead to war. Has any condition of affairs ever more strongly recommended caution? Moreover, Air Force officers operate equipment noted for its great speed and powerful effects. Recklessness often costs lives; it certainly costs millions of dollars annually. In these circumstances, no Air Force officer is justified in abandoning caution. A famous Air Force combat ace once said, "When I get in an airplane, I slow down."

Sense of Responsibility. Responsibility is one of the most valued characteristics in an officer. Its most frequent evidence is the execution of work that should be done whether or not you are directly charged with that work. How many times can you hear the phrase from the substandard officer: "Oh, well, it's not my headache"? But it *is* your headache, if it hurts the Air Force. The sense of responsibility found in the best of Air Force officers will not be satisfied with a job merely well done. The question is: Has the job been done to the best of my ability? If not, it isn't finished.

Teamwork. Teamwork is the means by which officers do the impossible more rapidly. Teamwork makes football champions of eleven people who, if they all insisted on being ball carriers, would gain nothing. Teamwork makes every officer's task easier, and yet the overall result is greater success. It is the nearest thing to getting something for nothing. If you insist on playing a lone hand, always want to carry the ball, and feel that associates should do their own work without bothering you, you will find that your path is rough and does not go very far. Cooperation with others is essential, as the Air Force is a team organization.

Ambition. To be ambitious is the mark of a superior officer. Every officer has a right to be ambitious and will be a better officer for it. People will tend to assess you according to the evaluation you place upon yourself. If you exert yourself to become qualified for higher positions and greater responsibilities, you will eventually become convinced that you are ready for advancement. Thus, ambition based on qualification will give you confidence and aggressiveness, qualities indispensable to superior officers. Stonewall Jackson said, "You can be what you determine to be." When Jackson used the word *determine,* he meant willingness to do the work, gain the qualifications, and seek the opportunity necessary for advancement to your goal. Ambition can and should be a driving force for self-improvement. Only one caution is relevant: Set the sights of your ambition no higher than the level of your willingness to work, for the two are linked.

Adaptability. One of the qualities that Air Force officers must employ the most is adaptability, the ability to make the best of any situation. Life in the Air Force is a rough-and-tumble of widely varying conditions. Officers serve in all parts of the world, in an almost infinite number of differing conditions. Equipment and technology change frequently, new maintenance problems arise, and all things are subject to change. As an officer, you must be prepared to adapt to the conditions you may find in any assignment. Living accommodations, offices, operational facilities, the quality of superiors and subordinates—all may differ radically from your previous assignment, yet you must work with these new factors. You, not they, must adapt. Adaptability and flexibility are essential to meet such different situations.

Ascendancy of the Civil Power. It is important that you know where your loyalty lies. Under our system of government, you have a dual allegiance to the U.S. Constitution, which you swore to uphold, and to the president as commander in chief.

In this system of divided civilian supremacy—between the president and Congress—over our armed forces, you must not allow yourself to become involved in the tug of war between an administration and Congress. You should keep informed about politics, and it is your duty to vote, but on active duty you should not speak publicly about your personal views on political policy. If you cannot support established policy, you should take the honorable course and resign your commission.

Relations with Civilians. One of the most important responsibilities expected of Air Force officers is the maintenance of favorable relations with civilians. This is very important when you realize that a significant part of the American public's attitude toward the Air Force is a reflection of the impression individual Air Force servicemembers make. The continued strength of the Air Force demands that American citizens hold a favorable view of the Air Force. The future of the service, in large measure, depends on the relations of Air Force personnel with their civilian neighbors.

All Air Force officers are public affairs officers, sources of information about the Air Force to civilians with whom they come in contact. If you, an Air Force officer, are irresponsible for your debts, conduct yourself in an obnoxious manner in your civilian neighborhood, display yourself in a drunken condition, or ignore the laws and the customs of the community, how much confidence would you expect a civilian observer of these antisocial behaviors to place in the Air Force you are a part of? On the other hand, if you conduct yourself as a sober, responsible citizen of the civilian community, your civilian acquaintances will tend to feel that the Air Force is an organization in which they can have confidence. Thus, by your *pattern of conduct,* you form important impressions regarding the Air Force.

Your civilian friends are interested in their Air Force. They have a right to be. It is one of their best hopes for averting war and one of their most effective instruments to win the nation's wars. The Air Force is close to their vital interests, for it is a force that stands between their homes and the enemy. As citizens and taxpayers, they have a lively and legitimate interest in the Air Force, and they frequently turn to the individual Air Force officer for information. The manner in which you meet that interest will have a decided effect on the future of the Air Force. Accordingly, each officer should welcome the opportunity to provide factual information about the Air Force to civilian friends, taking care always, of course, to avoid classified matters. If your civilian friends point with alarm to a report that an aircraft has crashed, explain how such things happen and how infrequently they happen. If civilians ask whether your quarters allowance is tax exempt, tell them yes. Also, explain to them the *overall* financial status of Air Force personnel. In other words, so far as security considerations permit, give your civilian friends the *whole* truth. Throughout, remember that the U.S. Air Force is the property of American citizens. They have built it, manned it, and paid for it. They have an awful lot of blue chips riding on its wings.

Air Force officers should seek to take a full part in the life of the civilian community. Be sociable with your neighbors. Become a member of their clubs, societies, and religious institutions. Take your share in community enterprises. In short, be a good citizen, a respected and desired neighbor. While doing so, you will not only perform a duty expected of you as an Air Force officer but also add greatly to your own enjoyment of life.

CODE OF CONDUCT IN WARTIME

The Code of Conduct for Members of the U.S. Armed Forces, which appears on the next page, was designed specifically for prisoner-of-war (POW) situations, so that POWs can survive honorably while resisting their captors' efforts to exploit them to the advantage of the enemy's cause and to the disadvantage of the POWs and the United States. However, the spirit and intent of the code are also applicable to servicemembers subject to other hostile detention; servicemembers can use the provisions of the code to avoid discrediting themselves and the United States.

Adherence to the Code of Conduct can help military personnel who are detained by unfriendly governments or groups survive with honor. Those detained during peacetime must take every reasonable step to prevent exploitation of themselves or the U.S. government. If exploitation cannot be prevented completely, every step must be taken to limit exploitation as much as possible. Detained U.S. military personnel often are catalysts for their own release, based on their ability to become unattractive sources of exploitation; in other words, one who resists successfully may expect detainers to lose interest in further exploitation attempts. Detainees, or captives, very often must make their own judgments as to which actions will increase their chances of returning

CODE OF CONDUCT FOR MEMBERS OF THE U.S. ARMED FORCES

I

I am an American, fighting in the forces which guard my country and our way of life. I am prepared to give my life in their defense.

II

I will never surrender of my own free will. If in command I will never surrender the members of my command while they still have the means to resist.

III

If I am captured I will continue to resist by all means available. I will make every effort to escape and to aid others to escape. I will accept neither parole nor special favors from the enemy.

IV

If I become a prisoner of war, I will keep faith with my fellow prisoners. I will give no information or take part in any action which might be harmful to my comrades. If I am senior, I will take command. If not, I will obey the lawful orders of those appointed over me and will back them up in every way.

V

When questioned, should I become a prisoner of war, I am required to give my name, rank, service number, and date of birth. I will evade answering further questions to the utmost of my ability. I will make no oral or written statements disloyal to my country and its allies or harmful to their cause.

VI

I will never forget that I am an American, fighting for freedom, responsible for my actions, and dedicated to the principles which made my country free. I will trust in my God and in the United States of America.

Notes: The secretary of defense has directed training under the code in three main phases: a general citizenship type of orientation; a formal course for combat crews likely to fall into enemy hands, which could include training in avoiding capture, survival while evading or during captivity, resistance to giving information and making false "confessions," and escape attempts; and a specialized course for selected students, which could include prisoner interrogation, and treatment courses of definite duration designed to toughen individual students and to let them test their resistance ability and determine their physical and mental weaknesses.

Because of the special status given them under the Geneva Convention, chaplains and medical personnel are granted a degree of flexibility with regard to some of the specific provisions of the code so that they are able to perform their professional duties.

home with honor and dignity. Without exception, military members must say honestly that they have done their utmost in detention or captivity to resist exploitation, uphold DOD policy, the founding principles of the United States, and the highest traditions of military service.

Once in the custody of a hostile government, regardless of the circumstances that preceded the detention situation, detainees are subject to the laws of that government. Detainees should maintain military bearing and should avoid any aggressive, combative, or illegal behavior. The latter might complicate their situation, their legal status, and any efforts to negotiate a rapid release.

Capture by terrorists is generally the least predictable and structured form of captivity. The captors qualify as international criminals. The possible forms of captivity vary from spontaneous hijacking to a carefully planned kidnapping. In such captivities, hostages play a greater role in determining their own fate, since the terrorists in many instances expect or receive no rewards for providing good treatment or releasing victims unharmed. If U.S. military personnel are uncertain whether captors are genuine terrorists or surrogates of a government, they should assume that they are terrorists.

AMERICA'S COMMITMENT TO POWs
The U.S. government also has responsibilities under the Code of Conduct. The government promises
- To keep faith with you and stand by you as you fight in its defense;
- To care for your family and dependents; and
- To use every practical means to contact, support, and gain release for you and all other prisoners of war.

3

Leadership

Leadership is the art of influencing and directing people to accomplish the mission. Management is the manner in which both human and material resources are used to achieve objectives. As an Air Force officer, you should be aware of your responsibility as a leader and manager. British Field Marshal Lord Slim made a clear distinction:

> There is a difference between leadership and management. The leader and the men who follow him represent one of the oldest, most natural, and most effective of all human relationships. The manager and those he manages are a later product with neither so romantic, nor so inspiring a history. Leadership is of the spirit, compounded of personality and vision—its practice is an art. Management is of the mind, more a matter of accurate calculation, statistics, methods, timetables, and routine—its practice is a science. Managers are necessary; leaders are essential.

In essence, you lead people, and you manage things. The Air Force needs people who can do both. The requirement is for the proper division of attention between the two, with the proportion dependent on the situation.

Leadership is essential to a successful officer. When considering other attributes of successful officers, there are specific exceptions to all but leadership. Ulysses S. Grant rarely wore his uniform properly and used liquor to excess, yet he knew how to win a war. Robert E. Lee had every desirable attribute of an officer, but of all his military attributes, that which shone brightest was leadership. Renowned Air Force officers such as "Hap" Arnold, Hoyt Vandenberg, and Curtis LeMay were men of many talents, but their outstanding talent was leadership.

A young officer should recognize that all officers are leaders, not just those in command positions. Leading is the most exciting and interesting experience the service can offer. The Air Force does not expect that every officer will equal Arnold, Vandenberg, or LeMay, but who can tell? Some writers have described the good, common, garden variety of leaders as officers who can inculcate those under them with knowledge of their tasks and imbue them with the spirit to do them well. That goal is not impossible. With application, a person who meets the standards for commissioned officers can be that sort of good leader.

A *leader* is one fitted by force of ideas, character, or genius or by strength of will or administrative ability to arouse, incite, and direct individuals in conduct and achievement.

Leadership means the art of imposing one's will upon others in such a manner as to command their respect, their confidence, and their wholehearted cooperation. The core of the definition is that leaders must impose their will on others, who must do what their leaders direct them to do.

Martinets accomplish this goal by simple reliance upon their positions of authority and their power of punishment. Leaders accomplish it through the quality of leadership the Air Force seeks. In the case of martinets, the people commanded do what the martinets direct them to do, but often in a sullen and grudging manner. In the case of leaders, the people carry out directions with enthusiasm, contributing their own ingenuity and drive to the task at hand.

THE AIR FORCE LEADERSHIP CONCEPT

As an effective leader, the basic concept you must keep in mind encompasses two fundamental elements: the mission and the people. This is the Air Force concept of leadership, and all facets of Air Force leadership should support these two basic elements.

The Mission. The primary task of a military organization is to perform its mission. This is paramount, and everything else must be subordinate to this objective. As a leader, your primary responsibility is to lead people to carry out the unit's mission successfully. Most missions involve many tasks that must be completed if the unit is to fulfill its responsibilities. Commanders set priorities for the mission's various components, but all officers, as leaders, support their commanders to accomplish their units' missions. Former Air Force Chief of Staff General Curtis LeMay emphasized, "No matter how well you apply the art of leadership, no matter how strong your unit or how high the morale of your men, if your leadership is not directed completely toward the mission, your leadership has failed." Yet you must never forget the importance of the unit's personnel.

The People. People perform the mission. They are the heart of the organization, and without their support a unit will fail. You cannot be totally successful at getting the most out of people without first knowing their capabilities and what motivates them. Your responsibilities also include the care and support of your unit's personnel. To be a successful leader, you must continually ensure that the needs of the people in your unit are met promptly and properly.

Clearly, the two "simple" parts of the leadership concept—mission and people—are actually two very complicated elements. Successful leaders who effectively deal with this complex concept have certain characteristics or traits.

LEADERSHIP TRAITS

The list of a leader's desirable qualities is long. Although these characteristics are also expected of all members of the military profession, six traits are vital to Air Force leaders: integrity, loyalty, commitment, energy, decisiveness, and selflessness.

Integrity. Integrity is a total commitment to the highest personal and professional standards. As a leader, you must be honest and fair. Integrity means establishing a set of values and adhering to those values. Air Force Chief of Staff General Charles Gabriel said, "Integrity is the fundamental premise of military service in a free society. Without integrity, the moral pillars of our military strength—public trust and self-respect—are lost."

Loyalty. Loyalty, a three-dimensional trait, includes faithfulness to superiors, peers, and subordinates. You must first display an unquestionable sense of loyalty before you can expect members of your unit to be loyal. General George Patton highlighted the importance of loyalty when he said, "There is a great deal of talk about loyalty from the bottom to the top. Loyalty from the top down is even more necessary and much less prevalent."

Commitment. Commitment means complete devotion to duty. As a leader, you must demonstrate total dedication to the United States, the Air Force, and your unit. Plato said, "Man was not born for himself alone, but for his country." Dedicated service is the hallmark of the military leader.

Energy. Energy is an enthusiasm and drive to take the initiative. Throughout history, successful leaders have demonstrated the importance of mental and physical energy. You must approach assigned tasks aggressively. Your preparation should include physical and mental conditioning that will enable you to look and act the part. Once a course of action is determined, you must have the perseverance and stamina to stay on course until the job is completed.

Decisiveness. Decisiveness is a willingness to act. As a leader, you must have the self-confidence to make timely decisions. You must then effectively communicate the decisions to your unit. British Admiral Sir Roger Keyes emphasized that "in all operations a moment arrives when brave decisions have to be made if an enterprise is to be carried through." Of course, decisiveness includes the willingness to accept responsibility. You are always accountable—when things go right and when things go wrong.

Selflessness. Selflessness requires sacrificing personal requirements for a greater cause. You must think of performing the mission and caring for the welfare of the men and women in your organization. As an Air Force leader, you cannot place your own comfort or convenience before the mission or the people. Willingness to sacrifice is intrinsic to military service. Selflessness also includes the courage to face and overcome difficulties. Although courage is often thought of as an unselfish willingness to confront physical dangers, equally important—and more likely to be tested on a daily basis—is the moral courage you need to make difficult decisions. General of the Army Douglas MacArthur said, "No nation can safely trust its martial honor to leaders who do not maintain the universal code which distinguishes those things that are right and those things that are wrong." It requires courage and strength of character to confront a tough situation head-on rather than avoid it by passing the buck to someone else.

These traits are essential to effective leadership. Developing these characteristics will improve your ability to employ the principles of leadership.

LEADERSHIP PRINCIPLES

Leadership principles are guidelines that have been tested and proven over the years by successful leaders. The most important of these principles are discussed below. Although some aspects of these principles apply only to commanders, most are universally applicable to all officers. All officers are not commanders, but all are leaders.

Know Yourself. Knowing your own strengths and weaknesses is important to successful leadership. You, the leader, must recognize your personal capabilities and limitations. Former Chief Master Sergeant of the Air Force Robert Gaylor put it this way: "Sure, everyone wants to be an effective leader, whether it be in the Air Force or in the community. You can and will be if you identify your strengths, capitalize on them, and consciously strive to reduce and minimize the times you apply your style inappropriately."

Know Your Job. People will follow you if you are a competent person who has the knowledge needed to complete the mission successfully. You should have a broad view of your unit's mission, and you must make sure all members of your unit understand how their jobs relate to mission accomplishment.

Between World War I and World War II, the United States Army Air Corps was fortunate to have men like General Hap Arnold and General Carl Spaatz. These men learned their jobs and knew how they could enhance the Air Corps mission. Their preparation and vision paid substantial dividends when they were charged with building a force to fight and win the air battles of World War II.

Just as important as your own competence is ensuring that assigned people know their responsibilities. Former Chairman of the Joint Chiefs of Staff General Maxwell Taylor stated, "One expects a military leader to demonstrate in his daily performance a thorough knowledge of his own job and further an ability to train his subordinates in their duties and thereafter to supervise and evaluate their work."

Set the Example. You must help set the standard for professional competence in your unit. People will emulate your standards of personal conduct and appearance. They will observe your negative characteristics as well as your positive ones. If you are arrogant or domineering, you will get no respect, only resentment. If you violate basic standards of morality, you will invariably end up in a compromising situation. If you drink excessively or abuse drugs, you send a dangerous message: "I cannot control myself; how can I control you?" Lack of self-discipline in a leader destroys the unit's cohesion and, ultimately, impairs its ability to perform the mission.

Self-discipline also pertains to physical fitness. When you are in good physical condition, you are better prepared for any assigned mission. Setting the right example includes supporting your unit's fitness program and enforcing Air Force fitness standards. As a military leader, you must be a positive example of professional conduct, appearance, and physical conditioning. As General George Patton once remarked, "You are always on parade."

Care for People. General of the Army George Marshall believed, "A decent regard for the rights and feelings of others is essential to leadership." Take care of the people. Find out what their requirements are and be sensitive to human needs. Are the people housed adequately? Are they well fed? Are there personal problems with which they need help? When people are worried about these conditions, they cannot focus their full attention on their jobs, and the mission will suffer. If people believe they are cared for as well as circumstances will permit, you, as leader, are in a position to earn their confidence, respect, and loyalty.

Communicate. Information should flow continuously throughout the organization. Former Air Force Chief of Staff General Thomas White believed, "Information is the essential link between wise leadership and purposeful action." Communication is a two-way process. Only as an informed leader will you be able to evaluate realistically your unit's progress toward mission accomplishment. You must listen to what your people have to say and always look for the good ideas that can flow up the chain. It is also key to emphasize the importance of feedback. The worker who is well informed concerning the quality of the work and its importance to the mission will be more effective and highly motivated. It is your job to keep all channels open. The more senior you become, the more listening skills will be required.

Educate and Train. People should be properly educated and trained to do their jobs. Professional military education, technical training courses, and on-the-job training are formal means by which Air Force personnel are prepared. Informal training, practice, and personal experience at the unit level are crucial reinforcements to formal training. General Douglas MacArthur observed, "In no other profession are the penalties for employing untrained personnel so appalling or so irrevocable as in the military."

Equip. It is also your responsibility to ensure that your subordinates are equipped properly. Just as an aircrew should never be expected to engage in combat without a well-armed aircraft, personnel should not be sent ill-equipped to the office, shop, or flightline. Your leadership responsibilities include identifying needs, securing funds, and then obtaining the necessary weapons, tools, and equipment.

Motivate. Your greatest challenge is motivating subordinates to achieve the high standards set for them. Motivation is the moving force behind successful leadership. In fact, the ability to generate enthusiasm about the mission may be the single most important factor in leadership. Recognition of the efforts people put forth is one positive way in which motivation toward mission accomplishment pays dividends. When you publicly applaud the efforts of unit personnel, you build a cohesive organization that will accomplish the mission.

To motivate people, you must understand their needs and work to align these needs with unit requirements. Most people will work for an organization that they know cares about them, and one in whose mission they believe. Remember, the most powerful form of lasting motivation is self-motivation. One of your goals as a leader should be to provide an environment that fosters and rewards self-motivation.

Accept Your Responsibility. General LeMay was once asked to provide a one-word definition of leadership. After some thought, he replied, "If I had to come up with one word to define leadership, I would say *responsibility*." As a leader, you are responsible for performing the unit's mission. If you fail, you are accountable for the consequences. Any unwillingness to accept responsibility for failure destroys your credibility as a leader and breaks the bond of respect and loyalty. Accountability also includes the requirement for discipline within a unit. A leader should reward a job well done and punish those who fail to meet their responsibilities or established standards. The former is easy and enjoyable; the latter is much more difficult, but equally necessary. George Washington observed, "Discipline is the soul of an army. It makes small numbers formidable, procures success to the weak, and esteem to all."

Develop Teamwork. As a leader, you must mold a collection of individual performers into a cohesive team that works together to accomplish the mission. The unit's mission will suffer if each person in your organization is doing his or her own thing. As the leader, you should know how the various functions within the unit fit together and how they must work in harmony. You should create and maintain an atmosphere of teamwork and cooperation to meet mission demands. Teamwork comes when people are willing to put the unit's mission before all else.

Be Flexible. There is no one perfect leadership style. Rather, the most effective style is the one that the leader tailors to the mission, the people, and the environment. You should carefully consider the environment in which you work. Leadership methods that worked in one situation with one group may not work with the same group in a different environment. Consider the squadron that is permanently based in the United States but deploys overseas for an extended period of temporary duty. Billeting or food service difficulties, equipment or parts shortages, family separation problems, challenging weather conditions, hostile local population, or other problems may occur. Any of these situations creates an entirely new environment with which you must cope. As a unit leader, you must alter your leadership behavior, as necessary, to accommodate changes in the environment of the given mission. Be sensitive to your surroundings.

Successful military leaders adapt their leadership styles to meet mission demands and use approaches that capitalize on their strengths. For example, if you are able to communicate effectively with people on an individual basis but are uncomfortable when speaking to large groups, then use personal conferences as much as possible. If you write well, take advantage of this skill by writing letters of appreciation or using other forms of correspondence. If you are a good athlete, organize and participate in unit sports activities.

In addition to capitalizing on your strengths and minimizing your weaknesses, your style of leadership must correspond to the people's job knowledge. When they lack sufficient knowledge to do the job at hand, you must spend much of your time directing their efforts to accomplish the mission.

On the other hand, if people have the requisite training or experience, you are not required to direct their every action and should not do so. Still, you must motivate them to complete the task. Work with them, but keep your eye on the objective.

Occasionally, you may discover that people are only moderately motivated to do a job they are capable of completing. In such circumstances, let them participate in planning the task. Motivate them by maintaining a job-related working relationship. Their capabilities will do the rest.

When the people have extensive experience and are enthusiastic about the task, you should provide them greater freedom to complete it the way they choose. Nevertheless, you, as the leader, are still ultimately responsible for the mission, so stay informed of the group's progress.

LEADERSHIP PREPARATION

Now that we have examined some of the basics of Air Force leadership, here is how you can best prepare yourself to lead:

Think About Leadership. What would you do in a given situation, and why? If you were placed in charge of your work unit tomorrow, how would you act? Remember the concepts, traits, and principles of Air Force leadership.

Observe Leaders in Action. How does your boss handle a given situation? Why did a particular action succeed or fail? How do your wing commander, squadron commander, first sergeant, and supervisor lead?

Study Leadership and the Profession of Arms. The military has a long tradition of leadership. Read about the successful leaders in our history and how they led. Alfred Thayer Mahan wrote, "The study of history lies at the foundation of all sound military conclusions and practice." You must have detailed professional knowledge to develop perspective and to meet the challenges of the future.

Practice Leadership. Look for opportunities to exercise leadership. It can be as simple as taking the initiative and leading one person to complete a task. Learn from your efforts, seek feedback, and evaluate your efforts. Always lead by positive example.

The United States was fortunate that between the two world wars, several members of its military services prepared themselves to be leaders. Their preparation resulted in strong leadership during some of the most crucial years in our history. The Air Force has inherited a legacy of strong, dynamic leadership from the early air pioneers. As one of today's leaders, you must continue this tradition of excellence.

Do not confuse leadership with management. Leadership is about people; management is about things.

The Air Force depends on positive, effective leaders at all levels to perform the mission. Leadership is not the private domain or responsibility of senior officers. It is a responsibility for which every member of the Air Force must prepare. General LeMay's words continue to serve us well: "I'm firmly convinced that leaders are not born; they're educated, trained, and made, as in every other profession." To ensure a strong, ready Air Force, we must always remain dedicated to this process.

4

Responsibilities of Command

To most junior officers of the Air Force, nothing seems more remote from current or prospective duties than does command of an Air Force unit. Command is indeed a rare assignment for Air Force officers of any grade. The officer strength of the Air Force is many times the number of Air Force units available to command, hence the rarity of command jobs. Yet consider another aspect of command. Command is not a function exercised solely by one officer, such as the squadron commander. The squadron commander cannot exercise command other than through the officers and noncommissioned officers of the squadron. Each officer of the squadron not only is subject to command, but also helps exercise command. Thus, every officer participates in the function of command. For this reason, all officers, whatever their grades, ranks, or assignments, should understand the basic elements and objectives of the command function. They are part of the command operation, and it is one of their most important responsibilities. The command function has to do with the mission of the unit, with training, discipline, supply, and morale. How could an officer not be involved in these factors? All officers should appreciate the responsibilities of their unit commanders to better comprehend the reasons for their commanders' decisions. One of the hallmarks of a professional is the ability to appreciate the responsibilities of other members of the team and to assist in the discharge of those responsibilities.

During the Cold War, the Air Force became accustomed to operating from large, fixed bases with extensive infrastructure. Missions became almost inflexible, operations routine; leadership gave way to management. Foreign officers occasionally voiced their contempt of American officers as clerks, not officers—clerks whose expertise was confined to knowing the applicable regulation or standing operating procedure. The Korean and Vietnam wars temporarily brought us back to the timeless nature of all wars—confusion, unpredictability, uncertainly, and unreliability. But these "limited wars" and contingency operations were largely dismissed as aberrations and sideshows. For those who are still caught up in the Cold War mentality, much of this chapter may seem

28

anachronistic. For those, however, who have focused on Grenada, Panama, the Gulf, Haiti, the Balkans, Afghanistan, and Iraq the prospects of assuming command and operating semiautonomously—modern communications notwithstanding—may seem more descriptive of the present and the future than of the past. Commanders may find themselves left to their own resources and forced to act without the enormous "tail" that has defined the Air Force for much of its independent existence. And wise young officers will prepare themselves to operate in this uncertain, changing environment.

ASSUMPTION OF A COMMAND POSITION

Almost every Air Force officer must anticipate being assigned without warning to assume command of an Air Force unit. By U.S. law, chaplains may not command, and medical corps officers may command only medical units. All other officers are eligible to command. This opportunity may arise as a result of combatlike situations, or less dramatically, a sudden need to shift personnel. As an Air Force officer in such a situation, you may find that the command position given is a larger one than normally associated with your grade. Therefore, you should develop the habit of getting to know the problems of command of your unit whenever you assume any new assignment. Commanders should learn the problems of command of the next higher unit.

Assumption of Command in Combat. During operations in a hostile environment, your superior may become a casualty. If you are the next senior officer down the chain of command, your immediate duty is to take over the responsibility of your senior. This need could result from any one of several situations, such as a flight leader's plane going down, the commander of a security forces squadron being struck by hostile gunfire on the ground, or the commander of a maintenance squadron becoming ill. In any case, you, as the next in command, must act at once to ensure that the unit continues to perform its mission. Although such assumption of command under conditions of combat may prove to be only a temporary expedient, you must never allow a break in the continuity of command during combat. Like almost every other officer, you must be prepared to step in and take over when necessary.

Assumption of Command Under Conditions Other Than Combat. Whenever the commander of an Air Force unit is detached from command of the organization for any reason, the next senior officer present for duty automatically assumes the command function, pending orders from higher authority. In such a situation, the officer assuming the command function shoulders the responsibility and the authority previously held by the officer replaced. Such a situation is, of course, extremely rare.

Transfer of Responsibilities. Other than under conditions of combat, officers assuming command take over all standing orders, the unit fund, all government property pertaining to the unit, and the organization's records. The transfer of these responsibilities, especially for property and funds, should proceed in a careful and thorough manner, with the outgoing and the incoming commanders reaching jointly acceptable conclusions. As the new commander, you should decline to accept responsibility until you have satisfied yourself that the property, the funds, and the records of the unit are in an understandable and proper order.

Do Not Hasten to Change Things. Sometimes officers assuming command of an Air Force unit are overly quick to disrupt standing operating procedures (SOPs), to radically modify policies the unit personnel have become familiar with, and generally to create confusion. As the new commander, you should allow a reasonable period of time to study the organization, the personnel, and the practices that preceded your command before launching into major changes.

THE SQUADRON COMMANDER

The commander is responsible for the execution of all activities pertaining to the unit, including the successful accomplishment of all missions assigned in either training or war. Commanders are responsible in every way for all that their organizations do or fail to do.

To a greater degree than commanders at higher levels, squadron commanders must be in intimate touch with their people and know their individual characteristics and capacities, their degree of training, their morale, and their discipline. They must provide for the welfare of their people under all conditions. In training, they must prepare their own people to succeed despite the most rigorous hardships. In war or even in training, they must save them from all unnecessary trials to preserve their stamina. The conditions airmen experience in their own squadrons determine their opinions of the Air Force as a whole.

There are several duties commanders cannot decentralize, such as responsibility for organization property, responsibility for the unit fund, nonjudicial punishment under Article 15 of the Uniform Code of Military Justice, and the authentication of many records.

Use of Subordinate Leaders. Highly successful commanders are adept at obtaining maximum efficiency from subordinate leaders. Their responsibilities should be clearly defined so that each may proceed with confidence.

Events that depart from routine must be disclosed to subordinate leaders in time to permit them to make their plans and prepare to do their parts. A meeting may be held at which the requirement is discussed. Thought should be given to the manner of presenting the project before the group assembles. At the assembly, the commander should state the mission, with its time and place of execution. Opportunity to ask questions should be provided. At the end of the meeting, the commander will probably have announced the decision and plan for the execution of a mission for which the commander alone is responsible.

Meetings of the key officers of a squadron should be held frequently. This is an opportunity for the commander to announce new work to be undertaken, specific small tasks to be completed in anticipation of a later action, and inspections and other matters that affect the squadron as a whole. Opportunity to make suggestions for improvement in conditions should be extended. A healthy reaction is obtained by asking opinions as to matters of general concern and interest. These meetings should be informal and brief. They provide an opportunity for the commander to obtain the cooperation of all subordinate leaders, because they will know exactly what is wanted.

Understudies and Replacements. The services of key persons are often lost to an organization with surprising suddenness. The Air Force must maintain itself so that any officer, noncommissioned officer, or specialist may be immediately replaced without adversely affecting the efficiency of the unit. The training of understudies must be continuous.

The best people must convince themselves that they will receive consideration for appointment to higher responsibility or position if they prepare themselves for the task. Some regular procedure must be followed for the training of ambitious airmen who wish to demonstrate their capacity for advancement. As opportunities arise, airmen should be given a chance to exercise leadership or control of others to provide a means of further development. When this is done, the selection of the best people for advancement or for replacements is made more likely.

Preparations to Be Relieved of Command. The conditions of military service often result in a limited tenure of command by individual officers. Although one should approach each current duty as if it would continue for a lifetime, commanders know well that one day they must turn their units over to their reliefs.

The efficiency of commanders can be better judged after their relief from command. When command is relinquished, it should be clean, with no hidden skeletons, no loose ends to confound a successor unfamiliar with the problems. Property should be in good condition, with no shortages, all required entries should be made in official records, and the unit fund should be built up and its exact status made entirely clear.

It would seem to be a questionable practice for an officer about to be relieved to embark upon a program of expenditure of the unit fund. The successor may have ideas on these matters and be prevented from carrying them into execution.

The new commander should not be embarrassed by requests that are just within permissible practices. It is an imposition to ask a new commander to receipt for overages or shortages, and if such request is made, it should be refused. The successor should not be asked to complete transactions that should be finished by the officer being relieved.

It is reprehensible to criticize the predecessor in command. Even in those few instances when it may be well deserved, it should be strictly avoided. But the officer being relieved can eliminate much of the chance of such criticism by being certain to complete every required transaction, to inform the successor of

every helpful bit of information (not forgetting the special desires and requirements of the immediate commander), and finally, to transmit to the new commander an organization to be proud of.

THE SOUND OF COMBAT

Air Force officers who have seen the sights and heard the sounds of battle
understand the reactions of untried Air Force officers. Most experienced officers state that inexperienced officers show more bravery, more unconcern for
enemy fire than do those who have sweated through more deadly circumstances on a number of earlier occasions.

Combat is too often described as being only the event of deadly encounters
between two adversaries. Not so. Combat is more often the tiresome struggle to
supply aviation materiel, such as fuel, at the proper time and place in the combat zone. Combat is frequently the effort to produce sanitary water and food in
an area where it is almost impossible to do so; to build revetments around aircraft; to operate a decent eating facility in indecent surroundings; to furnish
needed parts for inoperable aircraft when the parts are many miles away. In
today's warfare, especially in unconventional warfare, frustration can build
because of the near impossibility of distinguishing friend from foe or the seem-
ing ingratitude or hostility of the local population. Combat is doing the best
you can under the circumstances. It is a sharp realization that your life or death
or someone else's hangs in the balance between your performance and that of
your enemy.

Air Force officers need not be unduly afraid of combat, provided they have
done their best to prepare themselves professionally, physically, emotionally,
and spiritually for the test.

IMPORTANCE OF THE MILITARY MISSION

In the exercise of command, the first necessity is to perform the mission.
Orders may assign the mission. If so, just go ahead and do it. Occasionally, the
assignment is general with an overall objective. You may then need to select
and adopt successive missions, the sum of which will accomplish the requirement. Successful commanders are the ones who accomplish their missions on
time, with minimal expenditures of personnel and other resources, and in a professional manner.

TRAINING

Purpose of Military Training. The ultimate purpose of all military training is the assurance of victory in war. We want a fighting Air Force composed
of officers and enlisted people who can do their complex jobs better than the
enemy. If we train well, the task of winning will require far less time than that
which will be necessary if we train poorly.

One of the outstanding lessons derived from experiences in World War II,
Korea, Vietnam, the Gulf War, and the wars in Afghanistan and Iraq is that the

state of training of units is the governing factor determining the combat capability of a military unit. Air Force equipment in general is excellent in quality and adequate in quantity. Air Force morale is high. Supply and maintenance standards are superior. Discipline is commendable. Leadership, from the top down to the lowest unit, is superb. In training, however, lapses may be noted. Every commander should recognize this: *Training is never good enough; improvement is always possible.* Training is a round-the-clock function for the unit. A great deal of it may seem dull and tiresome. Nonetheless, it must be accomplished thoroughly, for it pays off in lives saved and in missions accomplished.

War also points up the tremendous importance of the less dramatic aspects of Air Force training. Officers controlling support activities, such as the supply of munitions and aviation fuel, actually hold the throttle of the Air Force. It is of critical importance that officers commanding support organizations realize the controlling nature of their units' performance and bring those units to the highest possible state of readiness and performance. Aircrews cannot fly without fuel, ammunition, spare parts, operable weapons, well-maintained air bases, and in-commission aircraft. The Air Force is a chain made of many links, only one of which is the operating combat force. Air depots, engineers, researchers, administrators, hospital staffs, maintenance crews, tactical control parties, intelligence agencies—all of these and many more are absolutely indispensable links in the chain of airpower. Everyone has a crucial job to do; everyone must be highly trained to do it.

Joint Training. Most commanders of combat units will sooner or later find their units engaged in some form of joint training with the Army, Navy, or Marine Corps. In the past, there was too little emphasis given to joint training. In part, this attitude stemmed from a false belief that the Air Force could win wars alone, that joint training was superfluous. Many felt that there was already too much to be accomplished in the training program without adding joint training. If any single fact stood out in Korea, Vietnam, and again in the Gulf War, it was the need for more and better joint training. The Air Force, Army, Marines, and Navy fight in close coordination. Each depends upon the others.

For the unit commander, the point is this: Wars are won by teamwork among the services; your unit not only must want to take part in this teamwork, but also must be well trained in joint operations. Mere willingness to cooperate in an emergency will never take the place of practiced know-how. It would be a sickening thing to think that Americans were dying because of a low state of joint training of *your* unit; nor would you find it any solace to reflect that such Americans were in the Army, the Navy, or the Marines rather than in the Air Force.

THE CONDUCT OF INSTRUCTION
Every commander has responsibilities for the conduct of instruction. Airmen will have received instruction in their specialties, through the formal training processes of the Air Force. But instruction never ceases. All airmen should be

brought to a higher state of competence as rapidly as possible, particularly in respect to the specific tasks they must perform in the unit of assignment. Commanders must engage themselves in this process, either through direct participation or through supervision of the noncommissioned instructors who perform the training tasks.

Instruction includes explanation, demonstration, practice, and correction. It is the responsibility of all officers to ensure that within their areas of responsibility instruction is carried on constantly and well. They cannot safely assume that this will be automatically accomplished by noncommissioned officers or that the formal training of airmen is sufficient. In the Air Force, change is constant, and almost every change requires new instruction of airmen. This is a prime responsibility of command.

LOGISTICS

The United States has been lavish with money and effort to make our armed forces the best equipped and maintained. Most individuals understand this point clearly when they consider outstanding single items. The total number of separate items is infinite, and the cost is prodigious. The job of commanders is to obtain the items allowed for their units, see that they are issued to their people, and see that they are maintained in top-notch condition.

Supply officers can provide all the necessary information on what is authorized. The unit commander, however, must supply the energy, care, and attention to detail that are necessary to attain the required results. Unit commanders must find out the equipment authorized for their units, and then ensure that it is obtained, distributed, inspected, and maintained, always ready for use.

Supply in the United States. Unit commanders constantly face supply problems. The supply procedures require considerable bookkeeping and responsibility. It cannot be otherwise. The whole problem revolves around accomplishing two primary objectives: first, to equip the unit with the items needed; and second, to keep every item of equipment in serviceable condition.

Supply in the Field. As soon as a unit enters field conditions, it faces a different sort of supply problem. But if any officers conclude that their responsibility has been left behind, they are in for a rude awakening. An officer is responsible for seeing that the enlisted personnel are provided with the items of equipment they require, in combat especially. The penalty for carelessness or inefficiency may be to do without, which in combat may mean the difference between life and death, victory and defeat.

Even if a unit reaches an overseas area fully equipped, at once things will happen that must be handled promptly. People are careless and lose things. Property is pilfered. Sympathetic American airmen may be tempted to give clothing, food, and other necessities to poverty-stricken locals. The airmen may feel that they can obtain replenishment or have more equipment than they will need. There is even the temptation to sell articles to locals. In any event, the commander is responsible for having personnel of the unit fully equipped.

Training to impress personnel with the importance of guarding their equipment jealously will help. Frequent property checks will also reduce losses and inform the commander of the unit's situation.

Wear and tear is a most difficult problem, especially in combat zones. The unit commander must reduce waste and present the needs in time for the supply or repair machinery to respond.

The problems of supply of food, ammunition, fuel, and clothing are with unit commanders day and night. They must provide for them and plan for them. In combat, supply lines are lifelines. Most items are in short supply. Squadrons unaccustomed to frugality with supplies pay for this failing in inconvenience, inefficiency, and sometimes lives.

Importance of Maintenance. In combat, any failure to maintain equipment in safe and operable condition may be disastrous. A gun that fails to fire may result in loss of life. Missiles or bombs that malfunction can waste the effort and increase the risk involved in a mission. A landing gear that is improperly maintained will be subject to unnecessary breakage and wear. It may fail in a crucial moment. Continual training and inspection are necessary. Adequate maintenance will reduce the necessity for returning vast quantities of supplies to the United States for extensive overhaul. Unit commanders, who are in direct charge of the equipment and the people who use it, must understand the whole problem, see the need for maintenance, and acquaint themselves with the condition of their equipment by unremitting inspections and corrective action. Maintenance may mean the difference between success and failure.

MILITARY SECURITY
There is always the problem of security. Personnel must be ready to detect attack from the air or the ground, on and off military installations. The repeated sudden attacks in Afghanistan and Iraq are sufficient examples of the necessity for vigilance. Security in combat-like situations, such as those that have proliferated since the end of the Cold War, pose many hazards, especially if airmen are complacent. Teach your people thoroughly the difficult art of security. The Royal Air Force concept that all airmen are soldiers first has its merits.

UNIT ADMINISTRATION
Administration begins in the squadron. That is where the airmen work and where changes in their status take place. That is where they are disciplined and trained to become efficient, high-spirited fighting teams. The entire process of administering their affairs depends in large measure upon the initial action of the commander. If that first action by the commander and his staff is speedy and accurate, the administrative process may then become a smooth-running operation of which the tactical commander is scarcely conscious.

Command of a unit includes a diversified responsibility over several different but interdependent phases of operation. The breakdown of one will have an injurious effect upon the others. Balance is required. These phases are organization, morale, discipline, training to develop battle efficiency, security, administration, and supply.

Classification and Assignment. The Air Force has an excellent classification system that identifies special skills possessed by airmen. After classification, people are assigned to units or other assignments in accordance with these skills. This knowledge is of inestimable value, because the use of skills reduces the training burden. Classification follows airmen wherever they go.

The Air Force is vitally interested in placing all members where they can best use their talents. In so doing, we use the training of our industry, our schools, and our colleges. Don't be guilty of hiding an experienced computer expert or an airplane mechanic.

TAKING CARE OF THE TROOPS

Next to the mission, welfare of the troops, especially in combat situations, is a leader's most important responsibility because of its effect on their morale and their consequent ability to perform the mission. Leaders must interest themselves in all matters affecting the welfare of their people, including food, adequate clothing and equipment, health and sanitation, recreation and entertainment, career guidance, and personal problems. This responsibility involves planning, procuring and distributing necessary supplies, training, frequent inspections, and corrective measures, which may include disciplinary action.

Consideration and, when possible, help must be given in dealing with personal problems. Young people away from home for the first time will most likely need unsolicited advice.

The spirit behind the leader's interest must be one of genuine helpfulness and thoughtfulness. In matters involving the proper care of government property, protection of health, and fitness of the airmen to perform assigned duties, stern measures should be taken, if necessary.

MORALE

Personal Appearance and Morale. The uniform is prescribed to improve the appearance and standing of the wearer. It will do so only to the extent that it is clean, pressed, and worn properly. Airmen cannot feel pride in their service unless they look the part of good airmen.

Health as an Aid to Morale. Commanders are responsible for the health and physical well-being of the members of their units. In this responsibility, they are assisted by the medical officers. Medical officers serve as staff officers and advisers of the commanders in all matters that pertain to the care of the sick and wounded and the evacuation of the wounded, as well as in matters of sanitation or hygiene, all in addition to their professional duties within medical facilities serving the needs of the armed forces. There is nothing so destructive of the morale of service personnel as the knowledge or even the suspicion that the sick or wounded are being inadequately attended. In the execution of normal command functions, officers of the Air Force have, in the medical officers, a material source of assistance upon which they may draw.

Athletics and Morale. Provision for athletics is an important factor in the physical fitness of the individual airman and in maintaining high morale. In addition to the mandated Air Force Fitness Program, commanders must sponsor and develop athletic facilities. For the most part, airmen are young, strong, and energetic. They need constructive outlets for their energies. A variety of fitness and athletic facilities should be available to meet the varying preferences of members of the unit. The use of the facilities should be encouraged.

Religion and Morale. Freedom of religion and of religious belief is one of the most important principles in our national philosophy. This principle must be extended to the airman and proper respect extended to religious convictions. The religious and spiritual welfare of the members of a command is an important factor in the development of individual pride, morale, and self-respect, all essentials in a military organization. Unfortunately, the Air Force environment in some instances leaves a little to be desired. There is a relation between morals and morale, just as there is a relation between fair and just treatment and morale, or cleanliness and morale. Organization commanders who are mindful of the religious and spiritual needs of their people will be able to make a strong appeal to the better instincts of all.

The Chaplain. Chaplains are charged with religious responsibility and a host of other duties. Although they conduct religious worship services and attend to baptisms, marriages, and funerals, their most important work may lie in the close, personal contacts they make throughout a command. Unless they receive the cooperation of commanders, their work cannot possibly achieve the utmost. The tasks of chaplains can be difficult ones. A word of suggestion to a chaplain as to a needed service for an individual will often result in the solution of a baffling problem. A word of encouragement to the chaplains to let them know their services are recognized and valued will stimulate further effort. Commanders who cooperate with the chaplains and seek to improve the spiritual, religious, and moral standards of their units will receive important dividends for their efforts.

Morale, Welfare, Recreation, and Services. The morale, welfare, recreation, and services officer leads the recreational services, including voluntary athletics. Close coordination and support should be developed between commanders and the services officer. The overall mission of the services officer is to provide an attractive, wholesome off-duty environment for personnel. Such a program should have a direct effect upon reenlistment rates, which are a matter of direct continual concern to commanders. Commanders of small units are their own services officers. They should be thoroughly familiar with facilities available for their use and make it possible for their people to make use of them to the fullest degree.

Athletic programs that encourage maximum participation by individuals constitute the heart of all recreational activities. The recreation center should be the hub around which many activities of interest to airmen revolve. The library is taken for granted at most bases and its popularity accepted. Hobby shops with manual arts programs should be encouraged.

The goal is to increase the degree of satisfaction experienced by all military personnel. The effect should be that airmen find interesting, constructive leisure activities on their bases, rather than seek every opportunity to visit nearby civilian communities.

Use of the Organization Fund. Through nonappropriated fund channels, commanders receive allotments of funds applicable to units on their bases for the purpose of improving morale. Squadron commanders can apply for an allocation from this fund for specific morale-building activities of the squadron. A typical use of such a fund allocation would be to hold a squadron picnic or party. Any worthwhile, enjoyable entertainment for squadron personnel can be financed in this manner. The squadron commander must make application for the allocation of funds, indicating the intended use.

Members of a unit are entitled to know the status of the fund at all times because, after all, it is *their* fund. They should be informed of the intent to make future purchases. The commander who announces, however, that a purchase will be made and fails to make it soon nullifies any beneficial effect such announcements can provide.

The American Red Cross and Morale. The American Red Cross acts as the means of communication between the military and the civilian community. This organization has chapters or representatives in all parts of the United States and its territories. At many bases, there is a Red Cross field director to serve the needs of the base. Although this nationwide organization always stands ready to perform a wide variety of worthy missions, its services are often useful in cases where airmen are troubled about conditions at home. In such instances, it is common practice to call upon the representative of the Red Cross, explain the problem fully, and ask for an investigation of the actual conditions. The situation can often be adjusted. In any event, the officers will obtain reliable information that will enable many baffling human problems concerning the airmen of their organizations to be handled in a judicious manner based upon facts.

Air Force Aid Society. The work of the Air Force Aid Society is another valuable adjunct to the efforts of commanders to provide for the welfare and morale of their airmen. (See chapter 26, "Legal Documents and Assistance.")

Family Support Centers. Family Support Centers are a result of the Air Force's recognition that family issues have a direct effect on the morale and productivity of Air Force members and on decisions for making the Air Force a career. They serve as a focal point for responding to family issues that affect the Air Force mission. (See chapter 26, "Legal Documents and Assistance.")

Leave and Passes. The Department of the Air Force authorizes commanders to grant leaves so that people receive 30 days' leave a year. Leave is a privilege and not a right. However, except as a consequence of war or unpredictable contingencies, something is wrong in the management of a unit and its personnel if every member does not have the opportunity to take the full annual leave. Commanders should ensure that each airman plans, schedules, and takes annual leave. Commanders should be informed thoroughly on the procedures governing leaves prescribed by the department and local senior commanders. Commanders should study the program of the organization and determine periods most suitable for granting leaves and those periods when they should not be granted except for important emergency reasons. They must plan their leave procedures. Personnel who are designated for reassignment overseas are required to be granted leave before departure unless they have had a recent absence or military necessity prohibits a delay in departure. Military necessity must govern, and it will not always be possible to grant these absences. It is most unwise for commanders to announce leave policies in a manner that can be interpreted as a promise. Broken promises are themselves a cause for some absences without leave. Commanders can inform unit personnel of the regulations, tell them of their plans and their intentions, inform them that circumstances at the time the leave is desired must determine their action, seek opportunities to send personnel on leave, and see to it that opportunities are equitably distributed to all personnel. These measures will replace ignorance with understanding and serve to reduce the causes for unauthorized absence.

Personal Problems of Servicemembers. Many servicemembers have left interests or problems behind that may require their attention or action while in military service. At home, they would turn for advice to parents, friends, clergy, lawyers, or other people in whom they have trust and confidence. In the service, they frequently turn to their commanders.

These occasions provide an opportunity for commanders to show true interest in the welfare of their troops. They should adopt an impersonal and kindly attitude in hearing these problems. If the matter is confidential, it must never be divulged improperly. They should give the counsel they feel is correct, obtain the necessary information, or refer the airmen to authorities who can supply the information.

Good leaders must have a genuine understanding of human relations. Their tools are people, and therefore they must be able to deal with people. The necessary warmth of military leadership may be demonstrated when individuals carry their baffling personal problems to their commanders for advice or solution.

Complaints. The commander must be accessible to members of the unit who wish to make complaints. Some of the complaints may be petty or even deliberate attempts to injure the reputation of another with a charge that is without foundation. Others will be substantive; after all even in the best organizations there can be genuine cause for dissatisfaction. This is information the commander must obtain so that the morale of the unit is not seriously impaired and the unit's mission is not jeopardized. Personnel must know that they may state a cause for complaint to their commander with the knowledge that the commander will give them a fair, impartial hearing and correct the grievance if convinced of its truth. They must believe that the commander will wish to remove causes for dissatisfaction.

When ideas, suggestions, or reports are stated to the commander that affect the welfare, efficiency, or morale of the unit, or any individual, they must be heard sympathetically. If the condition reported can be corrected or deserves correction, action should be taken at once.

Absence Without Leave. Commanders must face and solve the problem of unauthorized absences from duty. Particularly, commanders must analyze the causes and find solutions to the AWOL situation in their own units. It is not a new problem, and it exists during times of peace as well as in times of war. It is "the status of a person subject to military law who has failed to repair at the fixed time to the properly appointed place of duty, or has gone from the same without proper leave, or has absented himself from his command, guard, quarters, station, or camp without proper leave." In time of war, the punishments authorized in Article 86 of the Uniform Code of Military Justice depend upon the circumstances of the absence, but in a crucial situation in contact with the enemy, this is a most serious offense.

But the punitive approach is inadequate and will not provide the cure. Commanders who rely on punishment will fail to eliminate the cause of unauthorized absence. Officers must get acquainted with unit personnel. It is important for reasons of administration and leadership, but is especially necessary in connection with understanding the AWOL problem. They may facilitate this process by get-acquainted interviews preceded by an analysis of the servicemember's records and related forms so that they will know in advance of the interviews the individual's age, education, aptitudes, length of service, training status, dependent situation, and conduct as shown by the disciplinary record. With that information in mind, commanders should proceed with an informal interview to get acquainted with the airmen and let the airmen get acquainted with them. Seek to find the views of the airmen as to family responsibilities and any worries they may have with respect to their families. By so doing, commanders may be able to correct oversights in dependents' benefits provided by the government and thus remove at once a cause for people absenting themselves without leave. Inquire of the servicemembers as to their career progress, and determine whether they are satisfied that they are contributing a maximum of talents. Encourage them to talk freely, and take the time to explain to the servicemembers those misunderstood things that may confuse or disappoint young people. Knowledge of leave regulations should be tested, for it is true that some personnel absent themselves without leave when by asking they might have received an authorized absence. In these interviews, the servicemembers should be invited to bring problems to the commander when in need of help or advice so that they will feel they have someone to lean on when confused by personal problems.

The whole subject of eliminating unauthorized absences is of primary importance in building an effective Air Force. It is likewise of importance in developing pride in an organization. Success will identify the commanders who study causes of AWOL and remove them. Few people will absent themselves without leave from a well-commanded organization.

DISCIPLINE

Discipline Defined. Military discipline is intelligent, willing, and positive obedience to the will of the leader. Its basis rests upon the voluntary subordination of the individual to the welfare of the group. It is the cohesive force that binds the members of a unit, and its strict enforcement is a benefit for all. Its constraint must be felt not so much in the fear of punishment as in the moral obligation it imposes on the individual to heed the common interests of the group. Discipline establishes a state of mind that produces proper action and prompt cooperation under all circumstances, regardless of obstacles. It creates in the individual a desire and determination to undertake and accomplish any mission assigned by the leader.

Discipline is a controlling factor in the combat value of airmen. The combat value of a unit is determined by the military qualities of the leader and members and its "will to fight." A point too often overlooked is the fact that poorly trained and poorly disciplined units reap the defeats and greatest losses. The greater the combat value of the organization, the more powerful will be the blow struck by the unit.

People are and always will be the vital element in war. In spite of the advances in technology, the worth of the individuals is still decisive. They must be disciplined and must have good morale.

In war, discipline is a matter of the gravest importance, affecting the questions of life and death of individuals. Pilots must be briefed to obey rules of engagement, for example. Discipline is the cement in the structure of the Air Force. Without it, the Air Force would be merely a mob. We *must* have a disciplined Air Force; otherwise, ultimately, we shall have none.

Relationship of Superiors Toward Subordinates. Superiors are forbidden to injure those under their authority by tyrannical or capricious conduct or by abusive language or sexual harassment. While maintaining discipline and the thorough and prompt performance of military duty, all officers, in dealing with airmen, must bear in mind the absolute necessity of preserving their self-respect. A grave duty rests on all officers and particularly upon organization commanders in this regard. Officers must impress upon the young airmen lessons of patriotism and loyalty and above all the necessity of obedience. These lessons must be repeated again and again. The difference in the status of airmen compared with that of civilians must be carefully explained to make them understand that in becoming airmen they are subject to a new control and have assumed obligations they did not have as civilians. Officers must keep in as close touch as possible with the personnel under their command, take an interest in their unit's life, hear their complaints, endeavor on all occasions to remove the existence of those causes that make for dissatisfaction, and strive to build such confidence and sympathy that their people will come to them for counsel and assistance, not only in military and organizational matters, but also in personal or family distress or perplexity. This relationship may be achieved and maintained without relaxing the bonds of discipline.

Punishment. The maintenance of control requires instructions and policies for the guidance of members of the organization. These must include positive matters, things to do, and negative matters, things not to do. Good management requires that instructions and policies be few, entirely justified by conditions, easily understood, necessary for the accomplishment of unit objectives, and at least reasonably in harmony with those in use by neighboring organizations. Of course, all instructions and policies must meet the test of legality. There is little occasion for the adoption of additional restrictive orders that serve only to gratify the personal interests of the commander. The application of restrictive policies on an entire organization because of the transgressions of one or of a small number is a lazy and ineffective form of control. Mass punishment is poor leadership, as is the use of threats or naming a penalty in issuing an order. Such practices cause antagonism. The *Manual for Courts-Martial,* instructions and policies of the Air Force, and the orders of higher authority prescribe the methods of control. They should be carefully studied. An understanding of the requirements that must be enforced is an important part of the maintenance of control.

In any organization, there will be violations of standing orders and offenses committed that are punishable under the Uniform Code of Military Justice. In dealing with offenders against military law, officers should be guided wholly by a desire to serve the best interests of the Air Force. Vengeance has no place in such a consideration. The object is not to punish for the sake of retribution, but to deter servicemembers from offenses, to exact recompense when government property has been lost, and to rehabilitate offenders when possible. It is usually wise to be lenient with first offenders, particularly when the subsequent attitude of the offender is commendable. It is equally wise to be rough on second offenders. Do not seek a reputation for mercy or one for ruthlessness. Rather, advance the reputation of the Air Force for level-headed action in the interests of the national security.

The proper exercise of command requires that personnel be fully informed of what is required of them. The commander must be alert to prevent offenses, for very often a kind word of caution may prevent an offense. Offenses may be committed in ignorance, through carelessness, or with deliberate intent. The skilled commander can eliminate many of those that might be done through ignorance or carelessness.

An immediate recognition and reward of the deserving does much to prevent the commission of offenses. A softly spoken "good work" may be more stimulating to pride than a flowery and lengthy speech. The award of extra privileges or mere recognition of merit has much to do with the development of both sound discipline and high morale.

When considering disciplinary action, commanders must consult the staff judge advocate for legal advice and guidance. The commander should prefer to take disciplinary action under Article 15, Uniform Code of Military Justice, rather than submit charges that will result in a trial by court-martial. For first offenders or for petty offenses, this will usually suffice. Careful investigation must be made before any decision as to punishment is made. This investigation must be impersonal, fair, and just, and it must include an opportunity for the accused airman to refute the charge.

Methods of maintaining discipline must stand the test of battle or the courtroom. Reliance upon trial by court-martial as the sole means of securing obedience to law will fail. When faced with a disciplinary problem, commanders should consider all the alternatives and choose that which best corrects the problem and prevents its recurrence. In any case, where serious action or punishment is considered, commanders should consult the staff judge advocate to ensure that the procedure is appropriate and is legally justified.

There is a distinction between *punitive* and *administrative* procedures. Punitive actions include nonjudicial punishment and trial by court-martial, and necessitate compliance with the *Manual for Courts-Martial.* In all cases, the staff judge advocate should be consulted before taking punitive action. Administrative procedures are not governed by the UCMJ or the standards of criminal justice administration, yet they often require legal coordination and review. This is especially true in initiation of administrative discharge action or a demotion action.

In handling any disciplinary matter, commanders must be careful to remain objective. Haste and partiality can do much to harm commanders' images and respect in the eyes of their subordinates. It may also cement a bad attitude where airmen feel they cannot get a fair hearing or equitable treatment, thereby nullifying any rehabilitative effect that might otherwise result from the commander's action.

A common pitfall for some commanders and supervisors is failure to proceed through a graduated course of action employing the different levels of disciplinary tools. Generally speaking, a gradual increase in severity of action against a person with a disciplinary problem is the most effective method of getting the attention of those who can be rehabilitated. Too often, a supervisor will "forgive and forget"—that is, stay at the level of oral counseling—until some breaking point is reached, whereupon the supervisor wants the individual "hanged at sunrise" and discharged immediately thereafter. Some supervisors at this point have a strong feeling of being personally betrayed by the individual, who "has not appreciated all the chances I gave him." Since Air Force policies, instructions, and manuals are written in contemplation of a graduated response, there is often difficulty in meeting the requirements of these directives where there are erratic swings in the commander's response to a given discipline problem.

Disciplinary Tools. Commanders are responsible for maintaining good order and discipline within their commands. Military discipline refers to a person's self-control and ability to conform to the standard of conduct demanded by the service. Commanders are expected to set good examples, provide instructional guidance, and when necessary, impose disciplinary action upon personnel subject to their authority.

Commanders faced with problems of discipline, job performance, or maintenance of order have a number of administrative and disciplinary tools at their disposal. In connection with, but never in place of, disciplinary actions are counseling and other assistance with problems that underlie many discipline problems. For instance, valuable information, advice, and assistance is available from *The Military Commander and the Law (http://milcom.jag.af.mil),* the chaplain, military equal opportunity, the hospital, the staff judge advocate, the area defense counsel, family services, and the personal financial management counselor. Commanders should be aware of the range of disciplinary tools and when the use of each is appropriate. These tools include the following:

- Oral counseling by the commander, first sergeant, or supervisor.
- Written counseling (AFI 36-2907).
- Admonitions and reprimands (AFI 36-2907).
- Control roster and unfavorable information files (UIF) (AFI 36-2907).
- Administrative demotion (AFI 36-2503).
- Administrative discharge (AFI 36-3208).
- Nonjudicial punishment (AFI 51-202).
- Trial by court-martial (AFI 51-201).
- Discharge of commissioned officers (AFI 36-3206).

Punishment Under Article 15. Article 15 of the UCMJ provides authority to certain unit commanders to impose punishment of a degree less than that for which court-martial action is required. This authority, however, is qualified by the fact that any airman may demand trial by court-martial rather than accept punishment under Article 15. Nonetheless, when commanders have conducted a preliminary inquiry or are otherwise satisfied that court-martial action is not desirable, they should inform the offender in writing of the intent to impose punishment under Article 15. The offender must state, in writing, a willingness to accept Article 15 punishment or a demand for court-martial. If the offender demands court-martial, the matter is then handled by preferring formal charges. If the offender certifies willingness to accept Article 15 punishment, the commander proceeds to impose the punishment. In this correspondence, the commander does not indicate what punishment is intended until after the offender has accepted punishment under Article 15.

Commanders may impose a wide variety of punishments under Article 15. Commanders in general officer grade may, under Article 15, punish officers under their command by imposing restriction for up to sixty days, arrest in quarters for thirty days, or forfeiture of half pay for sixty days. Colonels may impose on officers in their commands a reprimand and restriction for thirty days.

Commanders in the grade of major or above may adjudge punishment to airmen of their command as follows: not more than thirty days' correctional custody, forfeiture of half of their pay for two months, extra duty of forty-five days, restriction for two months, or reduction in grade (an E-4 or higher may not be reduced more than two grades).

Commanders below the grade of major may, under Article 15, punish airmen of their command by imposing not more than one week of correctional custody, forfeiture of one week's pay, extra duty for two weeks, restriction to limits for two weeks, detention of two weeks' pay, or reduction of one grade (provided the commander has the authority to promote to the grade from which the airman is to be demoted).

The commander should consult with the staff judge advocate if the punishment intended approaches the levels for which court-martial action is required. In general, the use of Article 15 is preferred by commanders, as opposed to court-martial, when it is an appropriate procedure. The court-martial procedure is costly to the government and consumes the time of valuable people. Article 15 should be employed when the offender accepts it, when the punishments available under Article 15 are considered adequate, and when court-martial is not mandatory.

Administrative Discharges. Commanders are given authority to eliminate the unfit and the undesirable from the Air Force and to remove airmen who are mentally or psychologically unable to perform acceptably as airmen. Such people may well want to perform properly, but cannot. They should be discharged.

Air Force policy, instructions, and procedures provide for the separation of those who can be useful airmen but will not do so. These are the alcoholics, the drug users, the rebels, the repeating offenders, the undisciplined. They should be removed from the Air Force as quickly as possible. The Air Force also authorizes the separation of airmen who are sentenced by civil authorities to confinement for more than one year.

In preparing action to eliminate airmen, commanders must compile a record of offenses, instances, or other evidence of unsuitability. Usually, it will be necessary to show that efforts have been made to correct the situation, through counseling or other methods. This record is attached to a letter to the discharge authority, asking that a board of officers be formed to review the case and determine disposition.

Officers dealing with cases of unsuitability should be guided entirely by the needs of the Air Force. An unfit airman stands in a space that might be filled by a productive airman. There is no room for the unfit or the undesirable. Each person in the total strength of the Air Force must be first class.

Military Courts-Martial. There are three kinds of courts-martial: the summary court, the special court, and the general court. Officers may serve as members of any court-martial. Enlisted personnel may serve on a general or a special court-martial for the trial of enlisted personnel when, before the convening of the court, the accused requests in writing that enlisted personnel be so detailed. When so requested, the membership of the court must include at least one-third enlisted personnel. Punishing power of the two inferior courts, summary and special, is limited by statute. The punishing power of the general court is usually, by the wording of the Uniform Code of Military Justice denouncing a particular offense, left to the discretion of the court. That apparently unlimited power does not exist, however. In a few instances, the article itself prescribes the punishment for a particular offense. In all other cases, the president, under authority given him by an article of the Uniform Code of Military Justice, has prescribed a table of maximum punishments. The punishment of nearly all offenses that are denounced by the civil common law and by nonmilitary codes has been similarly limited by the president. In the rare event that an offense is committed that is not covered by the president's limit of punishment order, the punishment may not exceed that fixed as a maximum for the offense by the U.S. Penal Code or the Criminal Code for the District of Columbia. The sentence of a court-martial has no validity until it has been approved by the officer appointing the court. The sentences of all general courts-martial are subject to a series of reviews and approvals or disapprovals in which the record of trial is examined not only to determine its legal sufficiency, but also to ensure that no sentence of unnecessary harshness is finally executed.

Restraint. Any person in the military service may sign and swear to charges that are an offense under military law. Usually, however, the person having knowledge of the alleged offense makes the information known to the immediate commander of the accused enlisted servicemember or officer. Ordinarily, this commander would be the squadron commander. The commander must then make an immediate decision as to whether the accused person should be put under any degree of restraint, such as confinement to quarters. If restraint seems indicated, the commander should issue the necessary orders at once.

Informal Inquiry. The commander (or a representative) must promptly make a preliminary inquiry of the accusations. This inquiry may be no more than a consideration of the charges and such evidence as is offered by the accuser. It may include a search of dormitories, quarters, or other pertinent areas. Collection of documentary evidence may be desirable, depending on the nature of the charge. Individuals may be questioned informally. It is most important to remember, however, that before questioning accused persons, they must be informed of the accusations made and warned that any statement they make may be used against them if a trial results (Article 31, UCMJ).

The commander must reach decisions as matters proceed. If the preliminary inquiry leads to a conclusion that court-martial action is not indicated, the commander may wish to adopt lesser punitive procedures or none at all. In many cases, accusations will be found to lack substance and may simply be dismissed.

Charges for Courts-Martial. If commanders believe that court-martial procedure is proper, they should have formal charges executed at once and so inform the accused. In carrying out this action, commanders must consult with the office of the staff judge advocate.

Area Defense Counsel. The Area Defense Counsel (ADC) is a certified judge advocate performing defense counsel duties for courts-martial, administrative actions, Article 15 actions, interrogations, and any other adverse actions in which counsel for an individual is required or authorized. Active-duty servicemembers under any type of investigation should be referred to an ADC.

ADCs, who are outside any local chain of command, are responsible to vigorously represent their clients within the bounds of professional ethics. ADCs are advocates for their clients, not advisors for the command.

Commanders may talk to ADCs directly. ADCs can often fill in the "rest of the story," but they cannot reveal client confidences. Remember that ADCs are bound to represent their clients honestly and fairly and that your discussions will be on the record.

5

The Air Force of the Future

Many opportunities and challenges will face the Air Force officer as the United States moves farther into the twenty-first century. Some challenges are of a near-term nature, and others are focused on the long term. This chapter outlines some of the special reviews that have been conducted by the Air Force to help it meet its future national and international missions, including recognition of the important role Air Force personnel will play in future initiatives. Also discussed are other initiatives that are being pursued by the senior leadership to enhance the quality of life for those who serve.

AIR FORCE POSTURE STATEMENT

Each year, the secretary of the Air Force and the chief of staff of the Air Force issue a posture statement that is both a vision for the coming year and an overview of the Air Force's contribution to protecting the United States, deterring aggression, assuring our allies, and defeating our enemies. The 2007 posture statement focused on fighting and winning the Global War on Terror, developing and caring for our airmen and their families, and recapitalizing and modernizing USAF's aging aircraft, spacecraft, and equipment. More substantively, the posture statement states that "we see a long-term strategic mismatch between national strategy and defense resources." The secretary of the Air Force and the chief of staff elaborate that "the 2006 Quadrennial Defense Review calls for a DOD to defend the homeland, operate in and from forward areas, swiftly defeat enemies in tow regions, and win one conflict decisively." They conclude that neither the existing or projected force structure can achieve these missions.

Earlier posture statements have been specific about what the United States and the U.S. Air Force face. The reality of today's world necessitates an emphasis on the Global War on Terror, asymmetric threats from terrorists and rogue states, and the threat of the combination of radicalism and technology, specifically the proliferation of weapons of mass destruction in the hands of unfriendly states and nonstate entities. To counter these threats, the posture statement outlines the contributions of professional airmen, investment in state-of-the-art warfighting technologies, and the necessity to employ active-reserve, joint, and combined forces that are fully integrated.

For the foreseeable future, the Air Force will continue to have to deal with the stresses and disorders of the world as it continues the transition from the Cold War era. Defense intelligence analysts predict that no power, circumstance, or condition is likely to emerge in the short term that will be capable of overcoming post–Cold War stresses and creating a more stable global environment.

Within this environment, the "Big C" issues will continue to dominate America's political and military attention. These are (1) counterterrorism operations, especially against threats directed against the United States and its citizens, businesses, and military forces at home and abroad; (2) counter-proliferation of weapons of mass destruction; (3) counterintelligence against the growing variety of potentially hostile forces; and (4) counterdrug operations.

Globalization is the principal force driving the "Big C" issues. On the one hand, globalization means the increasing flow of ideas, money, people, information, and technology. It is generally a positive force that will most help the world to advance economically and democratically. The Internet and the explosion of information available at the click of a mouse have added to and accelerated the drive toward globalization.

On the other hand, the explosion of information can exacerbate local and regional tensions, increase the prospects and capabilities for conflict, and be used by those who would do America harm. The transfer of information and technology may allow smaller states, nonstate entities, and individuals to gain access to destructive capabilities of weapons of mass destruction-a capability previously limited to major world powers-and to use the inherent vulnerabilities of Western democracies with their complex economies and infrastructures-such as was done on 11 September 2001.

Some of the more specific threats facing the United States for the foreseeable future include:

International Terrorism. The possibility for the foreseeable future of a major terrorist attack against U.S. interests, either here or abroad, perhaps with a weapon designed to produce mass casualties, is considered likely.

The Middle East. Deterioration of conditions in the Middle East, specifically in Israel-Palestine, Afghanistan, and Iraq, could increase the risk of anti-American violence throughout the region and lead to a wider regional conflict. Furthermore, militant Islamic fundamentalism has demonstrated its potential to spread the security threat outside the region. A continued commitment of the U.S. military forces to the region can be expected.

Korea. The United States will closely monitor the Korean peninsula. A breakdown in the growing rapprochement between North and South Korea or failure to resolve nuclear issues may mean a return to high tensions. On the other hand, the United States and its allies must be prepared for an accelerated move toward reunification of the two countries. This too will have security implications, as U.S. national interests in this region are high.

India and Pakistan. The United States will be alert for an expanded military conflict between India and Pakistan over regional disputes. This is more serious now since both India and Pakistan have nuclear weapons and the means to deliver them. Both sides retain large forces in close proximity across a tense line of control. The potential for a mistake or miscalculation by either side remains relatively high.

Russia. Things are still not settled in Russia regarding the relationship of ethnic minorities and the Russian state and the degree of political and economic liberalization that the Russian state will tolerate. These issues have the potential for negative consequences in the European Union and the Middle East, and with the United States.

China. There will remain a possibility of conflict between China and Taiwan if Beijing increases its pressure on Taiwan for reunification or if Taiwan takes a more assertive stance on the issue of its independence from Beijing. The continuing modernization of Chinese military capabilities is also of great concern for the United States.

The Balkans. There is a possibility of more conflict in the Balkans, a region of long-standing animosities based on religious, linguistic, national, and ethnic differences and on the distribution of various ethnic groups. The commitment of NATO forces to peacekeeping and peace enforcement operations in this region is unlikely to end soon.

PART II

Air Force Organization

6

The Departments of Defense and the Air Force

The U.S. Constitution establishes a basic principle that the armed forces be under civilian control. By giving the president the position of commander in chief, the Constitution provides the basic institutional framework for military organization. This chapter outlines the organization of the Air Force and its role in national defense.

THE COMMANDER IN CHIEF

Following World War II, an increasing need to integrate military policy with national policy compelled the president to assume a much more active role as commander in chief of the armed forces. As commander in chief, the president has the final word of command authority, but as head of the executive branch, he is subject to the checks-and-balances system of the legislative and judicial branches of government. The heavy demands of domestic and foreign duties require the president to delegate authority broadly and wisely. Responsibility for national defense matters is delegated to the Office of the Secretary of Defense (OSD) and to the Department of Defense (DOD).

THE DEPARTMENT OF DEFENSE

The basic purpose of the National Security Act of 1947, and its later amendments, was to establish the Department of Defense. This cabinet agency establishes policies and procedures for the government relating to national security. It includes the Office of the Secretary of Defense; the Joint Chiefs of Staff (JCS); the Departments of the Army, the Navy (including the Marine Corps), and the Air Force; unified, specified, and combined commands; defense agencies; and DOD field activities. As the civilian head of the DOD, the secretary of defense reports directly to the president.

Office of the Secretary of Defense. The president appoints the secretary of defense, with the advice and consent of the Senate. As the principal assistant to

Department of Defense Command Lines

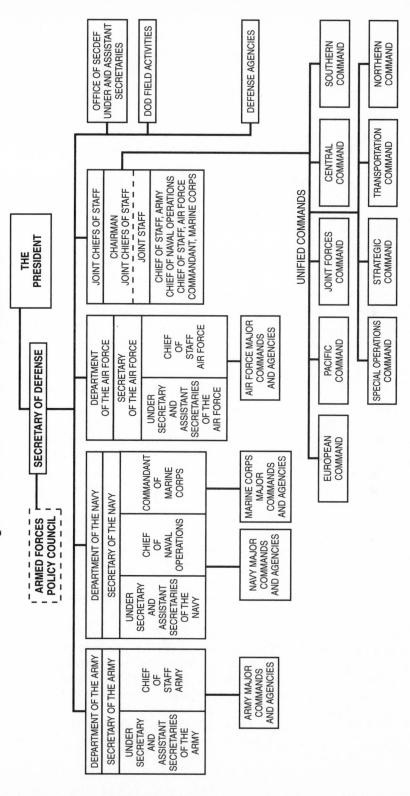

the president for military matters, the secretary has the authority to exercise direction and control over all elements of the DOD. The line of operational command flows from the secretary of defense *through* the JCS directly to the specified and unified commanders. The JCS is *not* in the chain of command. The secretary also delegates authority. For example, the responsibility for strategic and tactical planning is given to the JCS. The military departments have responsibility for training, administrative, and logistic support of the forces assigned to the unified and specified commands.

In the performance of his demanding duties, the secretary requires the help of many assistants, chief of whom is the deputy secretary of defense. When considering matters requiring a long-range view, and in formulating broad defense policy, a number of advisory bodies and individual advisors also assist the secretary of defense. The most important policy advisory body working directly with the secretary of defense is the Armed Forces Policy Council.

The *Armed Forces Policy Council* advises the secretary of defense on matters of broad policy relating to the armed forces and considers and reports on any other matters that, in the opinion of the secretary, need attention. The council consists of the secretary of defense (chairman); the deputy secretary of defense; the secretaries of the Army, the Navy, and the Air Force; the chairman of the Joint Chiefs of Staff; the undersecretaries of defense; the Army and Air Force chiefs of staff; the chief of naval operations; and the commandant of the Marine Corps. Officials of the DOD and other departments and agencies in the executive branch may be invited to attend appropriate meetings of the council.

Joint Chiefs of Staff. The chairman of the Joint Chiefs of Staff is the principal military advisor to the president, the National Security Council, and the secretary of defense. Subject to the authority and direction of the president and the secretary of defense, members of the JCS serve as advisors and military staff to the unified and specified commanders. The JCS prepares strategic plans and provides for the strategic direction of the armed forces. It reviews the plans and programs of unified and specified commands, reviews major personnel and logistic requirements of the armed forces, and establishes unified doctrine. The JCS is also responsible for assigning logistic responsibilities to the military services, formulating policies for joint training, and coordinating military education.

The members of the JCS consist of the chairman; the chief of staff, U.S. Army; the chief of naval operations; the chief of staff, U.S. Air Force; and the commandant of the Marine Corps. The chairman of the JCS serves as a member of, and presides over, the JCS and furnishes the recommendations and views of the JCS to the president, the National Security Council, or the secretary of defense. Other members of the JCS may also provide advice to these bodies, when requested. If a member disagrees with an opinion of the chairman, the chairman presents that advice along with his own.

When the chairman is not present, the vice chairman of the JCS serves as chairman. The vice chairman may participate in all meetings of the JCS but may not vote on a matter before the JCS except when acting as chairman. JCS duties take precedence over all other duties; therefore, as the military heads of their respective services, JCS members delegate appropriate duties to their vice chiefs of staff, but retain responsibility.

The Joint Staff supports the JCS. The Defense Intelligence Agency provides intelligence support, over which the JCS has operational control. The Joint Staff is composed of officers in approximately equal numbers from all the services. The Joint Staff neither operates nor is organized as an overall armed forces general staff, and it has no executive authority. It performs such duties as the JCS prescribes. However, the Joint Staff is structured in such a way that it is responsible for many key agencies within the DOD. One of the agencies most vital to military success is the National Military Command System.

National Military Command and Control. The National Military Command System provides our command authorities with all the information they need to make decisions and the means to transmit those decisions to subordinate levels. At the peak of its communication system is the National Military Command Center (NMCC), which receives data from various command and control centers of the unified and specified commands. The NMCC also receives data from such defense agencies as the National Security Agency and the Defense Intelligence Agency. Members of the Joint Staff analyze and process this information and pass pertinent messages on through the State Department Operations Center and the National Indications Center of the Central Intelligence Agency to the Situation Room in the White House. To ensure command and control survivability, the NMCC has an Alternate NMCC.

Unified, Specified, and Combined Commands. The president, with the advice and assistance of the chairman of the JCS, through the secretary of defense, establishes unified and specified commands for the performance of military missions.

A *unified command* has a broad, continuing mission and is under a single commander. The unified commands are the U.S. Strategic Command, U.S. Joint Forces Command, U.S. European Command, U.S. Pacific Command, U.S. Southern Command, U.S. Central Command, U.S. Northern Command, U.S. Special Operations Command, and U.S. Transportation Command. Unified commands also consist of significant assigned components of two or more services and are normally organized on a geographical basis. A component consists of the component commander and those individuals, organizations, or installations under the military command that have been assigned to the unified command. Other individuals, organizations, or installations may operate directly under the component commander.

A *specified command* also has a broad continuing mission but normally consists of forces from only one service and is functionally oriented. It may include units and staff representation from other services. If the allocation of such staffs or units is to be major or of long duration, it will be established as a unified command. There are currently no specified commands designated.

The secretary of defense assigns the military mission to unified and specified commands. The commander of a unified or specified command deploys, directs, controls, and coordinates the action of the command's forces; conducts joint training exercises; and controls certain support functions. The unified or specified commander is responsible to both the secretary of defense and the president. The component commanders or the commanders of subordinate commands exercise operational command. After a force has been assigned to a unified command, it cannot be transferred except by authority of the secretary of defense or under special procedures of that office with the approval of the president. All units not assigned to a unified or specified command remain with their respective services.

Each military service furnishes administrative and logistic support for its forces assigned to a unified command. The individual services continue to issue assignment orders, logistic support orders, personnel change orders, and similar documents. DOD agencies, such as the Defense Logistics Agency and the Defense Communications Agency, perform certain logistic and administrative support functions. Even though the individual services furnish logistic support to their respective components of the unified command, a unified commander can exercise directive authority to ensure effectiveness and economy of operations.

The logistic authority of unified commands expands under wartime conditions and when critical situations make it necessary. Unified commanders have authorization to use the facilities and supplies of all forces assigned to their commands as necessary to accomplish their wartime missions. Achieving maximum effectiveness from our armed forces requires that the efforts of all the services be integrated closely. The authority of the president and the secretary of defense maintains unity of effort; the secretaries of the military departments and the JCS exercise this authority.

The capability of a unified commander can expand through the formation of either a *subordinate unified command* or a *joint task force* (JTF). Each is composed of joint forces under a single commander. The primary difference between the two lies in the scope of the operation. The subordinate unified command has a continuing mission and command arrangement. The JTF is limited by specific time, place, and mission.

Another structure within the DOD is the *combined command,* which consists of forces from more than one nation. For example, the U.S. European and U.S. Joint Forces Commands contribute forces to the NATO combined commands. Combined commands operate similarly to unified commands, except that command is much less structured in combined commands. Units from the member nations retain their national identities, and much negotiation between nations is necessary to make the command function effectively.

The Military Departments. Although operational command rests with the DOD, the military departments—the Army, the Navy (including the Marine Corps and, in wartime, the Coast Guard), and the Air Force—continue as separate agencies. Although service secretaries are not responsible for military operations, they assist the secretary of defense in managing the administrative, training, and logistic functions of the military departments. Except in operational matters, the secretary of defense issues orders to a service through its secretary. The service secretaries are responsible for the economy and efficiency with which their departments operate.

The traditional roles and mission of each branch of service are commonly referred to as "functions." In addition to specific combat roles, they furnish operational forces to unified and specified commands. The secretary of defense and the JCS established the functions of the armed forces in the 1948 Key West Agreement, which was revised the National Security Act in 1953 and again in 1958. The general functions of the armed forces are the following:

- Support and defend the Constitution of the United States against all enemies, foreign and domestic.
- Ensure, by timely and effective military action, the security of the United States, its possessions, and areas vital to its interests.
- Uphold and advance the national policies and interests of the United States.
- Safeguard the internal security of the United States.

In addition to the general functions, the military services also have some specific functions they share. These include the following:

- Preparing forces and establishing reserves of equipment and supplies for the effective prosecution of war, and planning for the expansion of peacetime components to meet the needs of war.
- Maintaining, in readiness, mobile reserve forces that are properly organized, trained, and equipped for employment in an emergency.
- Providing adequate, timely, and reliable department intelligence for use within the DOD.
- Organizing, training, and equipping interoperable forces for assignment to unified or specified commands.
- Providing, as directed, administrative and logistic support to the headquarters of unified and specified commands, including direct support of the development and acquisition of command and control systems for those headquarters.
- Preparing and submitting (to the secretary of defense) budgets for their respective departments, and justifying (before Congress) budget requests as approved by the secretary of defense.
- Administering the funds made available for maintaining, equipping, and training the forces of their respective departments, including those assigned to unified and specified commands.
- Conducting research; developing tactics, techniques, and organization; and developing and procuring weapons, equipment, and supplies.
- Developing, supplying, equipping, and maintaining bases and other installations, including lines of communication. Providing administrative and logistic support for all forces and bases.

- Assisting in training and equipping the military forces of foreign nations.
- Assisting each other in accomplishing their respective functions, including the provision of personnel, intelligence, training, facilities, equipment, supplies, and services.
- Preparing and submitting, in accordance with other military departments, mobilization information to the JCS.

Each service develops and trains its forces to perform the primary functions that support the efforts of the other services. Carrying out their primary functions helps to accomplish overall military objectives. The assignment of collateral functions may not be used as the basis for additional force requirements.

THE DEPARTMENT OF THE AIR FORCE

The Air Force is responsible for preparation of air forces necessary for the effective prosecution of war and military operations short of war, except as otherwise assigned. In accordance with integrated joint mobilization plans, the Air Force is also responsible for expansion of its peacetime components to meet the needs of war. The *primary functions* of the Air Force include the following:

- To organize, train, equip, and provide forces for the conduct of prompt and sustained combat operations in the air—specifically, forces to defend the United States against air attack in accordance with doctrines established by the JCS; to gain and maintain general air supremacy; to defeat enemy air forces; to conduct space operations; to control vital air areas; and to establish local air superiority except as otherwise assigned herein.
- To organize, train, equip, and provide forces for appropriate air and missile defense and space control operations, including the provision of forces as required for strategic defense of the United States, in accordance with joint doctrines.
- To organize, train, equip, and provide forces for strategic air and missile warfare.
- To organize, train, equip, and provide forces for joint amphibious, space, and airborne operations, in coordination with other military services, in accordance with joint doctrines.
- To organize, train, equip, and provide forces or close air and air logistic support to the Army and other forces as directed, including airlift, air support, resupply of airborne operations, aerial photography, tactical air reconnaissance, and air interdiction of enemy land forces and communications.
- To organize, train, equip, and provide forces for air transport for the armed forces, except as otherwise assigned.

Department of the Air Force—Secretariat and Field Operating Agencies

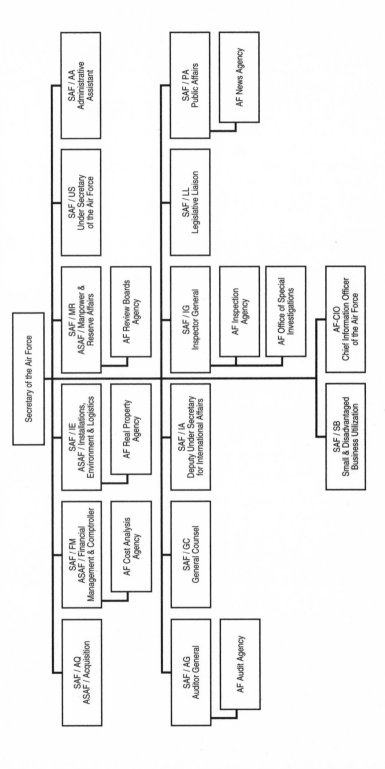

Department of the Air Force—Air Staff and Field Operating Agencies

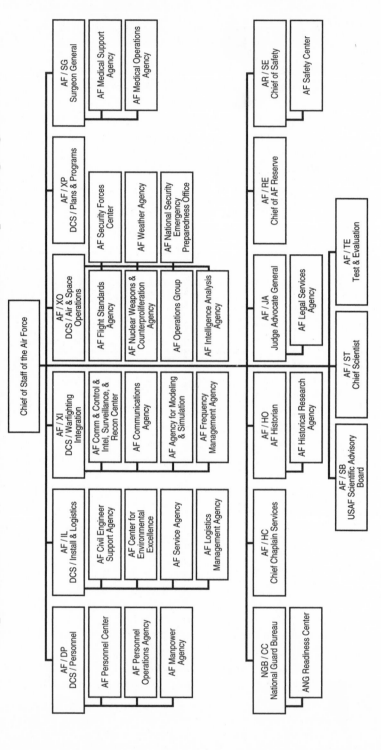

Chief of Staff of the Air Force

AF / DP
DCS / Personnel
- AF Personnel Center
- AF Personnel Operations Agency
- AF Manpower Agency

AF / IL
DCS / Install & Logistics
- AF Civil Engineer Support Agency
- AF Center for Environmental Excellence
- AF Service Agency
- AF Logistics Management Agency

AF / XI
DCS / Warfighting Integration
- AF Comm & Control & Intel, Surveillance, & Recon Center
- AF Communications Agency
- AF Agency for Modeling & Simulation
- AF Frequency Management Agency

AF / XO
DCS / Air & Space Operations
- AF Flight Standards Agency
- AF Nuclear Weapons & Counterproliferation Agency
- AF Operations Group
- AF Intelligence Analysis Agency

AF / XP
DCS / Plans & Programs
- AF Security Forces Center
- AF Weather Agency
- AF National Security Emergency Preparedness Office

AF / SG
Surgeon General
- AF Medical Support Agency
- AF Medical Operations Agency

NGB / CC
National Guard Bureau
- ANG Readiness Center

AF / HC
Chief Chaplain Services

AF / HO
AF Historian
- AF Historical Research Agency

AF / JA
Judge Advocate General
- AF Legal Services Agency

AF / RE
Chief of AF Reserve

AR / SE
Chief of Safety
- AF Safety Center

AF / SB
USAF Scientific Advisory Board

AF / ST
Chief Scientist

AF / TE
Test & Evaluation

- To develop, in coordination with the other services, doctrines, procedures, and equipment for air defense from land areas, including the United States.
- To organize, train, equip, and provide forces to furnish aerial imagery for use by the Army and other agencies as directed, including aerial imagery for cartographic purposes.
- To develop, in coordination with the other services, tactics, techniques, and equipment of interest to the Air Force, and if not provided for elsewhere, for amphibious operations.
- To develop, in coordination with the other services, doctrines, procedures, and equipment employed by USAF forces in airborne operations.
- To provide launch and space support for the DOD, except as otherwise assigned.
- To develop, in coordination with the other services, doctrines, procedures, and equipment employed by USAF forces in the conduct of space operations.
- To organize, train, equip, and provide land-based tanker forces for in-flight refueling support of strategic operations and deployments of aircraft of armed forces and Air Force tactical operations, except as otherwise assigned.
- To organize, train, equip, and provide forces, as directed, to operate air lines of communications.
- To organize, train, equip, and provide forces for the support and conduct of special operations.
- To organize, train, equip, and provide forces for the support and conduct of psychological operations.
- To provide equipment, forces, procedures, and doctrine necessary for the effective prosecution of electronic warfare operations and, as directed, support of other forces.

Collateral functions of the Air Force include conducting the following:
- Surface sea surveillance and antisurface ship warfare through air operations.
- Antisubmarine and antiair warfare operations to protect sea lines of communications.
- Aerial minelaying operations.
- Air-to-air refueling in support of naval campaigns.

Air Force responsibilities *in support of space operations* include the following:
- Organizing, training, equipping, and providing forces to support space operations.
- Developing, in coordination with the other military services, tactics, techniques, and equipment employed by USAF forces for use in space operations.

- Conducting individual and unit training of Air Force space operations forces.
- Participating with the other services in joint space operations, training, and exercises as mutually agreed to by the services concerned, or as directed by competent authority.

Other responsibilities of the Air Force include the following:

- With respect to amphibious operations, the Air Force will develop, in coordination with the other services, tactics, techniques, and equipment of interest to the Air Force and not provided for by the Navy and the Marine Corps.
- With respect to airborne operations, the Air Force has specific responsibility to provide USAF forces for air movement of troops, supplies, and equipment in joint airborne operations, including parachute and aircraft landings; and to develop tactics and techniques employed by USAF forces in the air movement of troops, supplies, and equipment.
- With respect to close air support of ground forces, the Air Force has specific responsibility for developing, in coordination with the other services, doctrines and procedures, except as provided for in Navy responsibilities for amphibious operations and in responsibilities for the Marine Corps.

COMMON SERVICE FUNCTIONS

The Army, Navy, Air Force, and Marine Corps, under their respective secretaries, are responsible for the following functions:

- Determining service force requirements and making recommendations concerning those requirements to support national security objectives and strategy and meet operational requirements of unified and specified combatant commands.
- Planning for use of the intrinsic capabilities of the other services' resources that may be made available.
- Recommending to the JCS the assignment and deployment of forces to unified and specified combatant commands established by the president through the secretary of defense.
- Administering service forces.
- Providing logistic support for service forces, including procurement, distribution, supply, equipment, and maintenance, unless otherwise directed by the secretary of defense.
- Developing doctrines, procedures, tactics, and techniques employed by service forces.
- Conducting operational testing and evaluation.
- Providing for training for joint operations and exercises in support of unified and specified combatant command operational requirements, including the following:

— Development of service training, doctrines, procedures, tactics, techniques, and methods of organization in accordance with policies and procedures established in service publications.

— Development and preparation of service publications to support the conduct of joint training.

— Determination of service requirements to enhance the effectiveness of joint training.

— Support of joint training directed by commanders of the unified and specified combatant commands and conduct of such additional joint training as is mutually agreed upon by the services concerned.

— Operating organic land vehicles, aircraft, and ships or craft.

— Consulting and coordinating with the other services on all matters of joint concern.

— Participating with the other services in the development of the doctrines, procedures, tactics, techniques, training, publications, and equipment for joint operations that are the primary responsibility of one of the services.

The forces developed and trained to perform the primary functions hereafter will be employed to support and supplement other military service forces in carrying out their primary functions, wherever and whenever such participation results in increased effectiveness and contributes to the accomplishment of overall military objectives. As for collateral functions, while the assignment of such functions may establish further justification for stated force requirements, such assignment will not be used as the sole basis for establishing additional force requirements.

AIR FORCE ORGANIZATION

The Department of the Air Force is made up of the Office of the Secretary of the Air Force, Air Staff, and USAF field units.

The U.S. Air Force is organized on a functional basis in the United States and on a geographic basis overseas by major commands (MAJCOMs), as well as a number of field operating agencies (FOAs) and direct reporting units (DRUs). There are 9 MAJCOMs, 31 FOAs, and 4 DRUs.

MAJOR COMMANDS

Air Combat Command (ACC). Headquarters: Langley AFB, Virginia. ACC is the USAF's principal offensive war machine. ACC organizes, trains, equips, and maintains combat-ready forces for rapid deployment and employment to meet the challenges of peacetime air sovereignty and wartime air defense. ACC provides combat airpower to the five U.S. warfighting commands (Central, European, Northern, Pacific, and Southern), as well as nuclear, conventional, and information operation forces to the U.S. Strategic Command and air defense forces to NORAD. ACC operates all USAF bombers and CONUS-based fighter and attack, reconnaissance, battle management, command-and-control aircraft, and intelligence and surveillance systems. ACC's 27 wings are organized under the 1st, 8th, 9th, and 12th Air Forces.

Air Education and Training Command (AETC). Headquarters: Randolph AFB, Texas. AETC recruits, accesses, commissions, trains, and educates USAF enlisted and officer personnel, providing basic military training, technical training, and officer and flying training. AETC also provides professional military education and degree-granting professional education. AETC's 10 flying wings and five technical training units are organized under the 2nd and 19th Air Forces, plus Air University, Air Force Recruiting Services, and a medical wing.

Air Force Materiel Command (AFMC). Headquarters: Wright-Patterson AFB, Ohio. AFMC manages the integrated research, development, test, acquisition, and sustainment of weapon systems; produces and acquires advanced systems; and operates major product centers, logistics and test centers, and the Air Force Research Laboratory.

Air Force Space Command (AFSPC). Headquarters: Peterson AFB, Colorado. AFSPC operates and tests the ICBM force for the U.S. Strategic Command; operates missile warning radars, sensors and satellites, national space-launch facilities and operational boosters, worldwide space surveillance radars and optical systems, and worldwide space environmental systems; provides command and control for DOD satellites; and provides ballistic missile warning to NORAD and the U.S. Strategic Command. AFSPC is organized into the Space and Missile Systems Center, the Space Innovation and Development Center, and the 14th and 20th Air Forces.

Air Force Special Operations Command (AFSOC). Headquarters: Hurlburt Field, Florida. AFSOC is the Air Force component of the U.S. Special Operations Command, a unified command. As such, it provides forces for worldwide deployment and assignment in regional unified commands to conduct agile combat support, combat aviation advisory operations, information warfare, personnel recovery and rescue operations, precision aerospace fires, psychological operations, and specialized aerospace mobility and refueling. AFSOC is organized into one wing, three groups, and two squadrons, as well as the USAF Special Operations School.

Air Mobility Command (AMC). Headquarters: Scott AFB, Illinois. AMC provides rapid global mobility and sustainment through tactical and strategic airlift and aerial refueling for U.S. armed forces, is the USAF component of the U.S. Transportation Command, and in wartime provides forces to theater commands. AMC provides peacetime and wartime aeromedical evacuation, as well as global humanitarian support. AMC's 13 wings are organized under the 18th Air Force and the 15th and 21st expeditionary mobility task forces.

Pacific Air Forces (PACAF). Headquarters: Hickam AFB, Hawaii. PACAF provides ready air and space power to promote U.S. interests in the

Air Combat Command

Air Mobility Command

Air Force Space Command

Pacific Air Forces

U.S. Air Forces in Europe

Air Education and Training Command

Air Force Material Command

Air Force Special Operations Command

Air Force Reserve Command

Emblems of Major Air Commands

Asia-Pacific region during peacetime, crisis, and war. PACAF's nine wings are organized under the 5th, 7th, 11th, and 13th Air Forces.

U.S. Air Forces in Europe (USAFE). Headquarters: Ramstein AB, Germany. USAFE provides the joint force commander rapidly deployable expeditionary aerospace forces. It plans, conducts, coordinates, and supports air and space operations to achieve U.S. national and NATO objectives based on tasks assigned by the commander in chief, U.S. European Command. To do so, it supports U.S. military plans and operations in Europe, the Mediterranean, the Middle East, and Africa, and develops and maintains light, lean, lethal, and rapid expeditionary aerospace forces. USAFE also established and maintains expeditionary bases. USAFE's ten wings are organized under the 3rd Air Force.

Air Force Reserve Command (AFRC). Headquarters: Robins AFB, Georgia. AFRC supports the active-duty force in missions such as fighter, bomber, airlift, aerial refueling, rescue, special operations, aeromedical evacuation, aerial firefighting, weather reconnaissance, space operations, airborne air control, flying training, flight testing, and aerial spraying. AFRC also provides support and disaster relief in the United States and supports national counterdrug efforts. Its 35 wings are organized under the 4th, 10th, and 22nd Air Forces. (See chapter 7 for additional information on the Air Force Reserve Command, as well as on the Air National Guard.)

SUBCOMMANDS AND LOWER LEVELS OF COMMAND
Below the MAJCOMs are the following levels of command, in descending order: numbered air force, wing, group, squadron, and flight.

Numbered Air Force (NAF). There are some 18 NAFs, which are strictly tactical echelons with an operations orientation.

Wing. Under the "one base, one wing, one boss" concept, most Air Force bases have only one wing. All assets are combined under one commander, usually a brigadier general or senior colonel.

Group. Combat wings are composed of four groups—operations, maintenance, mission support, and medical—each of which is usually commanded by a colonel. The groups are broken down into functional squadrons.

Squadron. The squadron is the basic unit in the Air Force. It is used to designate the mission units in the operations groups. Squadrons are also used as the units for functional entities, such as civil engineering; services and security police in the support group; or supply, maintenance, and transportation. Regardless of the functional area that uses it, the squadron has a vital mission.

Flight. There are two types of flights. The Air Force uses numerically designated flights primarily where there is a need for small mission elements to be incorporated into an organized unit. This is the lowest unit level in the Air Force. Alphabetically designated flights are components of squadrons and consist of several elements with identical missions. These flights are not units and are equivalent to branches.

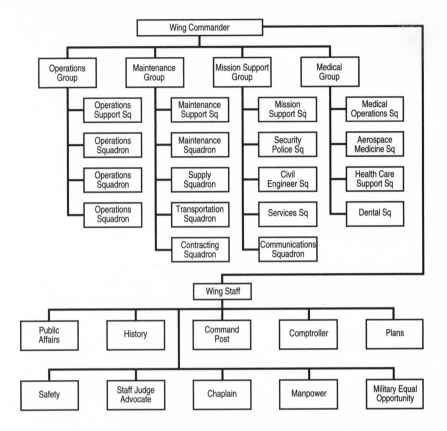

Objective Wing Organization

FIELD OPERATING AGENCIES

Field operating agencies (FOAs) are Air Force subdivisions that carry out field activities under operational control of Headquarters USAF functional managers, providing specialized services as their names indicate. Their missions are separate from major command missions. There are 31 FOAs.

Air Force Agency for Modeling and Simulation. Headquarters: Orlando, Florida. Supports Air Force modeling and simulation training, analysis, acquisition, and operations. Promotes modeling and simulation science and technology improvement and innovation, as well as professional development and education for Air Force modeling and simulation personnel.

Air Force Audit Agency. Headquarters: Washington, D.C. Provides independent internal audit evaluations for all levels of Air Force management. Produces audit products that evaluate the efficiency, effectiveness, and economy of Air Force programs and activities.

Air Force Center for Environmental Excellence. Headquarters: Brooks AFB, Texas. Provides Air Force leaders the comprehensive expertise to protect, preserve, restore, develop, and sustain the nation's environmental and installation resources.

Air Force Civil Engineer Support Agency. Headquarters: Tyndall AFB, Florida. Provides tools, practices, and professional support to maximize Air Force civil engineer capabilities in base and contingency operations.

Air Force Command and Control and Intelligence, Surveillance, and Reconnaissance Center. Headquarters: Langley AFB, Virginia. Develops the science of control to enable the art of command by influencing, integrating, and improving Air Force C4ISR capabilities. Represents major commands and provides operational warfighter perspective to Air Force C4ISR spiral development and system acquisition commands and processes. Delivers interoperability and combat capabilities to joint warfighters.

Air Force Communications Agency. Headquarters: Scott AFB, Illinois. Oversees ground, air, and space network. Deploys specialized strike teams and network assessment capabilities for assured Air Force communications and information combat power. Develops architectures and standards to ensure that systems are integrated into the network rapidly, securely, and reliably.

Air Force Cost Analysis Agency. Headquarters: Arlington, Virginia. Develops independent life-cycle cost estimates of major weapon and information systems; the estimates and cost factors for modernization planning, long-range planning, divestiture, and flying hour program; and cost estimation tools, techniques, methodologies, and databases. Conducts special cost reviews for the Air Force secretariat and for other organizations as directed. Researches emerging changes in technologies, acquisition priorities, and industry.

Air Force Flight Standards Agency. Headquarters: Oklahoma City, Oklahoma. Develops, standardizes, evaluates, and certifies Air Force policy, procedures, and equipment for flight operations and centrally manages the Air Force air traffic control and landing systems. Performs worldwide flight inspection of airfields and flight instrument/navigation systems. Represents the Air Force in Federal Aviation Agency airspace management and air traffic control issues and the DOD in international airspace and air traffic control issues. Provides procedures for air traffic control, airfield, operational evaluation of air traffic control systems, airspace management, and terminal instrument procedures.

Air Force Frequency Management Agency. Headquarters: Alexandria, Virginia. Obtains spectrum access for Air Force and selected DOD activities in support of national policy objectives, systems development, and global operations. Coordinates Air Force spectrum policy and guidance. Responsible for Air Force representation in spectrum negotiations with civil, military, national, and international regulatory organizations. Provides curriculum oversight for the Electromagnetic Spectrum Management Course and the Joint Force Spectrum Management Course.

Air Force Historical Research Agency. Headquarters: Maxwell AFB, Alabama. Collects, preserves, and manages the Air Force's historical document collection and oral history program. Researches, writes, and publishes books and other studies on Air Force history. Provides historical support to the Air Force, DOD, and other government agencies. Records and disseminates Air Force history. Operates research facilities and an automated historical data system. Determines the lineage and honors of USAF units, and maintains official emblem records. Verifies Air Force aerial victory credits.

Air Force Inspection Agency. Headquarters: Kirtland AFB, New Mexico. Provides Air Force leadership with independent assessments to improve the Air Force. Serves as the single, comprehensive inspection agency of USAF medical organizations. Recommends improvements to existing processes, practices, and programs for fulfilling peacetime, contingency, and wartime missions. Conducts special reviews and inquiries. Conducts compliance inspections for field operating agencies and direct reporting units that do not have major command oversight. Publishes *TIG Brief* magazine.

Air Force Legal Services Agency. Headquarters: Bolling AFB, D.C. Provides commanders and personnel with specialized legal services: administering military justice to protect individual rights and ensure good order and discipline; preserving command freedom of action through robust defense of Air Force interests in civil litigation; training and advising the headquarters and field in military justice and civil law matters; providing programs to benefit the Air Force family; and supporting legal services worldwide with state-of-the-art, specialized information technology.

Air Force Logistics Management Agency. Headquarters: Maxwell AFB, Gunter Annex, Alabama. Develops, analyzes, tests, evaluates, and recommends new or improved concepts, methods, systems, policies, and procedures to enhance logistics efficiency and effectiveness. Publishes *Air Force Journal of Logistics*.

Air Force Manpower Agency. Headquarters: Randolph AFB, Texas. Determines manpower requirements to support Air Force concepts of operations. Works with other USAF agencies to improve mission performance effectiveness and resource efficiency. Develops manpower programming factors and conducts special studies and competitive sourcing studies. Provides oversight for manpower and organizations' functional community needs.

Air Force Medical Operations Agency. Headquarters: Pentagon, D.C. Supports the Air Force assistant surgeon general, health care operations, and the Air Force surgeon general in the planning and execution of operational policies. Coordinates and tracks worldwide Air Force Medical Service expeditionary operations working with the services, unified commands, and Joint Staff. Creates and operates statistical tools to collect and analyze data to shape the delivery of health care. Directly supports health care professionals at military treatment facilities and special duty assignments worldwide.

Air Force Medical Support Agency. Headquarters: Bolling AFB, D.C. Oversees the execution of the Air Force surgeon general's policies and programs to support Air Force global capability and national security strategies. Provides consultative leadership for the Air Force Medical Service.

Air Force National Security Emergency Preparedness Agency. Headquarters: Arlington, Virginia. Facilitates Air Force support to civil authorities for natural or man-made disasters and emergencies.

Air Force News Agency. Headquarters: San Antonio, Texas. Creates, publishes, and broadcasts Web-based products that support Air Force and DOD communications goals. Provides news, information, and entertainment programs through the American Forces Radio and Television Service. Provides senior Air Force leaders with the means of communicating news and information to the Air Force community and to the public. Organizes, trains, and equips AFNEWS to accomplish its mission. Creates an environment that ensures the efficient and secure production and delivery of information.

Air Force Nuclear Weapons and Counterproliferation Agency. Headquarters: Pentagon, D.C. Oversees nuclear stockpile stewardship programs, including planning, development, and sustainment of Air Force nuclear weapons. Provides technical analysis on counterproliferation issues and leads all technical aspects of Air Force arms control process. Provides nuclear weapons, counterproliferation, and arms control issues technical advice to the Air Staff, major commands, unified command, and Office of the Secretary of Defense.

Air Force Office of Special Investigations. Headquarters: Andrews AFB, Maryland. Provides criminal and counterintelligence investigative services to the commanders of all Air Force activities. Identifies and resolves crime that impacts Air Force readiness or good order and discipline. Detects and provides early warning of worldwide threats to the Air Force. Combats threats to Air Force information systems and technologies. Defeats and deters fraud in the acquisition of Air Force prioritized weapons systems. Serves as the DOD's executive agency for the Defense Cyber Crime Center.

Air Force Operations Group. Headquarters: Pentagon, D.C. Supports Air Force chief of staff and deputy chief of staff for Air and Space Operations on current operational issues, including a 24-hour watch on all current operations as well as processing emergency messages. Provides facilities, policy, procedures, training, and staffing for the Crisis Action Team during crises, contingencies, and exercises. Coordinates actions among major Air Force organizations for JCS and USAF taskings. Prepares and provides weather data to the president, secretary of defense, JCS, NMCC, Army Operations Center, and other federal agencies.

Air Force Personnel Center. Headquarters: Randolph AFB, Texas. Provides service in worldwide personnel operations to Air Force commanders, military members, civilian employees, families, and retirees. Manages programs for individual career development.

Air Force Personnel Operations Agency. Headquarters: Pentagon, D.C. Provides analytical insight across the personnel life cycle to the deputy chief of staff for personnel decision makers. Develops and operates officer, enlisted, and civilian models.

Air Force Real Property Agency. Headquarters: Arlington, Virginia. Executes Air Force acquisition and disposal of all Air Force–controlled real property worldwide as well as environmental programs and real and personal property disposal of major Air Force bases being closed or realigned under the authorities of the Base Closure and Realignment Act of 1988 and the Defense Base Closure and Realignment Act of 1990. Assists communities in the conversion of closing and realigning bases from military to civilian use and ensures that property at these Air Force installations is made available for reuse as safely and efficiently as possible.

Air Force Review Boards Agency. Headquarters: Andrews AFB, Maryland. Manages military and civilian appellate processes for the secretary of the Air Force.

Air Force Safety Center. Headquarters: Kirtland AFB, New Mexico. Manages Air Force mishap prevention programs and the Nuclear Surety Program. Develops regulatory guidance. Provides technical assistance in flight, ground, and weapons and space safety disciplines. Maintains USAF databases for all safety mishaps. Oversees all major command mishap investigations and evaluates corrective actions for applicability and implementation USAF-wide. Directs safety education programs for all safety disciplines.

Air Force Security Forces Center. Headquarters: Lackland AFB, Texas. Develops USAF Security Forces guidance, policy, and training requirements to safeguard and protect personnel and resources. Prepares guidance on air base defense operations, security forces continuation training, mission-related security and law enforcement operations, resource protection, and antiterrorism. Develops and implements base-level and combat arms training and ground combat weapons maintenance programs. Manages the Air Force corrections program and activities, DOD military working-dog activities, and contingency tasking.

Air Force Services Agency. Headquarters: San Antonio, Texas. Provides community service programs that enhance the quality of life for Air Force members and their families. Manages Air Force nonappropriated central funds and operates central systems, such as banking, investments, purchasing, data flow, insurance, and benefits programs.

Air Force Technical Applications Center. Headquarters: Patrick AFB, Florida. Monitors compliance with several international nuclear treaties. Operates the U.S. Atomic Energy Detection System, a global network of subsurface, surface, airborne, and space-based sensors that detect nuclear explosions. Operates analytical laboratories that provide national authorities with technical measurements with which to monitor foreign nuclear tests.

Air Force Weather Agency. Headquarters: Offutt AFB, Nebraska. Maximizes the nation's aerospace and ground combat effectiveness by providing accurate, relevant, and timely air and space weather information to DOD, coalition, and national users and by providing standardized training and equipment to Air Force weather services.

Air National Guard (ANG) Readiness Center. Headquarters: Andrews AFB, Maryland. Provides combat capability to the warfighters and security of the homeland.

DIRECT REPORTING UNITS

Four direct reporting units (DRUs) are directly subordinate to Headquarters USAF. DRUs, which have the same administrative and organizational responsibilities as the major commands, are separate from the major commands and field operating agencies because of legal requirements or their unique missions.

Air Force District of Washington. Headquarters: Bolling AFB, DC. Air Force component to the Joint Force Headquarters-National Capital Region. USAF voice for planning and implementing cross-service solutions throughout the National Capital Region. Organizes, trains, equips, and deploys forces for AEFs and homeland defense, civil support, and national special security events.

Air Force Doctrine Center. Headquarters: Maxwell AFB, Alabama. Provides a focal point for air, space, and information operational doctrine. Develops basic and operational doctrine for USAF Total Force. Advocates doctrinally correct representation and execution at the operational level of war in service, joint, and multinational operations, exercises, and other events. Collects input from exercises and operations for lessons learned. Participates in the investigation of future operational concepts and strategies to capture emerging doctrine. Presents USAF doctrine to Air Force, other service, and joint audiences.

Air Force Operational Test and Evaluation Center. Headquarters: Kirtland AFB, New Mexico. Assesses the capabilities of new systems to meet warfighter needs by planning, executing, and reporting independent operational evaluations. Provides effectiveness, suitability, and operational impact expertise in the battlefield environment.

U.S. Air Force Academy. Headquarters: Colorado Springs, Colorado. Develops and inspires young men and women to become Air Force officers with knowledge, character, and discipline. Produces dedicated Air Force officers and leaders. Instills leadership through academics, military training, athletic conditioning, and character development.

AIR AND SPACE EXPEDITIONARY FORCE

Since the end of the Cold War, personnel cuts have forced every branch of the U.S. armed services to reexamine their roles as part of the national security puzzle. It quickly became clear that the Air Force would need to become more expeditionary (deployable) to meet future global challenges and to lessen operations tempo problems created by back-to-back deployments and operations. By definition, expeditionary means "sent on military service abroad." Being expeditionary means that the Air Force will conduct global aerospace operations with forces based primarily in the United States that will deploy rapidly to begin operations as soon as they arrive at a forward operating location. This includes deployment to and operations from austere locales.

As a result, the Air Force has evolved into an Air and Space Expeditionary Force (AEF) that is:

- Tailored to mission success with the right combination of capabilities and people to match the challenge.
- Rapidly deployable to any part of the world.
- Light and lean with the smallest possible footprint forward.
- Globally connected to reach back for worldwide information and support.
- Able to command and control the assigned forces in near real time.
- Led by a scheduled and seasoned air commander who can decisively apply the gamut of air and space capabilities across the spectrum of crisis.

Ten AEFs, or "buckets" of capability, grouped in five pairs have been formed. Each AEF rotates through a 20-month cycle in which each pair is assigned to one of five 120-day deployment vulnerability periods. Every wing in the Air Force will have personnel aligned under one or more AEFs. There is no one location or base for an AEF. Composed of geographically separated active-duty, Air National Guard, and Air Force Reserve units, AEFs have combat air forces, mobility air forces, and low-density, high-demand (LD/HD) forces. Because the LD/HD forces include battle management, combat search and rescue, command and control, and reconnaissance assets, they are in almost constant use and rotate more frequently than do most combat air forces and mobility air forces.

Role of Airmen in the AEF. Approximately 65 percent of Air Force personnel serve in deployable positions. The AEF should bring more stability and predictability in deployment schedules. Those who have traditionally high operational tempo jobs will probably experience a reduction in the frequency of deployments.

AFMAN 10-100, *Airman's Manual,* details information necessary to meet the challenges of Air and Space Expeditionary Force requirements: basic warfighting skills and knowledge, staying ready for deployment and dealing with field conditions, fighting, survival, and mission accomplishment in hostile situations.

SOURCES OF ADDITIONAL INFORMATION
AFI (Air Force Instruction) 38-101, *Air Force Organization*
AFMAN (Air Force Manual) 10-100, *Airman's Manual*

7

The Air Reserve Forces

The Total Air Force depends on personnel on active duty, in the Air Force Reserve, and in the Air National Guard, as well as civilians. The Air Reserve forces are the Air National Guard and the Air Force Reserve. All our reserve forces are placed in one of three categories: Active Reserve, Inactive Reserve, or Retired Reserve. The active Air Force alone is neither manned nor equipped to accomplish its missions without the full support of the Air Reserve forces. Downsizing of the active Air Force, combat tempo, number and geographic breadth of conflicts, and distribution of Air and Space capabilities have made the Total Air Force a reality, not merely a concept.

THE ACTIVE RESERVE

Active Reserve means that portion of our reserve forces that can be ordered to active duty under conditions short of a congressional declaration of war or national emergency. The *Air National Guard* is composed entirely of units organized and trained to be used as Active Reserve units. The Active Reserve portion of the *Air Force Reserve* includes not only Active Reserve units but also individual active reservists assigned to specific mobilization positions with regular Air Force organizations and other individuals earmarked as attrition replacements.

In peacetime, the Air National Guard is commanded by the governors of the various states; it is supported by the Air Force through the National Guard Bureau, under Air Force policies and regulations. It is trained under the supervision of the gaining commands, who also have the inspection responsibility. Thirty states also have state guards as backup to their National Guard units.

Both components are governed by Air Force policies, regulations, and training directives, and both are responsive to training standards and performance requirements prescribed by the gaining command.

The Air Force program for reserve forces puts into practice the concept of reliance on a "ready now" augmentation force.

THE INACTIVE RESERVE

In addition to the Active Reserve, there is within the Air Force Reserve an Inactive Reserve, which can be ordered to active duty *only* when Congress declares war or a national emergency, as some were for the Gulf War, and as others have been for the wars in Afghanistan and Iraq. Some of these inactive reservists would not be available because of critical needs of the government or the civilian community as a whole. Although a number of inactive reservists participate in correspondence courses or train with Active Reserve units, the majority of them would need refresher training to function in their Air Force specialties.

WHY AIR RESERVE FORCES?

One reason we have reserve units is that the Constitution and the Congress say that we will. But another very good reason is that reserve units provide an economical way to maintain a surge expansion capability for the Air Force during peacetime.

The reserves—even the Inactive and Retired Reserves—provide the Air Force a strong base of grassroots community support. They are an effective influence in favor of Air Force recruiting as well. By talking about the Air Force, reservists help to interest young people in Air Force careers.

The primary reason for reserves, however, is wartime support. Until a few years ago, the Air Force, like the other U.S. military services, traditionally relied on its reserve components to supply the extra manpower and capability needed for wartime expansion.

Under current concepts for their use, the "ready now" reserves are very much a part of our deterrent strength. Their readiness and usefulness are vital to the Air Force mission and, therefore, to the security of the nation. When the Air Force says its reserves are "ready now," it means that they can fight today. They can be and have been called up in hours. Call the roll: the Korean War, the 1961 Berlin Crisis, the 1962 Cuban Missile Crisis, the Vietnam War, Grenada, Panama, the Gulf War, the Balkans, and the wars in Afghanistan and Iraq.

The use of reserve forces to help keep the peace is sometimes thought to be a new concept. But it really isn't. The idea of the citizen-soldier was born as a "ready now" concept. As far back as 1607, the leaders of Virginia, following the practice in England, formed a local militia called the "train band." As rapidly as their populations could support them, "train bands" were formed in other nearby colonial settlements. The members of these organizations were not professional soldiers. They were farmers, craftsmen, and merchants. Their military obligation was a 24-hour-a-day affair, and there was hardly a period from 1622 until after the American Revolution when some of the members of the "train band" were not serving as soldiers on a full-time basis. There was no active colonial military establishment; the citizen-soldiers were the sole defense of their individual communities. During certain periods, British regulars were responsible for the frontiers or were stationed in Atlantic seaboard cities. As the American economy and population grew, a standing military force became a necessity if only to prevent constant disruption of the more and more complex national structure. With the oceans as effective barriers to sudden attack, our citizen-soldiers had time on their side and could become reserves, to be called upon only when the size and strength of the regular establishment had to be increased for war.

This, then, became the pattern for our military forces: an active-duty establishment strong enough to fend off the first attack, and a reserve that could be mobilized and quickly trained to expand the regular force to war-winning size.

But military weapons and concepts of war are constantly changing. Today, our Air National Guard and Air Force Reserve Command are much more than just a wartime mobilization force. They are, truly, an integral and vital part of our total aerospace power in being, supporting Army airborne training and airdrops, flying airlift missions at home and overseas, maintaining air defense units, and serving in the full spectrum of support specialties.

COMPOSITION OF AIR RESERVE FORCES

Air Reserve forces fly more than 1,700 aircraft (approximately three-quarters of which are Guard aircraft). One hundred percent of Total Force weather reconnaissance, aerial spraying, strategic interceptor force, and tactical reconnaissance aircraft are in the Air Force Reserves, as are approximately three-quarters of tactical airlift, half the aerial refueling/strategic tankers, almost half of tactical and strategic airlift, and over a third of our strike fighters.

Additionally, there are a wide variety of nonflying units—communications, medical, aerial port squadrons, and many other types. All have specific tasks to perform in the war and contingency plans of the major commands. Each major command of the Regular Air Force gets a sizable augmentation force from the reserve. Reserve medical units of various kinds are also distributed among the commands.

Air Force missions and responsibilities are so broad in scope and of such variety that they can be accomplished only by a completely responsive, instantly reacting, and highly flexible force. They can be accomplished only through the full use of all resources available to the Total Air Force, reserve as well as regular.

AIR RESERVE FORCES TRAINING

Realistic training for wartime readiness is now par for the course for reserve units and personnel. Airlift units carry high-priority cargo while training their personnel in airlift skills. Fighter and reconnaissance units take the place of regular units to support joint Army–Air Force exercises. Air Defense units fly air alert intercept missions under active Air Force control.

Management has been improved to give Air Force combat commands responsibility for supervising and training and operational inspection of those reserve units that would be assigned to them in wartime. Standards of performance are identical for regular and reserve units. Each aircrew, regardless of component, is required to meet the same rigid requirements as regular Air Force crews before it can be designated combat ready.

The operations room of a reserve outfit is almost indistinguishable from that of a regular outfit—except perhaps on weekdays. Reserve combat crews receive the normal 48 inactive-duty training periods and 15 days of active duty each year, plus 36 additional flying training periods. Even this is not enough for all flying requirements, and reserve personnel engage in training whenever they can get time off from their civilian jobs—because these part-time airmen have to meet exactly the same training requirements that the full-time Air Force crews must meet. They pass their operational readiness inspections exactly like active force units.

How is this possible with a part-time operation? A great deal of the reserve success is due to the stability of personnel. It takes a while longer to train reservists, but the reserves do not have the problem of frequent turnover that challenges regular units.

Another asset, and an extremely important one, is the technician program. The air technicians of the Guard and the Air Reserve have a dual status: They are full-time employees in a civilian capacity, as well as being reservists who train with units on weekends and during annual active duty. In other words, they wear two hats. They provide a permanent, hardcore base of skill and experience, not only for the day-to-day maintenance and operating functions, but also for training younger personnel. This valuable resource of experience is augmented by a handful of active Air Force advisors who assist in training and assure standardization with the requirements of the gaining commands of the Regular Air Force.

CIVIL AIR PATROL

Although Civil Air Patrol (CAP) members are not a part of the armed forces, they belong to the auxiliary of the U.S. Air Force and deserve mention here. CAP was formed in December 1941, just days before Imperial Japan attacked Pearl Harbor. Its first mission was to aid in the defense of America's coastline, which it did under the jurisdiction of the Army Air Forces. In 1946 Congress chartered CAP as a nonprofit civilian corporation, and two years later it was made the auxiliary of the new U.S. Air Force with three primary missions: aviation education, cadet programs, and emergency services.

Today, CAP accomplish its aerospace education mission by distributing an aerospace curricula for kindergarten through college, supporting college workshops, giving free aerospace training to America's teachers, and aiding in Air Force recruiting. The cadet program, which includes aviation education, orientation flights and flight training, provides about 10 percent of each year's new classes entering U.S. military service academies. CAP contributes aerial reconnaissance for homeland security, border patrol, and the war on drugs, as well as flies about 95 percent of all inland search and rescue sorties in the United States and provides disaster-relief to support local, state, and national disaster relief organizations.

CAP members are either cadets aged 12 to 21 or senior members over 21. They wear Air Force uniforms with a grade structure similar to the Air Force's, but wear distinctive CAP insignia. There are 1,500 units in 52 wings—for each state, the District of Columbia, and the Commonwealth of Puerto Rico. CAP's 34,000 senior members and 22,000 cadets fly more than 120,000 hours each year in 530 CAP aircraft and more than 4,000 member aircraft.

CAP national headquarters is at Maxwell AFB, Alabama, supported by CAP-USAF, an active-duty cadre. For further information, visit *www.cap.gov*.

PART III

Career and Advancement

8

Officer Professional Development

Officer professional development is essential to fulfill the Air Force mission and to provide the professional growth that officers expect. The officer who is most effective at carrying out the mission is one who is professionally prepared to assume the responsibilities that go with a particular rank. The officer professional development program is designed to support Air Force requirements and maintain maximum combat effectiveness while developing a well-rounded, professionally competent officer corps. An officer's professional development must harmonize with long-term Air Force requirements. *Officer Career Path Guide* provides detailed information regarding establishment of career goals and insight into career path options by technical specialty. The information that follows is for all Air Force officers, regardless of technical specialty.

OBJECTIVES OF PROFESSIONAL DEVELOPMENT
Professional development includes actions and experiences that improve officers' ability to perform their technical specialties and increasingly contribute to the Air Force mission. Professional development starts with concentrating on expertise in a primary skill, broadens throughout one's career, and ends, one hopes, with the officer being a generalist (if not a general!) with both depth and breadth of expertise. Officers grow by combining their career specialties with ability to lead and to manage in peace and in war. The Air Force offers officers numerous ways to enhance their professional credentials.

CAREER PATHS
The purpose of the officer assignment system is to fill Air Force requirements. Although one may express preference, officers volunteer only one time—when they take the oath of office. Officers should not concern themselves with mapping out their careers in detail but instead concentrate on their current duty. The

only assignment with which the officer should be concerned is the current one, and when available for a new assignment, the one that immediately follows. Qualifications and professional development are the primary factors in making assignments, and commanders play a key role in the process. The assignment system is an integral part of officer professional development, but officers must realize that assignments are made to fill Air Force needs with the best-qualified officers.

There are some steps officers can take to enhance their careers. In addition to studying the *Officer Career Path Guide,* officers should discuss their career aspirations, career plans, and assignment opportunities with their commanders. Mentors in the Career Broadening Program can also provide guidance on a wide variety of career and professional topics and share their knowledge of career development programs and initiatives.

PATH OF PROFESSIONAL DEVELOPMENT
The most important indicator of potential is the way an officer performs daily on the job and develops leadership abilities. This is certainly true for lieutenants, captains, and junior majors. A very limited number of captains will serve in lower-level staff assignments, and a larger number of majors will serve in staff jobs at all levels. Nevertheless, a staff job is not a prerequisite for promotion up through lieutenant colonel. A broader range of experience is more important for lieutenant colonels. In general, a demanding staff job as a senior major or lieutenant colonel will enhance the potential to perform as a colonel or above. Most colonel jobs require staff competence as well as skill in one's specialty and developed leadership talents.

Professional military education (PME) and graduate academic education should parallel and support job requirements. PME should build upon a solid foundation of officership laid during precommissioning programs. The uniqueness of the military profession and the particular values and culture of the officer corps are the bedrock on which all future professional development is based.

The focus for company-grade officers (lieutenants and captains) should be on developing the skills they need, especially leadership and communication skills. The emphasis for the field grades (majors and colonels) should shift to the effective management of people and resources, as well as skills needed for staff work. Lieutenant colonels and colonels must understand the elements of air and space force deployment and the policy considerations that drive them, so that is the role of the Air War College, the highest U.S. Air Force PME level.

THE OFFICER EVALUATION SYSTEM (OES)
The OES, an integral part of the officer professional development program, has three purposes: to furnish feedback to officers on how well they are doing and advise them on how to improve, to provide a long-term cumulative record of

performance and potential, and to provide central selection boards with sound information to help them pick the best-qualified officers for promotion. The OES focuses on performance and is a tool that officers can use in their own professional development.

THE PROMOTION SYSTEM

Objectives of the officer promotion system are to select officers through a fair and competitive process that advances the best qualified officers to positions of increased authority and responsibility and to provide the needed career incentive to attract and maintain an officer corps of high quality. Promotion boards are told that demonstrated leadership abilities and performance of primary duties are of overriding importance and far outweigh all other considerations. Therefore, officers should concentrate on duty performance in their current grade and not on "square-filling" maneuvering.

PROFESSIONALISM

The ultimate objective of career development is a quality called "professionalism," brought to its highest standard of excellence. All of us readily recognize the meaning of professionalism when we apply the term to a minister, a doctor, a lawyer, or a professor. What does it mean when applied to an Air Force officer? To assess this, it is first necessary to appreciate the unique scope of an Air Force officer's professionalism—the vast field of knowledge, experience, skills, and comprehension that is encompassed in an Air Force career. The armed forces of the United States constitute a significant effort of the American people. Approximately one-fifth of the federal budget is spent on our armed forces, and approximately 2.8 million active-duty, reserve, and civilian personnel maintain the armed forces of which about 700,000 serve in the Air Force. Currently, Air Force and Navy forces are declining, whereas Army and Marine Corps strength is increasing. The complicated, expensive tools of our military forces rest on the entire range of U.S. technology and industry, involving deeply other professional areas, such as medicine, engineering, law, education, and many scientific disciplines. Moreover, the armed forces are an integral, crucial part of U.S. diplomacy and international relations. "Peacetime" foreign policy cannot be separated from the existence and strength of U.S. armed forces. Finally, the armed forces exert, through their diverse requirements and activities, a major effect on the U.S. economy. Plainly, it is not enough that Air Force officers be expert in particular fields of Air Force operations; they are part of a vast complex that touches many aspects of American life and, therefore, must seek to achieve a professionalism that matches the uniquely multiple strands of responsibility and knowledge that characterize their profession.

Professionalism begins at less lofty levels than the ultimate responsibilities of the top officers of the Air Force. It begins with technical skill and knowledge relative to the particular task assigned to Air Force officers. It begins when Air

Force officers know how to perform their own jobs at maximum efficiency, routinely, prudently, smoothly. The reliable sign of the true professional is the calm, seemingly easy performance of tasks under all circumstances, without noise or heroics, without unnecessary risk or extravagant use of resources.

Professionalism is expanded and exploited when Air Force officers know how to create professionalism in the enlisted force. This task means training, careful supervision, discipline, and morale. It is the mark of officer pros that they have working with them enlisted personnel who are also pros.

Because of the vast field of concerns, Air Force officers must steadily increase professional competence by taking every opportunity to upgrade basic educational levels, attend military schools, read widely, and volunteer for a variety of additional duties. In particular, Air Force professionals should come to understand the very serious business management aspects of the Air Force, because the net capabilities of the Air Force will always be an expression of the efficiency with which Air Force officers use the resources made available by the Congress. These resources are used in a thousand ways: as pay, for procurement of equipment and supplies, for construction, for maintenance and operations, and for research and development. The business end of this problem is not only the thousands of contracts with U.S. industry, but also the accurate determination of requirements, the formulation of realistic plans, and the efficient use of available resources. All Air Force officers participate in this vast business of the Air Force. The Air Force can obtain the most national security from its huge annual budget only when all Air Force officers obtain the most efficient results from their use of their part of total resources.

In their fields of career development, all Air Force officers should constantly seek to heighten and broaden their competence so that at each succeeding level of their careers, they will fully deserve the accolade "a professional."

9

USAF Training and Education

For the Air Force to accomplish its mission requires that the service be highly organized; thus it is also a large bureaucracy. It must be equipped efficiently, so a close working relationship with science and industry is essential. Its men and women must be prepared by training and education, the subjects of this chapter. There are three main components—precommissioning programs, specialty training, and professional military education (PME)—as well as other opportunities to help officers enhance their skills.

PRECOMMISSIONING PROGRAMS

The U.S. Air Force Academy. The Air Force Academy graduated its first class in 1958. Enrollment at the school, located in Colorado Springs, is about 4,400 in a four-year college program leading to a bachelor of science degree. The academy commissions about one thousand second lieutenants each year, about a fifth of newly commissioned second lieutenants. Beginning with the class of 1997, academy graduates have been commissioned as reserve, rather than regular, officers. Most AFA graduates incur a five-year active-duty service commitment. However, graduates entering pilot training incur a ten-year commitment after completing Specialized Undergraduate Pilot Training, and graduates entering navigator training incur a six-year commitment after completing Specialized Undergraduate Navigator Training. The minimum service obligation for the Air Battle Management career field is also six years.

Air Force Reserve Officer Training Corps (AFROTC). Congress originally authorized ROTC on college campuses in 1916, just before the United States entered World War I. Thirty years later, after World War II, a separate Air Force ROTC came into being, now under Air University, Maxwell AFB, Alabama. There are two- and four-year programs, and in both, qualified applicants received AFROTC scholarships. There are 144 AFROTC detachments on American college and university campuses, with "cross-town" arrangements with slightly less than 1,000 other institutions. AFROTC usually commissions about 2,000 second lieutenants each year. Most AFROTC graduates incur a four-year active-duty service commitment. However, AFROTC graduates, like Academy graduates entering pilot training incur a ten-year commitment after completing Specialized Undergraduate Pilot Training, and graduates entering navigator training incur a six-year commitment after completing Specialized Undergraduate Navigator Training. The minimum service obligation for the Air Battle Management career field is also six years.

Officer Training School/Basic Officer Training (OTS/BOT). Located at Air University, Maxwell AFB, Alabama, OTS/BOT is a 12-week officer procurement program that recruits and trains non-AFROTC college graduates, including those from the Airman Education and Commissioning Program. Unlike the Air Force Academy and AFROTC, OTS/BOT has the capacity to quickly increase or decrease output of second lieutenants to meet changing Air Force requirements. OTS/BOT commissioned nearly 3,200 second lieutenants in 1985, but only 350 in 1991. OTS/BOT is now commissioning 500 to 700 second lieutenants each year. OTS/BOT graduates' service commitments are the same as for AFROTC graduates.

Officer Training School/Commissioned Officer Training (OTS/COT). Located at Air University, Maxwell AFB, Alabama, OTS/COT is a four-week course for chaplains, medical professionals, and judge advocates who have been given direct commissions. OTS/COT prepares these officers for service in the Air Force by providing training in leadership, professional military knowledge, defense studies, drill and ceremonies, and communication skills. OTS/COT is now graduating about 1,300 officers each year.

Academy of Military Science (AMS). Located at the Professional Military Education Center, McGhee-Tyson Airport, Knoxville, Tennessee, AMS commissions officers for the Air National Guard and the Air Force Reserve through an intensive six-week course. This Air National Guard institution opened in 1970 because the Air Force Academy, AFROTC, and OTS were unable to commission sufficient numbers of officers. Most current Guard and reserve officers, however, were commissioned by one of the three sources of active-duty officers and had prior active-duty service before joining the Guard or reserves. About 600 second lieutenants (480 Guard and 120 reserves) are commissioned each year by the Academy of Military Science. See *http://www.angtec.ang.af.mil.*

APPOINTMENT OF OFFICERS

Reserve and Regular Air Force Appointments. Reserve majors are eligible for regular commissions between an officer's 9th and 12th years. The exception to this timetable is that some medical officers, who are frequently commissioned as captains or majors, must wait until they become lieutenant colonels before receiving regular commissions. The Air Force automatically considers eligible officers and neither requires nor accepts applications for regular status. See AFI 36-2610, *Appointing Regular Air Force Officers and Obtaining Conditional Reserve Status.*

THE
PRESIDENT
OF
THE UNITED STATES OF AMERICA

To all who shall see these presents, greeting:
Know Ye, that reposing special trust and confidence in the patriotism, valor,
fidelity and abilities of   Lee R. Johnson   *, I do*
appoint   him   Second Lieutenant   *in the*

United States Air Force

to   date   *as such from the*   First   *day of*   June   *, two*
thousand   and Eight   . *This officer will therefore carefully*
and diligently discharge the duties of the office to which appointed by doing and
performing all manner of things thereunto belonging.
And I do strictly charge and require those officers and other personnel of lesser
rank to render such obedience as is due an officer of this grade and position. And,
this officer is to observe and follow such orders and directions, from time to time, as
may be given by the President of the United States of America or other superior
officers, acting in accordance with the laws of the United States of America.
This commission is to continue in force during the pleasure of the President of the
United States of America under the provisions of those public laws relating to
officers of the **Armed Forces of the United States of America**
and the component thereof in which this appointment is made.

Done at the city of Washington, this   First   *day of*   June
in the year of our Lord two thousand   and Eight   *and of the*
Independence of the United States of America the   Two Hundred and
     Thirty-two   *By the President:*

Lieutenant General, USAF
Deputy Chief of Staff, Personnel

Secretary of the Air Force

SPECIALTY TRAINING

Whatever their source of commission, most newly commissioned USAF line officers will go to either flying training or technical training schools, except the few who will learn their skills in on-the-job training, or "OJT."

Air Force Flying Schools. All undergraduate flight training is conducted by the Air Education and Training Command (AETC). Pilot training is conducted at Air Force, Navy, or Army bases under the supervision of Headquarters, AETC, Randolph AFB, Texas. Flight screening is conducted in Hondo, Texas, or at the Air Force Academy. Pilot training continues with an undergraduate pilot training program and ends with combat crew training in specific major weapons systems. Navigators train at NAS Pensacola, Florida, and conclude their training at NAS Pensacola or Randolph AFB.

Air Force Technical Schools. As the Air Force grows increasingly technical in its operations, the need for technically trained officers also increases. AETC operates a number of technical training schools to which officers may be assigned as students. Courses are designed to advance the officers' proficiency in their specialty fields, whether jet aircraft maintenance, electronics, missile maintenance and operation, intelligence, or scores of other technical and support field specialties. The main centers of such training are at Keesler AFB, Mississippi, and in Texas at Goodfellow AFB, Sheppard AFB, and Lackland AFB. Courses vary in length.

PROFESSIONAL MILITARY EDUCATION

Education in the discipline of the profession of arms is called professional military education, or PME, and is the systematic acquisition of theoretical and applied knowledge. In World War II, the United States surprised the German general staff with the ability of our armed forces to expand quickly from fewer than half a million men in 1940 to a well-organized and well-led force of more than 12 million in 1945. Three principal reasons that this rapid expansion was so successful were the Army and Navy PME systems between the two world wars, learning from our failures in industrial mobilization in World War I, and an available pool of about 74,000 reserve officers, 77 percent of them commissioned through ROTC.

The primary purpose of Air Force PME today is to train officers in the application of aerospace forces and to provide the opportunity to participate in joint service operations. The USAF officer PME system consists of three levels of instruction conducted through resident and nonresident programs. In addition some officers will participate in programs of the National Defense University, the other U.S. armed services, the U.S. State Department, NATO, foreign countries, and civilian institutions.

Air Force PME is divided into three levels: Primary PME (Squadron Officers Course and Squadron Officers College with its two components: Air and Space Basic Course and Squadron Officer School), Intermediate PME (Air

Command and Staff College), and Senior PME (Air War College). PME is a cumulative, coordinated process in which each level forms the foundation for the following level. All three levels are conducted by Air University at Maxwell AFB, Alabama, the center of Air Force PME programs.

Squadron Officers Course. The introduction to PME for newly accessioned officers, Squadrons Officers Course is taught at wing level and tailored to fit local requirements. It combines education in officership and leadership and the role of aerospace power with broad understanding of unit and installation operations and Air Force perspectives.

Air and Space Basic Course (ABC). ABC, the first resident phase of PME instruction for officers, inspires new USAF officers to comprehend their roles as airmen who understand and live by USAF core values, articulate and advocate USAF core competencies, and dedicate themselves as warriors. ABC creates an environment for second lieutenants to analyze and improve group and individual skills through seminars, lectures, exercises, simulations, and field activities. Because ABC emphasizes teamwork, there is no distinguished graduate program. All active-duty officers will have the priority to attend this six-week course, with nonline and civilian interns given the opportunity on a space-available basis. Second lieutenants within one year of commissioning are eligible and are selected by the Air Force Personnel Center.

Squadron Officer School (SOS). SOS, the third phase of Primary PME, is a five-week temporary duty (TDY) course that is attended by almost all active-duty line officers during their fourth to seventh years of commissioned service. In addition, a number of National Guard and Air Force Reserve officers attend SOS during the summer. SOS is designed to increase junior officers' dedication to the profession of arms by stepping back from individual technical specialties and offering a broader look at the profession. SOS's objective is to develop dynamic young officers ready to serve air and space forces in an expeditionary warfighting environment. Consequently, SOS's curriculum focuses on the profession of arms, military and international studies, and leadership and communication skills. The few officers who do not attend in residence are expected to complete SOS by distance learning through the Air Force Institute for Advanced Distributed Learning (AFIADL).

Air Command and Staff College (ACSC). ACSC is the Air Force's intermediate service school (ISS). This 10-month course is attended by about 600 U.S. and international officers whose performance clearly shows potential for further advancement. Active-duty line officers are chosen by Headquarters USAF Central ISS Designation Boards in a highly competitive selection process. Those eligible are majors with at least three years since their last PME education assignment, at least three years' retainability, and three years on station at projected departure date. Graduates incur a three-year active-duty service commitment upon completion of ACSC.

The college broadens the knowledge and increases the professional qualifications of future commanders and staff officers, emphasizing combat and combat support across the spectrum of service, joint, and combined operations. ACSC prepares officers to plan and execute warfare at the operational level; improves the communication, analytical, and problem-solving skills a staff officer needs; enhances command, leadership, and combat support skills; imparts an understanding of U.S. military power and our national interests; and fosters the understanding needed for joint duty assignments. For resident graduates, ACSC awards an academic degree of Master of Military Operational Art and Science. Each summer, ACSC conducts a Reserve Forces Course to update selected Air National Guard and Air Force Reserve majors on the USAF, its doctrine, and its weapon systems. Each academic year, selected Air Guard and reserve officers join the resident ACSC class for a week. All mid-level officers not selected for resident ACSC or other ISS should complete one of the associate programs, either by seminar or correspondence, which ACSC administers as an extension course.

School for Advanced Airpower Studies (SAAS). In 1992 this Air University school graduated its first class at Maxwell AFB, Alabama. The 11-month follow-on course for selected graduates of intermediate-level PME schools is to create warrior-scholars who have superior abilities to develop, evaluate, and employ airpower. The very demanding reading and seminar course focuses on theory, doctrine, and application of airpower at the operational level of war. A thesis and oral comprehensive examination are required. SAAS graduates are granted the academic degree of Master of Airpower Art and Science.

Air War College (AWC). AWC is the Air Force's senior service school (SSS). The student body is a carefully selected group of about 250 students, officers, and U.S. government civilians brought together for a 10-month course of graduate-level study. They are joined by officers from the other U.S. services and a number of other nations. Active-duty line officers are selected by annual Headquarters USAF Central SSS Designation Boards in a highly selective process. Students are colonels and lieutenant colonels; AWC graduates incur a three-year active-duty service commitment upon graduation. AWC prepares senior military officers to lead at the strategic level in the employment of air and space forces, including joint combined, coalition, and interagency operations, in support of national security. AWC offers an academic degree of Master of Strategic Studies. The AWC Department of Associate Studies in conjunction with the Air Force Institute for Advanced Distributed Learning (AFIADL) provides distance learning programs for eligible personnel not selected for resident schooling.

Joint, Other Services, and Non-DOD PME Courses. The Goldwater-Nichols Defense Reorganization Act of 1986 established a requirement for the joint specialty officer (JSO). To meet JSO educational requirements, the chairman of the Joint Chiefs of Staff, with the services, began a two-phase joint PME process whereby students receive Phase I Joint PME (PJE1) at both ISS and SSS and Phase II Joint PME (PJE2) at the Armed Forces Staff College (AFSC) and at the National Defense University's two senior service schools, the National War College (NWC) and Industrial College of the Armed Forces (ICAF), continuing both phase requirements. The JCS's aim is that AFSC, NWC, and ICAF graduates be used primarily in joint-duty assignments.

Armed Forces Staff College (AFSC). Located in Norfolk, Virginia, AFSC has the mission, prescribed by the JCS, of preparing selected officers of all services for joint and combined staff duty. The curriculum focuses on the strategic, doctrinal, and operational concerns of the JCS and the commanders in chief of unified and specified commands, the "CINC," in the likely environment graduates will encounter.

Industrial College of the Armed Forces (ICAF). Located at Fort McNair, D.C., ICAF, a major component of the National Defense University, is a joint Senior Service School operating under JCS direction. It began as the Army Industrial College after World War I with the mission to prevent future failures in military procurement. It became a joint service school after World War II, focusing on managing resources for national security. Its mission is to prepare selected officers from all services and senior career civilian governmental officials for positions of high trust in the federal government. Criteria for selection to ICAF are the same as for AWC and NWC, but officers attend only one of the three Senior Service Schools.

National War College (NWC). Also at Fort McNair, NWC is the only senior service school in the U.S. military educational system with the specific mission of studying national security policy preparation. It prepares selected personnel of the armed forces, State Department, and other U.S. government agencies for the exercise of joint and combined high-level policy, command, and staff functions for planning and carrying out national strategy. Criteria for attendance are the same as for AWC and ICAF, but officers attend only one of the three Senior Service Schools.

Other Service Schools. A few Air Force officers may be selected to attend the other services' intermediate service schools—Army Command and General Staff College, the College of Naval Command and Staff, or the Marine Corps Command and Staff College—and their senior service schools—the Army War College or the College of Naval Warfare.

Non-DOD PME Courses. A few Air Force officers may be selected to attend International PME courses, such as the ISS U.S. Army School of the Americas or the SSS Inter-American Defense College or NATO Defence College. The USAF also participates in a large number of allied PME courses, such as the RAF Staff College or German Staff College (ISS level), or the Royal College of Defence Studies, Canadian National Defence College, or French Air War College (SSS level).

Civilian PME Courses. These SSS equivalents for a chosen few are the U.S. State Department Seminar of National and International Affairs and the Harvard University Research Fellow Program.

OTHER TRAINING AND EDUCATION PROGRAMS

The Air Force sponsors a variety of training and educational opportunities for officers to develop their specialties and their military professionalism. Participation in some of the programs is selective; other programs are open to all officers. Each base's education services flight can provide general and location-specific information, including information on tuition assistance and veterans benefits.

Air Force Institute of Technology (AFIT). An Air University organization located at Wright-Patterson AFB, Ohio, AFIT supports national defense through graduate and professional education and research programs. AFIT provides consulting and research services to Department of Defense agencies and conducts nondegree and degree programs; the latter include undergraduate through the doctoral level. The resident program includes the Graduate School of Engineering, the Graduate School of Logistics and Acquisition Management, the School of Systems and Logistics, and the Civil Engineering and Services School.

AFIT's Civilian Institution Programs manage educational programs for students to meet specific Air Force requirements through civilian universities, research centers, hospitals, industrial and business organizations, and governmental agencies. Among these are the Graduate School Program for Air Force Academy graduates and the Education Delay Program for AFROTC graduates; both programs lead to graduate degrees, the former at Air Force expense and the latter at the expense of the individual officer. Civilian Institution Programs also encompass advanced degree programs in more than a dozen selected fields, legal and health-care education programs, research fellowship programs, education and industry programs, a Foreign Service Institute program, and professional continuing education programs in almost twenty fields.

The Ira C. Eaker College for Professional Development. This Air University college located at Maxwell AFB, Alabama, provides consultation services and specialized research, as well as seven professional educational programs: AF Human Resource Management School, International Officer School, Professional Military Comptroller School, USAF Chaplain Service Institute, USAF First Sergeants Academy, USAF Historian Development School, and USAF Judge Advocate General School. The College for Professional Development also conducts courses for commanders of wings, support groups, maintenance groups, and operations squadrons.

Air Force Institute for Advanced Distributed Learning (AFIADL). Headquartered at Gunter Annex, Maxwell AFB, Alabama, AFIADL offers hundreds of professional military education, specialized, and career development distance learning courses. PME courses include a USAF Reserve officer preparatory course, Squadron Officer School, Air Command and Staff College, Air War College, the Aerospace Power Course that is essential for officers assigned to joint billets, and a course on the history of U.S. airpower. Specialized and career development courses allow officers and enlisted personnel to develop skills in and knowledge of their technical specialties.

CAREER-LONG PROFESSIONAL EDUCATION

Air Force officers have two career-long educational obligations: They must develop expertise both in their specialties and in the profession of arms. Junior officers, of course, must concentrate on acquiring expertise in their specialties. But even they cannot neglect their professional education obligations. Day-to-day duties in officers' specialties are usually so demanding of time and energy that officers can easily neglect their professional obligations. But, by themselves, the formal professional military education schools are inadequate for developing warfighting expertise. The profession of arms is so broad, and it requires knowledge in so many fields, and familiarity in even more, that career-long self-study programs are necessary for officers who aspire to real professionalism. Although officers may supplement their individual professional education programs with formal courses, such as correspondence courses or classes at local universities, the bulk of officers' self-education is achieved by reading.

Career-long professional education should be centered on warfighting. Junior officers should focus their study on how leadership and management, strategy and tactics, and doctrine relate to their individual specialties during wartime. More senior officers, after fully understanding how their specialties contribute to the Air Force's capabilities to wage war, should focus on how airpower contributes to joint warfighting capabilities.

Understanding how military force is used as a political tool is achieved by a critical study of military history and by analysis of contemporary politico-military events. The "Professional Reading Guide," appendix B of this book, is a place to begin. The books in this appendix are particularly useful in developing an understanding of military history; critical study of these books can enlighten the reader regarding employment of military forces today and in the future. But a historical understanding is not enough; contemporary politico-military events must also be followed and analyzed. All officers must keep abreast of a vast spectrum of domestic and international issues (religious, social, ethnographic, political, economic, scientific, technological, and so on) that bear on the profession of arms. This cannot be achieved by reading the local newspaper or watching the news on television. All officers should read at least one weekly newsmagazine; *The Economist* is particularly good. They should read general professional journals and journals concerned with their specialties. Senior officers should read the *Early Bird* (*http://ebird.afis.mil*) and *Defense Daily* (*http://www.defensedaily.com*), as well as scholarly journals, such as *Foreign Affairs, Journal of International Affairs, Journal of Strategic Studies, Orbis,* and *Political Science Quarterly.*

Two lists follow: one of selected professional journals and other periodicals, and a second of selected professional associations, each of which publishes a periodical for its members. Neither list is inclusive of all professional journals and associations that may be of interest to Air Force officers. Furthermore, all officers should identify those additional publications related to their specialties and keep abreast of them as well. All officers should also consider joining one or more of the associations listed below, as well as those societies devoted to their specialties.

SELECTED PROFESSIONAL JOURNALS AND OTHER PERIODICALS

Ad Astra, National Space Society, 1620 I St., Suite 615, Washington, DC 20006, *www.nss.org.*

Air and Space Power Journal, AFRP 10-1, an official Air Force quarterly distributed widely within the Air Force. Air and Space Power Journal is now online at *http://www.airpower.maxwell.af.mil.*

Air Force Times, 800-424-9335.

Air Forces Monthly, 800-221-3148, *http://www.keypublishing.com.*

Airman, an official Air Force publication distributed widely within the Air Force; also see *http://www.af.mil/news/airman.*

Armed Forces Journal, 800-368-5718, *http://www.armedforcesjournal .com.*

Armed Forces and Society, the official journal of the Inter-University Seminar on Armed Forces and Society, *http://www.asafs.org,* 773-508-2930.

Aviation Week and Space Technology, http://www.aviationweek.com, 800-525-5003.

Citizen Airman, official magazine of the Air Force Reserve, *http://www .afrc.af.mil,* 800-616-3775.

Current News: Early Bird, http://ebird.dtic.mil.

Inside the Air Force, a weekly report of Air Force programs, procurement, and policymaking, *http://www.InsideDefense.com.*

Jane's Defense Weekly, 800-824-0768, *http://www.jdw.janes.com.*

Jane's International Defense Review, http://www.idr.janes.com.

Joint Forces Quarterly, an official Department of Defense publication distributed within the armed forces; see *http://www.dtic.mil/doctrine/jel/jfq _pubs/index.htm.*

Marine Corps Gazette, http://www.mca-marines.org/gazette.

Military Review, the professional journal of the US Army. Now available on line at *www.leavenworth.army.mil/MILREV.*

Naval War College Review, Code 32S, Naval War College, 686 Cushing Rd., Newport, RI 02841-1207, *http://www.nwc.navy.mil/press.*

Parameters, U.S. Army War College quarterly. *Parameters* is online at *http://www.carlisle.army.mil/uswc/Parameters.*

Surface Warfare, an official publication of the Department of the Navy, *http://www.navy.mil/navpalib/cno/n76.*

SELECTED PROFESSIONAL ASSOCIATIONS

Air Force Association, 1501 Lee Highway, Arlington, VA 22209-1198 (membership fees include subscription to *Air Force* magazine), *http://www.afa.org.*

Air Force Historical Foundation, P.O. Box 151150, Alexandria, VA 22315 (membership fees include subscription to *Air Power History*), *http://www .afhistoricalfoundation.com.*

Military Officers Association of America (formerly TROA—The Reserve Officers Association), (membership fees include subscription to *Military Officer*), 800-234-6622, *http://www.moaa.org.* MOAA, which represents all servicemembers to the U.S. government, is open to active-duty, as well as retired, officers.

National Guard Association of the United States, One Massachusetts Ave. NW, Washington, DC 20001 (membership fees include subscription to *National Guard*), 202-789-0031, *http://www.ngaus.org.*

Reserve Officers Association, One Constitutional Ave. NE, Washington, DC 20002-5618 (membership fees include subscription to *The Officer*), 202-479-2200.

Society for Military History, George C. Marshall Library, Lexington, VA 24450-1600 (membership fees include subscription to *Journal of Military History*), *http://www.smh-hq.org.*

BASE LIBRARIES

Although individual officers may choose to subscribe to several professional or specialty publications, or to buy several books in the "Professional Reading Guide" (See appendix B), financial considerations will limit acquisition of a large professional library. Fortunately, most base libraries have adequate collections of professional books and subscribe to a wide variety of professional and specialty publications.

Junior officers may be inclined to despair when confronted with professional education obligations in addition to day-to-day specialty obligations. But if professional reading is made a habit early in an officer's career, it will not be a burden, but something to enjoy, because it is at the heart of the officer's chosen profession. Moreover, professional self-study will inevitably relate to an officer's specialty, improving daily performance. The experiences of an ongoing Air Force career, and even the opportunities to broaden perspective afforded by foreign travel, will also contribute to developing professional military expertise.

PROFESSIONAL WRITING

All officers are frequently required to write and write effectively. As with expository and persuasive writing in the civil sector, writing in the Air Force should be well organized, clear, concise, and, of course, free of spelling, grammar, and punctuation errors. Avoid Air Force jargon, or militarese; rather, use plain, standard English. The Air Force has style rules and formats for a variety of written correspondence. Refer to AFMAN 33-326, *Preparing Official Correspondence,* and AFH 33-337, the *Tongue and Quill.* All officers need their own copies of the *Tongue and Quill,* which addresses military speaking and logic, as well as writing. Another popular practical guide is William McIntosh's *Guide to Effective Military Writing,* by Stackpole Books.

10

Health and Fitness

Many lists of attributes considered essential to a successful Air Force officer omit these critically important items: health and fitness—and happiness. The traditional picture of an officer of our armed services is that of a man or a woman so dedicated to duty, so disciplined, that the officer carries on despite illness of the body, or agonized turmoil of the mind, or sickness of the soul. An officer in such condition may indeed carry on, but he or she is a menace to all. Such an officer is really incapable of doing an adequate job. The Air Force *requires* all officers to guard their own physical and mental health. Thus, the Air Force recognizes a fact: Officers can't do their best work unless they're healthy, fit, and happy. Mental and physical fitness and health are connected, and both are also interrelated with happiness. Young, vigorous officers have some difficulty imagining themselves other than healthy when they are healthy. Still, though you're healthy now, you would do well to look ahead a bit. Actually, the Air Force is going to ensure that you maintain your health and fitness. The Air Force's emphasis on physical fitness can best be illustrated by the fact that an officer's physical fitness test results are recorded on the new Officer Performance Report (AF Form 707).

AIR FORCE FITNESS PROGRAM
In 2004, the Air Force instituted its new, comprehensive fitness program (AFI 10-248). It requires airmen to participate in a year-round physical conditioning program that emphasizes total fitness, which includes effective aerobic conditioning, strength and flexibility training, and healthy eating. Furthermore, the new program requires that commanders and supervisors incorporate fitness into Air Force culture to ensure that every airman is personally fit for expeditionary mission requirements. This fitness program differs from its predecessors by requiring that each airman follow a fit and healthy lifestyle. No longer will passing an annual fitness test suffice.

Physical Training. To establish and maintain a fitness environment, commanders are required to have unit-based physical training sessions at least three times each week, and each airman must participate in at least three weekly physical training sessions. Every airman is permitted to engage in 90-minute exercise sessions from three to five times a week—during duty hours. These physical training sessions aren't excuses for golf, rather they must be effective cardiorespiratory and weight training exercise, specifically running and doing push-ups and crunches.

Healthy Eating. Aerobic and anaerobic physical training is one component of Air Force Fitness Program. Healthy eating is another component; healthy eating includes what you eat, how much you eat, and when and how often you eat. Two-thirds of American adults are overweight, and about half of those are obese. We're naturally attracted to food that's unhealthy, because unlike our ancestors, we no longer engage in unrelenting physical activity and we're no longer threatened with starvation. Our innate propensity to eat when food is available is compounded because eating is almost inseparable from socializing and because portion sizes have increased dramatically. In general, we must curb our appetite for carbohydrates, calories, and fat. The greatest portion of our food should be grains and vegetables, followed by fruit and dairy products. Meats should be limited; fats, oils, and sweets should be strictly limited. This means, of course, limited or no soft drinks and fast foods. So consider the matter of fast lunches, eating at your desk, or erratic eating habits. In twenty years of service, you could just "grab a bite to eat" for lunch from the junk food vending machine more than 5,000 times! What does this procedure of eating rapidly and without regard to a balanced diet do to your health? Any doctor can give answers ranging over a wide variety of physical troubles. Which one would finally hit *you* depends on your particular makeup. Your base's health and wellness center has a nutritionist on staff to advise you in making healthy eating choices. See AFI 44-104, *Nutrition Education.*

Drugs. One of the most certain methods of destroying good health is to use legal and illegal drugs. The most frequently abused drug is *alcohol,* and it's legal for Americans 21 years of age and older. Unfortunately, there's no pat answer as to what is excessive. Life would be far simpler for most people if there were pat answers—if it could be said that two drinks during an evening are not dangerous, but that three drinks are dangerous. Not so. It all depends on you; for those who are genetically programmed for alcoholism, one drink is too much. One thing is certain, however: If you drink to the point of being "high" each evening, or even a few evenings a week, something is wrong, and something is going to give. Perhaps it will be your stomach, perhaps your heart, or perhaps, your liver. If you prefer, you need not drink at all. No one will think less of you. Even if they do, it's their problem, not yours. The Department of Defense is making a concerted effort to discourage servicemembers from using *tobacco* products. Tobacco products not only damage active abusers, but tobacco smoke also puts passive smokers' health at risk. Today in the military, nonsmoking offices and workplaces are the rule. During off-duty hours, it's your choice to smoke or not, but if you smoke, you're responsible for being considerate of those who do not, because passive smoking is also dangerous—and irritating. Just say no to *illegal* *drugs.* If you don't yet care about your health, at least consider the well being of your family and your career. Mandatory urinalysis is as deadly for an Air Force career as is drug abuse itself. See AFI 44-121, *Alcohol and Drug Abuse Prevention and Treatment Program*; AFI 40-102, *Tobacco Use in the Air Force*; and AFI 44-120, *Drug Abuse Testing Program.*

Fitness Testing. The Air Force's new fitness test is completely different than that with which airmen have been familiar. The test consists of three components. The most heavily weighted component is the test for aerobic fitness, which consists of a 1.5-mile timed run, or for those who cannot run, a stationary bicycle test. The aerobic fitness portion of the test has a maximum point score of 50.

The second component is a measurement for body fat. This is scored by measuring the waist at the level of the upper hip bone. The thinner that one is in the abdomen, the higher the component score, with the maximum component score being 30.

The last component tests muscular fitness through separately scored push-ups and crunches repetitions. Each portion of the muscular fitness component carries a maximum score of 10, for a component total of 20.

The test's total overall maximum point score is 100. Tests are rated by use of charts calibrated to the airman's gender and age. Scoring tables for men and women by age are shown in appendix G.

Members must complete all the components unless medically exempted. Test components and maximum possible points are shown on this table:

Component	Possible Points
Aerobic	50
Body Composition	30
Push-ups	10
Crunches	10

Fitness levels are correlated to total scores as shown on this table:

Fitness Level	Total Score
Excellent	>90
Good	75–89.9
Marginal	70–74.9
Poor	<70

Airmen's scores determine how often they need to retest. Those scoring in the good and excellent categories will retest after a year. Airmen scoring in the marginal category will retest after six months, and those scoring in the poor category will retest after 90 days.

In addition, airmen scoring marginally on the test will have to attend a two-hour healthy-living workshop that focuses on lifestyle behavior, time management, and fitness education. Remedial training for people scoring in the poor category involves attendance at a healthy-living workshop, an individualized exercise program, a weight-loss program for those who exceed body fat standards, and mandatory exercise five days a week.

MENTAL HEALTH

The Air Force Fitness Program focuses on aerobic conditioning, strength and flexibility training, and healthy eating. Health and fitness, however, have other components.

Duty. Combat tempo, especially, can produce tension and stress. Air Force officers lead lives characterized by long duty hours, steady pressure, sudden change, and tense occasions. Unless officers are more than usually careful of their health, the long years of tension may finally take their toll, perhaps grievously. Most doctors look on stress as the chief debilitating agent of modern times. Anxiety and worrying are probably the most expensive of all pastimes, because they not only prevent effective action to remove the cause of worry, but also degrade physical and mental strength, thus making those under stress less capable of taking action. Stress, however, is more a symptom than a disease. This thought brings us to the area of mental health—happiness. Mental health—serenity, happiness—is usually firm and stable when there's no cause for concern about health, family, career, or finances. An entire spectrum of special situations doesn't fall within these four categories, but a great deal of all unhappiness stems from these fatal four. Officers must take care of not only their own health, but also the health of others whose lives touch their own.

Dependents' Health. As an officer, don't allow your official duties to prevent your taking proper steps to ensure the health of your loved ones. Personal duty may necessitate absenting yourself from your place of work for a few hours to take your child to the doctor for a needed checkup. Do so. Your commander will approve; but ask beforehand. Here is the point: If you fail to see that your spouse or child gets proper medical attention at the time it can do the most good, sooner or later your spouse or child may become seriously ill. If you become deeply disturbed as a result, the Air Force loses your most effective services, not for a few hours, but for weeks or months. Obviously, your duty may separate you from your family. This is almost inevitable considering the missions that the Air Force faces today and the intensity of combat tempo. Minimize this possibility by keeping your legal and financial matters in order. See chapter 26, "Legal Documents and Assistance," and chapter 27, "Financial Security for Your Family."

Family Problems. No person enjoys the best mental health when family relationships are abnormal. The foremost consideration in this area is the relationship between husband and wife. Air Force officers can't live a daily home life full of strain and turmoil and at the same time do a top-notch job at work. If trouble persists between husband and wife, the two should discuss their problem with a chaplain or a counselor. False pride in officers is poor justification for suppressing a situation that can wreck lives, careers, and the health of all involved. Marital problems are the proper concern of the Air Force because these strains can and very often do result in poor health, poor efficiency, or both.

Officers suffering from appendicitis do not hesitate to lay this problem before a doctor. They should as quickly seek competent advice on family problems because these can be, in the long run, more damaging than most bodily ailments.

Career Satisfaction. Concern about your career and duty conditions (such as TDY frequency and combat tempo) can become a source of worry, of bitterness, or of frustration amounting to a major menace to mental health. Perhaps you feel you've been forced into a career channel to which you're unsuited. Perhaps you believe you've been mistreated in the matter of promotion. These thoughts often lead to a state of mind incompatible with mental fitness, and can markedly degrade your job performance. If such a problem develops, talk it over with your commander in complete frankness. The commander may not agree with you but will at least know your state of mind. By sharing your problem with someone, you lighten it somewhat. Better still, the commander may be able to do something about it. If you don't feel comfortable talking to your commander, go see a chaplain or a lawyer or a community mental health professional. But do something—don't just keep it inside until you make yourself ill.

Finances. Finances are perhaps the greatest single source of worry among officers, and the greatest single source of career and marital troubles. All officers should spend ample time *thinking*—not worrying—about their finances. Trite as it may sound, there's no good substitute for a budget. A budget is simply a financial plan, a program for matching financial obligations and income. All officers can draw up a budget for themselves. The trick is to stick to it.

Easy Credit. Foremost among the financial traps awaiting officers is easy credit. Officers are considered excellent credit risks, because the services require them to meet their debts. Officers can buy on credit almost anything they are willing to sign for. There's a great temptation, therefore, to go for the high-priced car, the deluxe television set, a state-of-the-art personal computer, and the best-quality furniture. The best help in resisting these temptations is the cold logic of a personal budget. A budget will show you exactly what you can afford to buy with your income.

If, however, you slip into debt, the best action is to consult with Family Services. When you pay off your credit cards, however, make sure you don't simply run them up again.

Other than by such notably stupid practices as spending too much money on liquor or gambling, the chief methods of encountering financial troubles are in connection with renting or buying a house, buying a car, and purchasing furniture or appliances.

Renting an Apartment or a House. Renting is an experience that Air Force officers often face, so consider these points. Begin at the base housing office, which will have leads regarding where to look, as well as where not to look—places that military personnel are forbidden to rent. A lease is binding on you as an Air Force officer unless you get permanent change of station (PCS) orders. Make sure your lease has a military clause.

Be very clear as to what the rent covers. How about utilities? Water? Heat? Who pays for these? If the landlord requires an extra month's rent as a deposit in advance, exactly what are the conditions under which you will be able to get your deposit back? Is fair wear and tear chargeable? Before renting, ask to see a few utility bills for the winter and summer months. These are, in effect, additional rent. Consider such matters thoughtfully before you sign the lease.

Buying a House. Buying a house is probably the most momentous financial decision you will ever make. Thorough investigation of all angles is imperative, especially in these days of conventional, variable rate, and creative financing in addition to your eligibility for VA and FHA guaranteed loans. Current four-year tours often make buying a house *seem* like a reasonable investment. But before you buy, research the housing market in your area to assess your chances of being able to resell or rent your house when you PCS.

Buying Cars. The primary mistake of many young officers in buying an automobile is to sign up for a luxury car on an economy model budget. Any fully equipped automobile is a very expensive item, especially if it's also equipped with finance charges. Further, the higher the initial price, the higher the upkeep cost. When it comes to spare parts, another factor sets in with a vengeance. Compare the cost of a new muffler for a Porsche with the same item for a Honda. Generators, starters, water pumps, tires—you must replace these, too, when they wear out. In this area you find a significant differential. Whatever your final decision, at least take these matters into account.

Buying Furniture. An officer can easily go overboard in purchasing furniture and appliances. Repeated moves or storage can reduce furniture to shambles. Buy only the items of furniture you really must have. Stay away from very expensive, delicate items. Don't try to match the Joneses, who may not move every few years.

Bad Checks. Zealously monitor your checkbook balance and your entire credit rating. Impress upon your spouse the need for responsibility, and if you share a checking account, be sure that each party knows the extent to which the other may use it. Keep an amount in your account as a cushion above your monthly expenditures. If possible, either arrange with your bank to notify you if there is a slipup before bouncing a check, or authorize it to cover the amount by drawing against your savings account.

In summary, the Air Force depends on officers and enlisted personnel who are physically and mentally healthy and fit. Because of the new demands made by the expeditionary mission, the Air Force is now taking a more active role to ensure that all airmen are capable of effectively accomplishing their duties. The fitness program addresses physical health and fitness. Although the fitness program does not directly address the issues of mental health, individual airmen are not left to deal with their problems by themselves. If you have a problem that threatens your mental health, seek competent advice, and seek it early. Remember that your health is a matter of proper and sincere concern to your superiors in the Air Force, your doctor, and your chaplain. Do not ignore the help they can and will gladly give if you ask. If troubles arise, do not just worry. Do something!

11

Promotion

The subject of promotion often comes up for discussion when officers gather. Such discussions are only natural because promotion is the avenue to increased responsibility and rank, including the pay that goes with increased responsibility. Promotion causes heated discussions, but often without full consideration of just what the promotion system is supposed to accomplish, the methods available, or the problems involved in the operation of a career promotion system. Understanding the promotion system—what it is, how it works, and some of the obstacles involved—requires a review of the laws and policies governing promotion. See AFPAM 36-2506, *You and Your Promotions: The Air Force Officer Promotion Program.*

DEFENSE OFFICER PERSONNEL MANAGEMENT ACT

To an extent unparalleled by any other profession, the law establishes the parameters of the careers of commissioned officers. These laws reflect the concern of the Congress and the nation in maintaining the high quality of our officer corps and the recognition that this quality is essential to national security. A landmark in the legislation governing officer personnel management was the enactment of the Defense Officer Personnel Management Act (DOPMA), which became effective on 15 September 1981.

DOPMA updated outmoded aspects of earlier law, introduced important new officer personnel management concepts, and completed the task begun with the Officer Personnel Act of 1947 of unifying and standardizing the law as it applies to officers of the four armed services. Although DOPMA deals in comprehensive fashion with all aspects of officer personnel management, the bulk of the legislation concerns the dimensions and characteristics of the career system for officers and the specific rules governing promotion procedures. The changes from earlier systems and procedures were evolutionary, building on experience under previous laws to improve the overall quality of the officer corps.

DOPMA created a single system of permanent promotions for all officers on active duty. This system replaced a complex and sometimes confusing system of temporary and permanent promotions. With DOPMA, all active-duty officers are considered under the same rules governing promotion eligibility and consideration.

With DOPMA in force, the officer corps will continue to have a mix of regular and reserve officers on extended active duty, although all officers selected for promotion to major will be offered regular appointments. Most officers, who enter active service as reservists, will first be considered for a regular appointment before the eighth year of active service (approximately at the seventh year). The final consideration point is on selection for major.

PROMOTION SYSTEM OBJECTIVES

Air Force promotion plans have these objectives:

- To fill Air Force positions. The primary purpose of the active-duty promotion system is to select the best-qualified officers available to fill Air Force positions. Therefore, the system must be responsive to the needs of the Air Force. Promotion is not a reward for past service; it is based on demonstrated potential to serve in positions of greater responsibility.
- To provide reasonably stable, consistent, and visible career progression opportunities. The active-duty promotion system must also provide incentive to the officer. It must provide reasonable opportunity for promotion, including accelerated promotion from below the promotion zone for officers possessing exceptional potential. The active-duty promotion system should be relatively stable, so as to offer each year group of officers opportunity comparable with that of other year groups.
- To maintain force vitality. To carry out its role in support of national objectives, the armed forces have a unique requirement to maintain a young and dynamic officer corps that is capable of developing and managing a large combat-ready force and of assuming wartime leadership. The Air Force promotion system is designed to produce officers in sufficient quality and quantity while maintaining a well-balanced force in terms of age and experience.

The Air Force must continue to cultivate a promotion system that will select those who best meet the challenges for future leadership.

PROMOTION BOARDS

How does one officer get promoted and another not? No discussion of the subject is realistic that does not touch upon how officers get themselves promoted. Although cynics may say that the prerequisites are to be a general's offspring, in-law, or aide, you may reasonably doubt the truth of that point of view because there is too much evidence to the contrary. Others may subscribe to the philosophy that if they do a good job the system will take care of them, but this theory, too, is an insufficient explanation.

Discussing how a typical promotion board operates may help you understand better how the selection process—often shrouded in mystery and distorted by rumor—really works. First, to scotch some rumors, it does not help to have a friend on the board; job descriptions and word pictures *are* important as well as the blocks checked; and the process does not favor select groups.

A selection board uses the following officer records as instruments: all officer performance reports (OPRs) and training reports, citations or orders for approved U.S. decorations, the officer selection brief, letters pertaining to nonattendance at or ineligibility for professional military education, letters to the board from officers eligible in or above the promotion zone, and specified unfavorable information, such as court-martial orders and Air Force forms reflecting the imposition of nonjudicial punishment. The selection board also uses each officer's Promotion Recommendation Form that recommends "Definitely Promote," "Promote," or "Do Not Promote This Board."

All selection boards use the best-qualified method of selection. Because the board can recommend only a set maximum number, it must arrange those eligible in an order-of-merit listing (best to least qualified), apply the quota to this listing, and promote those officers above the line where the quota runs out. Boards evaluate officers using the whole-person concept. Board members carefully review each officer's selection folder, especially in the areas of job responsibility and performance, leadership, breadth of experience, professional competence, and academic and professional military education.

The board knows that records contain evaluations under several different assignments. The ratee's job, unit of assignment, and level of responsibility all play a part in evaluation. The new OPR reflects the tremendous importance now being put on the officer's physical fitness test. The selection folder reflects each officer's level of academic and professional military education, but the board judges to what extent these achievements improve performance and potential to assume greater responsibility. The board does not give mere completion of such courses disproportionate credit, nor does the board penalize officers for not having obtained advanced degrees or PME diplomas. Some officers, such as those assigned to engineering or scientific areas or to some particular rated specialty, may not receive an opportunity for career broadening, so boards do not penalize them for that reason.

Boards must promote the best officers they review for consideration, and the board members—highly qualified officers who have the experience and mature judgment to make accurate assessments of potential—must take an oath to perform their duties without prejudice or partiality, having in view the fitness of the officers considered and the efficiency of the USAF. The Air Force takes pains to ensure that board panels make selections on a uniform basis. Of course, in the last analysis, individuals' views of the promotion selection process may depend upon whether they are selected or not, but the Air Force makes strenuous and conscientious efforts to ensure that the selection basis is the best one possible.

HOW TO GET PROMOTED

This question has no perfect and unequivocal answer, but some observations based on experience may help. First, hit the ground running when you go on active duty. Whether you go first to flight or technical training or get on-the-job training, master your *job* quickly and thoroughly and give it 100 percent effort. Although your seniors, peers, and subordinates should give you aid and comfort, don't assume that anyone is going to help you learn the ropes. After this step, begin learning your *profession,* the profession of arms. Even in this age of specialization, just being a specialist—a pilot, a maintenance officer, or an intelligence officer—is usually not enough. The military profession is an honorable profession. Learn it, understand it, and respect it.

Along the way, you may want to become an expert in some aspect of the military arts and sciences that few others know. If you are *the* expert, your expertise may lead you to some interesting experiences.

Strive for assignments at increasingly higher command and staff levels, including joint staff duties. When you can obtain advanced education and PME, go for it.

Because your fellow officer is at the same time your comrade, your peer, and your competitor for promotion, you must maintain a proper perspective about this business of promotion. Above all, keep a good sense of humor. Always be yourself, never forgetting Polonius's advice to Laertes in *Hamlet:* "This above all, to thine own self be true. Thou canst not then be false to any man." After your career has ended and if you have soldiered as a professional, not only will you cherish the worth of it all, having followed the path of duty, honor, country, but you will also cherish the camaraderie that was such an essential part of it.

12

Officer Evaluation System

.The measurement of an officer's performance, with potentials, strengths, and weaknesses, is a matter of importance to the Air Force, as well as to the individual officer. Next to expertise in career specialty, performance reports constitute the most important single source of information for selection and assignment of people to do the work of the Air Force. They are the means by which all members may be placed where their work will be of greatest value. Here also will be recorded the information that will determine selection for promotion, for favored assignment, for the higher schools, or for actions leading possibly to termination of service.

Junior officers are not so much concerned with why performance reports are necessary, or even with the responsibility imposed upon the rating officers, as they are with how to obtain favorable performance reports. This chapter will therefore discuss the Officer Evaluation System (OES), how the rating system's forms work, and how you can get higher evaluations. A full explanation of the Officer Evaluation System can be found in AFI 36-2406, *Officer and Enlisted Evaluation Systems,* and AFPAM 36-2506, *You and Your Promotions: The Air Force Officer Promotion Program.*

Officers who study this information and apply it will find themselves in the position of writing performance reports on other officers sooner than they may now think.

THE OES AND OFFICER PROFESSIONAL DEVELOPMENT

Because any appraisal system is an integral part of officer professional development, it is important to understand the Air Force concept of professional development. It has three basic objectives.

First, professional development must increase the officer's qualification and ability to perform duties, now and in the near term. Formal training and discussions with supervisors provide a foundation for building this competence. However, the most important contributor is likely to be the officer's experiences in day-to-day duties.

Second, professional development involves preparing officers for future leadership challenges. Professional military education and most other education assist this effort, but again, the key to growth in leadership and professionalism is experience in appropriate leadership positions.

The third objective of professional development is to ensure that the people who are best qualified are advanced in grade and responsibility. This is where the Officer Evaluation System fits in.

What makes an officer "best qualified" for promotion? The right kind of experience, training, education, and, of course, job performance at the right time.

Lieutenants and captains become best qualified for promotion by concentrating on depth of experience in their fields of specialization. Staff assignments and other career-broadening experiences are not needed for promotion to major. Some captains will serve in staff jobs because their expertise is needed, but the OES strongly emphasizes performance in the assigned job for company grade officers with neither credit nor penalty for staff jobs.

There is increased opportunity for field grade officers to fill command and staff jobs, with more diverse job opportunities and accompanying broadened career opportunities. Field grade officers who choose to forgo broader opportunities and remain in primary line duties should still have a reasonable prospect for promotion to lieutenant colonel, given a level of performance warranting promotion. The lieutenant colonel seeking promotion to colonel will generally need emphasis on broader considerations as well as job performance.

The point is that lieutenants and captains need not make a long-term career decision between a narrow focus on line jobs and broadening. Whatever their long-term goals, the right focus at the lieutenant and captain level is on their career specialty. The primary concern of all officers should be doing the very best possible job in their primary duties, day in and day out.

WHY AN OES?

The Air Force has a high-quality officer force, making competition for promotion inevitable. An evaluation system should not attempt to eliminate or even reduce the intensity of this competition. Rather, the OES must ensure that officers compete on the right basis by measuring the proper accomplishments and qualities.

The number of officers to be selected for promotion by any given board is limited because there is a ceiling imposed by law on the number of officers who can be serving in the field grades. Promotion opportunity and select rates to all grades remain relatively constant regardless of the evaluation system used. The purpose of an evaluation system is to ensure that promotion boards have the information to select, within these percentages, those officers who are the best qualified.

PERFORMANCE FEEDBACK

Performance feedback, for lieutenants to colonels, an important element of the OES, is provided during a private, formal meeting between an officer and the officer's supervisor. It is designed to provide a realistic assessment of the officer's performance. An initial session requiring the supervisor to let an officer know what is expected establishes the basis for later feedback on how well the officer is meeting these expectations. The second feedback meeting will occur midway through the officer's reporting cycle to allow for corrections in deficient areas. Additional feedback meetings can be initiated by either the ratee or the rater.

The supervisor prepares a handwritten form (AF Form 724) that provides an assessment of the subordinate's performance, and the two discuss the comments on the form. At the conclusion of the session, the rater gives the form to the officer being provided the feedback. The feedback form does not become part of an officer's record, nor can the rater show the form to anyone other than the officer on whom the form has been prepared.

Supervisors provide feedback on duty performance, job knowledge, leadership skills, organizational skills, judgment and decisions, professional qualities, communication skills, and physical fitness using a scale that ranges from "does not meet" to "clearly exceeds." The rater includes written comments to expand on these ratings. The rater also addresses the ratee's strengths, goals, education, and future assignments.

OFFICER PERFORMANCE REPORT

The Officer Performance Report (OPR) is designed to build a continuing record of performance. For lieutenants through colonels, the rater is an officer's immediate supervisor, the same person who provides performance feedback, so the person being rated should not be surprised with the content of the report. Furthermore, the performance factors rated on the new AP Form 707, Officer Performance Report, are identical with those addressed during performance feedback. Annotation is provided only if the ratee does not meet standards. The OPR requires a brief job description and short overall assessment. The ratee signs the report to acknowledge all required feedback was accomplished during the reporting period. This new feature of the AP Form 707 allows for correction of factual errors before the report is forwarded.

The additional rater is the supervisor's boss. For officers below the grade of colonel, the additional rater must be at least one grade senior to the officer being rated. A senior officer, called the reviewer, will perform quality control on the report. The reviewer will not normally provide a rating and does not make comments about the officer unless there is disagreement with the rating of the rater or additional rater. For lieutenants through majors, the reviewer is the wing commander or equivalent staff officer. For lieutenant colonels and colonels, the reviewer is the first general officer in the rating chain. The

PERFORMANCE FEEDBACK WORKSHEET (Lt thru Col)

I. PERSONAL INFORMATION

NAME	GRADE	UNIT

II. TYPES OF

INITIAL	MID-TERM	RATEE REQUESTED	RATER DIRECTED

III. PRIMARY DUTIES

IV. PERFORMANCE FEEDBACK

1. Job Knowledge. Has knowledge required to perform duties effectively. Strives to improve knowledge. Applies knowledge to handle non-routine situations.

N/A Initial Feedback	Does Not Meet	Meets	Above Average	Clearly Exceeds

2. Leadership Skills. Sets and enforces standards. Works well with others. Fosters teamwork. Displays initiative. Self-confident. Motivates subordinates. Has respect and confidence of subordinates. Fair and consistent in evaluation of subordinates.

N/A Initial Feedback	Does Not Meet	Meets	Above Average	Clearly Exceeds

3. Professional Qualities. Exhibits loyalty, discipline, dedication, integrity, honesty, and officership. Adheres to Air Force standards. Accepts personal responsibility. Is fair and objective.

N/A Initial Feedback	Does Not Meet	Meets	Above Average	Clearly Exceeds

4. Organizational Skills. Plans, coordinates, schedules and uses resources effectively. Meets suspenses. Schedules work for self and others equitably and effectively. Anticipates and solves problems.

N/A Initial Feedback	Does Not Meet	Meets	Above Average	Clearly Exceeds

5. Judgment and Decisions. Makes timely and accurate decisions. Emphasizes logic in decision making. Retains composure in stressful situations. Recognizes opportunities. Adheres to safety and occupational health requirements. Acts to take advantage of opportunities.

N/A Initial Feedback	Does Not Meet	Meets	Above Average	Clearly Exceeds

6. Communication Skills. Listens, speaks, and writes effectively.

N/A Initial Feedback	Does Not Meet	Meets	Above Average	Clearly Exceeds

7. Physical Fitness. Maintains Air Force physical fitness standards.

Does Not Meet	Meets	Exempt

AF FORM 724, 20070625   PREVIOUS EDITIONS ARE OBSOLETE (724A and 724B)

Performance Feedback Worksheet (front)

V. PROFESSIONAL DEVELOPMENT

STRENGTHS

SUGGESTED GOALS

ACADEMIC/PROFESSIONAL EDUCATION

DE (BDE, IDE, SDE RESIDENCE/SEMINAR/CORRESPONDENCE)

NEXT/FUTURE ASSIGNMENTS (BASE LEVEL, STAFF, JOINT, CONUS, OVERSEAS)

VI. ADDITIONAL COMMENTS

RATEE SIGNATURE	RATER SIGNATURE	DATE

AF FORM 724, 20070625   PREVIOUS EDITIONS ARE OBSOLETE (724A and 724B)

Performance Feedback Worksheet *(reverse)*

reviewer will be in a position to have personal knowledge, or access to such knowledge, of the officer's job performance.

The emphasis of the performance report is on how well officers accomplish their primary duties. The raters will not consider or evaluate the probable impact of professional military education, advanced degrees, or broadening assignments. This information is available elsewhere in an officer's record. The rater's task is to focus on performance and potential based on that performance.

Performance reports make up the cumulative record of an officer's performance. They will weigh heavily both in the promotion board's deliberations and in the senior rater's recommendation for promotion, which will be made on a separate form.

PROMOTION RECOMMENDATION

To assist promotion boards in selecting those officers best qualified for promotion, there is the Promotion Recommendation Form (PRF), which focuses strongly on duty performance. It is completed sixty days before a promotion board on all officers eligible for promotion in or above the promotion zone and on a specific percentage of those officers eligible below the promotion zone. The individual completing the form is the officer's senior rater. For lieutenants, captains, and majors, this will be the wing commander or equivalent staff officer. For lieutenant colonels, it will be the first general officer in the rating chain. The senior rater is the same individual who acts as reviewer for the OPR. A different term has been chosen to reflect the different function on the PRF. The senior rater completes the PRF based on knowledge of the officer and on a review of the officer's overall record of performance.

The Promotion Recommendation Form consists of a brief description of the unit's mission, the officer's job description, narrative comments about the officer's promotion potential, and one of three possible recommendations: "Definitely Promote," "Promote," or "Do Not Promote This Board." A "Definitely Promote" recommendation tells the central promotion board that an officer's performance and performance-based potential alone warrant promotion, with minimal regard for broader considerations, such as variety of job experience, PME, and academic education. A "Promote" recommendation means that the officer is well qualified for promotion and should compete on the basis of performance, performance-based potential, and broader considerations.

The number of "Definitely Promote" recommendations for in- and above-the-promotion-zone officers is limited to a number smaller than the total number of officers that a board can select for advancement. These percentages will vary by grade. Experience suggests that when promotion boards are given a vehicle to assist them in differentiating among officers on the basis of performance, they will use it. Therefore, officers in and above the promotion zone who receive a "Definitely Promote" assessment will probably be promoted at a high rate. Even if all officers with a "Definitely Promote" are selected, a specified number of

OFFICER PERFORMANCE REPORT (Lt thru Col)

I. RATEE IDENTIFICATION DATA (Read AFI 36-2406 carefully before filling in any item)

1. NAME (Last, First, Middle Initial)	2. SSN	3. GRADE	4. DAFSC	5. REASON FOR REPORT	6. PAS CODE

7. ORGANIZATION, COMMAND, LOCATION, AND COMPONENT	8. PERIOD OF REPORT	9. NO. DAYS SUPV.
	THRU	

II. JOB DESCRIPTION (Limit text to 4 lines)
DUTY TITLE

10. SRID

III. PERFORMANCE FACTORS

	DOES NOT MEET STANDARDS	MEETS STANDARDS	FITNESS EXEMPTION
Job Knowledge, Leadership Skills, Professional Qualities, Organizational Skills, Judgment and Decisions, Communication Skills, and Physical Fitness (see reverse if marked Does Not Meet Standards)			

IV. RATER OVERALL ASSESSMENT (Limit text to 6 lines)

Last performance feedback was accomplished on: _____ (IAW AFI 36-2406) (If not accomplished, state the reason)

NAME, GRADE, BR OF SVC, ORGN, COMMAND & LOCATION	DUTY TITLE	DATE
	SSN	SIGNATURE	

V. ADDITIONAL RATER OVERALL ASSESSMENT (Limit text to 4 lines)

CONCUR   NON-CONCUR

NAME, GRADE, BR OF SVC, ORGN, COMMAND & LOCATION	DUTY TITLE	DATE
	SSN	SIGNATURE	

VI. REVIEWER (If required, limit text to 4 lines)

CONCUR   NON-CONCUR

NAME, GRADE, BR OF SVC, ORGN, COMMAND & LOCATION	DUTY TITLE	DATE
	SSN	SIGNATURE	

VII. FUNCTIONAL EXAMINER/AIR FORCE ADVISOR
(Indicate applicable review by marking the appropriate box)

FUNCTIONAL EXAMINER   AIR FORCE ADVISOR

NAME, GRADE, BR OF SVC, ORGN, COMMAND & LOCATION	DUTY TITLE	DATE
	SSN	SIGNATURE	

VIII. RATEE'S ACKNOWLEDGMENT

I understand my signature does not constitute agreement or disagreement. I acknowledge all required feedback was accomplished during the reporting period and upon receipt of this report.

Yes No   SIGNATURE   DATE

AF FORM 707, 20070625   PREVIOUS EDITIONS ARE OBSOLETE (707A and 707B)   PRIVACY ACT INFORMATION: The information in this form is FOR OFFICIAL USE ONLY. Protect IAW the Privacy Act of 1974.

Company-Grade Officer Performance Report (front)

RATEE NAME:

IX. PERFORMANCE FACTORS (If Section III is marked Does Not Meet Standards, fill in applicable block[s])   **DOES NOT MEET STANDARDS**

1. Job Knowledge. Has knowledge required to perform duties effectively. Strives to improve knowledge. Applies knowledge to handle non-routine situations.

2. Leadership Skills. Sets and enforces standards. Works well with others. Fosters teamwork. Displays initiative. Self-confident. Motivates subordinates. Has respect and confidence of subordinates. Fair and consistent in evaluation of subordinates.

3. Professional Qualities. Exhibits loyalty, discipline, dedication, integrity, honesty, and officership. Adheres to Air Force standards. Accepts personal responsibility. Is fair and objective.

4. Organizational Skills. Plans, coordinates, schedules and uses resources effectively. Meets suspenses. Schedules work for self and others equitably and effectively. Anticipates and solves problems.

5. Judgment and Decisions. Makes timely and accurate decisions. Emphasizes logic in decision making. Retains composure in stressful situations. Recognizes opportunities. Adheres to safety and occupational health requirements. Acts to take advantage of opportunities.

6. Communication Skills. Listens, speaks, and writes effectively.

7. Physical Fitness. Maintains Air Force physical fitness standards.

X. REMARKS (use this section to spell out acronyms from the front)

XI. REFERRAL REPORT (Complete only if report contains referral comments or the overall standards block is marked as does not meet standards)

I am referring this OPR to you according to AFI 36-2406, para 3.9. It contains comment(s)/rating(s) that make(s) the report a referral as defined in AFI 36-2406, para. 3.9. Specifically, _____

Acknowledge receipt by signing and dating below. Your signature merely acknowledges that a referral report has been rendered; it does not imply acceptance of or agreement with the ratings or comments on the report. Once signed, you are entitled to a copy of this memo. You may submit rebuttal comments. Send your written comments to:

not later than 10 calendar days (30 for non-EAD members) from your date below. If you need additional time, you may request an extension from the individual named above. You may submit attachments (limit to 10 pages), but they must directly relate to the reason this report was referred. Pertinent attachments not maintained elsewhere will remain attached to the report for file in your personnel record. Copies of previous reports, etc. submitted as attachments will be removed from your rebuttal package prior to filing since these documents are already filed in your records. Your rebuttal comments/attachments may not contain any reflection on the character, conduct, integrity, or motives of the evaluator unless you can fully substantiate and document them. Contact the MPF career enhancement section, or the AF Contact Center if you require any assistance in preparing your reply to the referral report. It is important for you to be aware that receiving a referral report may affect your eligibility for other personnel related actions (e.g. assignments, promotions, etc.). You may consult your commander and/or MPF or Air Force Contact Center if you desire more information on this subject. If you believe this report is inaccurate, unjust, or unfairly prejudicial to your career, you may apply for a review of the report under AFI 36-2401, Correction of Officer and Enlisted Evaluation Reports, once the report becomes a matter of record as defined in AFI 36-2406, Attachment 1.

NAME, GRADE, BR OF SVC OF REFERRING EVALUATOR	DUTY TITLE	DATE
	SIGNATURE	
SIGNATURE OF RATEE		DATE

INSTRUCTIONS

ALL: Recommendations must be based on performance and the potential based on that performance. Promotion recommendations are prohibited. Do not comment on completion of or enrollment in Developmental Education, advanced education, previous or anticipated promotion recommendations on AF Form 709, OPR endorsement levels, family activities, marital status, race, sex, ethnic origin, age, or religion. Evaluators enter only the last four numbers of SSN.

RATER: Focus your evaluation in Section IV on what the officer did, how well he or she did it, and how the officer contributed to mission accomplishment. Write in concise "bullet" format. Your comments in Section IV may include recommendations for assignment. Provide a copy of the report to the ratee prior to the report becoming a matter of record and provide follow-up feedback to let the ratee know how their performance resulted in this final product.

ADDITIONAL RATER: Carefully review the rater's evaluation to ensure it is accurate, unbiased and uninflated. If you disagree, you may ask the rater to review his or her evaluation. You may not direct a change in the evaluation. If you still disagree with the rater, mark "NON-CONCUR" and explain. You may include recommendations for assignment.

REVIEWER: Carefully review the rater's and additional rater's ratings and comments. If their evaluations are accurate, unbiased and uninflated, mark "CONCUR" and sign the form. If you disagree with previous evaluators, you may ask them to review their evaluations. You may not direct them to change their appraisals. If you still disagree with the additional rater, mark "NON-CONCUR" and explain in Section VI. Do not use "NON-CONCUR" simply to provide comments on the report.

RATEE: Your signature is merely an acknowledgement of receipt of this report. It does not constitute concurrence. If you disagree with the content, you may file an evaluation appeal through the Evaluation Reports Appeals Board IAW AFI 26-2401 (Correcting Officer and Enlisted Evaluation Reports), or through the Air Force Board for Correction of Military Records IAW AFI 36-2603 (Air Force Board for Correction of Military Records) and AFPAM 36-2607 (Applicants' Guide to the Air Force Board for Correction of Military Records (AFBCMR)).

PRIVACY ACT STATEMENT

AUTHORITY: Title 10 United States Code, Section 8013 and Secretary of the Air Force and Executive Order 9397, 22 November 1943.

PURPOSE: Information is needed for verification of the individual's name and Social Security Number (SSN) as captured on the form at the time of rating.

ROUTINE USES: None. RATIONALE: This information will not be disclosed outside DoD channels.

DISCLOSURE: Disclosure is mandatory; SSN is used for positive identification.

AF FORM 707, 20070625   PREVIOUS EDITIONS ARE OBSOLETE (707A and 707B)   PRIVACY ACT INFORMATION: The information in this form is FOR OFFICIAL USE ONLY. Protect IAW the Privacy Act of 1974.

Company-Grade Officer Performance Report (reverse)

PROMOTION RECOMMENDATION

I. RATEE IDENTIFICATION DATA (Read AFI 36-2406, Officer and Enlisted Evaluation Systems, carefully before filling in any item.)

1. NAME (Last, First, Middle Initial)	2. SSN	3. GRADE	4. DAFSC
5. ORGANIZATION, COMMAND, LOCATION			6. PAS CODE

II. UNIT MISSION DESCRIPTION

III. JOB DESCRIPTION
1. DUTY TITLE:

2. KEY DUTIES, TASKS, RESPONSIBILITIES:

IV. PROMOTION RECOMMENDATION

V. PROMOTION ZONE	VI. GROUP SIZE	VII. BOARD	VIII. SENIOR RATER ID
BPZ [ ] I/APZ [ ]			

IX. OVERALL RECOMMENDATION	X. SENIOR RATER
	NAME, GRADE, BR OF SVC, ORGN, COMD & LOCATION
DEFINITELY PROMOTE [ ]	
PROMOTE [ ]	DUTY TITLE
DO NOT PROMOTE THIS BOARD [ ]	SSN SIGNATURE

Instructions
Senior Rater:
Review previous OERs, OPRs, Education/Training Reports, and Supplemental Evaluation Sheets. May consider other reliable information that is not contained in the record of performance when completing the PRF. Evaluate the officer's performance and assess his or her potential. Write Promotion Recommendation (Section IV) in concise "bullet" format. Enter only the last four numbers of senior rater's SSN.
Provide an accurate unbiased assessment free from consideration of race, sex, ethnic origin, age, religion, or marital status.
Provide the officer a copy of this report approximately 30 days prior to the board for which this report is prepared.

Officer:
Review record of performance, Officer Pre-Selection Brief, and PRF for accuracy. Prior to your board convening date, you must contact your senior rater to discuss if your PRF is not accurate, omits pertinent information or has an error. If your senior rater concurs, there are procedures to correct prior to the board (reference 36-2406, chapter 8). Per DOD Directive 1320.11 *Special Selection Boards*, paragraph 4.3., a supplemental promotion board "shall not consider any officer wh might, by maintaining reasonably careful records, have discovered and taken steps to correct that error or omission on which the original board based its decisi against promotion."

AF IMT 709, 20040415 V2   PREVIOUS EDITION IS OBSOLETE.   FOR OFFICIAL USE ONLY *(When filled in)*

Promotion Recommendation Form

people who receive a "Promote" recommendation will also be promoted. The latter is a mathematical reality based on the fact that more officers will be promoted than will meet the board with a "Definitely Promote" recommendation.

Senior raters also give a percentage of their below-the-promotion-zone (BPZ) candidates "Definitely Promote" recommendations. This amounts to a nomination for early promotion and means only that the officer's record will be reviewed by the selection board. Below-the-promotion-zone "Definitely Promote" recommendations are limited to 10 percent of eligible officers for promotion to major, lieutenant colonel, and colonel; this percentage is applied only to those officers eligible for BPZ consideration. PRFs on officers who are BPZ skip the evaluation board process discussed below and go directly to the central promotion board.

After the senior rater makes promotion recommendations on above- and in-the-promotion-zone candidates, the forms are sent to management-level review (MLR). This group, made up of senior raters, meets at major command or equivalent level. MLR board performs a quality control function and may, in certain circumstances, allocate a limited number of "Definitely Promote" recommendations. It cannot downgrade a recommendation given by a senior rater.

Allocation of additional "Definitely Promote" recommendations by MLR occurs in two cases. The first is when a subordinate unit is too small to earn an allocation of at least one "Definitely Promote." A minimum group size of three lieutenants, three captains, three majors, or four lieutenant colonels is required to earn an allocation. Units with fewer eligible officers are aggregated in order to produce a group size large enough for valid quality comparisons. This occurs at MLR.

The second case in which MLR allocates "Definitely Promote" recommendations is when additional "Definitely Promote" recommendations are available as a result of rounding down. When senior raters determine how many "Definitely Promotes" they can award, they must round down any fractions to the nearest whole number. For example, a senior rater who computes that 4.5 officers may receive "Definitely Promote" recommendations can give this rating to four people. Fractional remains accrue into whole number recommendations that are allocated by MLR based on job performance of officers whose records they have reviewed.

After MLR completes its tasks, it sends all the APZ and IPZ promotion recommendations to the selection board. By law, the central selection board is charged with selecting officers for promotion. Although a "Definitely Promote" recommendation will be a strong signal, it remains up to the selection board to determine which officers are selected for promotion.

Promotion recommendations for APZ and IPZ candidates are removed after the central promotion board has finished, whether or not the officer is selected for promotion.

QUESTIONS AND ANSWERS ABOUT THE PROMOTION RECOMMENDATION FORM

What types of comments are allowed in the "Promotion Recommendation" section of the PRF?

The senior rater is expected to make a decision on promotion potential based on the officer's performance. The rater first evaluates the cumulative record of job performance reflected in the file of performance reports and applies knowledge of the officer's most recent performance. The narrative section should explain why the senior rater feels the officer should be promoted. The narrative would most likely include a brief synopsis of the officer's cumulative record of performance, a statement linking that performance to advancement qualification, and an appropriate recommendation for promotion. The narrative would not address factors not related to performance, but rather should focus on performance. The rater may highlight any particular aspects of performance that set the officer apart from others and make the officer being rated best qualified for promotion.

How are senior rater positions and grades chosen?

These officers must be senior enough in grade to have the scope and breadth of experience to assess long-term performance based on the officer's record as reported on performance reports. At the same time, senior raters need to be close enough to the officers being rated to have reliable knowledge of their most recent performance or access to reliable knowledge and need to understand the significance of that performance as it relates to potential and promotion. The OPR reviewer and PRF senior rater are the same person. The terms are different to depict their different roles in the OES.

What is the significance of the three levels of recommendation the senior rater can make?

Definitely Promote. This recommendation indicates that the strength of the officer's performance and performance-based potential alone warrant promotion, with minimum regard for broader considerations.

Promote. This recommendation indicates that the officer is well qualified and should compete at the promotion board on the basis of performance, performance-based potential, and broader considerations. A "Promote" recommendation means exactly that—promote. The senior rater believes the officer should be promoted.

Do Not Promote This Board. This recommendation means that, based on the cumulative record of the performance and on personal knowledge of the most recent performance, the senior rater believes that the officer should not be promoted on the board for which the promotion recommendation is being prepared. As with all promotion recommendations prepared on IPZ and APZ officers, the "Do Not Promote This Board" recommendation is removed from the promotion file selection folder after the central promotion board reviews the record and makes final consideration. Thus, a "Do Not Promote This Board" does not become a permanent part of an officer's selection folder.

If an APZ or IPZ officer receives a "Definitely Promote" recommendation, does this mean promotion is virtually guaranteed?

"Definitely Promote" recommendations have a very powerful effect, and APZ and IPZ officers receiving such recommendations have a strong probability of promotion. However, by law, the promotion decision may be made only by the central promotion board. It is possible that an officer receiving a "Definitely Promote" will not be promoted. However, there will, in all likelihood, be some indicator in the officer's selection folder, other than performance, of why this has occurred.

Why are all Promotion Recommendation Forms pulled from the record once an officer is promoted?

The promotion recommendation is intended to be a direct communication between a senior rater and a specific central selection board. This recommendation evaluates the officer's potential for advancement to a specific rank at a specific point in time based on a cumulative record of performance. Removing recommendations eliminates any potential stigma from having been selected for promotion with a "Promote" versus a "Definitely Promote" recommendation.

Why are there limits for "Definitely Promote" recommendations?

Limits are the result of two facts of life. First, the services cannot promote everyone. Public law limiting the number of officers who may serve in the field grades forces choices. Second, without such limits, experience has shown that inflation is inevitable. Inflation tends to deny selection boards access to clear differentiation based on performance. To be assured their proper weight, "Definitely Promote" recommendations must be limited so that fewer officers meet the central board with a "Definitely Promote" than can be promoted. Said another way, value is associated with limited supply.

May I see my Promotion Recommendation Form?

Yes. You may have access to your Promotion Recommendation Form. Your senior rater will provide you with a copy of the form after review by the evaluation board.

How are the number of "Definitely Promote" recommendations for my unit computed?

For the BPZ category, your senior rater multiplies the total number of BPZ eligible officers in the wing or equivalent unit by the appropriate allocation percentage, rounding down. For the APZ and IPZ category, your senior rater multiplies only the number of in-the-promotion-zone eligible officers in the wing or equivalent unit by the appropriate percentage, again rounding down. If, for example, there are eight captains in your wing eligible for major IPZ and three eligible APZ, the number of "Definitely Promote" recommendations available to your senior rater is five (8 x .65). These five recommendations will go to the top performers among the 11 APZ and IPZ officers.

ADDITIONAL INFORMATION ON OFFICER EVALUATIONS

Unfavorable Information Files (UIFs). UIFs provide commanders a repository of substantiated derogatory information concerning the member's personal conduct and duty performance that may form the basis for administrative, personnel, or judicial actions. These files are "For Official Use Only" and are closely controlled at all levels to preclude unauthorized disclosure. UIFs may include these items, among others: documentation concerning placement on the control roster, failure to discharge a just financial obligation, misconduct or substandard performance resulting from emotional instability, drug or alcohol abuse, or similar deviations from accepted norms of behavior. UIFs are maintained by the military personnel flight and contain only that unfavorable information that has been verified for file by the individual's commander or higher authority. In addition, a summary of UIFs on officers is maintained at MAJCOM level. Except for documentation concerning court-martial convictions, certain (specified) civil court convictions, drug abuse, records of certain (specified) Article 15 UCMJ actions mandatory for file, and control roster actions, the documentation must be referred to the member for comments. The notification of "intent to file" optional information in the UIF will be sent by the commander to the member for comments.

WHAT CONDUCT PRODUCES A MORE FAVORABLE RATING?

Of obvious importance if you seek to obtain good performance reports—and you should—are the factors your rating official weighs. First, read an OPR form. If, with objectivity, you cannot rate yourself highly, you'd better start a self-improvement regimen quickly.

An Aid to Receipt of Good Performance Reports. You must earn good performance reports that lead to selection for promotion and preferred assignments.

Forbes Magazine, a publication for business executives, included the following helpful principles as developed by Rogers & Slade, Management Consultants. Observing these simple truths should help you not only in the execution of your responsibilities, but also in getting good performance reports.

In my relations with those who supervise me, I will—
- Accept my full share of responsibility.
- Make sure I know what is expected of me.
- Do what is requested in the best manner I know.
- Be agreeable when asked to do something difficult or unpleasant.
- Be honest—and not try to cover up my errors.
- Stand up for my decisions—but admit it promptly if they are shown to be wrong.
- Accept criticism in good spirit and not let a few rebukes get me down.
- Point to needed improvements but make sure my ideas are well thought out and clearly presented.

In my relations with those under my supervision, I will—
- Sell the job to be done, and not pull my rank.
- Be firm but reasonable.
- Treat those working under me as human beings—consider their feelings.
- Accept proffered suggestions—or explain why they should not be used.
- Give full job instructions and not pass the buck.
- Be friendly but not intimate—not play favorites.
- Set a good working example—not break rules I expect others to follow.
- Back up my people when they are right and give credit when and where due.

An Aid to Avoidance of Bad Performance Reports. Those who have had the opportunity of evaluating thousands of performance reports as they sat on selection boards for promotion or elimination have commented on the patterns that appear among officers whose records are below standard and have offered these tips for avoiding poor performance reports:
- Avoid unprofessional conduct, including intemperate use of liquor, questionable sexual practices, and obscenity or vulgarity.
- Avoid generating ill will among seniors, associates, or juniors.
- Avoid a reputation of mediocre or undependable performance of duty.
- Avoid a reputation of being a poor credit risk.

Summary. Officers may earn splendid reports that will lead to a successful career by establishing a reputation of always finding a legal and ethical way of getting things done; by winning the good will of those with whom they work, seniors and juniors alike; and by preparing themselves today and tonight for the discharge of the tasks of tomorrow or next week.

HOW TO WORK FOR AN "SOB"

In times past, readers have often asked for help in the delicate area of how to deal with the difficulties of working under certain officers. The editorial staff considered the matter and decided to attempt to offer something constructive. Surely, here was a field in which great good was possible. We invited an officer to write his views. Here is his answer:

> Dear Editor:
>
> You asked if I'd write a piece on how to work for an SOB. The mere thought raised wells of sympathy within me for those unfortunates who, as I did in times gone by, now suffer under a hair-shirt boss who is intolerable. How to live with the Grouchy, the Unreasonably Impatient, the Unfair, the Mean and Vicious— the summation of all the SOBs I've served under? My enthusiasm was quickened by the thought that I might be able to help those who had fallen on such evil times as to inherit an SOB as unit commander. Ah, the troubles I've known from SOBs!

Well, I began to cast about among the multitude of my SOB superiors to select the most horrendous one as my opening illustration, so as better to explain how I survived my painful ordeal while retaining my sanity. With elation upon discovering my perfect example, I began to describe old General Blank, the biggest SOB, surely, in all the world. As I wrote, however, I began to recall how, after I grew to know General Blank, I learned of his nerve-shattering war experiences, of his being finally relieved of his command and sent home more or less in physical collapse. These and other things about Blank occurred to me. On second thought, I decided he was not my candidate for Senior SOB.

When I remembered Major Dumguard, though, I knew I had my prize SOB. Dumguard's extreme impatience, his growled answers, his sudden violent anger over nothing, his indifference toward my problems—these and many other characteristics of a bonded 100-proof, aged-in-wood SOB came to mind. Yet, my resolve faded when I remembered Dumguard's young son hanging so long between life and oblivion with spinal meningitis; the deep shock of his wife's death; the fact that he lagged in promotion far behind his colleagues.

In fact, I must admit it, I can tell no one how to work for an SOB, because I've never worked for one. I have worked for people who were suffering from illnesses and who vented symptoms of these on me occasionally. I have worked for people who were bewildered, discouraged, tired, hurt, nervous, miserable, and afraid. These, too, made my life unpleasant. But I see now that these people were not true SOBs. They were human beings in some sort of trouble, people in pain, whether from real or fancied ills. Therefore, I must turn back to you unmarked pages on SOBs. I can't recall a one. Is it possible there aren't any?

Sincerely yours,

A LEGENDARY CLASSIFICATION SYSTEM

A distinguished military leader of the German army of a past era devised a classification of officers that applies even to the U.S. Air Force. According to this legend, officers fall into only four classes:

The brilliant and industrious. They make the best staff officers, for their talents provide maximum service to commanders.

The brilliant and lazy. They are the most valuable and constitute the commanders. Their tendency to avoid troublesome and time-consuming detail enables them to retain the perspective necessary in the art of making decisions. Their plans tend to the simple, the direct, and the most promising for easy success.

The stupid and lazy. Although this group will add little to military luster, they can be used on small tasks that are necessary to be accomplished. At least, they will do no great harm. They can be retained and used.

The stupid and industrious. Great damage may result from their actions. Attacking the ill-advised with zeal and energy, they may induce a disaster. They are the most dangerous. They must be eliminated!

PART IV

The Air Force Way

13

Military Courtesy

A very fine line distinguishes military courtesies from military customs. Both categories owe their existence to a common source: the respect for one another that is the proper attitude among military personnel. Military courtesies, however, are mandatory. Omission of them can bring disciplinary action. They are a part of an officer's duty; they are a strong strand in the mesh of discipline that holds a military organization together. Whoever ignores military customs will be privately censured. Whoever ignores military courtesies, however, will be officially disciplined.

Even though an officer has no choice about observing required military courtesies, a little thought would make this requirement no burden at all. Almost all the specifics of military courtesy reflect civilian etiquette. Such courtesies improve relations among people, ease the conduct of business affairs, and add smoothness to what otherwise could be awkward and undesirable situations. For example, people commonly address an elderly gentleman in civilian life as "Sir" or with his full title, such as "Mr. Smith." Few, if any, people of younger age would say to such a man, "Hey, you," or "Say, Mac . . ." Why? No discipline in civilian life requires it, but people have learned through experience that to be respectful is better than not to be. The Air Force and other military services have codified for you such lessons learned through long experience and made them mandatory so that you need not blunder along until experience teaches the proper reactions to all the many situations you may encounter. Consult AFMAN 36-2203, *Drill and Ceremonies,* for details.

CORRECT USE OF TITLES

Titles of Officers. Officially address lieutenants as "Lieutenant." Use the adjectives "First" and "Second" only in written communications. Address or refer to captains and majors by their titles. In conversation and in nonofficial correspondence, refer to and address lieutenant colonels and colonels as "Colonel" and brigadier generals, major generals, and lieutenant generals as "General."

Senior officers frequently address juniors by their first names, but this practice does not give juniors the privilege of addressing seniors in any way other than by their proper titles. If airmen are present, senior officers should address junior officers by their titles. Officers of the same grade, when among themselves, may address one another by their given names. Increasingly, servicemembers use first names. Junior officers, however, should always be conservative until they can sense what is appropriate. It is wiser to err by being too formal rather than too familiar.

Address chaplains as "Chaplain" regardless of their grades. Address as Roman Catholic chaplains and Episcopal chaplains who prefer it as "Father," and address Jewish Chaplains who prefer it as "Rabbi."

Titles of USAF Enlisted Personnel. In official communications, address enlisted personnel by their full titles. In conversation and in nonofficial correspondence, refer to and address enlisted personnel as follows:

Chief master sergeant	"Chief"
Senior master sergeant	"Sergeant"
Master sergeant	"Sergeant"
Technical sergeant	"Sergeant"
Staff sergeant	"Sergeant"
Senior airman	"Airman"
Airman first class	"Airman"
Airman	"Airman"
Airman basic	"Airman"

Identification and Titles of Officers of Other Services. You must also meticulously observe military courtesies with officers of the Army, Navy, Marine Corps, and Coast Guard in the same manner as for officers of the Air Force. The corresponding grades of commissioned officers in the Air Force, the Army, and the Navy are in the illustrations in chapter 14. The grades of commissioned officers in the Army and Marine Corps are the same as those of the Air Force. In the Coast Guard, the grades correspond to those of the Navy. Respective dates of commission determine relative rank within grades.

Titles of Cadets. Address cadets of the Air Force Academy and the Military Academy as "Cadet" officially and in written communications; informally, they are addressed as "Mister or Miss." Midshipmen of the Naval Academy are addressed as "Mister" or "Miss." In written communications, use the title "Midshipman."

MILITARY SALUTES

History of the Military Salute. For centuries, men of arms have used some form of the military salute as an exchange of greeting. Modern armed forces, which have inherited some of their military traditions from the Middle

Ages, have preserved the military salute and continued its use. The method of giving the salute has varied through the ages, as it still varies in form among the armed forces of today.

Although the genesis of the military salute is shrouded in the mysteries of the ages, historians do have some idea of how it began. In the Middle Ages, for example, knights were mounted and wore armor that covered the body completely, including the head and the face. When two friendly knights met, their custom was for each to raise the visor and expose his face to the view of the other. They always raised the visor with the right hand and held the reins with the left. It was a significant gesture of friendship and confidence, because it exposed the features and also removed the right hand—the sword hand—from the vicinity of the weapon. Also, in ancient times, the freemen (soldiers) of Europe could carry arms; when two freemen met, both would raise their right hands and then shake hands to show that neither held a weapon in his hand. Slaves could not carry arms, and they passed freemen without the exchange of a greeting. The knightly gesture of raising the hand to the visor came to be recognized as the proper greeting between soldiers. Its use continued even after modern firearms had made armor a thing of the past. The military salute is today, as it seems always to have been, a unique form of exchange of greeting between military people, between comrades in the profession of arms.

The Different Forms of the Salute. Although in this chapter, unless otherwise stated, *salute* means the hand salute, prescribed salutes can take several forms. All servicemembers use the hand salute. There are also several methods of saluting with arms.

When a salute is prescribed (except in formation), the military member either faces toward the person or flag saluted or turns the head so as to observe the person or flag saluted.

Covered or uncovered, military members exchange salutes in the same manner. People who are running come to a walk before saluting. The smartness with which officers and airmen give the salute indicates the degree of pride they have in their profession. A careless or half-hearted salute is discourteous.

In the Army and the Air Force, it is customary that newly commissioned officers give a dollar to the first enlisted member who salutes them.

Besides the hand salute, other means of saluting include Present Arms, Eyes Right, Present Saber or Sword (in the three other services), Present Guidons, dipping unit colors, Ruffles and Flourishes, the president's and vice president's marches, gun salutes, three rifle volleys at graveside, dipping airplane wings, and the ceremonial flyover.

Methods of Saluting Used by Officers. Officers salute by using the hand salute or, when in civilian clothes, by placing the right hand (and hat) over the left breast. The hand salute is the usual method. Although officers usually give the hand salute while standing or marching at attention, they may also give it while seated, such as when an officer seated at a desk acknowledges the salute of an officer or an airman who is making a report.

Officers in civilian clothes use the salute by placing the hat, held in the right hand, over the left breast under three conditions. At a military funeral, all military personnel dressed in civilian clothes use this form of the salute as a courtesy to the deceased. Members of the military service dressed in civilian clothes and wearing hats use the method to salute the national anthem or "To the Colors." While in the same dress, they also use this salute to pay respect to the national flag. Members in civilian clothing and without hats stand at attention, holding the right hand over the heart, as a courtesy to the national anthem or the national flag.

Execution of the Hand Salute. Salute within saluting distance, the distance within which recognition is easy. Begin the salute when you are about six paces from the person or the flag you are saluting or, if the approach is outside that distance, six paces from the point of nearest approach. Before the instant arrives to give the salute, stand or walk erectly, hold your head up, tuck in your chin, and pull in on your stomach muscles. Look squarely and frankly at the person to be saluted.

To execute the hand salute correctly, raise the right hand smartly until the tip of the forefinger touches the lower part of the hat or forehead above and slightly to the right of the right eye, thumb and fingers extended and joined, palm down, upper arm horizontal, forearm inclined at a 45-degree angle, hand and wrist straight; at the same time, turn the head toward the person saluted. To complete the salute, drop the arm to its normal position by the side in one motion, at the same time turning the head and eyes to the front.

If you are returning the salute of a servicemember junior to yourself, execute the two movements of the salute in the cadence of marching, ONE, TWO. If you are saluting a superior officer, execute the first movement and HOLD the position until the salute is acknowledged, and then complete your salute by dropping the hand smartly to your side.

Do these things correctly, and you will derive many rewards. Your airmen will be quick to notice your salute. Thus, you may set the example that may then extend to other matters. At the time of exchanging salutes, you should also say, "Good morning, (Sir/Ma'am)" or Good afternoon, (Sir/Ma'am)."

Try to avoid making these frequently observed errors in saluting: failure to hold the position of the salute to a superior until it is returned, failure to look at the person or color saluted, failure to assume the position of attention while saluting, failure to have the thumb and finger extended and joined (a protruding thumb is especially objectionable), a bent wrist (the hand and wrist should be in the same plane), and failure to have the upper arm horizontal. By all means, avoid these gross errors: saluting with a cigarette in the right hand or in the mouth, saluting with the left hand in a pocket, or returning a salute in a casual or perfunctory manner.

Meaning of Under Arms. The expression "under arms" means with arms in hand or having attached to the person a hand arm or the equipment pertaining directly to the arm, such as a cartridge belt, a pistol holster, or a rifle belt.

Uncovering. As a general rule, officers and airmen under arms do not uncover (remove their hats). They do uncover, however, in these circumstances:

- When they are seated as members of or in attendance at courts or boards.
- When they enter places of divine worship. (Honor guards, however, remain covered.)
- When they are indoors not on duty and want to remain informal.
- When they attend official receptions.

Members in uniform may salute civilians when appropriate, but they do not raise the uniform hat as a form of salutation.

Interpretation of Outdoors and Indoors. In the application of military courtesies, the military considers as "outdoors" structures such as hangars, gymnasiums, and other roofed structures when used for drill or exercise of troops. "Indoors" means offices, hallways, dining halls, orderly rooms, recreation rooms, libraries, and quarters.

COURTESIES AIRMEN GIVE TO OFFICERS

Occasions. Uniformed airmen give the hand salute outdoors both on and off military installations, except when the salute would be obviously inappropriate or impractical. Although it is appropriate to salute in civilian clothing, this practice has fallen into disuse. Airmen must also give the hand salute in all official greetings in the line of duty, for ceremonial occasions, and when the national anthem is played or the colors pass by.

Those entitled to the salute are commissioned officers of the Air Force, Army, Navy, Marine Corps, and Coast Guard. Saluting officers of friendly foreign countries, such as officers of the armed forces of NATO, when they are in uniform is also customary.

The Air Force urges its members to be meticulous in giving salutes to and returning salutes from personnel of the sister services. Such courtesy increases the feeling of respect that all members should feel toward comrades in arms.

Covered or uncovered, military members exchange salutes in the same manner.

Members salute only once if the senior remains in the immediate vicinity and no conversation takes place.

Among a group of airmen on a military base and not in formation, the first person noticing the approach of an officer calls the group to attention. If the group of airmen is in formation, the one in charge calls the group to attention and salutes. If outdoors and not in formation, they all salute. If indoors they come to attention.

Officers driving vehicles return the salutes of gate guards on military installations.

Uniformed servicemembers on foot salute senior officers whose automobiles have rank plates on their bumpers. The senior officer will return the salute.

Courtesies Exchanged When an Officer Addresses an Airman. In general, when a conversation takes place between an officer and an airman, the following procedure is correct: They exchange salutes; they complete the conversation; they exchange salutes again. *Exceptions:* An airman in ranks comes to attention and does not salute. Indoors, they do not exchange salutes except when an airman reports to an officer.

When NOT to Salute. The following cases require no salutes:

An airman in ranks and not at attention comes to attention when addressed by an officer but does not salute.

Details or individuals at work do not salute. The officer or noncommissioned officer in charge, if not actively engaged at the time, salutes or acknowledges salutes for the entire detail.

When actively engaged in athletic games, such as baseball, tennis, or golf, one does not salute.

When in churches, theaters, or other public places or when using public transportation, military members do not exchange salutes.

When carrying articles with both hands, or when otherwise so occupied as to make saluting impracticable, a military member does not salute. A nod and a greeting are, however, always courteous.

A member of the guard who is engaged in the performance of a specific duty, the proper execution of which would prevent saluting, does not salute.

Reporting to Officers in Their Offices. When reporting to officers in their offices, airmen (unless under arms) uncover, knock, and enter when told to do so. Upon entering, they march to within about two paces of the officer's desk, halt, salute, and report in this manner: "Sir, Airman Jones reports to Captain Smith" or "Ma'am, Airman Jones reports to the squadron commander." When the business is complete, the airman salutes, executes an about face, and withdraws. An airman uncovers (unless under arms) on entering a room where an officer is present.

Procedure When an Officer Enters a Dining Hall. When an officer enters the dining hall, airmen seated at meals remain seated at ease and continue eating unless the officer directs otherwise. *Exception:* An airman addressed stops eating and sits at attention until the conversation is completed.

Procedure When an Officer Enters a Dormitory. In a dormitory, airmen rise, uncover (if unarmed), and stand at attention when an officer enters. If more than one person is present, the first to perceive the officer calls, "Attention." On suitable occasions, officers command, "Rest" or "At Ease," when they expect to remain in the room and do not want the airmen to remain at attention. It is not strictly correct to call officers to attention when the commander enters a room. Instead, the person nearest the door should warn of the commander's approach by calling, "Ladies and gentlemen, the commander!" Officers will then come to attention.

Personal Courtesies. When accompanying a senior, a junior walks or rides on the left.

Entering Automobiles, Small Aircraft, and Small Boats. Military persons enter automobiles, small aircraft, and small boats in inverse order of rank; that is, the senior enters last and leaves first. Juniors, although entering first, take their appropriate seats. The senior is always on the right. Officers sit in the backseat of passenger cars driven by airmen unless the car is full.

COURTESIES AN OFFICER GIVES TO A SENIOR OFFICER

General. The courtesies exchanged between officers are prescribed in AFMAN 36-2203 and also include those observed through the force of custom, as discussed in chapter 14, "Customs of the Service." Of course, officers should return the salutes of airmen and junior officers.

Many of the courtesies airmen must extend to officers apply with equal force and in identical manner to junior officers in relations with senior officers. The junior salutes first. In making reports at formations, however, the person making the report salutes first regardless of rank. A squadron commander, for example, salutes first when reporting to the adjutant at a ceremony.

Several courtesies airmen extend to officers are not required between officers. The prescribed formalities airmen must observe in a dining hall while at meals, for example, do not apply to officers. Also, in an officer's quarters, courtesies prescribed when an officer enters a dormitory occupied by one or more airmen are not necessary.

Specific Courtesies Observed Between Officers. An individual officer outdoors must salute when meeting a person entitled to the salute or when addressed by a senior entitled to the salute.

When reporting in an office to an officer senior in rank, the junior follows the same procedure as described for airmen.

An officer who is outdoors in uniform and sees an occupied staff car with a senior officer's rank displayed either on a bumper plate or on a flag located on the right side of the fender, should salute. Hold the salute until the car has passed or the officer inside the car has returned the salute.

An officer (or a noncommissioned officer) in charge of a detail riding in a vehicle salutes for the entire detail.

Organization or detachment commanders salute officers of higher grades by bringing the organization or detachment to attention before saluting.

The officer (or the noncommissioned officer) in charge of a detail at work, if not actively engaged at the time, salutes for the entire detail.

The officer uncovers (unless under arms) on entering a room where a senior is present.

HONORS AND CEREMONIES ACCORDED DISTINGUISHED VISITORS (DVs)

Honors and ceremonies are often designed for greeting distinguished visitors on arrival and are accorded to some on departure. The intent of honors is to extend a mark of courtesy to a distinguished visitor. The military accords honors to individuals rather than to groups and honors committees and delegations in the person of the senior or ranking member. Commanders with the advice and assistance of protocol officers arrange the specific honors afforded visiting DVs.

COURTESIES TO THE NATIONAL FLAG AND
NATIONAL ANTHEM

The Flag of the United States. The term *flag* applies regardless of size, relative proportions, or manner of display. The national flag, in its various sizes and uses, is the base flag, the all-purpose flag, the ceremonial flag, and the interment flag.

Air Force bases fly the following flags from a staff:

- U.S. base flag: 10' hoist by 19' fly; used in pleasant weather.
- U.S. all-purpose flag: 5' hoist by 9'6" fly; used in stormy and windy weather and as prescribed by the commander.

A military unit carries these flags:

- Ceremonial flag: 4'4" hoist by 5'6" fly; carried when the Air Force ceremonial flag is appropriate.
- Organizational flag: 3' hoist by 4' fly; not a national but a unit flag; carried when the organizational flag is appropriate.

The interment flag used to cover a casket at a funeral has the same dimensions as the all-purpose flag.

Special-Purpose Flags. A guidon is a swallow-tailed organizational flag carried by smaller units, such as squadrons. Other special-purpose flags include Air Force Recruiting Service, chapel, chaplain, and Geneva Convention flags.

Flag Appurtenances. A silver spearhead tops the pike or staff of Air Force flags. Other flag appurtenances may include unit streamers and silver bands, cords and tassels, and flag slings.

Respect. Members of the armed forces meticulously observe the courtesies that the national flag or the national anthem require. Colors or standards of organizations receive the same courtesy as the national flag flown from a flagstaff. The trumpet call "To the Colors" receives the same courtesy as the national anthem.

When the national anthem sounds indoors, officers and airmen stand at attention and face the music or the flag if one is present. They do not salute unless under arms.

Officers and airmen show the same marks of respect to the national anthem of any other country played upon official occasions.

Courtesies at Retreat and Escort of the Colors. Retreat is a daily ceremony at bases during which all personnel must pay respect to the flag. The ceremony may include a retreat parade; if units on parade carry organization colors or standards, participants in the ceremony or spectators at the ceremony usually pay respect to those colors or standards. The ceremony of retreat includes a trumpeter sounding the trumpet call "Retreat" and then, if present, the band playing the national anthem; in the absence of the band, recorded music sounds the trumpet call "To the Colors." Personnel lower the flag slowly, as if reluctantly, whereas in the morning at colors, they raise it smartly, as if eagerly. After they lower the flag, they fold it into a triangular shape, supposedly commemorative of the Revolutionary War soldier's cocked hat.

At the first note of the national anthem, or its counterpart in field music, all officers and airmen present, but not in formation, face the colors or flag and give the prescribed salute. They hold the salute until the last note of the music sounds. For all officers and airmen not in formation, the prescribed salute is the hand salute. The prescribed salute for military personnel dressed in civilian clothes and wearing a hat is to stand at attention, remove the hat with the right hand, and hold it over the left breast.

Vehicles in motion halt, and occupants remain seated in the vehicle.

Salute to Passing Colors. When passing or being passed by an uncased national colors, personnel give honors in the same manner as described above. For purposes of protection, the colors may be furled and then covered with a special case. When so carried, they do not require honors.

Courtesies to the National Anthem. Whenever or wherever the national anthem or "To the Colors" sounds, at the first note, officers and airmen present, but not in formation, face the music, stand at attention, and give the prescribed salute. *Exception:* At the ceremony of retreat or escort of the colors, they face the colors or flag. They hold the position of salute until the last note of the music sounds. The prescribed salute is the same, in all cases, as those described for the ceremonies of retreat and escort of the colors.

Remembering this obvious rule can help prevent embarrassment: If you are paying respect to the flag, face the flag and salute; if you are paying respect to the national anthem or "To the Colors" played by field music, face the source of the music and salute.

Dipping the Flag or Colors. Do not dip the national flag by way of salute or compliment. Dip the organization colors as a salute when the reviewing officer has the rank of a general officer: Lower the pike (as the staff of a colors is called) to the front so that it makes a 45-degree angle with the ground.

The organization flag salutes in all military ceremonies while the national anthem or "To the Colors" sounds and when honoring its commander or a person of higher rank, but in no other case.

When not in use, the unit flag is usually on display in the commander's office.

Display and Use of the Flag. International usage forbids the display of the flag of one nation above the flag of another in time of peace. When the flags of two or more nations are on display, they should fly from separate staffs or from separate halyards of equal size and on the same level.

The national flag, when not flown from a staff or mast, should always hang flat, whether indoors or out, neither festooned over doorways or arches nor tied in a bow knot or fashioned into a rosette. When used on a rostrum, it should be above and behind the speaker's desk. It should never cover the speaker's desk or drape over the front platform. Bunting of the national colors, arranged with

How to Display the Flag

1. When displayed over the middle of the street, the flag should hang vertically with the union to the north in an east-and-west street or to the east in a north-and-south street.

2. When displayed with another flag from crossed staffs, the U.S. flag should be on the right (the flag's own right), and its staff should be in front of the staff of the other flag.

3. When flying the flag at half-staff, the flag detail should first hoist the flag to the peak and then lower it to the half-staff position, but before lowering the flag for the day, they should again raise it to the peak.

4. When flags of states or cities or pennants of societies fly on the same halyard with the U.S. flag, the U.S. flag should always be at the peak.

5. When the flag hangs over a sidewalk from a rope extending from house to pole at the edge of the sidewalk, the flag should go out from the building, toward the pole, union first.

6. When the flag is on display from a staff projecting horizontally or at any angle from the windowsill, balcony, or front of a building, the union of the flag should go to the peak of the staff (unless the flag is to be at half-staff).

7. When the flag covers a casket, the union should be at the head and over the left shoulder of the deceased. The flag should not be lowered into the grave or allowed to touch the ground.

8. When the flag is on display other than by flying from a staff, it should be flat whether indoors or out. When displayed either horizontally or vertically against a wall, the union should be uppermost and to the flag's own right—that is, to the observer's left. When displayed in a window, it should appear the same way—that is, with the union or blue field to the left of the observer in the street.

9. When carried in a procession with another flag or flags, the U.S. flag should be either on the marching right or, when there is a line of other flags, in front of the center of that line.

10. When a number of flags of states or cities or pennants of societies are grouped on display from staffs with our national flag, the U.S. flag should be at the center or at the highest point of the group.

11. When the flags of two or more nations are on display, they should fly from separate staffs of the same height, and the flags should be of about equal size. International usage forbids displaying the flag of one nation above that of another nation in time of peace.

the blue above, the white in the middle, and the red below, serves such purposes well. Under no circumstances should anyone drape the flag over chairs or benches, place any object or emblem of any kind above or on it, or hang it where something could easily contaminate or soil it. No lettering of any kind should ever appear on the flag. When metal or cloth replicas of the national flag are decorations for civilian clothing (such as costume jewelry) or an identifying symbol, the positioning and treatment should be with the greatest possible respect. When carried with other flags, the national flag should always be in front or on the right as color bearers are facing. When a number of flags are grouped on display from staffs, the national flag should always be in the center or at the highest point of the group. Strictly speaking, no one should ever degrade the national flag for advertising purposes. Today, however, the flag is everywhere, not just at military headquarters, post offices, and schools. Because it is everywhere, it has lost a great deal of its reverence, and the public no longer considers it disrespectful to use it for commercial purposes.

DISPLAY OF UNITED NATIONS FLAG

When the United States flag and the United Nations flag are on display together, the United States flag is on the right, best identified as "the marching right." The United States flag will be equal in size or larger, in the position of honor on the right (observer's left), and above the United Nations flag. Troops will carry the United Nations flag only on occasions honoring the United Nations or its high dignitaries. When so carried, the United Nations flag will be on the marching left and below the United States flag.

COURTESIES TO THE MILITARY DEAD

General. Military dead receive a dignified and ceremonial funeral service in keeping with military tradition, with the flag at half-staff and prescribed salutes to the deceased. At a military funeral, one salutes the caisson or hearse as it passes and the casket as it is carried. One also salutes during firing of volleys and playing of taps. If a unit or detail passes a burial procession or coffin, the officer or NCO in charge will give the command "Eyes Right (or Left)" and salute. When an officer dies, the commander details another officer from the unit to escort the remains to the place of burial.

Funerals. The national flag covers the casket at the military funeral of members of the military service. The flag is lengthwise on the casket with the union at the head and over the left shoulder of the deceased. Personnel do not lower the flag into the grave and do not allow it to touch the ground.

Occasions for the Flag at Half-Staff. On Memorial Day at all Air Force installations, the national flag flies at half-staff from reveille to retreat.

On the death of an officer at a base, the flag flies at half-staff and remains so between reveille and retreat or until completion of the burial service, after which the flag detail hoists it to the top. If the burial service is not at the base, the flag flies at half-staff until the remains depart the base.

Whenever instructions prescribe or proper authority orders military mourning for the death of any person entitled to personal honors, all flags are at half-staff.

The Flag at Half-Staff. When displaying the national flag at half-staff, the flag detail first hoists it to the top of the staff and then lowers it to the half-staff position. Before lowering the flag, they again raise it to the top of the staff. A flag in any position below the top of the staff is technically in the half-staff position. For an unguyed flagstaff of one piece, the middle point of the hoist of the flag should be midway between the top of the staff and its base.

14

Customs of the Service

A custom is an established usage. Customs include positive actions—things to do—and taboos—things to avoid doing.

Customs are those reasonable, consistent, widely accepted practices that make for a more pleasant life or more orderly procedures. Continued without interruption for a long time, they become compulsory. Some customs may even have the force of law.

AIR FORCE CUSTOMS

The Air Force has its own customs, some older than others. For instance, the dining-in, explained in chapter 17, "Social Life in the Air Force," is a relatively new American military custom. Those customs that persist stand on their own merits and are unwritten in the sense that they do not appear in official instructions or policy directives. Many Air Force customs complement procedures required by military courtesy. The breach of some customs merely brands the offender as uninformed or careless, but the violation of others brings official censure or disciplinary action.

Unquestionably, most Air Force customs derive from Army customs. Because the Air Force descended from the Army, most Air Force customs are almost identical to Army customs. The personalities of several early Air Force leaders directly influenced the behavior of all officers. The simplicity, cordiality, and human warmth, combined with personal dignity, displayed on all occasions and with all people by such leaders as Arnold, Doolittle, and Vandenberg have served as a broad pattern to emulate.

Sanctity of Official Statements. Ordinarily, people accept an officer's official word or statement without question. The knowledge that a false official statement not only is illegal but also is contrary to the ethics of the military profession has placed personal and official responsibility for an official statement on a high level.

The Officer-Enlisted Relationship. Good officers strive to develop their organizations to their maximum efficiency while providing for their people effective leadership, impartial justice, and wise and fair attitudes in every way. Good officers also strive to avoid things that work against this efficiency. Because undue familiarity breeds contempt, officers and enlisted personnel do not generally associate together in social activities. No officers can violate this custom with one or two people of their command and convince the others of their unswerving impartiality.

Civilians and the inexperienced cannot really understand the officer-enlisted relationship, nor can they realize that it often develops into something very deep and valuable. Only those officers and enlisted personnel who have endured together the hardships of service or the ordeals of battle can understand. Those conditions often develop a mutual trust and complete confidence between officer and airman that carries each forward to acts of sacrifice, courage, and leadership. This deep tie is a force that helps win wars.

Provide for the Needs of Enlisted Personnel. Officers must always provide for the needs and requirements of enlisted personnel. Officers in command of or responsible for airmen must provide for the airmen's housing, food, and comfort before taking care of their own personal needs.

Public Breaches of Discipline and Misconduct of Enlisted Personnel. Officers are responsible for making proper corrections and taking the necessary actions whenever and wherever they see airmen conducting themselves in an improper fashion. Officers must not fail to take the necessary preventive or corrective steps because the offenders are not from the same organization or because they are off duty. Officers are never off duty. Generally, it is a matter of protecting the airmen from their own indiscretions, to save them from more serious trouble.

Approach the delinquent offenders in a quiet, dignified, unobtrusive manner. Talk in an impersonal, officerlike way. Use a tone of voice no louder than necessary to be heard. Avoid threats. Do not scold or argue. Tell enlisted personnel that the things they have done bring discredit upon the uniform they are wearing. If possible get their names and organizations. Generally, a contact of this sort will be sufficient. Whatever action you take, you must follow up, or the deterring effect will likely vanish as soon as you are out of sight. No officers worthy of their positions of trust will fail or avoid their responsibilities, however unpleasant they may seem at the time. But do not get involved in an undignified shouting match or resort to physical measures. If your action may discredit the uniform or degrade the officer corps, back off.

Drunkenness, foul language and cursing, and other acts that discredit the uniform are things to avoid. For the most part, the standards of airmen are high, and they will give their loyal support to the necessary measures. Officers must distinguish clearly between acts that are merely unwise or on the boisterous side and those that are actually offensive. You should ignore the former. A word of caution should suffice for the borderline cases. You must handle the others with judgment.

RANK HAS ITS PRIVILEGES (RHIP)

The military system is a hierarchy. Leaders placed in charge of units in the military structure exercise control. These leaders are officers and noncommissioned officers. All must display disciplined obedience combined with loyalty, in accordance with law and policy. From the highest to the lowest, subordinates must extend an unfailing respect to the authority that issues their orders. Personal admiration is a voluntary tribute to another that the military service does not demand. But the service does demand respect for authority by unfailing courtesy to people who exercise it.

The privileges of rank do not include the privilege of abuse of position. The needs of the organization as a whole come first. Officers who use official transportation for personal use are abusing the position. Officers who divert equipment to their own use do likewise. In general, officers who take the stand that they are above the policies that guide others, especially their own subordinates, are abusing their positions, and other people will condemn their acts.

The privileges of rank and position are privileges indeed, well worth striving for and attaining. They may mean more in the Air Force than in many civil professions because, in most instances, civilian leaders receive far greater pay or other monetary benefits.

"I Wish" and "I Desire." When the commander states, "I wish," or "I desire," rather than, "I order you to do so-and-so," this wish or desire has all the force of a direct order.

The Place of Honor. The place of honor is on the right. Accordingly, when juniors walk, ride, or sit with seniors, they take the position abreast and to the left of the seniors. The deference young officers should pay to civilian elders pertains to this relationship. The junior should walk in step with a senior, step back and allow the senior to be the first to enter a door, and show similar acts of consideration and courtesy. Usually, in the relations between seniors and juniors, the senior will never think of the difference in rank; the junior should never forget it.

Addressing a Senior. In military conversation, junior officers address senior officers and all enlisted personnel address officers as either "Sir" or "Ma'am." The "Sir" or "Ma'am" precedes a report and a query; it follows the answer of a question. For example: "Sir, do you wish to see Sergeant Brown?" "Sergeant Brown, Ma'am." "Thank you, Sir." Address a general officer, however, as "General."

Departing After the Commander. Officers should remain at a reception or social gathering until after the commander has departed. The corollary: Thoughtful commanders leave early.

Reception of a Newly Joined Officer. Customarily, newly joined officers receive a cordial welcome, and most units extend courtesy to officers and families to make their arrival more pleasant and convenient. People assume that newly joined officers know their professional duties and that they have every intention of performing them ably.

Wing commanders or unit commanders customarily send letters of welcome to officers under orders to join, informing them of local conditions that may be important or interesting for them to know before arrival. The commander will inquire as to the date and hour of arrival and the number of persons accompanying. The commander will detail sponsor officers to assist newly joined officers.

Sponsors should take steps to provide temporary accommodations at the BOQ or temporary lodging facility. Sponsors usually introduce newly joined officers to the commander and to the other officers of their units. Sponsors should also inform the newcomers about local procedures they will need to know at once. Maps of the base are especially useful to strangers.

IMPORTANT PERSONAL EVENTS

Military Weddings. Military weddings follow the same procedures as any other formal wedding except for additional customs that add to their color and tone.

At military weddings, all officers should wear the prescribed uniform for the occasion. Officers may wear their medals or ribbons. Whether the wedding is held in the morning, afternoon, or evening has no bearing on the selection of appropriate uniforms. For the wedding party, the thoughtful servicemember should express a preference as to the uniform.

Birth of a Child. When a child is born to the family of an officer, the officer's commander sends a personal letter of congratulations to the parents on behalf of the command.

The same procedure is appropriate for a child born to the family of an airman, except that the organization commander writes the letter of congratulations, and the gift, if any, is from the airman's unit.

Death of an Officer or a Member of an Officer's Family. When an officer dies, the commander immediately designates an officer to give every possible assistance to the bereaved family. The officer's commander writes a letter of condolence on behalf of the organization.

Death of an Airman. When an airman dies, the immediate commander of the deceased writes a letter of condolence to the airman's nearest relative. Flowers sent in the name of the members of the deceased's unit accompany the body. All officers and members of the deceased airman's unit, the commander, and other members who so desire and whose duties permit attend the funeral if that is the wish of the airman's family.

SUPPORT OF BASE AND ORGANIZATION ACTIVITIES

Your commander expects you to support the activities of your unit, such as wing, group, squadron, or flight, as well as the activities of the entire base. Your unit is a closely knit group around which official duties and athletic and social activities revolve for the benefit of all. You are a member of an official family. Your assignment must mean more than the place where you perform required and official duties, important as they are. Your commander expects you to support and assist, at least by your presence, many events that form a part of military life. A proper interest and pride in activities of your unit and base stimulate morale. An officer should be a good military citizen, sharing with other good citizens responsibility for the unofficial life and activities of the base.

Officers' Club. An officers' club (officers' open mess) is a membership association of commissioned officers established to provide food and beverage services, entertainment, and social and recreation programs for its members and their families and guests. Installations extend membership to retired officers of all armed services of the United States, officers of the National Guard and reserve components, and authorized Department of Defense civilian employees working on the installation, as determined by the installation commander. Because all officers are eligible for voluntary membership, they cannot use the officers' club unless they become members. In this sense, the officers' club resembles a private civilian club because the members themselves generate funds from sales and dues to support the services and programs. Historically, the officers' club has been the social center of Air Force community life for officers and their families. As such, it is customary, but not mandatory, for every officer to join the officers' club on the base of assignment. Officers who decline membership may be authorized limited club use; many officers resent nonmember officers using the club, even on a limited basis, as they view these officers as freeloaders.

The scope of activities and programs offered by the officers' club vary from base to base. Membership in your installation's officers' club, as verified by your United States Air Force Clubs credit card, assures you of reciprocal privileges in all other officers' clubs. Usually, the benefits and services offered include dining and beverage services, private party catering, special events, check cashing, charge privileges, and perhaps swimming and tennis.

For financial reasons, the dining rooms of officers' clubs are increasingly open for enlisted personnel and their families and even for civilians. This sharing of facilities does not include bars. No officer should ever drink with enlisted personnel; the potential for awkward or unpleasant situations arising is just too great.

Attendance at Athletic Events. As a matter of policy, to demonstrate an interest in base affairs, as well as for personal enjoyment, officers should attend athletic events in which their units' teams participate.

Attendance at Chapel. Similarly, officers should show their support of base religious activities by periodic attendance at services at the base chapel, to the extent that individual religious preferences permit.

Armed Forces Day. The third Saturday in May is usually designated Armed Forces Day. Many bases host special celebrations on this day. This day unifies all the former service days and is symbolic of the unity of action and purpose of all our armed services.

Combined Federal Campaign (CFC). This annual fund drive, similar to the civilian United Way campaign, enables servicemembers to make tax-deductible contributions to numerous charitable and nonprofit institutions. Participation, through cash donation or military pay allotment, is voluntary. Officers, however, should seriously consider participation in this worthy program.

FAREWELL TO A DEPARTING OFFICER
Before an officer departs from his unit or station on change of assignment or upon retirement, the officers and spouses usually give a suitable function in honor of the departing officer and family. Customarily, the unit gives an inexpensive memento to the one departing.

RETIREMENT CEREMONY
Retirement of a servicemember is an occasion that merits special commemoration. It is a just reward for honorable service. For most individuals, it is also a day of serious reflection on the value of military friendships accompanied by heart tugs of regret that these fine associations will change. A suitable ceremony should mark the occasion.

Retirement of an Officer. The officer's unit should arrange for a final ceremony, such as a parade, in the officer's honor with a reception for the officer and family. The ceremony includes the reading of retirement orders, presentation of awards, remarks by a senior officer and by the officer retiring, and recognition of the support of the officer's family. Friends and family of the retiring officer may also wish to hold informal retirement parties.

TABOOS
Do Not Defame the Uniform. Officers must not disgrace their uniforms or their official positions. Conduct unbecoming an officer is punishable under the Uniform Code of Military Justice. The confidence of the nation in the integrity and high standards of conduct of officers is an asset that the military may permit no one to lower.

Do Not Criticize Members of Other Services. Never belittle members of the Army, the Navy, or the Marines. They are part of our team. For that matter, don't downgrade your own service.

Appointment with the Commander Only Through the Aide or the Executive. Customarily, officers ask the commander's aide or executive officer for an appointment with the commander. Often, you may do so informally by asking when the commander can see you.

Give No Excuses. Never volunteer excuses or explain a shortcoming unless someone requires an explanation. Giving unsought excuses does more damage than good.

Scorn Servility. Servility, "bootlicking," and deliberate courting of favor are beneath the standard of conduct expected of officers, and any who practice such things earn the scorn of their associates.

Say Things like "Old Man" with Care. Some commanders acquire the accolade "the old man" by virtue of their position and without regard to their age. Although the term, which is used infrequently today, usually implies approbation and admiration, using it in the presence of the commander is disrespectful.

Avoid "Going Over an Officer's Head." Jumping an echelon of command is called "going over an officer's head." For example, a squadron commander may make a request of the wing commander concerning a matter that should first have gone through the group commander. The act is contrary to military procedure and decidedly disrespectful.

Avoid Harsh Remarks. Gossip, slander, harsh criticism, and faultfinding are unofficerlike practices. In casual conversation, follow this guide: "All fellow officers are valiant and virtuous." Don't criticize or correct fellow officers in front of airmen.

Avoid Vulgarity and Profanity. Although you certainly will hear profanity in the military, foul language is repulsive to most self-respecting people, and to them its use by officers is reprehensible. Officers should avoid vulgarity if they are to gain respect, and officers cannot lead others without their respect.

Avoid Excessive Indebtedness. Few offenses injure the standing of an officer more than earning the reputation of being a poor credit risk. Officers are people, and they are subject to the same temptations and the same hazards of life as any other adult. Sometimes you may find that assuming debt is unavoidable and necessary, but you must, of course, repay all debts. When circumstances prevent payment, you and the creditor must make a mutually satisfactory arrangement. You should make some payment, however small, at the time a payment is due; this practice protects the legal standing of the obligation and shows your intention to pay. Permitting bills to accumulate, with no attempt to pay or to arrange a method of payment, is reprehensible and subject to official military censure.

Officers enjoy an exceptional individual and group credit standing earned and deserved because of the scrupulous care officers have taken through the years to meet obligations when due. An officer who violates this custom brings discredit upon the entire officer corps.

Never Lean on a Senior Officer's Desk. Avoid leaning against a senior officer's desk. Most officers resent such unmilitary familiarity. Stand erect unless invited to be seated. Don't lean.

Never Keep Anyone Waiting. Report on time when notified to do so. Never keep anyone waiting unnecessarily.

Avoid Having People Guess Your Name. Do not assume that someone whom you have neither seen nor heard from for a considerable period will remember your name when you renew contact. Say at once who you are, and then renew the acquaintance. If this act of courtesy is unnecessary, the other person will view it only as an act of thoughtfulness; if it happens to be necessary, you will save the other person and perhaps yourself embarrassment. At official receptions, always announce your name to the aide.

Don't Trade on Your Commission. Officers may not use or permit others to use their military titles in connection with commercial enterprises of any kind.

Stay Out of Politics. Don't become embroiled in politics. Political activity is contrary to American military tradition. As a citizen, you have a right to your opinions and a duty to vote, but keep your opinions to yourself, within your home, or within your own circle of friends. You can do this without being an intellectual eunuch. Also remember that criticism of the president is particularly improper because the president is, after all, the commander in chief of the armed forces. Article 88 of the Uniform Code of Military Justice makes it a punitive offense for an officer to use "contemptuous words" against the president and certain high-ranking government officials.

What Not to Discuss. Avoid talking shop at social occasions, and of course, never discuss classified matters, no matter how obliquely. Use great discretion in discussing politics and religion.

Look Smart in Public. Avoid smoking or chewing gum when on the street in uniform. Keep your hands out of your pockets, your uniform coat (blouse) buttoned, your tie tight, and your cap squared away properly.

CUSTOMS CONCERNING AIRCRAFT
A representative of Base Operations meets all transient aircraft and determines crew and passenger transportation requirements. If possible, the installation commander usually meets general officers.

Pilots of aircraft carrying classified material are responsible for safeguarding it unless they can remove it from the aircraft and store it in an adequately guarded area.

Regardless of grade, aircraft commanders are the final authority on operation of their aircraft. If they decide to alter their flight plans, passengers of whatever grade or service will not question their decisions.

Aircraft passengers must be prompt, obey safety regulations, and avoid moving around unnecessarily.

The pilot is the last to leave an abandoned aircraft.

Parades and other ceremonies honoring dignitaries often use aircraft flyovers.

When airplanes participate in the funeral of an aviator, they fly in tactical formation, less one aircraft, over the graveside service, but not so low as to drown out the service with noise.

CUSTOMS OF SISTER SERVICES
Although there are similarities regarding the customs of the separate armed services, there are significant differences as well. Before visiting an installation of

a sister service or before participating in a formal ceremony, ascertain what behavior is expected of you. Ask your host for guidance, and be observant during your visit. Take your cues from your hosts.

ORIGINS OF SOME MILITARY CUSTOMS

Military customs are more meaningful if you understand how the customs began. Although some of the stories may be apocryphal, they are of interest.

The dress parade was originally supposed to impress visiting emissaries with the strength of the monarch's troops, rather than to honor the visitor.

Inspecting the guard of honor began with the restoration of Charles II to the throne of England. When one of Oliver Cromwell's regiments offered its allegiance, the king carefully scrutinized the face of each soldier in ranks looking for signs of treachery. Convinced of their sincerity, he accepted the escort.

The "Sound Off," in which the band plays the "Three Cheers" and marches down the front of assembled troops, stems from the crusades. Those selected as crusaders were at the right of the line of troops, and the band marched past them in dedication while the populace gave three cheers. "The right of the line" was the critical side in ancient battle formations and is the unit place of honor in ceremonies.

The saber salute, still employed on occasion of ceremony in the other services, demonstrated the officer's dedication to Christ in his bringing the hilt (symbolic of the cross) to his lips, while dipping the saber tip signified submission to the liege lord commanding him.

Age generally determines precedence; the order of precedence of U.S. military services is based on the date founded—Army, Marine Corps, Navy, Air Force, and Coast Guard.

Raising the right hand in taking an oath stems from ancient days when the taker called upon God as his witness to the truth and pledged with his sword hand. If gloved, people taking the oath removed the right glove, supposedly because criminals were once branded on the right palm, and courts could thus determine whether the witness was reputable.

Wearing decorations and medals on the left breast also goes back to the crusaders, who wore their order's badge of honor over their hearts and protected by their shields, which they carried on the left arm.

The origin of the aiguillette and the fourragère is open to debate. One story has it that squires used to carry metal-tipped thongs (*aiguillette* is French for little spike or lace-tag) in a roll over their shoulders to lace their knights into their armor, and it thus became the badge of an aide-de-camp. Another story concerns the fourragère, which states that the Duke of Marlborough's foragers carried fodder sacks for their mounts attached to their shoulders by a looped-up cord hooked to the jacket.

The white flag of truce may derive from the Truce of God arranged on certain days by Pope Urban V in 1095 between warring medieval barons.

The use of the arch of sabers in military weddings recalls the days when the groomsmen pledged to protect the wedded couple, particularly elopers.

The term *chaplain* supposedly derives from Saint Martin of Tours, who gave half his military cloak, or "cappa," to a beggar. The kings of France made it a relic and war talisman guarded by special clerical custodians, who celebrated services in the field.

Saluting a ship's quarterdeck apparently derives from ancient times when the ship's stern carried a pagan altar to propitiate the gods. Later, it carried the Christian crucifix, and it is still the seat of authority.

At a military funeral, the national flag is on the coffin to indicate that the dead died in service of the country, which acknowledges its responsibility.

The firing of three volleys over the grave may derive from the Romans, who honored their dead by casting earth thrice on the grave, calling the name of the dead, and saying "Vale" (farewell) three times.

A military funeral plays taps to mark the beginning of the servicemember's last sleep and to express hope in the ultimate reveille.

15

Uniforms and Insignia

The Air Force requires all members to maintain a high standard of dress and personal appearance. Pride in each member's personal appearance and uniform greatly strengthen the esprit de corps essential to an effective military force. Today's uniform choices and the options given individuals have resulted in extremely detailed directions about what is and is not authorized; consequently consult AFI 36-2903, Dress and Personal Appearance of Air Force Personnel, for details.

The Air Force is currently making major changes to the uniform—something that long-serving airmen have come to expect. The most visible changes involve the service dress "heritage" coat and the airman battle uniform (ABU). Minor changes involve ABU boots, the flight suit, sweaters, women's mess dress, ceremonial coats, and physical training gear. Exactly how these changes will eventually materialize will be published in AFI 36-2903 and subsequently in the 36th edition of this Guide.

WEARING THE UNIFORM

When to Wear the Uniform. Air Force personnel must wear the prescribed service uniform at all places of duty during duty hours, except as specifically authorized by AFI 36-2903. The installation commander designates the appropriate uniform combinations in accordance with local climate and mission requirements. Special occasions require wearing the service dress uniform.

Standards of Dress and Appearance. Although all Air Force personnel must maintain a high standard of dress and appearance, officers in particular, whose manner of dress and personal appearance provide a visual example for enlisted personnel, must wear the uniform in a manner that emphasizes pride and must keep their personal appearance above reproach.

The elements of the Air Force standard are neatness, cleanliness, and military image. The first two are absolute, objective criteria. The third standard, military image, is subjective in that the American public draws certain conclusions based on the image presented by Air Force members. The military image, therefore, must instill public confidence and leave no doubt that Air Force members live by a common standard and respond to military order and discipline.

Appearance in uniform is an important part of the military image. Because judgment as to what constitutes the proper image differs in and out of the military, the Air Force must spell out what is and what is not acceptable. For example, when in uniform, servicemembers will not put their hands in their pockets. The image of disciplined and reliable servicemembers excludes the extreme, the unusual, or the faddish.

Uniform Standards. Keep your uniforms clean, neat, correct in design and specification, properly fitted, pressed, and in good condition—not frayed, worn-out, torn, faded, or stained. Keep uniform items, including pockets, buttoned, snapped, or zipped as appropriate. Keep your shoes shined and in good repair. Keep your badges, insignia, belt buckle, and other metallic devices clean and free from scratches. Keep your ribbons clean, and replace them when they begin to look frayed. Keep the gig line—shirt placket, belt buckle, and trouser fly—in alignment. Standard creases are required for shirt sleeves and trouser legs, but "military creases" are forbidden for shirts.

Of course, you may wear wristwatches and identification bracelets, but they should be of conservative design. Necklaces must be concealed under the collar or undershirt. An identification bracelet must be no wider than 1 inch and must not present a safety hazard. You may also wear rings, but only a total of three rings on both hands at any one time.

Women may wear small (not to exceed $1/8$ inch in diameter), matching, conservative gold, diamond, white pearl, or black spherical earrings. When worn, earrings must fit flat against the ear and must not extend below the earlobe. Do not wear earrings when safety considerations dictate. Women who choose to wear nail polish may use a single conservative color, in good taste and not containing any ornamentation.

Eyeglasses must be conservative in shape and style; frames and lenses are only authorized to have conservative ornamentation. Minor ornamentation on sunglasses as well as conservative, wrap-around sunglasses are authorized.

Except in the special pocket on the battle dress uniform (BDU) shirt, pens and pencils must be concealed. Headphones and earphones are prohibited unless required to perform duties. One small, black, nondescript pager or cellular phone can be worn on the uniform belt.

Commanders may restrict wear of visible and nonvisible body ornaments when they interfere with the performance of a servicemember's military duties. Factors to be considered include, but are not limited to, ornaments that impair the safe and effective operation of weapons, military equipment, or machinery; pose a health or safety hazard to the wearer or others; or interfere with the proper wear of special or protective clothing or equipment, such as helmets, flak jackets, flight suits, BDUs/ABUs, gas masks, wet suits, and crash rescue equipment.

PERSONAL APPEARANCE AND GROOMING STANDARDS

One of the most important elements of your personal appearance as an officer is your hair. Keep your hair clean, well groomed, and neat. Avoid extreme or faddish hairstyles. If you dye your hair, it must look natural. When groomed, your hair must not touch your eyebrows.

Men. Hair, which must have a tapered appearance on sides and back, must not touch the ears. Only the closely shaved hair on the back of the neck may touch the collar. The bulk of a man's hair may not exceed 1¼ inches in depth, regardless of length. Hair must not protrude in front below the band of a properly worn hat. Sideburns must be neatly trimmed and tapered, straight, not flared, and end with a horizontal line. They can be no longer than the lowest part of the exterior ear opening. In 2004, the Air Force changed its long-standing policy that forbade extreme, faddish hairstyles and authorized shaved heads and high-and-tight haircuts for men.

Men who choose to wear mustaches must ensure that they do not extend downward beyond the lipline of the upper lip, or extend sideways beyond a vertical line drawn upward from the corners of the mouth. Wigs or hairpieces are authorized only to cover baldness or disfiguration, and then only when documented in medical records. The Air Force does not allow its members to wear beards or handlebar mustaches. On the advice of a medical officer, however, the commander may authorize a beard, but it must not exceed ¼ inch in length.

Women. Hair must not extend in length on all sides below an invisible line drawn parallel to the ground at the bottom edge of the shirt collar at the back of the neck. Hair may be visible in front of a woman's flight cap. Minimum length/bulk is 1 inch; hair bulk may not exceed 3 inches. Hair ornamentation is not permitted. To keep hair in place, women may wear black conservative hairpins, combs, headbands, elastic bands, or barrettes with all natural female hair colors. Although dreadlocks are not authorized, conservative braids, microbraids, and cornrows are authorized in solid colors similar to the individual's hair color.

Tatoos/Brands/Body Piercing. In the recent past, body mutilation was considered incompatible with service in the Air Force. Members who failed to remove or alter unauthorized tattoos in a timely manner (or remove or alter inappropriate, excessive tattoos/brands) and/or who attached, affixed, or displayed objects, articles, jewelry, or ornamentation to or through the ear, nose, tongue, or any exposed body parts were subject to disciplinary action or involuntary separation. This prohibition of body mutilation also extended to alteration or modification to achieve a visible, physical effect that disfigured, deformed, or otherwise detracted from a professional military image, such as tongue splitting or forking, tooth filing, and acquiring visible, disfiguring skin implants. Failure to observe these mandatory provisions and prohibitions by active duty Air Force members, USAFR members on active duty, or inactive duty for training, and Air National Guard members in Federal service was a violation of Article 92, Uniform Code of Military Justice.

The previous prohibition of body mutilation has been relaxed. Neverthe-less, tattoos/brands anywhere on the body that are obscene or that advocate sexual, racial, ethnic, or religious discrimination are prohibited in and out of uniform. Tattoos/brands that are prejudicial to good order and discipline or of a nature that tends to bring discredit on the Air Force are also prohibited in and out of uniform. Members obtaining unauthorized tattoos will be required to remove them at their own expense. Using uniform items to cover unauthorized tattoos is not an option. In addition to these prohibited tattoos/brands, excessive tattoos and brands that are inappropriate for military image will not be exposed or visible (including visible through the uniform) while in uniform.

Excessive is defined as any tattoo/brand that exceeds one-fourth of the exposed body part and those above the collarbone and readily visible when wearing an open-collar uniform. Air Force members are not allowed to display excessive tattoos that detract from an appropriate professional image while in uniform. Air Force members with existing tattoos not meeting an acceptable military image are required to maintain complete coverage of the tattoos/brands using current uniform items (long-sleeved shirt/blouse, pants/trousers, dark hosiery) or remove their tattoos. Depending on the circumstances, commanders may seek Air Force medical support for voluntary tattoo removal. Upon notifi-cation by their commanders, servicemembers who receive tattoos/brands not meeting standards will be required to have them removed at their own expense; they may not use Air Force medical centers for removal.

Air Force servicemembers are prohibited from attaching, affixing, or dis-playing objects, articles, jewelry, or ornamentation to or through the ear, nose, tongue, or any exposed body part, including those visible through the uniform. (Women's conservative, matching earrings are excepted from this prohibition; although women may pierce their earlobes, piercing must not be extreme or excessive.) This prohibition is total: it applies in and out of uniform, on and off duty, on and off military installations.

Installation or higher commanders may impose more restrictive standards for tattoos and body ornaments, on or off duty, in those locations where the Air Force–wide standards are inadequate to address cultural sensitivities (such as overseas) or mission requirements.

Members not complying with these requirements will be subject to disci-plinary action for failure to comply with Air Force standards and may be invol-untarily separated.

CLASSIFICATION OF UNIFORMS

Uniforms worn by USAF personnel fall into three categories: service uniforms, mess dress uniforms, and utility uniforms.

Service Uniforms. Wear the service uniforms during regular duty hours. You may wear all service uniform combinations year-round, but the installation commander may prescribe when members will wear certain combinations. If the commander does not prescribe specific combinations, use good judgment, based on weather conditions and duties, when selecting the particular service uniform combination to wear.

Mess Dress Uniforms. The mess dress is for year-round wear for semiformal and formal occasions. As this uniform is the equivalent of civilian "black tie," it should be reserved for evening wear. Members may, however, choose to wear the mess dress for weddings at any time of day.

Utility Uniforms. Wear the flight suit or battle dress uniform (BDU)/airman battle uniform (ABU) whenever mission requirements make the service uniform inappropriate. These uniforms should not be worn off base, except to go to and from your residence. However, flight suits and BDUs/ABUs can be worn at gas stations, convenience stores, or drive-through fast-food establishments. The BDUs/ABUs can be worn for short convenience stops, including malls, and into fast-food establishments, or even restaurants, if customers are wearing comparable (work/utility) civilian attire. These utility uniforms cannot be worn to restaurants where customers are wearing business attire, nor can they be worn to establishments that primarily serve alcohol or into commercial airports. When wearing a utility uniform off base, you must present the proper standards of cleanliness, neatness, and military image. In practice, BDUs are frequently worn off base, but the best policy is to obey the rules.

SERVICE UNIFORMS

There are several service uniform combinations: the service dress uniform for men and women, long- and short-sleeved shirts with trousers for men, and long- and short-sleeved blouses with skirts or slacks for women. The cardigan and pullover sweaters are for indoor or outdoor wear; if worn outdoors, all of the cardigan's buttons must be buttoned.

Service Dress Uniform. The polyester/wool blend, serge weave, semi-drape, single-breasted coat has three buttons, one welt pocket on the upper left side, and two lower pocket flaps. The breast pocket is used to align ribbons and specialty badges (see chapter 16). The new metallic name tag is worn on the right side of the service dress jacket with the bottom of the name tag level with the bottom of the ribbons. Colonels and below wear regular-size metal grade insignia $5/8$ inch from the end of the epaulets, and $1/2$ inch of sleeve braid 3 inches from the end of the sleeve. With the exception of the satin-finished Hap Arnold (wing and star) buttons, the lapel U.S. and epaulet grade insignia, and specialty badges are highly polished. With arms hanging naturally, coat sleeves should end approximately $1/4$ inch from the heel of the thumb, and the bottom edge of the coat should extend 3 to $3^{1}/_{2}$ inches below the top of the thigh. The tie or inverted-V tie tab is worn with either the long- or short-sleeved light blue shirt or blouse with epaulets. Coat and trousers or skirt must match in shade and material. The front of the trouser legs rests on the front of the shoe, with a slight break in the crease; the back of the trouser legs will be approximately $7/8$ inch longer than the front.

Men's Service Dress Uniform
(Eventually, this coat will be replaced by
the four-button, belted "heritage" coat.)

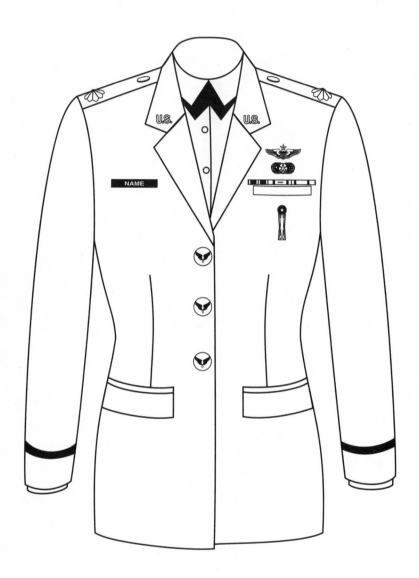

Women's Service Dress Uniform
(Eventually, this coat will be replaced by
the four-button, belted "heritage" coat.)

Men's Long-Sleeved and Short-Sleeved Shirts

Women's Long-Sleeved and Short-Sleeved Shirts

The "heritage" coat, inspired by the belted blouse of the 1940s, is replacing the three-button coat described above. It has a fourth button and is worn with a silk necktie.

Other Service Uniforms. In addition to the service dress uniform, there are numerous combinations of shirts or blouses and trousers, slacks, or skirts. Name tags are worn on the shirts or blouses, except for the service dress coat. Aeronautical and chaplain specialty badges are required; see chapter 16 for wear of ribbons and other specialty badges. Both men and women may wear the pullover sweater with or without tie or tab; if the shirt or blouse collar is open, it may be in or out of the sweater's V-neck. A blue cardigan sweater worn with or without tie or tab is for indoor and outdoor wear. If worn outdoors, all buttons must be buttoned. Men can wear the long-sleeved shirt with tie or the short-sleeve shirt with or without tie. The tie should end approximately in the middle of the belt buckle, and the tie tack or clasp (Air Force coat of arms, grade insignia, wing and star, or new Air Force symbol) should be placed halfway between the bottom of the knot and the tip of the tie. Women have more uniform combinations than men because there are several types of long- and short-sleeved blouses, slacks, and skirts, as well as maternity uniforms.

Footwear. Footwear for service uniforms must be black and made of smooth or scotch-grained leather or man-made material, of either high-gloss or patent finish. They must always be clean and polished; worn-down heels should be replaced. Shoe heels must not exceed one inch in height. Men may wear low-quarter shoes or dress boots; socks must be black, although white socks can be worn with BDUs/boots if they are not visible. Women may wear pumps, oxfords, or oxfords with low-wedge heels. Dress boots are authorized for wear with pants but not with skirts.

Headgear. Men wear the flight cap with all service uniform combinations. The flight cap is worn slightly to the wearer's right, with the vertical crease of the cap in line with the center of the forehead, in a straight line with the nose; the cap extends approximately one inch from the eyebrow in front. Indoors, the flight cap may be tucked under the belt above the officer's right thigh; the cap should be flush with the top of the belt or protrude only slightly so as not to fold over. Male field-grade officers (major through colonel) are required to have the service cap (wheel hat) with clouds and darts (scrambled eggs) on the visor. The service cap, with plain visor, is optional for company grade officers (lieutenants and captains). The U.S. coat-of-arms service cap insignia is satin-finished to match the buttons of the service dress uniform. The service cap is worn squarely on the head, with no hair protruding. Any type of religious head coverings must be approved by the individual's commander on a case-by-case basis in accordance with DOD Dir. 1300.17 and AFI 36-2903. (Basically, the servicemember requests permission of the installation commander after obtaining an endorsement from the installation chaplain.) Women wear a blue service cap or the female version of the flight cap. (Women in rated career fields may wear the men's flight cap with the flight suit.) Seven USAF career fields are authorized to

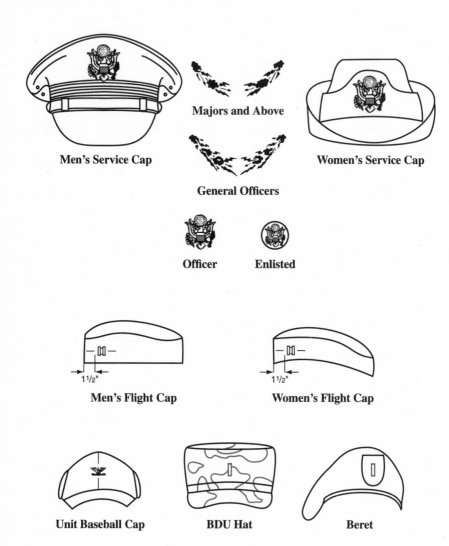

Men's Service Cap

Majors and Above

General Officers

Women's Service Cap

Officer

Enlisted

1½"

Men's Flight Cap

1½"

Women's Flight Cap

Unit Baseball Cap

BDU Hat

Beret

Men's and Women's Headgear

wear colored berets along with the crest of that particular field: combat control team, pararescue, security forces, survival evasion, tactical air command and control, tactical airlift liaison officers (ALO), and weather parachutist.

MESS DRESS UNIFORMS

Men's Mess Dress. *Required items:* Blue mess jacket with officers' silver sleeve braid, blue shoulder boards with grade insignia, miniature badges and decorations; blue trousers with striping; plain white pleat-fronted shirt; blue bow tie; blue cummerbund with open edge of pleats facing up (hence: "crumb-catcher"), silver studs and cuff links, and chain buttons; suspenders; plain black socks and low-quarter shoes. *Optional items:* Blue topcoat, gray gloves, and scarf.

Women's Mess Dress. *Required items:* Blue mess jacket with officers' silver sleeve braid, blue shoulder boards with grade insignia, miniature badges and decorations; blue ankle-length skirt; plain white pleat-fronted shirt with blue tie tab, blue cummerbund, with pleats facing down. Cufflinks and studs are optional; if worn, they will be wing and star design, oval, or plain with satin finish. *Optional items:* Blue topcoat, white gloves, and black vinyl, leather, or suede clutch handbag.

UTILITY UNIFORMS

Officers generally wear either the flight suit or battle dress uniform (BDU) as utility uniforms. The flight suit, which was originally worn as overalls to protect the service uniform worn underneath, is increasingly worn for nonflight duties. Nevertheless, the flight suit must not be worn off base for dining, shopping, or socializing. Off-base wear of the BDU is less restrictive.

Battle Dress Uniforms. There are several types of camouflage BDUs, including hot-weather desert (tan) and cold- or hot-weather woodlands (green). Desert BDUs are worn only in specified locations. Officer rank is worn on the collar of BDUs. Sewn-on name tags and USAF cloth tapes are required. The new Air Force symbol will be displayed on BDUs. When BDU sleeves are rolled up (just above the elbow), the tab on the sleeve must show; that is, the outside of the material will face out. This requires that the shirt be off to roll the sleeves up. The brown T-shirt is the issue, joint service standard; MAJCOMs may individually authorize wear of a black T-shirt, turtleneck, or dickey. Trouser legs may be bloused above the combat boots or tucked into the boots, but if they are tucked in they must create a bloused appearance. Consequently, blousing the trouser legs with blousing bands at the top or just above the top of the boots is more convenient and more comfortable. White socks, if worn, must not be visible. Gray or black gloves may be worn with the BDU. There are two standard styles of BDU caps in woodland camouflage. Colored organizational caps with emblem can be authorized on an individual basis; these baseball caps are authorized for home-base and for CONUS TDYs, but not for overseas.

Men's Mess Dress Uniform

Women's Mess Dress Uniform
(This jacket will eventually be replaced by a looser-fitting one.)

Men's and Women's Battle Dress Uniform
The BDU will eventually be replaced by the flame-resistant and
standard version of the airman battle uniform (ABU).

The new airman battle uniform (ABU) will be significantly changed from the BDUs. The fabric should be heavy enough to wear well, but light enough to breath. It should resist stains, shrinking, and rips; the flame-resistant version should protect the wearer in flash fires.

ADDITIONAL UNIFORM ITEMS

Outerwear. Besides the pullover and cardigan sweaters, there are several kinds of outerwear for men and women: the lightweight blue jacket with knit cuffs and waist; the lightweight blue jacket with knit cuffs (for women only); the double-breasted, belted all-weather coat; and the double-breasted, belted topcoat. The lightweight blue jacket must be zipped at least halfway up, preferably higher. When worn over a sweater, the sweater must not be visible.

Women have the option of wearing the men's lightweight blue jacket but also have one of their own, which does not have a knit waistband. Regular-size metal grade insignia are worn on all outergarments $5/8$ inch from end of the epaulet. The pullover sweater requires cloth shoulder marker grade insignia.

The lightweight blue jacket, pullover, and cardigan are the only outerwear garments authorized for indoor wear.

Leather Flight Jacket. The brown Army Air Forces' World War II–type leather flying jacket is authorized for aircrew members only. It is worn without grade insignia but with an embossed leather name patch showing the wearer's grade. The jacket must be zipped up at least halfway, preferably higher. Brown leather flying gloves are authorized for wear with the A-2 leather jacket.

Gloves. Gray or black gloves are authorized for wear with the BDU jacket and with the outerwear listed above, with the exception of the sweaters.

Distinctive Badges and Specialty Badges. See chapter 16, AFI 36-2803, AFI 36-2903, and AFI 36-2923 for distinctive badges and specialty insignia authorized for wear on the uniform.

Name Tags. An ultramarine blue plastic, $3^3/16$-inch by $5/8$-inch name tag with the servicemember's last name in $1/4$-inch block white letters is worn on long- and short-sleeved shirts. As a recent change, the Air Force adopted a metallic name tag for wear on pullover sweaters and the service dress uniform coat.

Identification Tags. All Air Force personnel must wear identification tags (dog tags) when engaged in flying or field training or when outside the continental limits of the United States when engaged in combat or contingency operations.

Aiguillettes. Aides and attachés wear aiguillettes of silver-colored rayon or metallic cord with service uniforms and with the mess dress uniform. Presidential and White House aides wear their aiguillettes on the right shoulder, while other aides and attachés use the left. The aiguillette is secured to the underside of the epaulet about midway between the epaulet button and the shoulder seam.

Men's and Women's Lightweight Blue Jackets
Men's and Women's All-Weather/Topcoat

OFFICER INSIGNIA OF GRADE

AIR FORCE	ARMY	MARINES	NAVY
General of the Air Force	General of the Army	(None)	Fleet Admiral
General	General	General	Admiral
Lieutenant General	Lieutenant General	Lieutenant General	Vice Admiral
Major General	Major General	Major General	Rear Admiral (Upper Half)
Brigadier General	Brigadier General	Brigadier General	Rear Admiral (Lower Half)
Colonel	Colonel	Colonel	Captain
Lieutenant Colonel	Lieutenant Colonel	Lieutenant Colonel	Commander
Major	Major	Major	Lieutenant Commander

OFFICER INSIGNIA OF GRADE

AIR FORCE	ARMY	MARINES	NAVY
Captain	Captain	Captain	Lieutenant
First Lieutenant	First Lieutenant	First Lieutenant	Lieutenant Junior Grade
Second Lieutenant	Second Lieutenant	Second Lieutenant	Ensign

(None)	SILVER AND BLACK	SCARLET AND SILVER	
	W-5 / W-4 / W-3 Chief Warrant Officer, Chief Warrant Officer, Chief Warrant Officer	W-5 / W-4 / W-3 Chief Warrant Officer, Chief Warrant Officer, Chief Warrant Officer	W-4 / W-3 Chief Warrant Officer, Chief Warrant Officer
	SILVER AND BLACK	SCARLET AND GOLD	
	W-2 / W-1 Chief Warrant Officer, Warrant Officer	W-2 / W-1 Chief Warrant Officer, Warrant Officer	W-2 / W-1 Chief Warrant Officer, Warrant Officer

COAST GUARD

Coast Guard officers use the same rank insignia as Navy officers. Coast Guard enlisted rating badges are the same as the Navy's for grades E-1 through E-9, but they have silver specialty marks, eagles and stars, and gold chevrons. The badge of the Master Chief Petty Officer of the Coast Guard has a gold chevron and specialty mark, a silver eagle, and gold stars. For all ranks, the gold Coast Guard shield on the uniform sleeve replaces the Navy star.

ENLISTED INSIGNIA OF GRADE

AIR FORCE	ARMY	MARINES	NAVY
Chief Master Sergeant of the Air Force (CMSAF)	Sergeant Major of the Army (SMA)	Sergeant Major of the Marine Corps (SgtMajMC)	Master Chief Petty Officer of the Navy (MCPON)
Chief Master Sergeant (CMSgt) — Command Chief Master Sergeant	Command Sergeant Major (CSM) — Sergeant Major (SGM)	Sergeant Major (SgtMaj) — Master Gunnery Sergeant (MGySgt)	Fleet/Command Master Chief Petty Officer — Master Chief Petty Officer (MCPO)
Senior Master Sergeant (SMSgt) — First Sergeant (E-8)	First Sergeant (1SG) — Master Sergeant (MSG)	First Sergeant (1stSgt) — Master Sergeant (MSgt)	Senior Chief Petty Officer (SCPO)
Master Sergeant (MSgt) — First Sergeant (E-7)	Platoon Sergeant (PSG) or Sergeant First Class (SFC)	Gunnery Sergeant (GySgt)	Chief Petty Officer (CPO)
Technical Sergeant (TSgt)	Staff Sergeant (SSG)	Staff Sergeant (SSgt)	Petty Officer First Class (PO1)
Staff Sergeant (SSgt)	Sergeant (SGT)	Sergeant (Sgt)	Petty Officer Second Class (PO2)
Senior Airman (SrA)	Corporal (CPL) — Specialist (SPC)	Corporal (Cpl)	Petty Officer Third Class (PO3)
Airman First Class (A1C)	Private First Class (PFC)	Lance Corporal (LCpl)	Seaman (Seaman)
Airman (Amn)	Private E-2 (PV2)	Private First Class (PFC)	Seaman Apprentice (SA)
Airman Basic (AB) (no insignia)	Private E-1 (PV1) (no insignia)	Private (Pvt) (no insignia)	Seaman Recruit (SR)

OPTIONAL ITEMS

Umbrellas. A solid black or dark blue umbrella with unobtrusive handle is authorized. Carry it in your left hand so that your right hand is free for saluting.

Women's Handbags. An Air Force–approved vinyl handbag, optional leather handbag, or clutch-style purse is authorized. Carry the handbag in your left hand so that your right hand is free for saluting.

Scarves. The scarf, which is worn only with the overcoat, should not be more than 10 inches wide, black wool or cotton, with or without napped surface. The scarf is worn folded flat and tucked in.

Earmuffs. Commercially designed earmuffs of any material, plain in solid dark blue, black, or gray are authorized but seldom worn.

Cuff Links. Men and women may wear cuff links with long-sleeved light blue shirts or blouses. The design may be plain, the Air Force coat of arms, or wing and star.

Physical Training Uniforms. Both Air Force uniform shorts/T-shirt and sweat suit physical training uniforms are available. Installation commanders set rules for wear of uniforms at sporting events.

Briefcases, Gym Bags, and Backpacks. Civilian briefcases are carried in the left hand. Air Force uniform black backpacks and gym bags are used with the blue uniform; either Air Force black, olive drab, or woodland camouflage backpacks and gym bags are used with BDUs. Backpacks and gym bags may be carried with a strap over the left shoulder or over both shoulders. The right hand must be kept free for saluting. Backpacks are also carried over the left shoulder or over both shoulders, except when on crutches or riding a two-wheeled vehicle, when both shoulder straps must be used.

UNIFORM WEAR POLICIES

Active Servicemembers. Air Force members may not wear the uniform, or any part, in situations that are counter to the interests of the United States or the U.S. Air Force, including the following:

- A meeting of, or sponsored by, an organization, association, movement, or group that the attorney general of the United States has named as totalitarian, fascist, communist, or subversive; that advocates acts of force or violence to deny others their rights under the Constitution; or that seeks to change the U.S. government by unconstitutional means.
- Activities such as public speeches, interviews, picket lines, marches, rallies, or any public demonstration not approved by the Air Force. To do so could imply the Air Force's sanction of the cause for which the demonstration or activity is conducted.
- When furthering private employment or commercial interests, if official sponsorship might be inferred.
- When engaged in off-duty civilian employment.
- When doing so would discredit the armed forces.

- Any public meeting, demonstration, march, rally, or interview if the purpose may be to advocate, express, or approve opposition to the U.S. armed forces.

Air Force members are also prohibited from wearing combinations of uniforms not prescribed in AFI 36-2903 and from wearing or mixing distinctive uniform items (grade insignia, cap devices, badges, insignia, and so forth) with civilian clothing.

Reserve Servicemembers. Except as otherwise prescribed, a reserve officer on active duty will wear the uniform, including insignia, prescribed for officers of the Regular Air Force.

Reserve officers not on active duty, when within the limits of the United States or its possessions, may wear the uniform when participating in inactive-duty training, on occasions of military ceremony, at social functions and informal gatherings of a military character, when engaged in military instruction, or when responsible for the military discipline at an educational institution.

Reserve officers will wear the uniform when participating in an inactive-duty training period, when performing equivalent or appropriate duties, or when engaged in equivalent training or instruction, when such duty, training, or instruction is within the confines of a military installation.

Reserve officers will wear the appropriate uniform when engaged in military flying activities.

Reserve officers not on active duty and outside the United States or its possessions, except when granted authority by the secretary of the Air Force, will *not* wear the uniform. These officers, on occasions of military ceremony or other military functions, upon reporting to the nearest military attaché and having their status accredited, may receive authority to appear in uniform. In a country without a military attaché, these officers should obtain authority to wear the uniform for a specific occasion from the proper civil or military authorities of the country concerned.

Special Occasions. The proper uniform for special occasions, such as ceremonies, weddings, funerals, and White House social functions and similar duties, depends on the circumstances in each case. Such occasions may also require white silk, cotton, or nylon gloves or gray suede or double-weave cotton gloves.

In Foreign Countries. Air Force personnel departing for foreign countries in official capacities will be responsible for getting information regarding uniform matters before they leave the United States. The U.S. air attaché or the defense attaché can answer questions regarding uniforms that arise in a foreign country.

Members of the Air Force, active or retired, visiting or residing in a foreign country in an unofficial capacity will *not* wear the uniform except when attending, by formal invitation, ceremonies or social functions that, by the terms of the invitation or by the regulation or customs of the service, require wearing the uniform.

Retired Officers. The uniform of retired officers will be, at their option, either that for officers of corresponding grade at date of retirement or that for officers on the active list, but not a mixture of the two uniforms.

Retired officers not on active duty are prohibited from wearing the uniform in connection with nonmilitary, civilian, or personal enterprises or business activities.

Retirees and honorably discharged veterans may on ceremonial occasions wear either full-size or miniature decorations and service medals on appropriate civilian clothing, such as "black tie" or "white tie" evening wear or equivalents.

Former Members of the Armed Forces. All persons honorably separated from the armed services of the United States may wear on ceremonial occasions the uniform of the highest grade held during that service. The uniform may be either that authorized at the time of separation or that authorized by current regulations. Ceremonial occasions means those with military significance. Persons honorably discharged from the service may wear their uniforms from the place of discharge to their homes, provided such wear is within three months of the date of discharge.

Illegal Wearing. Any person within the jurisdiction of the United States who wears a uniform or a distinctive part of a uniform of the armed services without authority is subject to the penalties prescribed by Title 18 U.S. Code 702. This policy is frequently violated, especially by veterans. Nevertheless, officers should scrupulously adhere to policy.

Illegal Manufacture, Sale, and Possession. The protection of law extends to wearing, manufacture, sale, possession, and reproduction in regular size of any U.S. decoration, medal, badge, or insignia that requires the approval of the secretary of the Air Force.

16

Awards, Decorations, and Badges

Decorations awarded to members of the armed services are an acknowledgment by the government for a job well done. They consist of awards for heroism, the highest of which is the Medal of Honor, and awards for meritorious achievement and meritorious service, the highest of which is the Distinguished Service Medal. Just as the degree of heroism or achievement above and beyond the call of duty varies, so too does the importance or rank of the several awards given for these three purposes. AFI 36-2903, *Dress and Personal Appearance of Air Force Personnel.*

HISTORY
The granting of awards dates at least as far back in history as classical times. The Greeks crowned citizens who were outstanding in war, athletics, literature, and oratory with the laurel wreath. Roman rulers also adopted the laurel wreath. The laurel wreath forms a part of America's highest award for valor. In the Middle Ages, a system of rewards emerged in the form of titles of nobility and membership in knightly orders, which often included a special badge.

Before the Napoleonic period, such military rewards were given mostly to the aristocracy, who were the principal military leaders. Rewards given to drafted fighting men were infrequent. Napoleon started the modern concept. He originated a decoration that could be worn by anyone, regardless of rank or social background—the *Légion d'Honneur.* It was the spearhead of the system he used to instill loyalty in the nation he led—because anybody could win it. The French Legion of Honor was followed by the Russian Order of Saint George, the German Iron Cross, and the British Victoria Cross. They were products of the era of nationalism, created to reward courage and loyalty.

In the United States, the custom of awarding military decorations dates from the American Revolution. A resolution of the Continental Congress

169

approved on 25 March 1776, gave the first medal to General George Washington. General Horatio Gates received the second on 25 November 1777, for the defeat of the British at Saratoga. The third went to General Henry Lee, "Light Horse Harry," who won his nickname on 24 September 1779, in recognition of his successful attack on the British at Paulus Hook, New Jersey, during which he captured 160 of the enemy without loss to his own forces. John Paulding, Isaac van Wart, and David Williams received the fourth, fifth, and sixth, known as the "André" medals. These three American militiamen captured the British intelligence officer Major John André, while he was en route to New York from West Point, after having plotted with Benedict Arnold to betray the American cause.

The Purple Heart was the first military decoration established in the United States. It was authorized by General Washington in 1782 as the Badge of Military Merit, a decoration for unusual gallantry or extraordinary fidelity. Three men received it in 1783. In 1932, the United States reestablished the Purple Heart on a permanent basis.

In the first winter of the Civil War, a feeling developed that a way must be found to recognize and honor the heroism and valor of American soldiers who had distinguished themselves on the battlefield. A Navy and Marine Corps medal was approved by President Abraham Lincoln on 21 December 1861, and on 12 July 1862, a Medal of Honor was provided for award to enlisted men of the Army "who shall most distinguish themselves by their gallantry in action, and other soldier-like qualities." It was amended by an act approved 3 March 1863, which extended its provisions to include officers as well.

The Medal of Honor, the first decoration since General Washington's Badge of Military Merit, is the highest military decoration awarded by the United States. Some 3,400 have been awarded since 1861. Now there are more than 50 other military awards and decorations.

PRINCIPLES GOVERNING THE AWARD OF DECORATIONS

The award of decorations is a powerful stimulus to pride of service and to encourage heroism or achievement. But if the greatest benefit is to be obtained, the process of making awards must be most carefully administered.

Awards must be made only to those who have truly earned them. The giving of unmerited awards is cheapening and destructive of the purpose for which the awards were authorized. But to fail to recognize true valor or merit promptly and make the awards also defeats the purpose. Both a proper evaluation of facts plus promptness in making awards are required.

This requirement presents a serious problem of decision to commanders of combat organizations. Evidence is often sketchy. The witnesses may be dead as a consequence of combat. The weighing of facts as to which of the several awards is most appropriate is also a delicate choice. To justify any award, the act must be above and beyond the call of duty. Final consideration of the facts before decision by a senior commander will rest with a board of officers who can establish a reasonable yardstick against which to measure and compare these events. Individual commanders, especially junior commanders, must recognize or identify those acts that are truly above and beyond the call of duty, make prompt recommendation for the awards they consider most appropriate, and document those awards with the statements of witnesses, so that the reviewers may arrive at an independent and accurate decision. Unless a careful process is followed by all, there will be many serious errors, anomalies, and variations among organizations, which may greatly reduce or even nullify the powerful stimulus to pride of individual service that may be attained through awards. AFI 36-2803 describes the policy on award of decorations.

Decorations, Service Medals, and Achievement Awards. *Decorations* are awarded in recognition of extraordinary, unusual, or outstanding acts or services. They are the visible evidence of such acts or services. Properly used, they are incentives to greater effort and instrumental in building and maintaining morale. Decorations are awarded for heroism and for achievement. Although most decorations are awarded for one or the other distinct purpose, the Distinguished Flying Cross and the Bronze Star Medal may be awarded for either reason.

Service medals are awarded to members of the active military service of the United States for performance of specified duty, usually during periods of war or national emergency.

Achievement awards are presented to recognize specific types of achievements for individuals serving on active duty in the Air Force or as members of the Air Reserve Forces.

Oak Leaf Clusters. The oak leaf cluster is awarded in place of a second award of the same decoration. It consists of a bronze twig with four oak leaves and three acorns on the stem. It is affixed to the ribbon. One silver oak leaf cluster is worn in place of five bronze ones.

Award by Foreign Governments. No one holding any office under the United States will, without the consent of Congress, accept any present, emolument, or title of any kind from any foreign government.

In this connection, special authority was granted by Congress with respect to foreign decorations awarded during World War II, the Berlin Airlift, the Korean War, the Vietnam War, and the Gulf War. Officers to whom such awards may be tendered are advised to obtain the advice of their headquarters personnel division or judge advocate. Awards from foreign governments can be accepted only for active combat service or outstanding or unusually meritorious performance, not for peacetime support of an ally.

Penalty for Unauthorized Wearing of Decorations, Service Medals, or Badges. A federal statute provides for a fine or imprisonment for individuals convicted of unauthorized wearing of any decoration, service medal, ribbon or rosette, or badge, or of wearing the uniform or decorations of a foreign nation for the purpose of deception.

USAF DECORATIONS FOR HEROISM

Medal of Honor (MH). The Medal of Honor is awarded for conspicuous gallantry and intrepidity at the risk of life above and beyond the call of duty while a member of the Air Force was engaged in action against an enemy of the United States, while engaged in military operations involving conflict with an opposing foreign force, or while serving with friendly foreign forces engaged in an armed conflict against an opposing armed force in which the United States is not a belligerent party. The Medal of Honor is a gold star with the head of the Statue of Liberty centered upon it and surrounded with green enamel laurel leaves suspended by rings from a trophy consisting of a bar inscribed with the word "Valor" above an adaptation of the thunderbolt from the U.S. Air Force coat of arms.

Air Force Cross (AFC). On 6 July 1960, Congress established the Air Force Cross to parallel the U.S. Army Distinguished Service Cross and the U.S. Navy Cross. Earlier, the Air Force had awarded the Distinguished Service Cross.

The Air Force Cross is our nation's second highest military decoration and is awarded to U.S. Air Force airmen for extraordinary heroism in an action against an enemy of the United States, while engaged in military operations involving conflict with an opposing foreign force, or while serving with friendly foreign forces engaged in an armed conflict against an opposing armed force in which the United States is not a belligerent party. The Air Force Cross may be awarded to members of foreign military forces and to American and foreign civilians serving with the armed forces of the United States. The Air Force Cross is a bronze cross on which is centered a gold-plated American bald eagle with wings spread against a cloud formation.

Silver Star (SS). The Silver Star was instituted by Congress in 1918. It is granted to persons serving in any capacity with the Air Force cited for gallantry in action that does not warrant the award of a Medal of Honor or the Air Force Cross.

Distinguished Flying Cross (DFC). *For Heroism.* The Distinguished Flying Cross has been awarded to airmen since 1917 for heroism or extraordinary achievement while participating in aerial flight. The heroism must be evidenced by voluntary action in the face of great danger and beyond the line of duty. The Distinguished Flying Cross is a bronze cross with rays on which is displayed a propeller. The DFC for heroism includes the "V" device.

Airman's Medal (AmnM). The Airman's Medal is awarded for heroism involving voluntary risk of life under conditions other than those of actual conflict with an enemy. The Airman's Medal is a bronze metal disk bearing a representation of Hermes, son of Zeus, releasing an American bald eagle.

Bronze Star Medal (BSM). *For Valor.* The Bronze Star Medal is awarded for heroism or meritorious achievement or service not involving participation in aerial flight while engaged in military action against an enemy of the United States.

Purple Heart (PH). The Purple Heart is our nation's oldest medal. It was first established by General George Washington on 7 August 1782. The Purple Heart is awarded for wounds received or death after being wounded in action against an enemy of the United States or as a direct result of an act of such enemy. The Purple Heart bears a gold replica of the head of General George Washington and the Washington arms.

USAF DECORATIONS FOR ACHIEVEMENT

Distinguished Service Medal (DSM). The Distinguished Service Medal is awarded to members of the armed forces who distinguish themselves by exceptionally meritorious service to the government in a duty of great responsibility.

The term "duty of great responsibility" means duty of such a character that exceptionally meritorious service therein has contributed in high degree to the success of a major command, installation, or project. The performance of the duty must be such as to merit recognition of the service as clearly exceptional. A superior performance of the normal duties of the position will not alone justify the award. The accomplishment of the duty for which the award is recommended should have been completed, or it should have progressed to an exceptional degree if the person rendering the service has been transferred to other duties before its full accomplishment.

The Air Force Distinguished Service Medal features a blue stone representing the firmament at the center of a sunburst of 13 gold rays separated by 13 white enamel stars. The center motif represents the vault of the heavens; the stars symbolize the 13 original colonies. The stylized wings on the ribbon bar are symbolic of the USAF.

Legion of Merit (LM). The Legion of Merit, without reference to degree, is awarded to members of the armed forces of the United States who, while serving in any capacity, distinguish themselves by exceptionally meritorious conduct in the performance of outstanding services. In peacetime, awards by the Air Force are generally limited to recognizing services of marked national or international significance, services that aided the United States in furthering national policy or national security.

This decoration, like the Purple Heart, stems from the Badge for Military Merit, America's oldest decoration, established by George Washington in 1782. As was the case with the Badge for Military Merit, it is awarded for "extraordinary fidelity and essential service." It will constitute a reward for service in a position of responsibility, honorably and well performed. The design of the Legion of Merit has been developed from the Great Seal of the United States, also approved by Congress in 1782.

Distinguished Flying Cross (DFC). *For Achievement.* The Distinguished Flying Cross is awarded to members of the armed forces who, while serving in any capacity with the Air Force, distinguish themselves by heroism or extraordinary achievement while participating in aerial flight. To warrant an award of the Distinguished Flying Cross for extraordinary achievement while participating in aerial flight, the results accomplished must be so exceptional and outstanding as to clearly set the individual apart from comrades who have not been so recognized. The DFC for achievement does not include the "V" device.

Bronze Star Medal (BSM). *For Achievement.* The Bronze Star Medal is awarded to members of the armed forces who, while serving in any capacity, distinguished themselves by meritorious achievement or meritorious service not involving participation in aerial flight in connection with military operations against an enemy of the United States. The required meritorious achievement or meritorious service for award of the Bronze Star Medal is less than that required for award of the Legion of Merit, but must nevertheless be accomplished with distinction. The Bronze Star Medal may be awarded to recognize meritorious service or single acts of merit.

Meritorious Service Medal (MSM). The Meritorious Service Medal is awarded for outstanding noncombat meritorious achievement or service to the United States. Normally, the acts or services rendered must be comparable to those required for the Legion of Merit, but in a duty of lesser though considerable responsibility. It must, nevertheless, be accomplished with distinction and be above and beyond that for the award of the Air Force Commendation Medal. The Meritorious Service Medal ranks with, but after, the Bronze Star.

Air Medal (AM). Authorized by executive order of President Franklin Roosevelt in 1942, the Air Medal is awarded to people who, while serving in any capacity with the armed forces of the United States subsequent to 8 September 1939, distinguish themselves by heroic or meritorious achievement while participating in an aerial flight. This decoration is awarded in those cases where the act of meritorious service does not warrant the award of the Distinguished Flying Cross.

Aerial Achievement Medal (AAM). The Aerial Achievement Medal may be awarded for sustained meritorious achievement while participating in aerial flight. The achievement must be accomplished with distinction above and beyond that normally expected of professional airmen.

Air Force Commendation Medal (AFCM). The Air Force Commendation Medal may be awarded for outstanding achievement or meritorious service rendered specifically on behalf of the Air Force, for acts of courage that do not meet the requirements for award of the Airman's Medal or the Bronze Star Medal, or for sustained meritorious performance by crew members. The medal is a bronze hexagon medallion bearing eagle, shield, and arrows from the Air Force seal. It is awarded to those below the grade of brigadier general.

Air Force Achievement Medal (AFAM). Awarded for outstanding achievement or meritorious service, this award is intended primarily for outstanding airmen and officers below the grade of colonel. The pendant is a silver-colored nebular disk bearing the winged thunderbolt from the USAF seal.

DOD DECORATIONS FOR ACHIEVEMENT

In addition to the USAF decorations listed above, the Department of Defense awards five military decorations that take precedence with their service counterparts but are worn before them.

Defense Distinguished Service Medal (DDSM). This medal may be awarded to any U.S. armed forces officer assigned to a joint staff or other DOD joint activity for exceptionally meritorious service in a position of unique and great responsibility.

Defense Superior Service Medal (DSSM). This medal may be awarded to U.S. military personnel who render superior meritorious service in a position of significant responsibility on a joint staff or in a joint activity. The pendant design is that of the DDSM, except that it is in silver.

Defense Meritorious Service Medal (DMSM). This medal may be awarded to U.S. military personnel who distinguish themselves by noncombat meritorious achievement or meritorious service on a joint staff or in a joint activity.

Joint Service Commendation Medal (JSCM). This medal is awarded to personnel on duty in the Office of the Secretary of Defense, the Joint Staff, the Defense Supply Agency, the National Security Agency, other joint agencies reporting to the Joint Chiefs of Staff, joint task forces, or NATO organizations for meritorious achievement or service. It takes precedence with the AFCM, but is worn before it. A bronze "V" is authorized for a combat award after 25 June 1963.

Joint Service Achievement Medal (JSAM). Worn before the AFAM, this medal may be awarded to any members of the U.S. armed forces below the rank of colonel who distinguish themselves by meritorious achievement or service while serving in specified joint activities after 3 August 1983.

UNIT AWARDS

The following types of unit awards are authorized as recognition of certain types of service and as a means of promoting esprit de corps:

- Unit decorations
- War service streamers
- Campaign and expeditionary streamers

U.S. Unit Decorations. The following U.S. unit decorations have been established to recognize outstanding heroism or exceptionally meritorious conduct in the performance of outstanding services:

- Presidential Unit Citation
- Joint Meritorious Unit Award
- Air Force Gallant Unit Citation
- Air Force Meritorious Unit Award
- Air Force Outstanding Unit Award
- Air Force Organizational Excellence Award

Presidential Unit Citation (PUC). The Presidential Unit Citation (formerly Distinguished Unit Citation) is awarded to units of the armed forces of the United States and co-belligerent nations for extraordinary heroism in action against an armed enemy. The unit must display such gallantry, determination, and esprit de corps in accomplishing its mission under extremely difficult and hazardous conditions as to set it apart and above other units participating in the same campaign. The degree of heroism required is the same as that which would warrant award of an Air Force Cross to an individual. Extended periods of combat duty or participation in a large number of operational missions, either ground or air, is not sufficient. Only on rare occasions will a unit larger than an air group qualify for award of this decoration.

Air Force Gallant Unit Citation (GUC). Established in 2004, this citation is awarded to Air Force active duty, Reserve, and Guard units for extraordinary heroism in action against an armed enemy of the United States while engaged in military operations involving conflict with an opposing foreign force on or after 11 September 2001. The GUC requires a lesser degree of gallantry, determination, and esprit de corps than required for the Presidential Unit Citation. Nevertheless, the unit must have performed with marked distinction under difficult and hazardous conditions in accomplishing its mission so as to set it apart from and above other units participating in the same conflict. The degree of heroism required is the same as that which would warrant award of the Silver Star, which is awarded for gallantry and heroism of high degrees, including risk of life in action. The GUC will normally be earned by units that have participated in single or successive actions covering relatively brief time spans. Only on rare occasions will a unit larger than a group quality for the GUC. Extended periods of combat duty or participation in a large number of operational missions, either air or ground, is not sufficient.

Air Force Meritorious Unit Award (MUA). Also established in 2004, the MUA is awarded to Air Force active duty, reserve, and Guard units for exceptionally meritorious conduct in the performance of outstanding achievement or service in direct support of combat operations for at least 90 continuous days during the period of military operations against an armed enemy of the United States on or after 11 September 2001. The unit must display such outstanding devotion and superior performance of exceptionally difficult tasks as to set it apart and above other units with similar missions. The degree of achievement required is the same as that which would warrant award of the Legion of Merit. Superior performance of normal mission will not alone justify award of the MUA. Service in a combat zone is not required, but service must be directly related to the combat effort. Squadrons, groups, and wings may be recommended for this award. The MUA is not awarded to any unit or unit component previously awarded the Air Force Outstanding Unit Award, the Air Force Organizational Excellence Award, or unit awards from other service components for the same act, achievement, or service.

Joint Meritorious Unit Award (JMUA). This ribbon is awarded in the name of the secretary of defense to joint activities of the Department of Defense for meritorious achievement or service, superior to that normally expected, during combat with an armed enemy of the United States, during a declared national emergency, or under extraordinary circumstances that involve the national interest.

Air Force Outstanding Unit Award (AFOUA). Established in 1954, this award recognizes units that distinguish themselves by exceptionally meritorious service or outstanding achievement that clearly sets the units above and apart from similar units. This award consists of a predominantly blue streamer with a narrow red band center bordered by white lines and red bands. Theater or area of operations is embroidered in white on the streamer. The individual emblem is a ribbon of the streamer color. It is awarded to units not larger than a wing for meritorious achievement or service in support of military operations or of great significance in accomplishment not involving combat operations.

Air Force Organizational Excellence Award (AFOEA). Established in August 1969, this ribbon is predominantly red with a narrow blue band center bordered by white lines and blue bands at each edge separated by white lines. It is awarded to Air Force internal organizations that are organizational entities within larger organizations in recognition of achievements and accomplishments of units that did not meet eligibility requirements of the AFOUA. The organizations are unique, unnumbered organizations or activities that perform staff functions and functions normally performed by numbered wings, groups, squadrons, and so on.

ACHIEVEMENT AWARDS

Air Force achievement awards recognize specific types of achievement by members serving on active duty in the Air Force or in the Air Reserve Forces.

Prisoner of War Medal (POWM). This award is authorized for all U.S. military personnel who were taken prisoner of war during an armed conflict and who served honorably during the period of captivity. An American eagle is surrounded by a border of barbed wire.

Combat Readiness Medal (CRM). This medal is authorized for members of combat crews of manned weapons delivery systems for sustained individual combat or mission readiness or preparedness for direct weapon system employment. The medal is a circle marked with arrowheads and the points of overlapping triangles to indicate the hours of round-the-clock duty and performance.

Air Force Good Conduct Medal (AFGCM). This medal is awarded only to enlisted persons in recognition of exemplary conduct. A distinctive clasp is awarded for each successive period of three years' service that meets the requirements.

Air Reserve Forces Meritorious Service Medal (ARFMSM). This medal is an award equivalent to the Air Force Good Conduct Medal for issuance to Air

Reserve personnel who demonstrate exemplary behavior, efficiency, and fidelity for four continuous years.

Outstanding Airman of the Year Ribbon (OAYR). This ribbon is awarded to airmen nominated by major air commands and field operating agencies for competition in the 12 Outstanding Airmen of the Year Program.

Air Force Recognition Ribbon (AFRR). This ribbon is awarded to named individual Air Force recipients of special trophies and awards.

Air Force Overseas Ribbon (AFOSR). This ribbon is awarded for completion of an overseas tour of duty.

Air Force Expeditionary Service Ribbon (AFESR). Established in 2003, the AFESR is awarded to Air Force active duty, reserve, and Guard personnel who complete a contingency deployment after 1 October 1999. Deployed status is defined as either deployment on contingency, exercise, deployment orders, or members sourced in direct in- or out-theater support of expeditionary operations with an overnight away from home station. Individuals must have deployed for 45 consecutive days or 90 nonconsecutive days on a deployed status. The time criteria can be waived for actual combat against an enemy of the United States. Any contingency (overseas or stateside) deployment qualifies regardless of the duty, destination, or location of the TDY. There is no time limit to accumulate the 90 nonconsecutive days. Permanent party overseas personnel are not eligible for the AFESR unless they are forward deployed on a contingency deployment. Members on an overseas short tour may receive both the AFESR and the Overseas Short Tour Ribbon, provided they meet the requirements of both. To receive both, the number of days forward deployed must be subtracted from the number of short tour days credited and still meet the minimum requirement for short tour credit. A gold border worn on the AFESR represents participation in combat operations. It is authorized for wear by individuals who were engaged in conducting or supporting combat operations in a designated combat zone or in a hazardous duty area. Combat action is defined as when a member is subject to hostile fire, explosion, or is engaged in employing lethal weapons. To receive the gold border, the individual must have been assigned to an Air Expeditionary Force or have been on Contingency Exercise Deployment orders.

Air Force Longevity Service Award (AFLSA). All members of the Air Force on active duty and all reservists not on active duty are eligible for this award. Requirements for the basic award are four years of honorable active federal military service with any branch of the U.S. armed forces. A bronze oak leaf cluster is worn on the ribbon for each additional four years of service. A silver oak leaf cluster is worn in lieu of five bronze clusters. No medal is authorized.

USAF Basic Military Training Instructor Ribbon. This ribbon is awarded to Air Education and Training Command personnel staffing basic military training.

Air Force Recruiter Ribbon. This ribbon is worn by active-duty, Guard, and reserve personnel on completing recruiting training and while serving as a recruiter, and on a permanent basis after serving for 36 months as a recruiter.

NCO Professional Military Education Graduate Ribbon (NCOP-MEGR). This ribbon is awarded to graduates of certified Noncommissioned Officer Professional Military Education Schools, Phases II, III, and IV.

USAF Basic Military Training Honor Graduate Ribbon (BMTHGR). This ribbon is awarded to honor graduates of BMT who, after 29 July 1976, have demonstrated excellence in all phases of academic and military training.

Small Arms Expert Marksmanship Ribbon (SAEMR). Awarded after 1 January 1963, to persons qualifying as "expert" in small arms marksmanship with either the M-16 rifle or issue handgun. Qualification as "expert" in both after 22 June 1972, is denoted by a bronze service star on the service ribbon.

Air Force Training Ribbon (AFTR). Awarded to Air Force members on completion of initial military accession training (BMT, OTS, ROTC, academy, medical services, judge advocate, chaplain orientation, and so on).

SERVICE MEDALS

Service medals are awarded to members of the armed forces of the United States to denote the honorable performance of duty. Most service medals pertain to federal duty in a time of war or national emergency. A person's entire service during the period for which the award is made must be honorable.

Service Medals Authorized Through the Vietnam War. Service medals that pertain only to wars or campaigns through the war in Vietnam are not included, since there are few airmen still on active duty who might wear such items. See AFI 36-2803 for details on these awards.

National Defense Service Medal (NDSM). This medal has been authorized for honorable active service for any period between 27 June 1950 and 27 July 1954. Persons on active duty for purposes other than extended active duty are not eligible for this award. The NDSM was also authorized for Cold War service from 1 January 1961 to 14 August 1974, and again for service during Operations Desert Shield and Desert Storm from 2 August 1990 to 30 November 1995. The NDSM is also authorized for honorable service from 11 September 2001, to a date to be determined. Servicemembers on active duty, members of the Selected Reserve in good standing, and members of other than the Selected Reserve who were called to active duty, including USAF Academy cadets are eligible. Ineligible are members called to active duty for physical examinations, training only, or to serve on boards, courts, or commissions. A bronze service star is authorized for persons who have served during more than one such period.

Antarctica Service Medal (ASM). This medal is awarded to members of any of the armed forces who, as members of a U.S. expedition, participated in scientific, direct support, or exploratory operations in the Antarctic or who participated in 15 missions to and from Antarctica in support of such operations. The medal includes a "Wintered Over" clasp for those who stayed in Antarctica during winter months. There is a corresponding circular device for wear on the ribbon bar, depicting the map of the Antarctic continent.

Armed Forces Expeditionary Medal (AFEM). This medal is awarded to members of the U.S. armed forces who, after 1 July 1958, participated in U.S. military operations, U.S. operations in direct support of the United Nations, or U.S. operations of assistance for friendly foreign nations. Generally 30 days, or the full period of the operation, in the following recent areas of operations are required:

El Salvador: 1 January 1981 to 1 February 1992

Grenada: Operation Urgent Fury from 23 October to 21 November 1983

Lebanon: 1 June 1983 to 1 December 1987

Libya: Operation Eldorado Canyon, 12 to 17 April 1986

Panama: Operation Just Cause from 20 December 1989 to 31 January 1990

Persian Gulf: Operation Earnest Will from 24 July 1987 (Bridgeton incident) to 1 August 1990

East Africa: Operation Restore Hope from 4 August 1992 to 31 March 1995

Haiti: Operation Uphold Democracy from 16 September 1994 to 31 March 1995

Operation Joint Endeavor from 20 November 1995 to 19 December 1996

Balkans: Operation Joint Guard from 20 December 1996 to 20 June 1998, and Operation Joint Forge from 21 June 1998, to a date to be determined

Iraq Operations from 1 December 1995 to a date to be determined: Operation Southern Watch, Maritime Intercept Operations, Operation Vigilant Sentinel, Operation Northern Watch, Operation Desert Thunder, Operation Desert Fox, or Operation Desert Spring

Participants are entitled to only one AFEM for assignment in Iraq operations. A second award of the AFEM is only authorized to individuals for nonconsecutive and nonconcurrent assignments to separate operations that were awarded the AFEM (for example, first awarded for Somalia Operations and second award for the Iraq Operations) provided that the participants meet the criteria for each. Multiple award of the AFEM for assignments or rotations to the same operations is not authorized. No servicemember may be awarded more than one of these four medals for service in the same approved expedition or operation to combat terrorism: the Global War on Terrorism Expeditionary Medal, the Global War on Terrorism Service Medal, the Armed Forces Expeditionary Medal, and the Armed Forces Service Medal.

Southwest Asia Service Medal (SWASM). This medal has been authorized to servicemembers who served in the Persian Gulf area in Operations Desert Shield and Desert Storm from 2 August 1990 through 30 November

1995. Those who served in Egypt, Israel, Jordan, Syria, and Turkey, including airspace, directly supporting combat operations between 17 January 1991 and 30 November 1995 are also eligible. Servicemembers who earned the SWASM on their initial tour in Southwest Asia and who later become eligible for the Armed Forces Expeditionary Medal are entitled to wear both awards, but not for a single tour in Southwest Asia.

Kosovo Campaign Medal. This medal is awarded for participation in NATO operations related to Kosovo from 24 March 1999 to a date to be determined. The award is for 30 days continuous or accumulated service on land, at sea, or in the airspace of Kosovo, or other territories of the Federal Republic of Yugoslavia (Serbia and Montenegro); Croatia; Bosnia and Herzegovina; Slovenia; Albania; Macedonia; and the Adriatic and Ionian Seas. Award is also for aircrews participating in Operation Allied Force, 24 March 1999 through 10 June 1999, with 15 sorties into Kosovo of the Federal Republic of Yugoslavia; and 90 days continuous or accumulated service in Italy, Greece, or Hungary in direct support of NATO operations conducted in the area of eligibility.

Afghanistan Campaign Medal. Servicemembers authorized the AFGM must have served in direct support of Operation Enduring Freedom on or after 24 October 2001 to a date to be determined. The area of eligibility encompasses all land areas of the country of Afghanistan and all air spaces above the land. Service members must have been assigned, attached, or mobilized to units operating in this area for 30 consecutive days or for 60 non-consecutive days and meet one of the following criteria: engaged in combat during an armed engagement regardless of time in the area of eligibility, been wounded or injured and required medical evacuation from Afghanistan, or while participating as a regularly assigned air crewmember flying sorties into, out of, within, or over the area of eligibility in direct support of the military operations (each day of operations counts as one day of eligibility).

Servicemembers qualified for the Global War on Terrorism Expeditionary Medal (GWOT-E) for service between 24 October 2001 and 30 April 2005, in the area for which the AFGM was subsequently authorized, shall remain qualified for that medal. On application, any such servicemember may be awarded the AFGM in place of the GWOT-E for such service. No service member shall be entitled to both medals for the same action, achievement, or period of service. Servicemembers serving in the qualifying area of eligibility for which the AFGM was subsequently authorized are no longer qualified to receive the GWOT-E after 30 April 2005.

Iraq Campaign Medal. The ICM is authorized for servicemembers directly supporting Operation Iraqi Freedom on or after 19 March 2003 to a date to be determined. The area of eligibility encompasses all land area of the country of Iraq as well as the contiguous water area out to 12 nautical miles and all air spaces above the land area of Iraq and above the contiguous waters out to 12 nautical miles. Service members must have been assigned, attached, or mobilized to units operating in this area for 30 consecutive days or for 60 non-consecutive days and meet one of the following criteria: engaged in combat during an armed engagement regardless of time in the area of eligibility, been wounded or injured and required medical evacuation from Afghanistan, or while participating as a regularly assigned air crewmember flying sorties into, out of, within, or over the area of eligibility in direct support of the military operations (each day of operations counts as one day of eligibility).

Servicemembers qualified for the Global War on Terrorism Expeditionary Medal (GWOT-E) for service between 19 March 2003 and 30 April 2005, in the area for which the ICM was subsequently authorized, shall remain qualified for that medal. On application, any such servicemember may be awarded the ICM in place of the GWOT-E for such service. Servicemembers serving in the qualifying area of eligibility for which the ICM was subsequently authorized are no longer qualified to receive the GWOT-E after 30 April 2005.

Global War on Terrorism Expeditionary Medal. The GWOT-E is awarded to active duty, reserve, and Guard servicemembers who have deployed abroad in service of Operations Enduring Freedom or Iraqi Freedom. Participants must have been assigned or attached to a unit in OEF/OIF and served 30 consecutive days or 60 nonconsecutive days (on or after 11 September 2001) in one of a large number of geographic areas, primarily in the Middle East, but also in the Balkans, northeast Africa, and the Philippines, as well as offshore areas. Also eligible are those who have engaged in actual combat against the enemy under circumstances involving grave damage or death or serious bodily harm from enemy action, regardless of time served in OEF/OIF. Service as a crew member flying sorties into, out of, within, or over the areas of eligibility in direct support of Operations Enduring Freedom or Iraqi Freedom are eligible, accruing one day's credit for the 30 or 60 day requirement for each day that one or more sorties is flown.

Note the restriction regarding the GWOT-E and the AFGM and ICM immediately above.

Global War on Terrorism Service Medal. While the GWOT Expeditionary Medal recognizes servicemembers who participated in an expedition to combat terrorism on or after 11 September 2001, the GWOT Service Medal recognizes service in DOD-designated operations to combat terrorism on or after 11 September 2001, from outside the area of eligibility designated for the GWOT Expeditionary Medal. Servicemembers must have been assigned or attached to a unit participating in or serving in support of designated operations for 30 consecutive days or 60 nonconsecutive days. Also eligible are those who have engaged in actual combat against the enemy under circumstances involving grave damage or death or serious bodily harm from enemy action, regardless of time served. Service as a crew member flying sorties into, out of, within, or over the areas of eligibility in direct support of Operations Enduring Freedom or Iraqi Freedom are eligible, accruing one day's credit for the 30 or 60 day requirement for each day that one or more sorties is flown.

No servicemember is entitled to more than one award of the Global War on Terrorism Expeditionary Medal or the Global War on Terrorism Service Medal, and no servicemember may be awarded more than one of these four medals for service in the same approved expedition or operation to combat terrorism: the Global War on Terrorism Expeditionary Medal, the Armed Forces Expeditionary Medal, and the Armed Forces Service Medal.

Korean Defense Service Medal (KDSM). Established in 2004, this medal is awarded to servicemembers who have been assigned, attached, or mobilized to units operating or serving all the land area of the Republic of Korea and the contiguous waters and airspace for 30 consecutive or 60 nonconsecutive days, or who were actually engaged in combat during an armed engagement or who were killed, wounded, or injured in the line of duty and required medical evacuation from the area of eligibility. Service is between 28 July 1954 and a future date to be determined.

Armed Forces Service Medal (AFSM). This medal is awarded to servicemembers who, after 1 June 1992, participated in military operations deemed to be a significant activity by the Joint Chiefs of Staff and who encountered no foreign armed opposition or imminent threat of hostile action. No servicemember may be awarded more than one of these four medals for service in the same approved expedition or operation to combat terrorism: the Global War on Terrorism Expeditionary Medal, the Armed Forces Expeditionary Medal, and the Armed Forces Service Medal.

Air Force Combat Action Medal. The AFCAM recognizes Air Force members below the general officer grades who actively participated in ground or air combat. The principal eligibility criterion is that the individual must have been under direct, hostile fire while operating in an unsecured space (outside a defended perimeter) or physically engaging hostile forces with direct, lethal fire. The AFCAM is awarded for qualifying service from 11 September 2001 to a date to be determined.

Humanitarian Service Medal (HSM). This medal is awarded to those who, after 1 April 1975, distinguished themselves by meritorious direct participation in significant military acts or operations of a humanitarian nature or who have rendered a service to mankind. Specifically excluded from eligibility are servicemembers remaining at a geographically separated location and who did not make a direct contribution to influence the action.

Military Outstanding Volunteer Service Medal (MOVSM). This medal is awarded to members of the armed forces of the United States who, subsequent to 31 December 1992, performed outstanding volunteer community service of a sustained, direct, and consequential nature. To be eligible, an individual's service must be to the civilian community, including the military family community; be significant in nature and produce tangible results; reflect favorably on the military service and the Department of Defense; and be of a sustained and direct nature. The MOVSM is intended to recognize exceptional community support over time, and not a single act or achievement, and to honor direct support of community activities.

Air and Space Campaign Medal (ASCM). This medal is awarded to members of the U.S. Air Force who, after 24 March 1999, participated in or directly supported a significant U.S. military operation designated by the chief of staff of the Air Force. The ASCM is awarded only to personnel who provided direct support of combat operations (such as sortie generation, intelligence surveillance, targeting, or computer network attack operations) from outside a geographic area determined by the Joint Chiefs of Staff: Operation Allied Force from 24 March 1999 to 10 June 1999; Operation Joint Guard from 11 June 1999 to a date to be determined; Operation Allied Harbour from 4 April 1999 to 1 September 1999; Operation Sustain Hope/Shining Hope from 4 April 1999 to 10 July 1999; Operation Noble Anvil from 24 March 1999 to 20 July 1999; and the Kosovo Task Forces Hawk from 5 April 1999 to 24 June 1999; Saber from 31 March 1999 to 8 July 1999; Hunter from 1 April 1999 to 1 November 1999; and Falcon from 11 June 1999 to a date to be determined. Servicemembers who provide direct support for at least 30 consecutive days or for 60 nonconsecutive days at their homestations or from outside the geographic area of combat qualify for the ASCM. No individual is eligible for both the ASCM and a DOD campaign/service medal awarded during a single tour in the designated operation.

Armed Forces Reserve Medal (AFRM). Required for this award is honorable and satisfactory service in one or more of the reserve components of the armed forces for a period of 10 years, not necessarily consecutive, provided such service was performed within a period of 12 consecutive years. Periods of service as a member of a regular component are excluded from consideration.

NON-U.S. SERVICE MEDALS

United Nations Medal (UNM). This medal is awarded by the United States to specific individuals for service with United Nations Forces. Each UN mission or action for which a UNM is awarded is commemorated by a suspension and service ribbon of unique colors and design. The ribbon and medallion combination takes on the name of the specific operation for which the combination was created; for example, the operation in the former Republic of Yugoslavia is the United Nations Protection Force (UNPROFOR), yielding the UNPROFOR Medal. U.S. servicemembers who meet the criteria may accept and wear the first UNM with the unique suspension and service ribbon for which they qualify. To recognize subsequent awards (if approved by the secretary of defense) for service in a different UN mission or action, the servicemember will affix a bronze service star to the first UN suspension and service ribbon awarded.

NATO Medal. Approved for U.S. military personnel who served under NATO command or operational control in direct support of NATO operations in the former Republic of Yugoslavia and in Kosovo, or as designated by the

DECORATIONS, AWARDS, AND SERVICE MEDALS

USAF AND DEPARTMENT OF DEFENSE
MILITARY DECORATIONS

**Medal of Honor
(Air Force)**

Air Force Cross

**Defense
Distinguished Service
Medal**

**Distinguished Service
Medal
(Air Force)**

Silver Star

**Defense Superior Service
Medal**

Legion of Merit

**Distinguished Flying
Cross**

**Airman's
Medal**

**Bronze Star
Medal**

Purple Heart

**Defense
Meritorious Service
Medal**

**Meritorious Service
Medal**

**Air
Medal**

**Aerial Achievement
Medal**

**Joint Service
Commendation
Medal**

**Air Force
Commendation
Medal**

**Joint Service
Achievement
Medal**

**Air Force
Achievement
Medal**

USAF AND DEPARTMENT OF DEFENSE UNIT AWARDS

**Presidential
Unit Citation
(Air Force)**

**Joint Meritorious
Unit Award**

**Air Force
Gallant Unit Award**

**Air Force
Meritorious Unit
Award**

**AF Outstanding
Unit Award**

**AF Organizational
Excellence Award**

MILITARY SERVICE AWARDS

**Combat Action Medal
(Air Force)**

**Prisoner of War
Medal**

**Combat Readiness
Medal**

**Good Conduct Medal
(Air Force)**

**Air Reserve Forces
Meritorious Service
Medal**

**National
Defense Service
Medal**

**Antarctica Service
Medal**

**Armed Forces
Expeditionary
Medal**

**Vietnam Service
Medal**

Outstanding Airman of the Year Ribbon

Air Force Recognition Ribbon

Air Force Overseas Ribbon (short tour)

Air Force Overseas Ribbon (long tour)

Air Force Expeditionary Service Ribbon

Air Force Longevity Service Award Ribbon

USAF Basic Military Training Instructor Ribbon

Air Force Recruiter Ribbon

NCO Professional Military Education Graduate Ribbon

USAF Basic Military Training Honor Graduate Ribbon

Small Arms Expert Marksmanship Ribbon

Air Force Training Ribbon

Southwest Asia Service Medal

Kosovo Campaign Medal

Afghanistan Campaign Medal

Iraq Campaign Medal

**Global War on Terrorism
Expeditionary Medal**

**Global War on Terrorism
Service Medal**

**Korean Defense Service
Medal**

**Armed Forces Service
Medal**

**Humanitarian Service
Medal**

**Military Outstanding
Volunteer Service Medal**

**Air and Space Campaign
Medal**

**Armed Forces Reserve
Medal**

NON-U.S. SERVICE MEDALS

United Nations Medal

NATO Medal

Multinational Force and Observers Medal

Republic of Vietnam Campaign Medal

Kuwait Liberation Medal (Kingdom of Saudi Arabia)

Kuwait Liberation Medal (Government of Kuwait)

Supreme Allied Commander Europe (SACEUR), beginning July 1992. Only one NATO service medal/ribbon is authorized for wear. Recipients should wear the one awarded first with a bronze service star for each subsequent award. Currently, two NATO Medals are authorized: NATO Medal–Former Republic of Yugoslavia and NATO Medal–Kosovo Operations.

Multinational Force and Observers Medal. This medal may be awarded to those who served with multinational forces and observers for at least 90 cumulative days after 3 August 1981. Subsequent awards are designated by numeral appurtenances.

Kuwait Liberation Medal, Kingdom of Saudi Arabia (KLM). Awarded to U.S. military personnel who served in the theater of operations of the Gulf War between 17 January and 11 April 1991.

Kuwaiti Liberation Medal, Kuwait. Awarded to U.S. military personnel who served in the theater of operations of the Gulf War between 2 August 1990 and 31 August 1993.

BADGES

Badges are appurtenances of the uniform. In the eyes of their wearers, several badges have significance equal to or greater than all but the highest decorations. Although there is no established precedence among badges, aerospace badges are worn above any others, with the exception of the chaplain insignia. New specialty badges for all USAF personnel were authorized in 1994, but only one may be worn at a time.

Six categories of badges and specialty insignia are currently approved for wear: aerospace, noncombatant designation, duty identification, Air Force specialty qualification, special service, and other badges. See AFI 36-2923 for eligibility requirements for wearing aerospace badges. Those granted aeronautical ratings no longer current are authorized to wear the aerospace badge that was in effect when the rating was granted.

Aerospace Badges. These include the pilot, navigator/observer, enlisted aircrew member, astronaut, flight surgeon, flight nurse, officer aircrew member, missileer, and air battle manager.

Noncombatant Designation Badges. These include the dental corps, nurse corps, enlisted medical, medical corps, medical service corps, biomedical science corps, chaplains, and judge advocate badges.

Duty Identification Badges. These include the combat crewmember, security police, AETC instructor, Air Force recruiting service, fire protection, Junior AFROTC instructor, Air Force Reserve recruiting service, and Defense Language Institute instructor badges.

Air Force Specialty Qualification Badges. These include air traffic control, acquisition and financial management, information management, operations support, band, intelligence, paralegal, chaplain service support, civil engineer, force protection, public affairs, command and control, logistics, services, communications and information management, space/missile, explosive ordnance disposal, manpower and personnel, supply/fuels, historian, meteorologist, transportation, and weapons director badges.

Special Service Badges. These include the presidential service, vice-presidential service, Office of the Secretary of Defense, Joint Chiefs of Staff, and permanent professor at the Air Force Academy badges.

Other Badges. These include distinguished international shooter, USAF distinguished rifleman, USAF bronze excellence-in-competition rifleman, USAF distinguished pistol shot, USAF distinguished-in-competition pistol shot, and USAF bronze excellence-in-competition pistol shot badges.

DEVICES

Service Ribbons. The service ribbon is a strip of ribbon identical to that from which the service medal is suspended. (Not all ribbons reflect the award of a medal, such as service longevity ribbons.) Service ribbons will not be worn with protective coverings.

Bronze Oak Leaf Cluster. Represents second and subsequent entitlements of awards.

Silver Oak Leaf Cluster. Represents the 6th, 11th, etc., entitlements or is worn in lieu of five bronze OLCs.

Service Stars. The service star is a bronze or silver five-pointed star that represents participation in campaigns or operations, multiple qualifications, or an additional award to any of the various ribbons on which it is authorized. A silver service star is worn in lieu of five bronze ones.

Wearing on Service Ribbons. Service stars are authorized to be worn on the service ribbons of some pre-Vietnam medals and the following medals only:

- National Defense Service Medal to represent a second award.
- Small Arms Expert Marksmanship Ribbon to represent qualification with M-16 rifle and with handgun.

Letter "V" Device. The bronze letter "V" device indicates an award for valor in combat.

Miniature Decorations, Service Medals, and Appurtenances. Miniature decorations, service medals, and appurtenances are replicas of the corresponding decorations and service medals on the scale of one half. The Medal of Honor is not worn in miniature. Its rosette is authorized for civilian wear.

Miniature Service Ribbons. Miniature service ribbons are replicas of corresponding service ribbons on a scale of about one half.

Lapel Buttons. *For All Decorations and Service Medals.* The lapel button is 2 $1/32$ inch long and $1/8$ inch wide, in colored enamel, being a reproduction of the service ribbon. Miniature appurtenances may be placed on lapel buttons.

Air Force Lapel Button. This is a small metal replica of the Air Force star and wings. It is authorized for wear by all active-duty and reserve personnel, including AFROTC cadets.

Air Force Retired Lapel Button. This button is presented to each retiree.

Presidential
Service Badge

Vice-Presidential
Service Badge

Office of the Secretary
of Defense Badge

Joint Chiefs of Staff
Badge

Headquarters Air Force
Badge

Commander's
Badge

Permanent Professor
USAF Academy Badge

Special Service Identification Badges

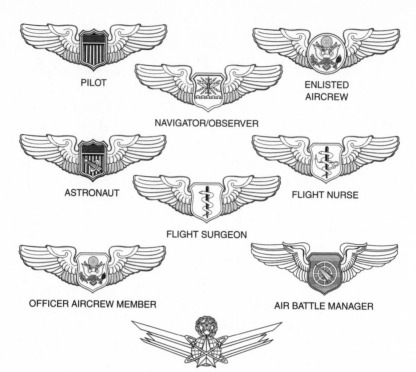

PILOT

NAVIGATOR/OBSERVER

ENLISTED AIRCREW

ASTRONAUT

FLIGHT SURGEON

FLIGHT NURSE

OFFICER AIRCREW MEMBER

AIR BATTLE MANAGER

SPACE & MISSILE OPERATIONS

MISSILE

MISSILE WITH
OPERATIONS DESIGNATOR

MASTER DESIGNATOR

SENIOR DESIGNATOR

COMBAT CREW MEMBER

ACQUISITION & FINANCIAL
MANAGEMENT

AIR TRAFFIC CONTROL

BAND

CHAPLAIN SERVICE
SUPPORT

CIVIL ENGINEER
READINESS

CIVIL ENGINEER

COMMAND & CONTROL

COMMUNICATIONS &
INFORMATION

EXPLOSIVE ORDNANCE
DISPOSAL

FORCE PROTECTION

HISTORIAN

INFORMATION
MANAGEMENT

INTELLIGENCE

JUDGE ADVOCATE

LOGISTICS

MAINTENANCE

MANPOWER & PERSONNEL

METEOROLOGIST

OPERATIONS SUPPORT

PARACHUTIST

PARALEGAL

PUBLIC AFFAIRS

SERVICES

SPACE/MISSILE

SUPPLY/FUELS

TRANSPORTATION

WEAPONS DIRECTOR

BIOMEDICAL SCIENCE
CORPS

DENTAL CORPS

ENLISTED MEDICAL

MEDICAL CORPS

MEDICAL SERVICE
CORPS

NURSE CORPS

BUDDHIST
CHAPLAIN

CHRISTIAN
CHAPLAIN

JEWISH
CHAPLAIN

MUSLIM
CHAPLAIN

Supply of Appurtenances. Only the following appurtenances will be supplied by the Department of the Air Force:

- Service ribbons
- Clasps
- Service stars
- Letter "V" device
- Arrowheads
- Lapel buttons for U.S. military decorations (except Medal of Honor)
- Air Force lapel button
- Air Force retired lapel button

An initial issue of the above appurtenances will be made with the corresponding service medals. Replacements for military personnel on active duty will be supplied to commanders on requisition in the usual manner. Replacements for retirees and veterans should be requested through Air Force Reference Branch, National Personnel Records Center, 9700 Page Ave., St. Louis, MO 63132-5100.

Manufacture, Sale, and Illegal Possession. There are restrictions on manufacture and sale of service medals and appurtenances by civilians and penalties for illegal possession and wearing of service medals and appurtenances.

GUIDE FOR WEARING AWARDS

Individuals entitled to wear decorations, service medals, ribbons, and badges should be certain that they place them on the uniform in the prescribed location and in the prescribed order. Ribbons are arranged symmetrically in rows of three, with the exception of wear on the service dress coat. When the coat lapel covers the usual symmetrical arrangement of three ribbons in a row, they can be staggered to the wearer's left and arranged in rows of four. This asymmetrical arrangement is authorized only for the service dress coat. For detailed information, see AFI 36-2903.

U.S. Military Service Medals. U.S. military and naval service medals are awarded by the Department of Defense Department and by the departments of the Air Force, Army, and Navy.

Occasions for Wearing. Commanders may prescribe the wearing of decorations and service medals on the following occasions:

- Parades, reviews, inspections, and funerals
- Ceremonies and formal occasions

The servicemember has the option of wearing decorations and service medals on the following occasions:

- Holidays when not on duty with troops
- Social occasions of a private nature ("black tie" or "white tie")

U.S. Nonmilitary Decorations. The following nonmilitary decorations may be worn only if military decorations or service medals are worn: the Medal for Merit, the National Security Medal, the Presidential Medal for Freedom, and decorations awarded by NASA, the Treasury Department, Public

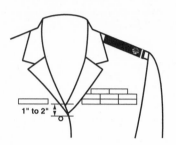

Women's Open Collar

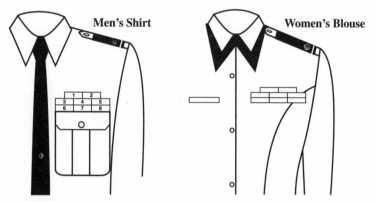

Men's Shirt   **Women's Blouse**

Wear of Ribbons on Service Uniform Combinations

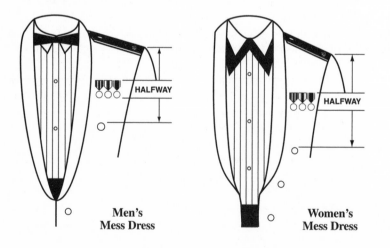

**Men's
Mess Dress**   **Women's
Mess Dress**

Wear of Miniature Medals on the Mess Dress Uniforms

Health, and Maritime Services. Nonmilitary service awards may not be worn on the Air Force uniform.

State decorations and service awards may be worn only by Air National Guardsmen in nonactive-duty status.

Foreign Service Medals. In general, the acceptance or wearing of foreign decorations and service medals for service performed while a member of the armed forces of the United States is prohibited. See AFI 36-2903.

Decorations and service medals awarded by the national government of a friendly country may be worn, provided such service medals were earned during service as a bona fide member of the armed forces of that friendly foreign nation. At least one U.S. decoration or service medal must be worn at the same time that a foreign service medal is worn.

The wearing of foreign service medals (except those indicated above), including civilian service medals awarded by a foreign national government and all service medals awarded by an inferior foreign jurisdiction, is prohibited.

Wear of Decorations and Service Medals. Decorations and service medals are worn on the service coat. The Medal of Honor is worn pendant from the cravat (ribbon placed around the neck) outside the shirt collar and inside the coat collar, the medal proper hanging over the necktie near the collar. Other decorations and service medals are worn in order of precedence from right to left of the wearer immediately above the pocket on the left breast in one or more lines, which are overlapped. The top line consists of those decorations and service medals highest in the order of precedence, which is as follows: decorations (in order listed at the end of this chapter); U.S. unit citations; achievement awards; service medals, in order earned; foreign decorations; USN service awards; and foreign service awards.

A *bronze oak leaf cluster* is authorized for wear for each additional Presidential Unit Citation received by a unit. A *silver oak leaf cluster* is authorized for wear in lieu of five bronze oak leaf clusters.

Wear of Decorations and Service Medals on Civilian Clothing. The wearing of decorations, service medals, or miniatures on civilian clothes should be limited to ceremonial occasions—and then only when strictly appropriate to the occasion.

When permitted by the employing agency, employees of federal, state, and city government who served honorably in active service and whose duties require that they wear special uniforms to denote their authority may wear U.S. service ribbons.

Wear of Unit Awards. An individual assigned to, or permanently attached to, and present for duty with a unit in the action for which a unit award was given may wear the award as a permanent part of the uniform.

The framed awards (the Presidential Unit Citation and the Joint Meritorious Unit Award) are worn with the laurel leaves pointing up. The unit award emblems may be worn with service ribbons or full-size medals but are not worn with miniature medals.

Wear of Badges. Only one U.S. aerospace badge may be worn at a time. Medical Corps and Nurse Corps officers may wear both the aviation medical badge and authorized medical insignia. For placement of badges, see the accompanying illustrations of placement of accoutrements, AFI 36-2803, AFI 36-2923, and AFI 36-2903.

BRASSARDS
A brassard is a cloth band worn around the upper arm to designate its wearer as a member of a special group or service and usually bearing an identifying mark, such as the Red Cross. Special duty brassards are worn centered on the left sleeve of the outergarment—overcoat, raincoat, coat, jacket, or shirt when worn as an outergarment—halfway between elbow and sleeve shoulder seam.

ORDER OF PRECEDENCE OF DECORATIONS AND AWARDS
There is a definite ranking among decorations and awards. Consult this listing and your base's military personnel flight before you assemble authorized decorations and awards on your uniform to be sure you have them in the proper sequence. U.S. military decorations of the Air Force, Army, Navy, and Coast Guard are worn by Air Force personnel in the following order:

Medal of Honor
Air Force Cross
Distinguished Service Cross
Navy Cross
Defense Distinguished Service Medal
Distinguished Service Medal (Air Force, Army, Navy, Coast Guard)
Silver Star
Defense Superior Service Medal
Legion of Merit
Distinguished Flying Cross
Airman's Medal
Soldier's Medal
Navy–Marine Corps Medal
Coast Guard Medal
Bronze Star
Purple Heart
Defense Meritorious Service Medal
Meritorious Service Medal
Air Medal
Aerial Achievement Medal
Joint Service Commendation Medal
Air Force Commendation Medal
Army Commendation Medal
Navy Commendation Medal

Coast Guard Commendation Medal
Joint Service Achievement Medal
Air Force Achievement Medal
Army Achievement Medal
Navy Achievement Medal
Air Force Combat Action Medal
Presidential Unit Citation
Navy Presidential Unit Citation
Air Force Gallant Unit Award
Joint Meritorious Unit Award
Air Force Meritorious Unit Award
Air Force Outstanding Unit Award
Air Force Organizational Excellence Award
Prisoner of War Medal
Valorous Unit Award
Navy Unit Commendation
Coast Guard Unit Commendation
Meritorious Unit Commendation (Army, Navy, Coast Guard)
Navy "E" Ribbon
U.S. nonmilitary decorations (see AFI 36-2803)
Combat Readiness Medal
Air Force Good Conduct Medal
Army Good Conduct Medal
Navy Good Conduct Medal
Marine Corps Good Conduct Medal
Coast Guard Good Conduct Medal
Air Reserves Forces Meritorious Service Medal
Army Reserve Component Achievement Medal
Navy Reserve Meritorious Service Medal
Selected Marine Corps Reserve Medal
Coast Guard Reserve Good Conduct Medal
Outstanding Airman of the Year Ribbon
Air Force Recognition Ribbon
National Defense Service Medal
Antarctica Service Medal
Armed Forces Expeditionary Medal
Southwest Asia Service Medal
Kosovo Campaign Medal
Afghanistan Campaign Medal
Iraq Campaign Medal
Global War on Terrorism Expeditionary Medal
Global War on Terrorism Service Medal
Korean Defense Service Medal
Armed Forces Service Medal

Humanitarian Service Medal
Military Outstanding Volunteer Service Medal
Air and Space Campaign Medal
Air Force Overseas Ribbon (short)
Air Force Overseas Ribbon (long)
Army Overseas Ribbon
Sea Service Deployment Ribbon (Navy, Marine)
Coast Guard Special Operation Service Ribbon
Coast Guard Sea Service Ribbon
Air Force Expeditionary Service Ribbon
Air Force Longevity Service Award Ribbon
USAF Basic Military Training Instructor Ribbon
Air Force Recruiter Ribbon
Armed Forces Reserve Medal
USAF NCO PME Graduate Ribbon
Army NCO Professional Development Ribbon
USAF Basic Military Training Honor Graduate Ribbon
Coast Guard Reserve Honor Graduate Ribbon
Small Arms Expert Marksmanship Ribbon
Navy Pistol Shot Medal
Air Force Training Ribbon
Army Service Ribbon
Foreign decorations (see AFI 36-2803)
Foreign unit citations (see AFI 36-2803)
United Nations Medal
NATO Medal (Yugoslavia)
NATO Medal (Kosovo)
Multinational Force and Observers Medal
Kuwait Liberation Medal (Saudi Arabia)
Kuwait Liberation Medal (Kuwait)
Foreign service medals (see AFI 36-2803)

17

Social Life in the Air Force

Air Force social life helps bind individuals into units and individual families into the larger Air Force family. It is an outward sign that service in the Air Force is more than a job, that the Air Force is a way of life.

Air Force social life, coupled with interaction among officers in the workplace, especially under conditions of shared adversity, binds individuals in lifelong friendships. Invariably, officers cite these friendships as being among the most rewarding aspects of their Air Force service.

Social activities and relationships in the Air Force are similar to those of society in civilian communities. Although officers and their spouses will find little need for adjustment from their civilian habits with respect to social activities while on duty in the Air Force, there are a few differences. Many air bases are in themselves small communities in which everyone knows almost everyone else. This makes for tight-knit social relations and close scrutiny by all of each family's activities. In this sense, officers and their families live in goldfish bowls. Bear this carefully in mind at all times.

SOCIAL LIFE ON THE BASE
How to Be a Good Citizen of the Air Base. The following tips can make the officer and spouse a helpful unit in air base social life. Strive to be on good terms, if not good friends, with all. Choose your close associates with great care. Do not openly express your personal dislike of individuals. Do not become a member of a clique. Keep your dinner guests, your running partners, and your tennis matches open to a broad sweep of the families on your base. Do not attempt to live beyond your means. In repaying your social obligations, do so within your means. Call on newly arrived families, and offer them your assistance. Don't merely sit there for 15 minutes making conversation. See what you can do to help when members of officers' families are ill. Take appropriate part in the community activities on base.

The Geography of Military Social Life. As soon as the officer and family arrive at a base, they will observe that people fall into one of two categories:

those that live on base in government quarters and those that live off base. Regardless of which category your family may fall into, you may find that the officers' club is the center of your social activity. At the officers' club, you can find a program of entertainment. Traditionally, military social life consisted of either visiting the homes of friends on or off base or attending some kind of entertainment at the officers' club. Today this is more likely to be the case for unmarried junior officers and for married senior officers. Many midgrade officers and their spouses no longer participate in evening and weekend activities at officers' clubs. The base gymnasium or sports center has also become a social center for many officers and their spouses.

SOCIAL LIFE IN THE CIVILIAN COMMUNITY
Because many married Air Force officers live in civilian communities rather than on base, a substantial amount of their social life pertains to their civilian neighbors. In such circumstances, officers are well advised to become active participants in the social activities of their communities. The idea that an officer on duty in a foreign country is an ambassador of the United States is well advertised. Less emphasized, but just as important, is the fact that officers living in civilian communities are ambassadors of the Air Force to the American public. Accordingly, Air Force officers should constantly seek to create a good impression with their civilian neighbors. In the main, this good impression is accomplished through conduct of the officer and family that is above reproach. It is also helpful, however, if officers become members of the churches, societies, and clubs of the civilian community and participate in the civic activities and with the schools and youth activities of their children. (Of course, on-base gymnasiums, sports centers, golf courses, rod and gun clubs, aeroclubs, bowling alleys, hobby shops, youth centers, and chapel programs also play roles in Air Force social life.) It is perhaps more important that Air Force officers discharge their social obligations to their civilian neighbors in ways that reflect credit on the Air Force than it is that they meet these criteria in respect to other Air Force personnel. In a sense, all social niceties can be summed up in the phrase "Be a good neighbor." This notion certainly applies to your civilian friends as well as to your Air Force associates.

TIPS ON ETIQUETTE
Manners matter; courtesy counts. Etiquette is merely an aspect of good manners, the essence of which is helping create an atmosphere in which everyone is comfortable, an atmosphere of mutual respect. Before commissioning, every officer candidate learns that officers always return salutes, that junior officers initiate an exchange of salutes with their superiors, that juniors walk to the left of their superiors, that they stand in the presence of their superiors, that when riding in the backseat of an automobile the senior officer sits on the right. Knowing these customs makes everyone comfortable. Social etiquette is the

same; it is not a way to separate those in the know from the uninformed or the in-group from outsiders. It is not to embarrass anyone, although ignorance of customs and courtesies, manners and etiquette does make individuals uncomfortable. If you do not know the rules of social etiquette—standard table manners, introductions, social correspondence such as thank-you notes, telephone manners, responsibilities of hosts and guests, and other social practices—the remedy is to expand your comfort zone by learning the rules.

In addition to AFI 34-1201, *Protocol*, and AFPAM 34-1202, *Guide to Protocol*, the following references are very helpful. All three reflect current practice. Consult them in your base library, and you will probably decide that you want your own copies.

Ann Crossley and Carol A. Keller, *The Air Force Wife Handbook: A Complete Social Guide.*

Mary Jane McCaffree and Pauline Innis, *Protocol: The Complete Handbook of Diplomatic, Official and Social Usage.*

Oretha D. Swartz, *Service Etiquette.*

There are several general rules about etiquette:

- Follow the Golden Rule: Do unto others as you would have them do unto you.
- Do not do or say anything that would embarrass anyone or make someone uncomfortable.
- Be gracious; take second place.
- Do not act superior; to do so puts another in a place of inferiority.
- If you do not know, ask; try to find out what is expected beforehand.
- If you do not know, observe; follow the lead of those who do know.
- Junior officers defer to senior ones; youth to age; hosts to guests; gentlemen to ladies—even today.
- Be conservative, not avant-garde.

Some practices occur so often, and are so often flubbed, that they need special mention.

Reaction to Invitations. You must respond to an invitation promptly. *Promptly* means within 24 hours. If the invitation is received orally, respond orally. If received in an informal note, respond by informal note (unless a telephone response is specified in the invitational note). If the invitation is received in the form of a formal note or card, respond fully, in writing, on formal note paper, and in the third person: "Lieutenant Jones is happy to accept the kind invitation of Colonel and Mrs. Smith to dinner on 3 June 2002, at seven o'clock." RSVP or R.S.V.P. (*Répondez s'il vous plaît,* which literally translates "Respond if it pleases you") means that *you must respond whether or not you will attend.* Your host deserves the courtesy; not to do so is extremely rude. If the invitation says "Regrets" or "Regrets only," you are expected to respond only if you will not attend. Even in this case, a short note expressing your appreciation of the invitation is acceptable but, of course, is not required.

Always explain a regret to an informal invitation; normally, you do not give reason in regretting a formal written invitation. *Do not* regret an invitation issued by your commander unless official duties unavoidably prevent your attendance.

If the invitation is informal, ask if there is anything that you can bring. If not, a bottle of wine or flowers that can easily be put in a vase are appropriate symbols of your appreciation for the invitation.

If invited to dinner and you are a bachelor, inquire of your hosts whether they wish you to escort anyone to the function. After attending a private social function, it is essential to write a note to your hostess (or make a telephone call) thanking her for the entertainment.

Remember to return the courtesy extended to you. It is not necessary that this be in exactly the same form as the courtesy you received.

Introductions. Introducing your wife to any man (except chiefs of state and very high church dignitaries): "Mary, this is Colonel Brown."

Introducing your husband to another man: "Colonel Brown, may I introduce my husband, Jack," or "Jack, this is Lieutenant Black." The correct order is to introduce the junior to the senior or the younger to the older.

Introducing one lady to another: "Mrs. Jones, may I present Mrs. Green," or "Mary, this is Mrs. Green."

Introducing one officer to another: "Major Smith, this is Captain Brown."

Introducing yourself to an officer senior to you: "Sir, may I introduce myself? I am Captain Jones." (Wait for the other to extend a hand.)

Introducing yourself to an officer of equal or lesser rank: "I'm Captain Margaret Jones." (Extend your hand.)

Introducing children or teenagers to adults: "Lieutenant Jones, this is Mary Smith."

Gentlemen are introduced to ladies, not the reverse. This holds even though the gentleman may be very distinguished and the lady very young. Exceptions: the president of the United States, a royal personage, a high church dignitary.

The most common way to make introductions, always in good taste, is to state the names in proper sequence, the lady, the senior, more distinguished, or more elderly first. "General Smith—Captain Jones." "Miss Youthful—Colonel Adams." "Mrs. Elderly Lady—General Cole." Use a rising inflection for the first name pronounced. The more formal method: "General Smith, may I introduce Captain Jones?"

Acknowledgment of an introduction by saying, "How do you do?" is always appropriate.

When men are introduced, they shake hands, standing without reaching across another person, if possible. They may say nothing, just look pleasant or smile, or say a courteous "It is nice to meet you" or "How do you do?"

When women are introduced to each other, with one sitting, one standing, the seated one rises to greet her hostess, or a very distinguished lady, as an act of respect. This would apply, for example, to the wife of a very senior officer.

In the usual case, the seated lady does not rise. The reply to an introduction may be a simple "How do you do?"

When a gentleman is introduced to a lady, he does not offer his hand unless the lady offers hers. In Europe, gentlemen are taught to take the initiative in shaking hands. A lady does not refuse an extended hand.

A lady or gentleman, introducing husband or wife to another, may say, "This is my husband," or "May I introduce my wife?"

At a social occasion, host and hostess should shake hands with guests in greeting and upon their departure.

Using titles with names:

Major General Black: "General Black"

Brigadier General White: "General White"

Colonel Smith: "Colonel Smith"

Lieutenant Colonel Jones: "Colonel Jones"

First Lieutenant Brown: "Lieutenant Brown"

Second Lieutenant Green: "Lieutenant Green"

Social Functions. Receptions, dinners, dances, and other such social functions are conducted in the Air Force in essentially the same manner as in civilian society.

It is a courtesy to your host or hostess to accept or regret invitations as soon as you possibly can, preferably within 24 hours of receiving the invitation. *You must fulfill this obligation without fail.* If regretting an informal invitation, be sure to state clearly a sound reason why you cannot accept it, such as illness in the family, a previously accepted engagement, or military duty.

Often a reception includes a receiving line. The line is based upon the position taken by the senior officer or honored visitor. Other members of the receiving line form on the left of the senior or honored person in order of rank of the officers, with their spouses on their left. An aide or an officer acting in that capacity usually greets the guests and introduces them to the first person in the receiving line. In Air Force receiving lines, the officer precedes the spouse in passing through the line. To avoid embarrassment and confusion, be certain to announce your name very clearly to the aide, who may then present you accurately to the receiving line. Greet each person in the receiving line before proceeding into the main area of the reception. In greeting the members of the receiving line whom you do not already know, repeat their names, as for example, "Colonel Smith, I am very happy to meet you, sir."

At dinner dances, guests should invite their dinner partners, their hostesses, guests of honor, and houseguests to dance, regardless of dancing ability.

At cocktail parties, circulate as much as possible, conversing with as many people as you can. Do not retire to a corner to tell jokes, discuss flying, or talk shop.

Upon leaving a social function, bid your host and hostess farewell, expressing thanks for the hospitality you have received. Do not leave the function before the senior officer present leaves. Thank your host and hostess when departing a social function by saying, "Thank you for a delightful evening." If you *must* leave a function noticeably early, say, "Mrs. (Hostess), I'm sorry I must leave early." (Then give your reason, and make it good!)

It is customary to reciprocate an invitation received, regardless of whether you accepted or regretted the invitation. Furthermore, you extend to house-guests of officers invitations to social gatherings to which their host has been invited.

Social Behavior and Foreigners. Although etiquette and manners are based on making everyone comfortable because they know what is expected of them and what to expect of others, etiquette and manners are not the same the world over. Military officers and their families often come into contact with foreigners. First recognize that the practices of one culture or nationality, such as those of the United States, are not right, logical, reasonable, and civilized while the practices of another are wrong, illogical, irrational, and barbarous. The customs are merely different. Try to learn the customs of your foreign guests and hosts. Do not assume that things are what they appear to be; always be attentive and observant. You and your family represent not just yourselves, but also the Air Force and the United States.

DINING-IN AND DINING-OUT

Certain ceremonies and traditions are part of the Air Force way of life. One of these is the dining-in, a formal, ceremonial dinner for members of an organization *only*. The dining-out is a similar function for servicemembers and their spouses and guests. The dining-out, a relatively new function, has largely replaced the dining-in.

The material here was prepared at Air University, Maxwell Air Force Base, to assist officers who desire to hold a dining-in or dining-out for their units, or whose commanders have assigned them the duty of making preparations for such a function.

Background. The custom of dining-in is a very old tradition in England, but it is not exclusively military. Dining-in probably began as a custom to welcome new members in monasteries, was adopted by early colleges, and later spread to military units of the country when the officers' mess was established.

General Hap Arnold is considered to have started the dining-in within the Army Air Forces when he used to hold his famous "wing-dings." The contacts of U.S. Army Air Forces personnel with the British and their dinings-in during World War II gave additional impetus for the growth of this custom in the USAF. Dinings-in provided situations where ceremony, tradition, and good fellowship could play an important part in the life of military organizations.

The dining-in provides an occasion for officers to meet socially at a formal military function. Further, it provides an opportunity to recognize individual and unit achievements. All of these are very useful in building high morale and esprit de corps.

PROPER DRESS

Event	Civilian	Air Force	Army	Navy	Marines
Formal:* official formal evening, state occasions (white tie)	Men: tails and white tie Women: long dress	Mess dress	Blue mess	Formal dress	Evening dress "A" or blue dress "A"
Semiformal: social function of general or official nature (black tie)	Men: tuxedo/dinner jacket Women: long dress or cocktail dress	Mess dress	Blue mess or Army blue with bow tie	Dinner dress, blue jacket, or dinner dress, white jacket	Evening dress "B," blue dress "B," or white dress "B"
Informal:** receptions, daytime/early evening occasions	Men: dark suit Women: tea-length, short dress or suit	Service dress	Army blue, with four-in-hand tie	Dinner dress, blue, or dinner dress, white	Blue dress "B" or white dress "B"
Informal:** ceremonies, military parades, reviews, official visits of civilian dignitaries, change of command	Men: business suit/coat and tie Women: short dress or suit	Service dress	Class A	Full dress, blue, or full dress, white, or service dress, blue, or service dress, white	Blue dress "A" or "B" or white dress "A" or "B," or service uniform "A"
	Men: open collar/sport shirt Women: short dress	Short-sleeved shirt, with or without tie	Class B	Short-sleeved shirt, without tie (uniform of day)	Blue dress "D"
Casual:** barbecues, picnics, parade spectator	Men: sport shirt/open collar (with jacket or sweater, as needed) Women: blouse and skirt	Short-sleeved shirt, without tie	Class B	Short-sleeved shirt, without tie	Blue dress "D"

*Because formal (white tie/tails) is unusual today, semiformal (black tie/tuxedo) is occasionally referred to as "formal." Invitations specifying formal are likely to mean semiformal, so confirm exactly what the host means.

**Be specific about what you expect your guests to wear if you host an event. If attending an event, ensure that you know exactly what your host expects you to wear.

Planning. Preparation for a dining-in or dining-out should begin well in advance. Date, location, and speaker should be selected, and reservations made. Details for the various arrangements should be allocated to individuals and their specific duties outlined. An order of events, or agenda, should be prepared.

Attendance. Traditionally, attendance at a dining-in was mandatory, and many commanders still consider this function a mandatory requirement, similar to a commander's call. Other commanders feel that since a goal of the dining-in or dining-out is to bring members closer together, attendance should be voluntary to avoid having persons who feel that they were forced to attend dampen the spirit and enthusiasm of the others. The decision whether a dining-in is voluntary or mandatory rests with the commander.

Dinings-out are attended by officers assigned to the unit holding the dining-out. They are the "members of the mess." Officers not assigned to the unit or of similar units, as well as spouses, invited to participate by the commander are not members of the mess, and may attend only if invited as guests. Most dinings-out are held at the officers' club.

There are two types of guests: official and personal. Official guests are honored guests of the mess. The guest speaker is an official guest. All official guests are seated at the head table, and their expenses are shared by the members of the mess. Because of the costs and limited space at the head table, the number of official guests should be limited. Personal guests may be either military officers or civilians. They are not seated at the head table, and their expenses are paid by the sponsoring member.

Senior officers from other units and organizations and civic leaders from the local community should be considered when inviting guests. It is a good way to enhance relations among base units and with civilian neighbors.

Guest Speaker and Other Guests. The guest speaker should be a military member or a civilian who can be expected to address the mess in an interesting manner on an appropriate subject. The guest speaker should be invited well in advance and advised of what is expected of a dining-out guest speaker. Arrangements should be made for the guest speaker and for other invited guests as protocol and custom dictate.

Dress. The dress for the dining-out should be the mess dress uniform. Civilian guests usually wear semiformal wear (dinner jackets or tuxedos), but business attire may be acceptable. The proper dress for civilians should be clearly stated in the invitation. Retired officers may wear the mess dress or civilian attire.

The Formal Dinner. All members of the mess should arrive within 10 minutes after the opening time. When the signal is given for dinner, the members should enter the dining room and stand behind their chairs. Members, unless properly excused, should not leave the mess before the guest of honor and the president have departed.

The guest of honor and the president of the mess are the last to join the head table. The president formally opens the mess and continues according to the agenda. The president remains standing while speaking but seats the other members of the mess after the last formal toast.

Toasting. The custom of toasting is universal. It is believed that this custom came into wide acceptance after the effects of poison were discovered. When two persons, who might be antagonists, drank from the same source at the same instant and suffered no ill effects, a degree of mutual trust and rapport could be established. With this foundation laid, discussions could continue on a more cordial basis. Today, toasting is a simple courtesy to the person being honored.

It is not proper to drain the glass at the completion of each toast. A mere touch of the glass to the lips satisfies the ceremonial requirements. Toasts, which are drunk standing, not seated, should be proposed in sequence and at intervals during the program of the evening.

The president proposes the first toast. If a toast to the colors is done, it is always the first toast, to which the members of the mess respond, "To the colors."

The second toast, in order of precedence, is to the heads of state of the allied nations represented. The toasts are made in the order determined by the seniority of foreign officers present. Remember that Commonwealth nations toast the British sovereign (head of state), not an elected official (head of government). Consult the installation protocol office or the individual foreign officers for the proper terminology to be used in toasting their heads of state.

After the president of the mess has toasted the head of each allied nation represented, the senior foreign officer then proposes a toast to the president of the United States. The response is "To the president." If no allied nations are represented, the president proposes the toast to the commander in chief, rather than to the president of the United States. The response is "To the president."

Following the president's or senior allied officer's toasts, Mister or Madam Vice proposes a toast to the chief of staff, Air Force. The response is "To the chief of staff." If officers of other services are present at the mess, toasts to their chiefs of staff would precede the toast to the chief of staff, United States Air Force: A toast to the chief of staff of the Army, chief of Naval Operations, and commandant of the Marine Corps is appropriate. The senior-ranking officer representing a sister service would then propose a toast to the chief of staff, United States Air Force.

Excessive toasting can make for a long evening. Although other toasts may be appropriate, too many toasts can cause the evening to run behind schedule and dampen the enthusiasm of the members of the mess. At some locations, there may be a large number of foreign officers present. In this case, it is appropriate to collectively propose a toast to the heads of state of all allied nations represented. The absolute last of the formal toasts is the prisoner of war (POW) toast, which is customarily drunk with water, rather than wine.

Following the formal toasts, the president seats the mess with one rap of the gavel.

President's Opening Remarks. Besides setting the tone for the evening, the president's remarks provide the opportunity to officially welcome guests. After the head table is introduced, the president should either personally introduce the remaining guests or poll the host officers. When all guests have been recognized, Mister or Madam Vice proposes a toast to the guests. Members of the mess stand, guests remain seated. The response to this and all future toasts is "Hear, Hear!"

The president then seats the mess and invites the members to eat.

Informal toasts are also an important part of the occasion. They should be humorous, but in good taste. It may be advisable to "plant" some impromptu toasts to set the tone of the evening.

Dinner. The first course may be placed on the table while the mess assembles in a nearby room. However, salad should not be wilted. Consider the capabilities of the club.

Courses are always served to the head table first. Mister or Madam Vice should be served immediately after the head table. Toasts requested by the mess during dinner and related activities will take up so much of the vice's time that he or she simply will not have a chance to eat unless served early. The president always has the option to limit toasts to keep the evening on schedule or to permit members to eat uninterrupted.

Before serving the main course, the president may wish to add some humor to the meal by asking Mister or Madam Vice to sample the meal to make sure it is fit for consumption by members of the mess. The vice may compose a short poem to the meal. There are numerous variations that are best left to the imagination of the planning committee and the dictates of the president. But if these are not really witty, unoffensive, and well done, they should be omitted.

The Grog Bowl. Although a "grog bowl" has been used by many organizations, it is not required. If there is no grog bowl, however, some other means of punishment for infractions should be considered.

The contents of the grog bowl are best left to the imagination of the planning committee, but the contents must be nonalcoholic so as not to dampen the spirits and participation of those individuals who do not consume alcoholic beverages.

Some organizations have successfully used a "grog mixing ceremony," in which the individual contents of the grog are combined along with a humorous narrative by Mister or Madam Vice.

At various points during the evening, a member may be sent to the grog bowl as punishment for violating the rules of the mess, such as the following:
- Arriving late at the cocktail lounge.
- Carrying drinks into the dining room.
- Wearing the cummerbund inverted (the pleats should face up for men and down for women).

- Wearing an ill-fitting or discolored mess jacket.
- Toasting with an uncharged glass.
- Starting a course before the president.
- Applauding a particularly witty, sarcastic, or succinct toast (unless following the example of the president).
- Discussing business, referred to as "opening the hangar doors."
- Talking while another person has the floor.

Certain members of the mess seem to be frequent violators, such as Mister or Madam Vice. It is not uncommon for the president and the guest speaker to be charged with at least one violation. If the president must leave his or her position at the head table, he or she must appoint another individual to assume the position.

Infractions warranting a trip to the grog bowl may be noted at any time by the president, vice, or any member of the mess. Members bring infractions to the attention of the president by raising a "point of order." If the validity of the charge is questioned, members vote by tapping their spoons on the table.

When the president directs a violator to the grog bowl, the individual proceeds to the bowl promptly. The bowl is usually located on Mister or Madam Vice's table.

Upon arriving at the grog bowl, the violator does the following:

- Does an about face and salutes the president.
- Turns to the bowl and fills the cup.
- Does another about face and toasts the mess, with "To the Mess."
- Drains the contents of the cup without removing it from the lips.
- In some messes, the officer turns the cup upside down on the head.
- Replaces the cup, again salutes the president, and returns to his or her seat. With the exception of the toast, the violator is not permitted to speak during this process.

Recess. At the time scheduled for recess, the president raps the gavel three times to gain attention. When the mess is silent, the president raps twice and announces a short recess so the dishes may be cleared and dessert served. Members stand by their places until the head table departs. Everyone then proceeds to the cocktail lounge, where the bars have reopened.

Reconvening the Mess. At the end of the recess, Mister or Madam Vice sounds the chime and directs everyone to return to the dining room. Traditionally, drinks should not be brought into the dining room following the recess.

When members reach their places, they stand directly behind their chairs. The president then leads the head table party into the dining room. The president then seats the mess with one rap of the gavel. Coffee is immediately served, and dessert is eaten.

Recognition and Awards. If individual and unit achievements are to be recognized, an appropriate time would be after the dessert. Individual recognition may be those officers selected for promotion or an award such as Junior

Officer of the Year. A toast to those recognized may also be appropriate. Following the formal toasts at the beginning of the dinner, all others may be made either in a serious vein or through the use of a humorous poem.

Guest Speaker's Address. After recognition and awards, and any scheduled entertainment, the president introduces the guest speaker. The speaker's address typically lasts 15 to 20 minutes and should be of a patriotic or entertaining nature. After thanking the speaker for his or her time and thoughts, the president presents a gift to the speaker. The president then asks the vice to propose an appropriate toast to the guest speaker.

Closing the Mess. After the toast to the guest speaker, the president can have the color guard post the colors before adjourning the mess.

Rules of the Mess. The following is a list of the original "thou shalt" rules under which the mess will be conducted. They are designed to conform to tradition and promote levity. Violators of these rules are subject to the wrath and mischievousness of Mister or Madam Vice. All assigned penalties will be carried out before the membership.

- Thou shalt arrive within 10 minutes of the appointed hour.
- Thou shalt make every effort to meet all guests. (The number of guests and members of the mess may make this impractical and burdensome to the guests. Before introducing yourself, ascertain if the members of the mess, especially junior officers, are actually introducing themselves. As always, be observant.)
- Thou shalt move to the mess when you hear the chimes and remain standing until seated by the president.
- Thou shalt not bring drinks into the mess.
- Thou shalt not leave the mess while it is convened. Military protocol overrides all calls of nature; plan ahead.
- Thou shalt participate in all toasts unless you or your group is honored with a toast.
- Thou shalt ensure that thy glass is always charged when toasting.
- Thou shalt keep toasts and comments within the limits of good taste and mutual respect. Degrading or insulting remarks will be frowned upon by the membership. However, good-natured needling is encouraged.
- Thou shalt not murder the Queen's English.
- Thou shalt not open the hangar doors (talk business).
- Thou shalt always use the proper toasting procedure.
- Thou shalt fall into disrepute with thy peers if the pleats of thy cummerbund are not properly faced (up for men, down for women).
- Thou shalt also be painfully regarded if thy clip-on bow tie rides at an obvious list. Thou shalt be forgiven, however, if you also ride at a comparative list.
- Thou shalt consume thy meal in a manner becoming a gentleman or lady.

PART V

Benefits and Restrictions

18

The U.S. Air Force as a Career

The relative attractiveness of a military career is the subject of continuing national debate. It should be. The officer corps of the U.S. armed forces plays a central role, and a crucial one, in the security of the country. For this reason, the officer corps must be of the highest quality. Only you know whether you might improve that quality. Furthermore, only you know whether a military career appeals to you. If you are undecided, perhaps the following considerations will help you reach a decision.

Whatever careers people may choose, certain criteria seem to apply to their choices:
- Pay
- Security
- Advancement possibilities and use of one's talents
- Living conditions
- Prestige of the career
- Challenge of the career
- Associations
- Retirement benefits

Rarely do young people deliberately choose a career in which, in their minds, most of the above criteria seem unfavorable. Yet, few career fields offer positive favors in all of the criteria cited. Each career emphasizes some and slights others of these criteria. This chapter takes an objective look at a military career in light of the above criteria.

PAY AND BENEFITS
Military officers receive comparatively good pay and benefits.
- Medical expenses are normally a minor item to most active-duty officers and their families. The Air Force provides medical attention for officers and their families, thus almost eliminating the financial hazard of serious illness. Though officers may suffer extended illnesses, their pay continues in full, except for flight pay.

- Insurance costs are lower because of the availability of government term life insurance and certain survivor benefits.
- Commissaries and base exchanges offer food and merchandise at costs lower than those in the average civilian establishment.
- Travel and transportation expenses usually match government allowances, although the average officer can suffer a net loss in this regard, especially if the officer's spouse is employed.
- Leave with pay is available to each officer, 30 days a year.
- Travel to foreign countries and in the United States is an experience that officers take as a matter of course, but one that would cost a shocking amount of money if undertaken privately. Civilians spend many hard-earned dollars globetrotting for pleasure and education.

SECURITY

Officers enjoy a relatively high degree of job security. They cannot be separated from the service except by due process of applicable laws. Although physical disability incurred in the first eight years of service results in separation without retirement benefits, important VA benefits accrue. After eight years of service, the officer who becomes physically disabled receives retirement status and pay depending on the degree of disability. For all practical purposes, a regular officer has job security, barring only serious misconduct and incompetence.

Security may seem an insignificant quality to a young person contemplating a vigorous career. Yet, with the addition of a family, even the young must give due concern to the certainty of their income. Officers never grow rich on their military pay, but they can enjoy the peace of mind that comes from an assured income for themselves and their families. As an officer, you can plan a stable future with confidence. Realistically considering not only the merits of security in your present job but also the needs of retirement and even security for your yet unborn children may convince you that security is a career criterion of high value.

ADVANCEMENT

For the career officer, advancement in rank is available at stipulated periods, and the opportunity to advance more rapidly challenges the most competitive. You do not need to seek help through special influence. Merit alone will take you upward. Of course, the competition is keen and grows sharper as you reach higher grades. Nevertheless, you may aspire to any military position to which your capabilities can carry you.

On the other hand, not every officer can be a general; mathematics points this fact out inexorably. Most officers end even full careers as lieutenant colonels. Therefore, if you assess yourself as no better than average, you cannot reasonably expect to wear stars. The stars are there, however, waiting for officers with the ability and the will to earn them.

Advancement in the Air Force is more than a matter of promotion; it also includes advancement in responsibility. Whereas in some professions advancement takes the form of a steadily increasing income, often these increases are not associated with increased responsibility or authority. In some careers, men and women may labor at essentially the same level of responsibility for their entire careers, doing work that grows dull and burdensome. Not so in the Air Force.

LIVING CONDITIONS

The living conditions of Air Force officers and their families range across a wide spectrum. Not all married officers can expect to have quarters on base because not that many quarters exist. Consequently, officers may find themselves occupying housing in civilian communities near air bases.

Although housed off base, many officers and their families find the base the center of their activities. The various facilities of the base, the exchange, the officers' club, athletic/sports facilities, hobby shops, and social gatherings may appeal to you and your family.

Your children may attend schools on base or, more likely, will enroll in schools of the civilian community. Your children's schooling may include numerous shifts among schools in various parts of the world.

Perhaps the most notable "living condition" of an Air Force career is the frequent changes of station. These moves often mean temporary (and not so temporary) separation of the family.

Hazard is also part of Air Force life. As a member of the Air Force, each officer is subject to being dispatched suddenly into danger. Indeed, hazard is a greater factor in an Air Force career than it is in almost any civilian vocation.

PRESTIGE OF THE CAREER

Officers of the Air Force generally hold a place of high respect in the minds of Americans. The career officer is a member of an honorable profession, the importance of which is beyond question. The officer is accepted in any social group, is considered an excellent credit risk, and is assumed to be an intelligent and responsible citizen. These are the basic attributes of prestige in its actual application. Public opinion polls continue to reflect the public's high rating of the military officer in the United States.

CHALLENGE OF THE CAREER

Few, if any, career fields offer greater challenges to the individual than does the Air Force. Never before in the history of mankind has so much power been assembled in organized fashion as by the U.S. Air Force. Making ready, or employing if need be, this almost incredible power is a job of endless ramifications. The task fully embraces the fields of engineering, law, medicine, political science, personnel management, industrial production, research, science, and even advertising. Hardly any aspect of American resources is not reflected in the operation of the Air Force. At the same time, the Air Force does not have a single solution for every situation, because nothing is static. Events and the progress of technology do not permit or tolerate stereotyped procedures. The problems are many, difficult, and urgently in need of solution. If you seek a challenge to your own abilities, you need look no further than an Air Force career.

CAREER ASSOCIATIONS

Probably the most satisfying aspect of an Air Force career lies in the associations it offers with a company of fine men and women. They are honorable people who adhere to a high code of conduct. They are loyal people who serve the nation without stint. They are able people who meet the great tasks of the Air Force and the realities of Air Force life with sure competence. They are interesting people who contribute to the knowledge and the culture of the nation from their worldwide experiences. They are, on the whole, good people whom it is good to know. Comradeship of the Air Force is truly a great attraction.

Not only does a career offer fine associations with the people of the Air Force, but also it affords a matchless opportunity to meet and know men and women of many backgrounds, talents, and interests. Few civilian Americans compare with the average Air Force officer in the cosmopolitan nature of friendships. Almost any Air Force officer of 20 years' service can name personal friends in many states and in several foreign countries.

RETIREMENT BENEFITS

Officers of the Air Force enjoy excellent retirement prospects. Subject to the approval of the Department of the Air Force, an officer may retire after 20 years' service. Retired officers receive a substantial percentage of their active-duty pay and retain privileges of access to clubs, commissaries, exchanges, and athletic and some medical facilities. Taken together with a reasonable investment and insurance program, these provisions permit a retired officer to live comfortably, though not luxuriously.

Medical benefits, however, are in flux. TRICARE appears to be increasingly unsatisfactory, so retirees, if not active-duty servicemembers, will probably have to carry medical insurance, as well as long-term care insurance.

As an Air Force officer, you may retire after 20 years' service at about 42 years of age and can look forward to retirement early enough to permit you to embark on another career.

19

Rights, Privileges, and Restrictions

When citizens enter military service, their legal status changes. Some civilian rights are restricted or modified. They take on additional hazards and obligations that are balanced by additional benefits not enjoyed by civilians. To a lesser degree, officers in inactive status and retired officers enjoy benefits and are also subject to restrictions. Some former members of the armed forces whose separation was honorable enjoy important benefits administered by the Department of Veterans Affairs.

JUSTIFICATION FOR BENEFITS
Strong reasons justify granting military rights and privileges called benefits. Those citizens who are members of the Army, the Navy, the Marines, or the Air Force have the primary mission of protecting and preserving the United States, including our institutions and way of life, the prosecution of wars with the incidental hazard, and the service of the federal government wherever duty is directed. They give up many freedoms of choice that civilians take for granted.

The active-duty armed forces consist of the officers and enlisted members who are volunteers. They are backed up by the several categories of reserves, also volunteers. Volunteers will not be obtained in the number required or the quality necessary unless the conditions of their lives are acceptable. Because of international tensions and recurrent wars, our country needs the armed forces to protect itself. These armed forces must be strong enough, courageous enough, and proud enough to do their job.

As long as the nation has need of the best military leadership of all grades and ages, it will be wise to recognize that all officers are volunteers by granting appropriate benefits, first to attract good people to service and then to hold them.

There is an inescapable difference between the individual in civilian employment and the member of the armed services. The civilian may quit or refuse a task with no greater penalty than loss of employment, then being free to choose another job. But members of the armed forces can do so only at the peril of punishment by action of court-martial.

JUSTIFICATION FOR RESTRICTIONS

There is a sufficient case also for imposing restrictions upon military people, especially commissioned officers, that civilians do not bear. The government must have a clearly defined rationale to deploy its forces and require individuals to perform specific missions, however unpleasant or hazardous such duties or locations may be. The government must insist upon full service of its officers and thus is justified in defining and prohibiting improper outside activities of individuals.

Since procurement officers and others in the business end of the armed forces have many prerogatives related to the letting of contracts, the government requires high standards of ethics as well as clearly codified methods of conducting these affairs.

To assure fair treatment for all and to prevent abuses in the exercise of federal power, limitations must be placed on authority, especially in the field of punishments, sentences of courts-martial, and the like.

RIGHTS

Although there are many obligations of service, there are not many actual rights. A right is a benefit established for military people by federal law. Unless a benefit is established by law, in contrast to a departmental policy that is subject to administrative change or withdrawal, it is something less than a right.

Acquisition of Military Rights. A citizen who has subscribed to the oath of office as an officer becomes entitled at once to certain rights of military service, such as the right to wear the uniform. Other rights accrue only by completing specified requirements, such as the right to retire after completing a stipulated period of service.

The Right to Wear the Uniform. Members of the military service have the right to wear the uniform of their service. That the department may require the wearing of the uniform is beside the point. First of all, it is a right.

Members of the reserve components on inactive status, retired personnel, and former members of the service who have been honorably separated have the right to wear the uniform only at stipulated times or circumstances, and unless these conditions exist, the right is denied.

The Right of Officers to Command. In the commission granted an officer by the president are these words: "And I do strictly charge and require those officers and other personnel of lesser rank to render such obedience as is due. . . ." The commission itself may be regarded as the basic document that gives military officers the right to exercise command and to exact obedience to proper orders.

The Right to Draw Pay and Allowances. Pay scales for grade and length of service are established by law (see chapter 20, "Pay and Personal

COMPARISON WITH CITIZENS' DUTIES

As a Civilian   **As a Servicemember**

1. To take part in civic affairs.

1. Modified—duty and right to vote remains; may express private opinions informally.

2. To serve on a jury.

2. Modified—may be exempted from jury duty; subject to appointment on court-martial.

3. To respect and obey laws; to assist public officials in preventing crime and assist courts by giving evidence.

3. Unchanged—sometimes officially assigned to assist public officials.

4. To pay taxes.

4. Modified—may be exempted by statute from certain taxes of state where stationed, if not a legal resident of that state.

COMPARISON WITH CITIZENS' RIGHTS

As a Civilian   **As a Servicemember**

1. Freedom of worship.

1. Unchanged.

2. Freedom of speech and press.

2. Altered slightly by duty to maintain respect toward the president, vice president, Congress, and other officials.

3. Right to assemble peaceably and to petition government.

3. Subject to maintenance of good order and military discipline; must not go beyond "petition" stage.

4. Right to keep and bear arms.

4. Unchanged within the United States, although a servicemember may need specific permission to keep personal weapons in government quarters, and they will probably have to be registered with the base's security force.

5. Protection against unreasonable search and seizure of person and property.

5. Similar safeguards applied by executive order.

6. Right to vote secretly in national and local elections.

6. Unchanged—military authorities required to facilitate absentee voting.

7. Freedom to make contracts, start and manage businesses, etc.

7. Some limitations—must not do business with government, reflect discredit on the uniform, interfere with duties, or use military titles (other than in authorship).

Allowances"). The rights as to pay and allowances may be suspended, in part, by action of a court-martial or forfeited in part by absence without leave.

The Right to Receive Medical Attention. Members of the armed services and, with restrictions, their families are entitled to receive appropriate medical and dental care for the treatment of wounds, injuries, disease, or illness. In fact, refusal to accept treatment ruled to be necessary may be punishable by court-martial. For rights of dependents to receive medical care, see chapter 22, "Medical Care."

The Right to Individual Protection Under the Uniform Code of Military Justice (UCMJ). All members of the military service are under the jurisdiction established by the Articles of the Uniform Code of Military Justice. Many persons regard the *Manual for Courts-Martial,* which contains this code, merely as the authorization of courts-martial and the implementation of their procedures as a means of maintaining discipline or awarding punishment for crime. This view is incomplete. Except for the punitive articles, the Uniform Code of Military Justice pertains in considerable measure to the protection of individual rights, such as these:

- No people may be compelled to incriminate themselves before a military court.
- No people shall without their consent be tried a second time for the same offense.
- Cruel and unusual punishments of every kind are prohibited.
- Although the punishment for a crime or offense is left to the discretion of the court, it shall not exceed such limits as the president may prescribe.

The Soldiers' and Sailors' Civil Relief Act. The Soldiers' and Sailors' Civil Relief Act, passed in 1940 and still in effect, has as its purpose the relief of draftees, enlistees, and reservists on active duty of some of the pressure of heavy financial obligations they may have assumed in civil life.

Redress of Wrong. Each of the armed services provides a procedure by which any members of the armed services may seek redress of wrong. Officers may have occasion to register official objections or complaints with respect to their own treatment, although such occasions should be rare because most officers complete their entire service without finding it necessary to use this right. But officers should certainly know that their juniors also enjoy this right and that if they take action that is grossly injurious to an individual or action that is so considered, they may be obliged to endure the process as the injuring party.

There may come a time in the service of all people when they feel that they have been wronged by a superior, such as in these situations: an unfavorable ruling regarding pay or allowances, unsatisfactory living conditions, undeserved stigma, or treatment by a superior that is directly contrary to military laws or policies. Any person contemplating registering an official complaint should first get the facts straight and be quite certain of sustaining them. It is contrary to policy to punish anyone for filing a complaint. But a person can be punished for knowingly making statements that are unfounded, untruthful, or unjustly harmful to another person's good name. No person should fear the effects of filing an honest complaint or stating a genuine grievance. But the basis of the grievances must be factual and subject to proof.

After getting the facts straight, the person should normally state the entire situation to the commander and seek advice. In most instances, this step will end the matter because, if the grievances are real, the commander should correct the situation.

If the conference with the commander is unsatisfactory or for some sufficient reason is not held, the person may bring the problem to the attention of the inspector general who serves the organization. More than likely, the inspector general will require a written statement. This officer will advise the complainant of the final action taken on the complaint or grievance. Nor need this be all. The officer or airman may write directly to the inspector general of the major command or to the inspector general of the Air Force.

Right to Request Correction of Military Records. Military records serve as the basis for recording the fact, nature or character, and duration of military service. Accordingly, the military records that pertain to each individual are of inestimable value. Therefore, when any individual military record contains an error, means have been made available to petition for correction.

Each service secretary, acting through boards of civilian officers or employees of his service, is authorized to correct any military record where such action is necessary to correct an error or remove an injustice. In the Air Force, this board is known as the Air Force Board for Correction of Military Records.

Application for correction should be submitted by the person requesting corrective action or by other persons as authorized by the board when the person concerned is unable to submit application. In general, a statute of limitations of three years applies to applications. There must be a showing of exhaustion of normal administrative remedies. Hearing on an application may be denied if a sufficient basis for review has not been established or if effective relief cannot be granted. When an application has been found to be within the jurisdiction of the board, and sufficient evidence has been presented indicating probable error or injustice, the applicant will be entitled to a hearing before the board either in person or by counsel or in person with counsel.

The Right to Vote. Air Force personnel are encouraged to exercise the privilege of voting in federal, state, and primary elections. To encourage and assist eligible servicemembers to vote, the Department of Defense maintains liaison with the various state election authorities to obtain current voting information, which, through Air Force channels, is disseminated to all Air Force installations for the information of all personnel. Voting officers are available at squadron level to answer pertinent questions concerning forthcoming elections in the servicemember's state of domicile and to provide printed postcard applications for state absentee ballots, which are transmitted, postage free, to the appropriate state. Every effort is made to ensure that all personnel are protected against coercion of any sort in making their political choices and to maintain the integrity and secrecy of the ballots cast.

Although the Air Force provides information and assistance concerning elections and voting procedures, the actual decision to vote rests with the individual servicemember. Voting must be entirely voluntary; no servicemember will be required or ordered to participate in political elections.

The determination of eligibility and the specification of requirements for voting are completely governed by the appropriate state. To vote, all servicemembers must meet such requirements and must be declared eligible to vote by the state in which they desire to exercise their voting privilege.

The Right to Retire. After satisfying specific requirements of honorable service or having endured physical disability beyond a fixed degree, commissioned officers of the armed forces have the right to retire. See chapter 24, "Retirement."

The "GI Bill of Rights." Former members of the armed forces and retired personnel may obtain benefits under the "GI Bill of Rights." VA benefits for *eligible* veterans, their dependents, and beneficiaries include these:

- Servicemembers' Group Life Insurance
- Educational aid
- Guarantee of loans for the purchase or construction of homes, farms, or business property
- Readjustment allowances for veterans who are unemployed
- Disability compensation
- Vocational rehabilitation
- Physical examinations, hospital care, and outpatient medical and dental treatment
- Domiciliary care and guardianship service
- Pensions
- Death benefits to survivors

Social Security Benefits of Retired Personnel. Retired officers, including those who are employed or self-employed, qualify for Social Security benefits in the same manner as other citizens. See chapter 24, "Retirement."

The Right to Be Buried in a National Cemetery. The rights of a deceased servicemember to be buried in a national military cemetery are discussed in chapter 25, "Benefits after Separation."

PRIVILEGES

The Privileges of Rank and Position. That "rank has its privileges" is a concept as old as the armed forces. It is similar to the deference in all walks of life to one's elders or seniors. It is no more or less pronounced, although it may be more codified, than among faculty members, in a business establishment, in legislative bodies, or among doctors, lawyers, and ministers.

Leave. Under current laws and regulations, military people become entitled to accumulate leave and to take it when their duties permit (see chapter 21, "Leave"). But people in uniform must apply for permission to take leave, regardless of how much leave they have accumulated. Their applications may be denied. The training or tactical situation will govern the decision. If they absent themselves without permission, they are subject to forfeiture of pay and to disciplinary action. Hence, it is a privilege, rather than a right.

Election to Public Office. Members of the Air Force other than the Regular Air Force, while on active duty, may become candidates for election to public office without resigning and may file such evidence of their candidacy as required by local laws. Their candidacy must not interfere with duty. If elected, the officers must not, while in active-duty status, act in their official capacity as the holders of the offices or perform any of the duties. Members of the Regular Air Force on the active list do not enjoy this privilege.

Because this particular privilege has been questioned several times in recent years, servicemembers considering becoming candidates for office should consult local military authority, for otherwise they may lose their commissions.

Membership in Officers' Clubs. Officers have the privilege of club membership, if clubs are provided. They must follow the rules of the club as to payment of dues, bills, and other matters, and unless they do so, this privilege may be curtailed or denied.

The Privilege of Writing for Publication. Traditionally, active-duty officers have been permitted to write for publication, as long as it was done on their own time and was not part of their official duties. One need only remember William J. Hardee, West Point commandant of cadets before the Civil War, whose *Rifle and Light Infantry Tactics* became the officer's manual for both Union and Confederate armies; General John J. Pershing's World War I and Dwight D. Eisenhower's World War II memoirs; and Colonel John A. Warden's *The Air Campaign: Planning for Combat.* Major General A. J. Kinney, the first author of this *Guide,* wrote it for more than 20 years on active duty.

In 1992, in an effort to clean its own house, the U.S. Congress passed a law prohibiting federal officials and employees from accepting honoraria for public appearances, speeches, or articles. Enforced throughout the U.S. government, the law proved unworkable and was challenged as a violation of the First Amendment. The U.S. Court of Appeals did find the law unconstitutional. Today, Air Force officers can again accept remuneration for their writing.

Publishing Articles on Military Subjects Is Authorized. Subject to restrictions stated below, any member of the armed services may publish articles on military subjects that contain nothing prejudicial to military discipline. If publication is not objectionable, such permission will be granted, but no reference to approval by the Department of the Air Force will appear in the publication.

If the author offers the work to the Department of the Air Force and it is accepted and published by the Department of the Air Force in original form, proper recognition will be given to the individual.

The inclusion of classified military information (Top Secret, Secret, or Confidential) in any article published by a member of the Air Force is prohibited.

Manner of Obtaining Clearance on Proposed Addresses and Military Publications. The Office of Public Affairs, Department of Defense, is responsible for reviewing for security and coordination with existing policies of the Department of Defense and its components information disseminated to the public on a national scale by individuals or agencies of the Departments of the Army, Navy, and Air Force.

The agency is charged with reviewing manuscripts, speeches, advertising material, radio scripts, and films submitted for clearance by individuals and agencies of the Department of Defense and its components.

Active-Duty Personnel. All material containing information about the Air Force prepared by officers or airmen on active federal service will be submitted to appropriate public affairs authority for review before publication.

Attention is called to a long-standing policy prohibiting military and civilian personnel assigned to public affairs divisions from accepting direct remuneration from civilian agencies for any type of public affairs activity without approval. Exceptions may be granted in cases where the subject matter is in no way related to the official duties of the personnel.

Inactive Personnel. Inactive Air Force Reserve and National Guard personnel assume civilian status upon completion of terminal leave and are not required to submit for review material that they have prepared. This, of course, does not relieve them of the responsibility to protect sensitive or classified information.

Retired Personnel. Retired military personnel are responsible for the security and propriety of material that they have prepared.

Inventions and Rights to Profit Therefrom. Another way active-duty personnel may seek to add to their income is through an invention. It is likely that many good ideas are unexploited because of lack of information on how to proceed. An officer who makes an invention has the same right as any other citizen to profit if it does not refer to and is not evolved in the line of duty. However, if it was created or evolved in the line of duty, the Air Force has certain ownership rights. Contact your staff judge advocate for information.

A free pamphlet on the subject is issued by the Commissioner of Patents, Washington, D.C. Novice inventors should obtain it before disclosing anything about their projects.

Defense Department Exchange Privileges. The following are entitled to all exchange privileges:

- Uniformed personnel on active duty more than 72 hours and their families.
- Officers and airmen of foreign nations when on duty with U.S. armed services under competent orders issued by one of the armed services.
- Widows and widowers of servicemembers of the following categories who have not remarried: members of the uniformed services who at the

time of death were on active military duty for a period exceeding 72 hours, members of the reserve components of the armed forces who died in line of duty while on active duty, and retired personnel.

Retired personnel entitled to the privilege include these people:

- Personnel carried on the official retired lists of the armed services.
- Uniformed personnel of the Red Cross assigned to duty within an activity of the armed services.

Patrons Entitled to Limited Privileges. The following are entitled to make limited purchases at exchanges:

- Honorably discharged veterans who are receiving medical treatment at a facility where exchanges are operated.
- Exchange employees.

Snack bar privileges may be extended to the following when civilian facilities are not conveniently available: civilian employees, Red Cross nonuniformed personnel working in offices within an activity of the armed forces, visitors, and reserve component members on duty for periods less than 72 hours.

Members of reserve components not on active duty are entitled at all times to purchase such necessary articles of uniform clothing, accoutrements, and equipment as would be required immediately when called to active duty.

Unlimited exchange privileges are authorized for Reserve component personnel who participate in regularly scheduled inactive-duty training. This training must be appropriately documented by the individual's commander.

Identification. All patrons must identify themselves as entitled to full or restricted privileges at the time purchase is made. Family members and nonuniformed people are required to obtain an official identification card. Widows and widowers and retired personnel will be obliged to establish their right to purchase by the same card. Uniformed people should be prepared to display their official identification cards or official orders before sales are made.

Private Practice by Medical and Dental Officers. Private practice by medical and dental officers is strictly regulated by the Air Force. Established application procedures must be followed. Approval is not ordinarily granted unless there is demonstrated community need, including a letter to support the need from the local medical or dental society. In no case may such practice be in conflict with military requirements, and the establishment of an office for the purpose of engaging in civilian practice is prohibited. Medical officers engaging in private practice must be licensed in that state and must provide their own professional liability insurance. The same provisions govern private practice for dental officers.

Concessions and Scholarships at Civilian Educational Institutions. Several civilian educational institutions offer concessions to service children and grant scholarships to discharged airmen whose records and educational qualifications justify the action. Any person in the military service who desires information relating to scholarships should apply directly to the sponsoring activity or, at base level, go through the personal affairs office or the education office.

Privileges Extended by Civilian Organizations. In many localities, civilian professional, civic, golf, or social clubs may extend the privilege of membership to officers stationed at a nearby military establishment. This custom, which is by no means universal, is of great importance to officers. In some instances it enables officers to obtain membership without the costly entrance fees. Before accepting the offered privileges, officers are morally obligated to ascertain that these organizations have no discriminatory practices, such as restricting membership because of race, gender, religion, etc.

Abuse of Privilege. The evil that has been practiced by a few and that has discredited many of the officer corps is *abuse of privilege.* It consists of taking advantage of position or rank to secure pleasures or facilities to which one is not entitled by law, policy, or custom. It is "getting away with something." This chapter is an attempt to clarify what is meant by proper benefits so that officers may observe and evaluate alleged rights and privileges before practicing them. The selfish and grasping may not be deterred. But officers who might offend innocently may be helped on a correct course.

Here is a simple way to determine whether an alleged benefit or privilege is genuine or spurious. Find the answers to these two questions:

- Can you establish authorization in any current departmental or major command document?
- Observe the five or ten best officers of experience known to you whom you observe frequently. They must have high standing as good officers among their colleagues. Is the questioned privilege used or practiced by them?

RESTRICTIONS

There are many *Thou shalt nots* in the military life. They consist for the most part of restrictions or standards of conduct inapplicable to civilians. Some are in federal laws. Others are in departmental policies. A few are in observed customs. They need not be regarded as onerous. They have come about through experience and necessity. In any event, they are well balanced by military benefits. Because their violation would be regarded as a serious matter, at the worst resulting in trial by a court-martial, officers should know of them.

Conduct Unbecoming an Officer. Article 133 of the Uniform Code of Military Justice reads as follows: "Any officer, cadet, or midshipman who is convicted of conduct unbecoming an officer and a gentleman shall be punished as a court-martial may direct" (*Manual for Courts-Martial, United States,* 1951).

There are certain moral attributes common to the ideal officer, a lack of which is indicated by acts of dishonesty or unfair dealing; of immorality, indecency, or indecorum, or of lawlessness, injustice, or cruelty. Not everyone is or can be expected to meet ideal standards or to possess the attributes in the exact degree demanded by the standards of the time, but there is a limit of tolerance below which individual standards of officers or cadets cannot fall without their being morally unfit to be officers or cadets. This UCMJ article contemplates such conduct by officers or cadets that, taking all the circumstances into consideration, satisfactorily shows moral unfitness.

This article includes acts made punishable by any other article of the code, provided such acts amount to conduct unbecoming an officer; thus, an officer who embezzles military property violates both this and the article dealing with embezzlement. Instances of violation of this article include knowingly making a false official statement, dishonorable neglect to pay debts, opening and reading another's letters without authority, giving a check on a bank where one knows or reasonably should know there are no funds to meet it and without intending that there should be, using insulting or defamatory language to other officers in their presence or about them to other military persons, being grossly drunk and conspicuously disorderly in a public place, public association with prostitutes, cruel treatment of airmen, committing or attempting to commit a crime involving moral turpitude, and failing without good cause to support one's family.

Racial Discrimination. Racial prejudice and discrimination are facts of life in American society. The armed forces have made great strides since the late 1940s, and today they are positive examples to the nation as a whole of the harmony that can exist in a multiracial and multiethnic society that is based on equal opportunity for all. Although the Air Force cannot control what personal opinions individual servicemembers may have, the institution itself does not practice racial discrimination, nor does it tolerate any form of racially discriminatory behavior among servicemembers.

Sexual Harassment. Sexual harassment is a form of sex discrimination that involves unwelcome sexual advances, requests for sexual favors, and other verbal or physical conduct of a sexual nature when submission to such conduct is made either explicitly or implicitly a term or condition of a person's job, pay, or career; submission or rejection of such conduct by a person is used as a basis for career or employment decisions affecting that person; or such conduct has the purpose or effect of unreasonably interfering with an individual's work performance or creates an intimidating, hostile, or offensive working environment.

It is rather easy to recognize sexual harassment of the type of "submit to my sexual requests or you will be (fired, demoted, intimidated, denied a promotion, and so on)." To recognize hostile environment sexual harassment is more complicated. Such a hostile environment can be created by discussing sexual activities, unnecessary touching, commenting on physical attributes, displaying sexually suggestive pictures, using demeaning or inappropriate terms, using unseemly gestures, members of one gender ostracizing workers of the other gender, granting job favors to those who participate in consensual sexual activity, and using crude and offensive language. The particular facts of each situation determine whether offensive conduct has crossed the line to unlawful gender discrimination.

Servicemembers should avoid all sexually offensive conduct or any behavior that is in any way demeaning to others. All complaints, regardless of whether they meet the legal test of hostile environment sexual harassment, must be quickly investigated and appropriate action taken to stop offensive conduct.

Sexual Misconduct. Congress has directed a program to deal with unacceptable sexual conduct. The program includes education on prevention and how to respond to complaints, as well as how complaints are to be investigated, medical care for victims, confidential reporting of incidents, and provisions of advocates for victims. The program also addresses the use of alcohol to diminish the victim's ability to resist sexual assault (rape).

Fraternization and Unprofessional Relationships. Fraternization is a personal relationship between officers and enlisted members in violation of acceptable behavior in the Air Force that prejudices good order and discipline or discredits the armed services. If good professional judgment and common sense indicate that a relationship is causing, or may reasonably result in, damage to morale, good order, discipline, unit cohesion, or mission accomplishment, corrective action will be taken. Criminal charges can be brought under Article 134, Uniform Code of Military Justice.

Unprofessional relationships encompass all relationships between military members (officer-officer, officer-enlisted, enlisted-enlisted, or certain military-civilian relationships) that result in inappropriate familiarity or create the appearance of favoritism, preferential treatment, or impropriety. These relationships create the appearance that personal friendships and preferences are more important than individual job performance and contribution to the mission. They are, therefore, matters of official concern because unprofessional relationships erode morale, discipline, and the unit's ability to perform its mission. Unprofessional relationships can occur whether or not the members are in the same chain of command, unit, or closely related units. Officers may not gamble with, lend money to, borrow from, date, engage in sexual relations with, or enter into business enterprises with enlisted members. Additional guidance can be gotten from a staff judge advocate and AFI 36-2909, *Professional and Unprofessional Relationships.*

Homosexual Conduct. The legal status of homosexuals and homosexual behavior in the armed services and the United States as a whole is evolving. The so-called "Don't Ask, Don't Tell, Don't Pursue" policy considers sexual orientation as a personal and private matter. Homosexual orientation is, therefore, not a bar to service entry or continued service unless manifested by homosexual conduct. Conduct is defined as an act or statement or as marriage or attempted marriage. A homosexual act is defined as any bodily contact, actively undertaken or passively permitted, between members of the same sex for the purpose of satisfying sexual desires, or any bodily contact that a reasonable person would understand to demonstrate a propensity or intent to engage in homosexual acts. A statement includes language or behavior that a reasonable person would believe intends to convey that the person engages in or has a propensity or intent to engage in homosexual acts. A statement such as "I am a homosexual" or "I have a homosexual orientation" fits this criteria. Propensity is more than an abstract preference or desire to engage in homosexual acts; it indicates the likelihood or will to engage in homosexual acts.

Although applicants for entry into the armed forces are not asked to reveal their sexual orientation or whether they have engaged in homosexual conduct, all applicants are informed of the separation policy for homosexual conduct, as defined above. Commanders must initiate separation action if there is probable cause to believe a servicemember engaged in homosexual conduct (acts or statements, or marriage or attempted marriage).

Servicemembers should be aware that this legal position is subject to change.

Searches and Seizures. Servicemembers are subject to searches and seizures when legally authorized. These are usually authorized by installation commanders only after they have consulted with the staff judge advocate.

Searches are examinations of an individual, property, or premises with the purpose of finding criminal evidence: contraband, stolen property, and evidence of a crime. Searches may be consensual—that is, with the written or oral consent of the individual whose person, property, or premises are to be searched. Searches without consent can be made with or without probable cause. Without-probable-cause searches are those of government property, within jails, incident to a lawful stop or apprehension, or an entry or exit from military installations, aircraft, or vessels. Probable-cause searches exist when there is reasonable belief that the person, property, or evidence is currently located in a particular place or on a particular individual. Drug dogs can be used at any time in common areas where there is no reasonable expectation of privacy, and they may be used during inspections anywhere within the scope of the inspection, including dormitory rooms, whether the occupant is present or not.

Seizures are the meaningful interference with an individual's possessory interest in property. Individuals, property, and evidence associated or believed to be associated with a crime can be seized.

Urinalysis Program. This program is to detect and deter drug use by servicemembers. There are several categories of urinalysis testing: inspection urinalysis, in which individual members are not singled out for inspection and the entire unit or part of it is tested by random selection; command-directed urinalysis for servicemembers who have displayed aberrant, bizarre, or unlawful behavior or are suspected by their commanders of such behavior; probable-cause urinalysis, in which there is reasonable belief that illegal drugs will be present in the individual's urine; consent urinalysis testing, in which the individuals are told that they do not have to give their consent; and medical urinalysis, in which urine collected for medical reasons is subject to drug testing. Positive urinalysis tests can be the basis for administrative and Uniform Code of Military Justice action.

Smoking. Department of Defense and Air Force policy is to promote a healthy work environment and healthy and fit servicemembers. Smoking cessation programs are offered to help smokers quit. Educational programs are aimed at discouraging smoking; tobacco products cannot be advertised in Air Force publications. Nonsmokers are protected from passive smoking by the prohibition of smoking in almost all facilities, including Air Force vehicles. Smokers and nonsmokers will not be billeted together, and if they must be, smoking is prohibited in the billet. During normal duty hours, smoking is also prohibited to students at the Air Force Academy, basic military training, Officer Training School, Undergraduate Pilot Training, and professional military education courses. Flagrant violations of these policies occasionally occur.

Religious Accommodation. The Air Force recognizes the importance of worship, spiritual health, and religious growth of servicemembers. The Air Force promotes the whole-person concept, which recognizes that individuals reach their full potential when they have developed the emotional, intellectual, physical, and spiritual aspects of their nature.

Commanders attempt to accommodate servicemembers' religious practices, such as holidays and dietary restrictions. Still, respect for religious beliefs should not infringe on military readiness, unit cohesion, standards, or discipline. When accommodation is not possible, the individual must conform to military requirements or face disciplinary action, administrative separation, or reassignment or reclassification.

Religious apparel that is part of the religious faith practiced by a servicemember may be worn if it is not visible and if it does not interfere with the proper wear of the uniform. Visible items of religious apparel must be authorized individually.

Liability Regarding Classified Documents. By the very nature of their duties, most officers are required to have access to and use classified documents. Officers must be mindful of the restrictions placed upon such documents and the punitive actions that may be taken against them for improper handling or use.

The inclusion of classified military information in any article, speech, or discussion by a member of the Air Force is prohibited unless specifically authorized:

> Whoever, being entrusted with or having lawful possession or control of any document, writing, code book, signal book, sketch, photograph, photographic negative, blueprint, plan, map, model, note, or information, relating to the national defense, through gross negligence permits the same to be removed from its proper place of custody or delivered to anyone in violation of his trust, or to be lost, stolen, abstracted, or destroyed, shall be punished by imprisonment and may, in the discretion of the court, be fined.

Effect of Disrespectful Language Concerning Certain Government Officials. The 88th Article of the Uniform Code of Military Justice reads as follows:

> Any officer who uses contemptuous words against the President, Vice President, Congress, Secretary of Defense, or a Secretary of a Department, a Governor or a legislature of any State, Territory, or other possession of the United States in which he is on duty or present shall be punished as a court-martial may direct.

Restrictions on Outside Activities. Officers will not engage in or permit their names to be connected with any activity in which participation is incompatible with the status of an officer.

There are limitations on officers and other personnel subject to military law relating to the activities outside of their military duties in which they may properly engage and upon the outside interests they may have without impropriety. Some outside activities and interests are specifically prohibited by statute or policy or both; there are many others from which certain military personnel are barred by the high standards of conduct required of persons in the armed services. The general principle underlying the limitations mentioned above is that every member of the military establishment, when subject to military law, is bound to refrain from all business and professional activities and interests not directly connected with military duties in which participation would tend to interfere with or hamper in any degree full and proper discharge of such duties or would normally give rise to a suspicion that such participation would have that effect. Any substantial departure from this underlying principle would constitute conduct punishable under the articles of the Uniform Code of Military Justice.

It is impossible to enumerate all the various outside activities to which this restriction applies. The following examples are typical: (1) acceptance by an officer or, with the approval of the officer, by a member of the officer's immediate family of a substantial loan or gift from a person or firm with whom it is the officer's duty as an agent of the government to carry on negotiations, or (2) acquisition or possession by an officer of a financial interest in any concern whose business includes the manufacture and sale of articles that it is the duty of the officer to purchase for the government.

An officer who is engaged or who contemplates engaging in outside professional or business activities should learn pertinent laws, policies, and standards of the service to determine whether such activities or interests might be considered in any way incompatible with the proper performance of official duties or in any sense adverse to the interests of the government. If after such investigation there is any doubt, the individual concerned should report all pertinent facts to the Department of the Air Force and request instructions. An officer who has certain outside interests that have no bearing upon the performance of military duties at the time of acquiring such interests, and who is later assigned to duties in the performance of which the possession of such interests might normally be suspected of having an influence adverse to the interests of the government, will immediately dispose of such outside interests and report the facts to superior military authority or without disposing of such interests will report all pertinent facts and circumstances to superior authority with a view to change assignments or such other action as may be deemed appropriate.

Acting as Consultant for Private Enterprise Prohibited. No member of the military establishment on active duty or a civilian employee of the Department of the Air Force shall act as a consultant for a private enterprise with regard to any matter in which the government has an interest.

Assistance to Persons Preparing for Civil Service Examinations Prohibited. No officer or employee of the government will, directly or indirectly, instruct or be concerned in any manner in the instruction of any person with a view to his or her special preparation for the examination of the U.S. Civil Service Commission or of the boards of examiners for the diplomatic and consular services. *The fact that any officer or employee is found so engaged will be considered sufficient cause for removal from the service.*

Solicitation for Contributions for Gifts. Servicemembers are prohibited by law from soliciting contributions from government employees, including fellow servicemembers, for gifts to be presented to those in a superior official position. Very restricted exceptions are made to this policy: Government employees may voluntarily contribute nominal amounts to purchase a superior an inexpensive memento. These mementos are customarily given to superiors, especially commanders, on their departure or retirement. Expensive gifts and involuntary contributions are absolutely forbidden.

Acceptance of Gifts from Subordinates. Superiors do not solicit or accept gifts from subordinates. Not only is pressure, favoritism, or bribery forbidden, but so too is the appearance of illegal behavior. Under restricted circumstances, such as a PCS move or retirement, a superior can accept a nominal gift from subordinates. These customary gifts must have little monetary value; they are merely mementos of service, command, and camaraderie.

Receiving Gifts from Civilian Sources in Recognition of Services Prohibited. The practice of receiving presents from persons not in the military establishment or in the employ of the government in recognition of services or from firms or their representatives with whom the officer has negotiated as an agent of the government is prohibited. Furthermore, officers should ensure that members of their immediate families do not receive or accept contributions or gifts from such persons or firms.

Effect of Refusal of Medical Treatment. A servicemember may be brought to trial by court-martial for refusing to submit to a surgical or dental operation or to medical or dental treatment at the hands of the military authorities if it is designed to restore or increase fitness for service and is without risk of life.

Communication with Members of Congress. Communication with members of Congress by personnel of the Air Force on matters of personal interest is slightly restricted. "No person may restrict any member of an armed force in communicating with a member of Congress, unless the communication is unlawful or violates a regulation necessary to the security of the United States." All members of the Air Force, however, are advised that all legislative matters affecting the Department of the Air Force program shall be conducted through the Office of the Secretary of the Air Force or as authorized by that office. See AFI 90-401, *Air Force Relations with Congress.*

Action on Attempts to Secure Personal Favor. Except when properly made by the officers themselves, requests for personal favor or consideration for any officers will be referred to the officers in question for statement whether they directly or indirectly procured the requests to be made and whether they avow or disavow the request as one on their behalf.

Writing Checks with Insufficient Funds and Payment of Debts. When servicemembers write checks against accounts with insufficient funds or fail to clear their personal accounts before departing for a permanent change of station, they are contributing to a reputation that adversely affects other servicemembers. Such irresponsible financial dealings are intolerable for officers. Creditors can attach a servicemember's bank account or personal property in pursuit of bad debts. Furthermore, up to 25 percent of a servicemember's paycheck (excluding subsistence and housing allowances) can be attached by private creditors to pay overdue debts. To involuntarily garnish a servicemember's pay to satisfy a debt, a creditor must have a court judgment and pay all processing expenses. Base exchanges can garnish up to 67 percent of a servicemember's paycheck. Needless to say, this situation must be avoided; it is morally wrong to incur debts that cannot be paid on time, and to do so negatively reflects on an officer's ability to manage personal affairs.

Restrictions on Using Franked Envelopes and Letterheads. All Department of the Air Force letterheads, envelopes, and other stationery are for OFFICIAL USE ONLY and may not be used as personal stationery.

STANDARDS OF ETHICAL CONDUCT

It is fundamental Air Force policy that personnel will not engage in any personal business or professional activity that places them in a position of conflict between their private interests and the public interest of the United States. To preserve the public confidence in the Air Force, even the appearance of a conflict of interest must be avoided. Air Force personnel shall not use inside information to further a private gain for themselves or others if that information is not generally available to the public and was obtained by reason of their Air Force position.

- Active-duty members may not make personal commercial solicitations or solicited sales to DOD personnel junior in rank at any time (on or off duty, in or out of uniform), specifically for insurance, stocks, mutual funds, real estate, or any other commodity, goods, or services.

- Accepting any gift, entertainment, or thing of value from any person or company that is engaged in procurement activities or business with any agency of the DOD is prohibited. Because interpretation of this paragraph is sometimes difficult, do not hesitate to consult the staff judge advocate.
- Solicitation of contributions for gifts to an official superior (except voluntary gifts or contributions of nominal value on special occasions like marriage, illness, transfer, or retirement) is prohibited.
- Active-duty military or civilian personnel may not use their grades, titles, or positions in connection with any commercial enterprise or for endorsing a commercial product.
- Outside or off-duty employment, if it interferes with or is not compatible with the performance of government duties, or if it might discredit the government, is prohibited. Squadron commanders are normally the approving authority for requests for off-duty employment.
- Air Force personnel, on base or while on duty, may not participate in any unauthorized gambling activity, including football pools. Although this prohibition is widely ignored, especially regarding football pools, the best policy is always to follow established Air Force standards.

20

Pay and Personal Allowances

The most current source for pay and allowance information is Defense Finance and Accounting Services' myPay website at *https://mypay.dfas.mil.* To access this site for your personal pay and allowances you will need your Social Security number and your personal identification number (PIN). If you need a new PIN, just click "need new pin." For help using this site, call 877-363-3677 or 800-321-1080 (retired).

MYPAY PROGRAM
MyPay is a flexible and reliable program; participation is mandatory. It is the primary means for you to view and print your Leave and Earnings Statement, as well as conduct online financial transactions. MyPay allows you to make these online transactions: view and print tax statements, change federal and state tax withholdings, update bank account and electronic fund transfer information, manage allotments, make address changes, purchase U.S. Savings Bonds, view and print travel vouchers, control Thrift Savings Plan enrollment, view and print retiree account statement, view and print annuitant account statement, and update certificate of annuitant eligibility.

FUNDAMENTAL ELEMENTS
An officer's pay and allowances consist of four fundamental elements:
- Basic pay
- Basic allowance for subsistence (BAS)
- Basic allowance for housing (BAH)
- Incentive and special pay

Basic Pay. Basic pay is set by grade and longevity, or years in service. Because of inflation, military pay has increased annually since 1964 to reflect the increased cost of living. This trend seems likely to continue, so consider the accompanying pay table as merely a guide, a reflection of 2008 military pay.

MONTHLY BASIC PAY TABLE (EFFECTIVE 1 JANUARY 2008)

GRADE	<2	2	3	4	6	8	10	12	14	16	18	20	22	24	26
Commissioned officers															
O-10	0.00	0.00	0.00	0.00	0.00	0.00	0.00	0.00	0.00	0.00	0.00	14137.20	14206.30	14501.70	15016.50
O-9	0.00	0.00	0.00	0.00	0.00	0.00	0.00	0.00	0.00	0.00	0.00	12364.80	12542.70	12800.10	13249.20
O-8	8748.90	9035.10	9225.60	9278.70	9516.00	9912.30	10004.70	10381.20	10488.90	10813.50	11282.30	11715.40	12004.20	12004.20	12004.20
O-7	7269.60	7607.40	7763.70	7887.90	8112.60	8334.90	8591.70	8847.90	9105.00	9912.40	10594.20	10594.20	10594.20	10594.20	10647.90
O-6	5388.40	5919.30	6307.80	6307.80	6331.80	6603.30	6639.00	6639.00	7016.40	7683.60	8075.10	8466.30	8688.90	8914.50	9351.90
O-5	4491.60	5059.80	5410.50	5476.20	5694.60	5825.70	6113.10	6324.00	6596.40	7013.70	7212.00	7408.50	7631.10	7631.10	7631.10
O-4	3875.70	4486.50	4785.60	4852.50	5130.30	5428.20	5799.00	6088.20	6288.90	6404.10	6471.00	6471.00	6471.00	6471.00	6471.00
O-3	3407.40	3862.80	4169.40	4545.60	4763.10	5002.20	5157.00	5411.40	5543.40	5543.40	5543.40	5543.40	5543.40	5543.40	5543.40
O-2	2943.90	3353.10	3861.90	3992.40	4074.30	4074.30	4074.30	4074.30	4074.30	4074.30	4074.30	4074.30	4074.30	4074.30	4047.30
O-1	2555.70	2659.80	3215.10	3215.10	3215.10	3215.10	3215.10	3215.10	3215.10	3215.10	3215.10	3215.10	3215.10	3215.10	3215.10
Officers with more than 4 year' active duty as enlisted or warrant officer															
O-3E	0.00	0.00	0.00	4545.60	4763.10	5002.20	5157.00	5411.40	5625.60	5748.60	5916.00	5916.00	5916.00	5916.00	5916.00
O-2E	0.00	0.00	0.00	3992.40	4074.30	4204.20	4423.20	4592.40	4718.40	4718.40	4718.40	4718.40	4718.40	4718.40	4718.40
O-1E	0.00	0.00	0.00	3215.10	3433.80	3560.40	3690.30	3817.80	3992.40	3992.40	3992.40	3992.40	3992.40	3992.40	3992.40

On the other hand, as federal budget constraints increase, cost-of-living allowance (COLA) increases could decrease or end.

Basic Allowances. The basic allowance for subsistence (BAS) is the same for all officers of all grades, with or without dependents.

Basic allowance for housing (BAH) is for officers authorized but not occupying government quarters. The BAH rate is based on the member's rank, marital status, dependency status, and where the member and dependents reside. The tax-free monthly housing allowance follows either of two schedules, with dependents and without dependents. The dependents' schedule is the same regardless of the number of dependents. A "partial rate" BAH is paid to officers living in government bachelor quarters; this BAH is extremely small. "BAH differential" is paid to officers entitled to without-dependent housing or residing in government single quarters and paying court-ordered child support.

Incentive and Special Pay. *Flight pay,* or *aviation career incentive pay,* for aircrew officers ranges from a minimum of $125 a month to a maximum of $840 after 14 years on flying status and at 22 years' service decreases to $585, falling gradually to $250 after 25 years' service. *Hazardous duty incentive pay* is $150–$250 per month for officers. A variety of other hardship, incentive, and special pay is offered to nonrated flying personnel, medical and dental officers, veterinarians, pharmacists, nurses, lawyers, some officers with critical nuclear skills and foreign language proficiency, and so on.

INTERMITTENT AND NONRECURRING ELEMENTS OF PAY AND ALLOWANCES

Uniform Allowance. On commissioning, all officers are entitled to a one-time payment to purchase required uniforms and insignia.

Advance Pay. If authorized by a servicemember's commander, a servicemember may draw permanent-change-of-station (PCS) advance pay of not more than three months' basic pay minus standard deductions (FICA, etc.).

Travel Allowance. A daily allowance (per diem) for each member, as well as a standard mileage reimbursement for the official distance is authorized for servicemembers moving under PCS orders by private vehicle. Per diem rate for dependents is based on age (under 12, 50 percent of member's rate; over 12, 75 percent of member's rate). Two vehicles are authorized for CONUS travel.

Dislocation Allowance. This allowance is to partially reimburse servicemembers for the expense incurred in relocating households from one permanent change of station to the next. Officers' allowances depend on grade and dependent status. It is paid only once in connection to any one PCS and only when dependents have completed travel in connection with a PCS that authorizes transportation of dependents or travel allowances. Dislocation is not paid for the move from home of record to first duty station or from last duty station to retirement home.

Temporary Lodging (Stateside). Servicemembers on PCS orders with families can draw advance payment of temporary lodging expenses.

Temporary Lodging (Overseas, including Alaska and Hawaii). Servicemembers on PCS orders with families can draw advanced payment of temporary lodging allowance.

Advanced Housing Allowance. If authorized by a servicemember's commander, this allowance is paid if money is needed for rental housing in the United States. In the United States, the amount can be as great as 3 months' basic allowance for housing. Overseas, advance housing allowance can be up to 12 months of the overseas housing allowance. Your commander's approval is required on AF Form 1039.

CONUS COLA. This cost-of-living allowance is paid to those living in selected high-cost areas in the United States.

Overseas COLA. Servicemembers stationed in a number of foreign countries, as well as Alaska and Hawaii, may receive an allowance to equalize the overseas cost of living and housing with that in the United States if the overseas cost is greater.

Family Separation Allowance. This allowance is payable only to servicemembers with dependents. It is paid to servicemembers assigned to locations where the Air Force will not move their families or whose military orders separate them from their military spouses. The family separation allowance is a partial reimbursement for daily expenses incurred during the servicemember's separation from family. The family separation allowance is tax free.

Hardship Duty Pay/Hostile Fire Pay. When serving in an officially declared "imminent danger area," at several overseas locations, hardship duty pay varies by location, whereas hostile fire pay is a set amount for all servicemembers. To qualify for the entitlement for the entire month, a member need only be assigned or on TDY to a designated area for one day a calendar month.

DEPENDENTS
Definition. The term "dependents" includes the lawful spouse, and unmarried children and wards of court under 21 years of age, of any member of the uniformed services, and the father or mother of the member, provided he or she is in fact dependent on the member for more than half of his or her support. It also includes unmarried children over 21 years of age who are incapable of self-support because they are mentally or physically incapacitated and who are in fact dependent on the member for more than half of their support. The term *children* includes stepchildren, adopted children, and wards of the court dependent upon the member. The term *father* or *mother* includes a stepparent or parent by adoption and any other person, including a former stepparent, who has stood *in loco parentis* to the person concerned at any time for a continuous period of not less than five years during the minority of the member.

Credit for Dependent Parents. An officer will receive credit for basic allowance for quarters because of a dependent parent only when the dependent parent actually is residing in the household of the officer claiming the increased allowance.

DEDUCTIONS

Social Security Tax. The law requires the Air Force to deduct Social Security taxes (FICA and Medicare) from individual basic pay.

Federal Income Tax. Members of the armed services are subject to the federal law providing for payroll deductions for income tax. Taxable income includes all pay (basic, flight, hazardous duty, incentive, and so on), but does not include subsistence, housing, or family separation allowances.

In special situations, limited federal income-tax relief is granted for servicemembers on duty in designated war zones. For example, officers can exempt an amount not to exceed the amount paid to the highest paid enlisted member. Officers serving in designated income-tax exclusion combat zones should carefully examine Box 1 of their W-2 forms. If their taxable incomes appear too high, they should consult their finance officers or the myPay website.

State Income Tax. Members of the armed services are subject to the laws of their state of legal residence providing for payroll deductions for state income taxes.

INCOME TAX EXEMPTION

Combat Zone Tax Exemption. Members are entitled to CZTE for any month in which they are either in a designated combat zone or assigned to a unit, either permanently or on TDY, in direct support of operations conducted in a combat zone. Servicemembers not entitled to Hazardous Duty Pay or Hostile Fire Pay (due to leave, TDY, etc.) are not entitled to CZTE for that period. For officers, there is a monetary limit for CZTE. Social Security and Medicare withholdings are not impacted by CZTE benefits.

Taxation of Pay for Retired Service Personnel. Members of the armed services who are retired for length of service or age pay the same federal income taxes as other citizens. The same tax withholdings as for active-duty officers are made.

Members retired for physical disability receive an important exemption in the computation of federal income tax. The amount of the exemption depends upon the degree of disability and applies to their active-duty base pay at the time of retirement.

ALLOTMENTS AND STOPPAGES

Allotments. Air Force regulations permit you to make allotments from your pay for various purposes; in fact, they are the preferred method to pay your bills and save money. The word *allotment* means a definite portion of your pay that you authorize the Air Force to pay a financial institution by electronic funds transfer. Of course, you must provide the routing number, account number, and type of account when you complete the allotment paperwork. The *allotter* is the person who makes the allotment, in this case you. The *allottee* is the person or institution to whom you make the allotment. The allottee will receive the full amount of the allotment on the first of the month, although your pay will have been deducted at mid-month and at the end of the month. Generally, you can make an allotment for an indefinite time.

Allotments can make life simpler for you, as you may have to go anywhere in the world at any time for temporary duty or permanent change of station. With allotments, although you still have control of your money, you do not have to write out the checks and mail them every month. You may want to consider making allotments for the following purposes:

- Buying U.S. Savings Bonds
- Donating to charity, including the Combined Federal Campaign
- Supporting dependents
- Repaying home loans
- Paying commercial life insurance premiums
- Adding to savings accounts or investments

Allotments are made on the myPay website.

While Prisoner of War or Reported Missing. Any officer who is interned, taken prisoner of war, or reported missing and who has made an allotment of pay for the support of dependents or for the payment of insurance premiums is entitled to have such allotments or insurance deductions continued for a period of 12 months from the date of commencement of absence. Allotments of officers under any of the above conditions may not continue beyond 12 months following the officially reported date of commencement of absence, except that when that 12 months is about to expire and the Air Force has received no official report of death or of being a prisoner of war or of being interned, the Air Force can fully review the case. Following such review, and when the 12 months' absence has expired, or following any subsequent review of the case, the Air Force may direct the continuance of the officer's missing status if it can be reasonably presumed that the officer is still alive. Such missing officers continue to be entitled to have pay and allowances credited and payment of allotments as authorized to be continued, increased, or initiated.

In the absence of an allotment, or when the allotment is not sufficient for reasonable support of a dependent and for the payment of insurance premiums, the Air Force may direct payment of an appropriate allotment, not to exceed the total basic pay of the person concerned.

Authorized Stoppages. The Air Force may withhold the pay of officers on account of an indebtedness to the United States admitted or shown by the judgment of a court, but not otherwise unless specifically ordered by the secretary of the Air Force.

CREDITABLE SERVICE FOR BASIC PAY

The Department of Defense Financial Management Regulation (DODFMR) establishes the rules for counting the various conditions of active duty in computing cumulative years of service for credit toward basic pay.

Active Duty. You will receive full-time credit for all periods of active duty served in any reserve or regular component of any uniformed service in any military status, commissioned or enlisted.

Retired Status. You will receive additional credit for any period of time you are on any retired list. This provision does *not* increase retired pay, but if you return to active duty from a retired list, you benefit from inclusion of your time on the retired list in computing basic pay.

Academies. Service as a cadet or midshipman in the service academies or ROTC is *not* creditable.

Fraudulent Enlistment. You may receive credit for service in a fraudulent enlistment not voided by the government.

Beginning Dates of Service. Service as an officer begins from the date of acceptance of appointment; as an enlisted member, from the date of enlistment.

REIMBURSEMENT FOR OFFICIAL TRAVEL EXPENSES

Government Travel Card (GTC). The GTC will be used by all U.S. government personnel to pay for costs incident to TDY and PCS official business travel. Fees for the use of this VISA card are reimbursable on completion of your settlement vouchers. Your unit will have a program coordinator who will assist you in card issuance and instruct you on how to use the card.

Per Diem. The per diem allowance, the "Lodging-Plus" system, within the United States and overseas depends upon the city. Rates are updated frequently. Per diem covers the cost of lodging and meals plus incidental expenses. Within the United States, members using commercial air are granted one travel day. Authorized automobile travel days are determined by the number of official miles traveled divided by 350.

Reimbursable Travel Expenses. When traveling under orders, keep a detailed record of all expenses, however minor. Many are reimbursable. Note the following list of reimbursable items:

Lodging. In instances requiring certificates of availability of government quarters and messing facilities, you must adhere to the provisions of the Joint Federal Travel Regulations (JFTR) if you wish to receive proper per diem reimbursement. For PCS moves, Temporary Lodging Expense (TLE) allowance is authorized for a total of 10 days in connection with PCS moves within the United States. Overseas' TLEs differ. If government quarters are not available, commercial lodging must be in the vicinity of the old and/or new PCS station. If you stay with a relative or friend, you will not receive the TLE allowance.

Taxi Fares. You may receive reimbursement for taxi fares between home or business and stations, airports, other carrier terminals or local terminuses of the mode of transportation used, between carrier terminals, while en route when free transfer is not included in the price of the ticket or when necessitated by change in mode of travel, and from carrier terminals to lodgings and return in connection with unavoidable delays en route incident to the mode of travel. Itemization is required.

Allowed Tips. You may receive reimbursement for tips incident to transportation expenses as follows: tips of 15 percent to taxi drivers and tips to baggage porters, not to exceed customary local rates, but not including tips for baggage handling at hotels. Itemization is required, including the number of pieces of baggage handled.

Excess Baggage. When excess baggage is authorized in the orders, actual costs for such excess baggage in addition to that carried free by the carrier are reimbursable.

Telephone and Other Electronic Communication. Cost of official telephone and similar communication services is reimbursable when incident to the official duty or in connection with items of transportation. Such services when solely in connection with reserving a hotel room and so on are not, however, considered official. Copies of messages sent are required for all electronic transmissions unless the message is classified, in which case a full explanation and a receipt will suffice. Local official calls are allowable when itemized. Long-distance calls require full explanations and certification by the orders-issuing official.

Local Public Carrier Fares. Expenses incident to travel by bus or other usual means of transportation may be reimbursable in lieu of taxi fares under certain conditions and limitations. Itemization is required.

Tolls. Ferry fares and road, bridge, and tunnel tolls may be reimbursable. Itemization is required.

Local Transportation. Reimbursement is sometimes authorized on orders for transportation obtained at personal expense in the conduct of official business within and around either the permanent or temporary duty station.

Nonreimbursable Travel Expenses. The government cannot reimburse you for the following travel expenses:

- Travel under permissive orders to travel, in contrast to orders directing travel.
- Travel under orders but not on public business, such as travel as a participant in an athletic contest. Unit or command welfare funds, which come from such sources as operation of exchanges and movie theaters, may reimburse you for such travel, but appropriated funds cannot.
- Return from leave to duty abroad. Unless government transportation is available, such as space on a transport, you must pay your own return expenses from leave in the United States.
- Attendance at public ceremonies or demonstrations paid for by the sponsoring agency.

Certificates of Nonavailability. When government quarters are available, the government will reduce the per diem allowance. If government quarters are not available, you must get certificates or a contact number from the billeting officer of an installation at which you perform temporary duty if you want reimbursement for nongovernment lodging and meals.

Amount of Overseas Travel Allowances. The allowances for TDY travel costs overseas vary. You may expect allowances for necessary expenses provided you use reasonable care. Before undertaking travel outside the United States, you should consult local transportation or financial services officers to determine the exact amount of the expected allowances, which appear in the Joint Federal Travel Regulations.

Preparation of Vouchers for Payment. Consult the local financial services office. Save every receipt from your trip, keep them together with your draft voucher paperwork, and take everything to finance when you file your voucher. Go to finance *before* your TDY trip, get a copy of the voucher, and ask the people at finance what they will need from you. They usually prefer to help travelers before the trip. Occasionally, installations have hand checklists or how-to-take-a-TDY-trip booklets for you. PCS settlement vouchers are paid within 10 days of your in-processing.

WEIGHT ALLOWANCES FOR CHANGE OF STATION

The first table shows weight allowances authorized for shipment of unaccompanied baggage at government expense on change of station; this baggage consists of items you will need immediately on arrival at your destination. The second table below shows weight allowances authorized for shipment of household goods at government expense on change of station.

UNACCOMPANIED BAGGAGE TABLE OF WEIGHT ALLOWANCE (POUNDS)

Grade	Permanent Change of Station
Colonel and above	800
2nd Lieutenant–Lieutenant Colonel	600

HOUSEHOLD GOODS TABLE OF WEIGHT ALLOWANCES
(POUNDS)

Grade	Temporary Change of Station	Permanent Change of Station With Dependents	Without Dependents
General	2,000	18,000	18,000
Lieutenant General	1,500	18,000	18,000
Major General	1,000	18,000	18,000
Brigadier General	1,000	18,000	18,000
Colonel	800	18,000	18,000
Lieutenant Colonel	800	17,500	16,000
Major	800	17,000	14,000
Captain	600	14,500	13,000
1st Lieutenant	600	13,500	12,500
2nd Lieutenant	600	12,000	10,000

21

Leave

The privilege of taking leave is a valuable benefit of military service, and the Air Force encourages its members to take leave. Leave should be used as you earn it and not hoarded to build up large cash payments for unused leave upon discharge or retirement. Periods of cessation from routine work for the purpose of travel, healthful recreation, and diversion are essential to the efficiency of people in the military service. Arrange duties so that both you and your subordinates can take all leave earned. Particularly encourage any members who are exhibiting signs of physical or mental stress to take leave to help lessen the effects of job stress leading to burnout.

Conversely, if you are reluctant to take leave because you are afraid your unit cannot get along without you for two weeks or a month, consider these thoughts: Your unit survived before you arrived; your unit will survive after you leave; if you die today of a heart attack at your duty station, your unit will survive and find time to do the paperwork for your death, attend your funeral, request a replacement, and do your work in the meantime. It is your responsibility to organize your work so that both your seniors and your subordinates can function well in your absence; sometimes, it is good to let them miss you for a while.

AIR FORCE POLICIES

Commanders will ensure that members of their commands have an opportunity and the encouragement to take leave. Commanders at all levels should encourage people in their commands to avail themselves frequently of accrued leave, and subject only to military necessity, all commanders will approve such requests of leave.

Commanders should bear in mind that the persistence of conditions within their commands in time of peace that preclude granting leave to their officers is an indication of poor organization, administration, or leadership. No military organization should rest on seemingly indispensable people. Moreover, commanders who grumble that they are so short of officers that they "can't afford" to permit their officers to take leave are admitting that they have no workable plan to meet the occurrence of sickness, accident, or death among their officers.

TYPES OF LEAVE

Ordinary Leave. Leave the Air Force grants upon your request at any time during a fiscal year to the extent of the leave that you may earn during that fiscal year, plus your leave credit from previous years.

Sick or Convalescent Leave. Leave the Air Force grants for absence because of illness or convalescence upon recommendation of the surgeon. It is not chargeable as leave.

Advance Leave. The Air Force may grant advance leave in anticipation of the future accrual of leave. In the case of officers, such leave would apply in case of emergency leave and pre-embarkation leave.

Emergency Leave. Leave the Air Force may grant upon assurance that an emergency exists and that granting of such leave will contribute to the alleviation of the emergency. The total leave advanced, including emergency leave, may not exceed 45 days. Emergency leave does not affect granting future leave, but the Air Force does charge it against present or future accrued leave.

Excess Leave. Leave the Air Force grants that is in excess of the amount you have accrued, except for such advance or ordinary leave as specifically authorized, without pay and allowances, and that you may take only under exceptional circumstances upon authority of commanders up to 30 days and of the Department of the Air Force for more than 30 days. Of course, this leave is chargeable.

Prenatal and Postpartum Leave. Women who become pregnant while on active duty can go into "sick in quarters" status about four weeks before delivery, if determined necessary by the attending physician. Time spent in the hospital for delivery is duty time. Following completion of inpatient care, the member receives convalescent leave until her medical condition permits her to return to duty, normally not more than six weeks after her release from the hospital.

Delays En Route in Executing Travel. The Air Force counts and charges as leave authorized delays stated in travel orders.

COMPUTATION OF LEAVE CREDITS

The Air Force credits leave on a fiscal year basis. In any case in which the Air Force considers only a part of the fiscal year, it will prorate earned leave at the rate of $2^1/2$ days for each month of active (honorable) service.

Leave may not accumulate in excess of 60 days (except that personnel in a combat zone may accumulate 90 days). Members of USAF Reserve Forces ordered to active duty for periods of 30 days or more will receive leave in accordance with these computations. Those ordered to active duty for periods of less than 30 days will not receive leave.

COMPENSATION WHILE ON LEAVE

Personnel in the following circumstances shall receive the same pay and allowances while on leave that they would receive if on duty status: when absent on sick or convalescent leave; absent with leave not exceeding the aggregate number of days of leave standing to their credit or authorized to be advanced to their credit; and absent awaiting orders on disability retirement proceedings in excess of the number of days of leave accrued or authorized.

Personnel granted excess leave shall receive no pay or allowances while absent from duty. The Air Force may, however, grant advance leave with pay and allowances, but if the member is separated before accruing sufficient leave to cover the advance leave, the Air Force will consider the unaccrued portion excess leave without pay and allowances.

APPLICATION FOR LEAVE

Airmen throughout the Air Force use an automated online leave system called *LeaveWeb,* which allows airmen to submit leave requests, coordinate leave with supervisors and orderly rooms, receive approvals, and notify the finance office electronically, thus saving time and improving customer service.

LEAVE TO VISIT OUTSIDE THE UNITED STATES

Air Force officers may visit foreign countries on leave, either from the United States or from their overseas stations. Such leaves are chargeable as ordinary leave.

WARNINGS

As an officer, you are responsible to report to your duty station, not just any Air Force base, at the expiration of your leave. You may use military air transport on a space-available basis during leave, but a delay in securing a flight is no excuse for failing to return from leave on time.

HOLIDAYS

The following days in each year are public holidays established by law. The Air Force observes them except when military reasons prevent:

New Year's Day—January 1
Martin Luther King's Birthday—third Monday in January
Washington's Birthday—third Monday in February
Memorial Day—last Monday in May
Independence Day—July 4
Labor Day—first Monday in September
Columbus Day—second Monday in October
Veterans Day—November 11
Thanksgiving Day—fourth Thursday in November
Christmas Day—December 25

When a holiday falls on a Sunday, the following day is a holiday. When a holiday falls on Saturday, the preceding day is a holiday.

Above all, use your leave and holidays as time for relaxation and rejuvenation. Have fun, but take it easy.

22

Medical Care

Servicemembers cannot function at peak performance if they are not fit and in good health. Individuals who are distracted by sickness or health problems of family members are also incapable of full concentration on their work duties. Consequently, the Air Force provides medical and dental care, in varying degrees, to servicemembers and their families. Many consider medical and dental care as primary benefits of service in the Air Force.

Medical and dental care for servicemembers is free of charge. If the required specialists are unavailable at your duty station, you will be medevaced to a regional military hospital or referred to local civilian physicians or hospitals.

As the Air Force is concerned with preventive medicine, periodic medical and dental examinations are required of servicemembers. Frequency varies depending on job specialty; flying personnel, for example, are given annual flight physicals. Fitness and weight programs, as well as antitobacco campaigns and emphasis on use of alcohol in moderation, are also efforts to maintain the health and fitness of servicemembers.

Medical and dental care for families of active-duty servicemembers and for retirees and their families has been provided on an as-available basis. For some years the capacity of Air Force medical facilities has been overloaded. Several programs have been tried to remedy the deteriorating situation.

TRICARE

TRICARE is DOD's health-care program for active-duty and retired military personnel, their families, and their survivors. The program's objectives are to improve beneficiary access to health care, assure affordable and high-quality care, provide choice, and contain costs to both beneficiaries and the DOD. For the most up-to-date information on TRICARE, see *http://www.tricare.mil.* The TRICARE system is underfunded; conflicting solutions are being proposed. The system is and can be expected to be in flux for the indefinite future, but all servicemembers, active and retired, should assume that benefits will be further eroded rather than confirmed or expanded.

TRICARE's Health Service Regions, each with a lead agent, coordinate regional health-care delivery between military treatment facilities (MTFs) and civilian health-care providers. The regional lead agents oversee contracts with civilian managed care companies that establish civilian health-care networks for beneficiaries to use when care is not available in the MTFs. TRICARE service centers are established at or near each military installation to assist beneficiaries in obtaining care and services.

Beneficiaries have options for seeking care: TRICARE Standard, TRICARE Extra, and TRICARE Prime. In addition to these three options, there are other TRICARE coverages, such as TRICARE Prime Remote, TRICARE Senior Pharmacy, and TRICARE for Life. The latter is for retirees over 65 years of age who are enrolled in Medicare Part B. Each TRICARE option has different cost-sharing features and degrees of freedom for using civilian providers. All options require that participants be listed as eligible in the Defense Enrollment Eligibility Reporting System (DEERS), which is accomplished at the nearest Uniformed Services Personnel Office (military personnel flight) and can be updated online at *http://www.tricare.mil/mybenefit/ProfileFilter.do.* Comparison and contrast of the three options is complicated; the decision is extremely important. Before selecting an option, an officer should study the informational materials available from the health benefits advisor at the nearest military medical facility, from the beneficiary counseling and assistance coordinator at your TRICARE region's lead agent office, from the regional TRICARE contractor's local TRICARE service center, and from *http://www.tricare.mil.*

TRICARE Standard has no annual enrollment fee. Beneficiaries can use non-network civilian providers of their choice, but pay a deductible and cost share. Standard is especially useful to beneficiaries who do not live within an established physicians' network area. This option offers the most freedom to choose a provider, but costs will be higher than with the other two TRICARE options. You may have to file your own claim forms and perhaps pay up to 15 percent more for allowable charges if your selected provider does not participate in TRICARE Standard. Providers that do participate accept the TRICARE Standard allowable charges as the full fee for care provided and will file the claims. TRICARE Standard beneficiaries must meet an annual outpatient deductible.

TRICARE Extra has no annual fee. Beneficiaries maintain their freedom of choice, but can elect to occasionally use network providers. Extra is exactly like Standard, but beneficiaries can seek care from a provider that is part of the TRICARE network (listed in the TRICARE contractor's directory of providers, on the contractor's website, or at the TRICARE service center); get a discount on services; and pay reduced cost shares (5 percent below those of TRICARE Standard) in most cases. TRICARE Extra beneficiaries do not have to file claims. Beneficiaries must meet an annual outpatient deductible. TRICARE Extra beneficiaries can use a military medical facility on a space-available basis.

TRICARE Prime is the only option that requires enrollment, and approximately two-thirds of TRICARE participants select Prime. Active-duty members and their families do not pay an annual enrollment fee or annual deductibles, and they do not pay co-pays or cost shares when using a military medical facility. Retirees (under 65 years of age) and their families selecting TRICARE Prime do pay an annual enrollment fee, but they do not pay annual deductibles. Prime is similar to a civilian health maintenance organization (HMO). TRICARE Prime beneficiaries either choose or are assigned a primary care manager (PCM), who will provide routine health care. The PCM will manage all aspects of the beneficiary's care, including referrals to specialists before care can be given. Except in emergency situations, if care is received before approval, there is an annual deductible, and after the deductible is met, the TRICARE Prime beneficiary must meet 50 percent of the TRICARE allowable charge. In addition to the services covered by TRICARE Standard, TRICARE Prime offers preventive and primary care services.

Before TRICARE Prime was an option, it was wise for servicemembers to carry a supplemental insurance to cover medical expenses of their families that would not be reimbursed by the Air Force. Retirees and their families also were wise to carry supplemental insurance. Theoretically, this is no longer so critical for those selecting TRICARE Prime, but those selecting TRICARE Standard or Extra, may want to continue carrying supplemental insurance through military-associated insurance companies and service associations that offer such services to their members. Those carrying TRICARE Prime should also seriously consider supplemental insurance.

TRICARE for Life, a Medicare wraparound coverage, is available worldwide for Medicare-eligible uniformed services beneficiaries, their eligible family members, and survivors. Participation requires annual purchase of Medicare Part B coverage. In most cases, Medicare pays first and TRICARE for Life pays its share of the remaining expenses second.

TRICARE ACTIVE-DUTY FAMILY MEMBER DENTAL PLAN

Dental care is provided to all servicemembers. At overseas locations, dental care for the families of active-duty servicemembers is provided on a very limited, space-available basis. (Dental care is essentially nonexistent for retirees and their families.)

The TRICARE Active-Duty Family Member Dental Plan is available for the families of active-duty servicemembers for a monthly premium for the servicemember's spouse only or for spouse and children. Premiums change from time to time. What dental services are covered, the limits of co-payments for specific services, and so forth are rather complicated. A pamphlet is available at your base medical facility. The monthly premium is so reasonable—it is supplemented by the government—that you should decline participation only in the most unusual circumstances.

23

Voluntary and Involuntary Separations

There are voluntary and involuntary separations from the Air Force, as well as retirement.

From time to time, active duty service commitments for some specialties are reduced or waived to reduce Air Force end strength to conform to Congressional manpower authorizations. These programs are the Palace Chase and the Limited Active Duty Service Commitment Waiver Programs. Officers interested in these programs should consult their military personnel flights.

INVOLUNTARY SEPARATION
Under the provisions of pertinent sections of Title 10, U.S. Code, the Air Force may discharge officers for moral or professional dereliction, in interests of national security, or for substandard performance of duty. The following are reasons for initiating action to determine whether a regular or reserve officer should be retained in the Air Force:
- Financial irresponsibility.
- Mismanagement of personal or government affairs.
- Recurrent misconduct.
- Drug or alcohol abuse.
- Failure at any school, when attendance at the school is at government expense, if the failure resulted from factors over which the officer had control.
- Failure to conform to prescribed standards of dress, personal appearance, or military deportment.
- Defective attitude.
- Retention is not clearly consistent with the interests of national security.
- Misrepresentation or omission of material facts in official written or oral statements or documents.

- Failure to demonstrate acceptable qualities of leadership required of officers of that grade.
- Failure to demonstrate acceptable standards of professional (including technical) proficiency required of officers of that grade.
- A progressive falling off of duty performance resulting in an unacceptable standard of efficiency.
- Homosexual behavior.
- A record of marginal service over an extended period of time as indicated by performance reports.
- Failure to properly discharge assignments commensurate with grade and experience.
- Fear of flying.

Commanders may recommend initiation of action when they determine that action is appropriate.

Officers against whom separation action is initiated may submit written statements or other documentary evidence they feel should be considered in evaluating their cases, may tender their resignations, or may apply for retirement, if eligible.

If an officer does not tender resignation or apply for voluntary retirement, and if the major commander determines that further action is warranted, the case is referred to a selection board. If the selection board determines that the officer should be required to show cause for retention in the Air Force, the major commander convenes a board of inquiry. The board of inquiry examines witnesses and documentary evidence and then recommends that the officer be retained or removed from active duty. The major commander sends the board of inquiry report to Headquarters USAF, where the case is reviewed by a board of review and final action is taken by the secretary of the Air Force.

Rights of Officers Required to Show Cause for Retention. The recorder invites witnesses, both for the officer and for the government, to appear if the legal advisor judges that they are reasonably available and that their testimony can contribute materially to the case.

Officers may tender their resignations or apply for voluntary retirement, if eligible, before the secretary of the Air Force makes a final decision.

Involuntary Release of Nonregular Officers. Air Force policy requires the involuntary release from active duty of reserve officers not promoted to the next higher grade, due to insufficient retainability for permanent change of station, and because of failure to complete flying or technical training.

Officers serving in the grade of second lieutenant, first lieutenant, or captain are released from active duty when they are not promoted to the next higher grade. Second lieutenants are released when they do not qualify for promotion. First lieutenants and captains are released when they are passed over twice.

Involuntary Discharge of Regular and Nonregular Officers—Failure of Promotion to Their Next Higher Permanent Grade. Title 10, U.S. Code, requires the involuntary discharge of first lieutenants, captains, and majors who are twice passed over for promotion to their next higher grade and who are not eligible for retirement or for retention to qualify for retirement.

Second lieutenants are honorably discharged when they are not qualified for promotion.

Active Duty Service Commitments for New Officers. Newly commissioned officers' active-duty service commitments vary from four to ten years following their date of commissioning depending on source of commission, service training, and speciality (AFSC). See chapter 9.

SELECTIVE CONTINUATION PROGRAM

Captains and Majors. Officers with the regular grade of captain or major who are subject to discharge or retirement because they were not selected for promotion may, subject to the needs of the service, continue on active duty if they are chosen by a selection board with the approval of the secretary of the Air Force. Captains may not continue on active duty under this program for a period that extends beyond the last day of the month in which they complete 20 years of active commissioned service unless they are promoted to the regular grade of major. Majors may not continue on active duty under this program for a period that extends beyond the last day of the month in which they complete 24 years of active commissioned service unless they are promoted to the regular grade of lieutenant colonel.

Officers selected for continuation on active duty who are not subsequently promoted or continued on active duty and who are not on a list of officers recommended for continuation or for promotion to the next high grade shall, unless sooner retired or discharged under another provision of law, be discharged upon the expiration of the period of continued service or, if eligible, be retired. Officers who would otherwise be discharged and who are within two years of qualifying for retirement under some provision of law shall continue on active duty until qualified for retirement under that law, and then be retired.

Lieutenant Colonels, Colonels, Brigadier Generals, and Major Generals. Officers with the regular grade of lieutenant colonel, colonel, brigadier general, or major general who are subject to retirement for years of service may, subject to the needs of the service, defer retirement and continue on active duty if chosen by a selection board with the approval of the secretary of the Air Force.

Above Major General. Officers subject to retirement for years of service who are serving in a grade above major general may, subject to the needs of the service, defer retirement and continue on active duty by order of the president.

Length of Deferral. Any deferrals of retirement and continuation on active duty under the Selection Continuation Program shall be for a period not to exceed five years, and not to extend beyond the date of the officer's 62nd birthday.

Declining Deferral. Officers selected for continuation on active duty who decline to continue on active duty shall be discharged, retired, or retained on active duty, as appropriate.

VOLUNTARY SEPARATION

The right of officers to resign their commissions or to request release from active duty is subject to certain restrictions growing out of their military status. The president or the secretary of the Air Force may accept a resignation or request for release, as appropriate, through any properly designated office.

Normally, a tendered resignation or request for release from extended active duty will be approved. However, an application for separation may be disapproved when an officer is under investigation; is under charges or awaiting result of trial; is absent without leave; is absent in hands of civil authorities; is insane; is in default with respect to public property or funds; is serving under a suspended sentence to dismissal; has an unfulfilled active-duty service obligation or agreement; is serving in time of war or when war is imminent, or in a period of emergency declared by the president or Congress; or in any other instance where the best interest of the Air Force requires retention.

A resignation or request for release must contain a complete statement of reasons and, when appropriate, documentary evidence to substantiate the reasons given.

Resignation for Hardship. Officers may tender their resignations when their retention in the service causes undue hardship to themselves or to members of their families. In such instances, they must include documentary evidence with their applications.

Resignation as Conscientious Objector. A tender of resignation based on conscientious objection is handled on an individual basis. The secretary of the Air Force makes the final determination based on the facts and circumstances. The officer must be conscientiously opposed to participation in war in any form; opposition must be founded on training and on a sincere and deeply held belief.

Resignation in Lieu of Demotion or Elimination from Service. Officers under consideration for demotion or elimination may tender their resignations in lieu of further proceedings.

Presumably, officers who believe their cases are worthy would elect to have the proceedings continue. But if they consider elimination or demotion almost a certainty, and are unwilling to accept demotion, they may choose to resign rather than submit to the embarrassment of having their shortcomings aired before a board of fellow officers.

Resignation for the Good of the Service. A resignation "for the good of the service" is a serious matter. Such resignations are used under the following conditions: Officers who can be tried by court-martial for their conduct may tender their resignations for the good of the service if charges have not been preferred; or they may tender their resignations for the good of the service in lieu of trial if formal charges have been preferred or if they are under suspended sentence.

The Air Force will not usually accept such a resignation when the offense or conduct is such that a court-martial would result in a punishment more severe than dismissal. For example, an officer accused of fraud that might result in confinement in a penitentiary would not be permitted to resign for the good of the service. Historically, this form of resignation has been used in lieu of trial when an officer is accused of serious transgressions of moral codes or other unofficer-like conduct that would result in no greater sentence than dismissal after a court-martial.

24

Retirement

Retirement from the Air Force, in most cases, ends a successful military career and opens the way to a new career or to years of modest leisure. There are, however, other mandatory or voluntary versions of retirement. Some such retirements are the result of dire physical disability: Dangers inherent in Air Force life make disability retirements not uncommon.

The Air Force Personnel Center at Randolph Air Force Base offers retirees a web page designed specifically for information on retiree issues: *http://www .afpc.randolph.af.mil/AFretire.* The website has a directory assistance, which lists telephone numbers and addresses to a variety of resources. Retirees will also find the *Retired Military Almanac* useful. It can be purchased in most exchanges. AFRP 36-1, *USAF News for Retired Personnel (Afterburner),* the official Air Force retiree newsletter, is published periodically and mailed to every retiree who receives retired pay. It is also available online at the Randolph website above. *Afterburner* is an excellent way to keep current on legislative and other changes that affect retired members and their dependents and survivors.

TRANSITION TO RETIRED STATUS
Retirement can be a time of pleasure or difficulty, depending on your attitude, how well you have prepared yourself, and the resources that are available to you. The following actions can help you enjoy your retirement more:

Have a positive attitude. A positive attitude is a good starting point for a successful retirement. People often think about retirement as an end of a career, the beginning of a lifestyle of leisure, or a transition from the past to the future. Those who think of retirement as an end to a career may find their retirement rather difficult as they try to hang on to the past. Those who think of retirement only as a time for relaxation may fail to face future responsibilities. A more realistic outlook toward retirement is to think of it as a time of transition and a time of moving out of past responsibilities and relationships into new ones. In other words, it is a time of change during which you let go of some of the past, take part of the past with you, and develop new strategies for the future. The way you go about making this transition will influence how successful your retirement will be. Remember that it is natural to experience anxiety due to the uncertainties of retirement.

Prepare early. You began preparing for retirement as a young officer when you started your career and realized that at some time in the future you would retire. Over your years of active service, you should take a number of steps to prepare for retirement. The more preparation you make, the easier your retirement transition will be. Every career officer needs to have a retirement plan.

Develop a variety of interests. People who put 100 percent into their work may experience a highly successful career but a devastating retirement. On the other hand, those who develop a variety of skills and interests while remaining dedicated to their work will experience an easier transition into retirement. Think about your interests and start developing activities you want to participate in during your retirement.

Make a realistic appraisal of your accomplishments. Retirement is often a time when people think about what they wanted to accomplish during their career and compare their desired accomplishments with what they have actually achieved. Be realistic about what you have accomplished and focus on your achievements. You cannot go back and change the past. Now is the time to think about the future and set realistic goals for your retirement.

Structure your activities. People who retire with the idea that they will do what they want when they feel like it often become dissatisfied. On the other hand, those who have made some decisions about what activities they want to do, and have scheduled specific times for them, usually experience more satisfaction in retirement. Many people follow through with their past work skills by working part-time, consulting, or doing volunteer work. Others use different skills they have developed, and many people go back to school.

Live within your means. Many people look forward to a comfortable retirement only to find that their retirement pay does not go as far as they thought it would. Those who saved, invested, and insured themselves for their retirement will be more comfortable financially than those who did not. Regardless of your financial resources, it is important that you adapt to a lifestyle that is within your means.

Be prepared for different levels of responsibilities. The levels of responsibility people experience after retirement are often much different than during their military career.

Understand the impact of your retirement on your family. Your family and friends will also need to adjust to your retirement. The changes associated with retirement will have an impact on each of them. Discussing these changes with them can ease potential problems in your relationship with them.

Develop new support systems. Next to your family, your work group may be the strongest emotional support system you have experienced. The loss of your work group can be emotionally painful and leave a void in your life. Getting involved in new groups, such as clubs, sports, or church, can be very important for a successful retirement transition.

Prepare for a move. If you move to a new geographical location in conjunction with your retirement, there will be many more factors to adjust to than if you remain in the same community. There are often a number of community resources that can ease your move and help you and your family get established. Find out about these resources, and get involved in your new community.

The success of your transition into retirement will be directly influenced by your own choices and actions. By preparing early and developing a sound retirement plan, you can significantly reduce the problems many retirees face.

VOLUNTARY RETIREMENT

After 20 Years' Service. Twenty years' service is still the basis for a full military career and retirement. After 20 years on active duty, officers are eligible for retirement pay. Retirement pay is tied to basic pay, but not to bonuses and allowances. Whereas active-duty officers begin drawing retired pay immediately after separation, eligible reservists must wait until their 60th birthday to begin drawing retired pay.

In efforts to reduce the burden of military retired pay on the federal treasury, the Congress changed the retired pay compensation formulas twice in the 1980s. The formula may, of course, be changed again. Currently, there are three formulas for computing 20-year retired pay. Which formula is used depends on the date an officer entered military service, usually the day reporting for active duty. Reservists, military academy cadets, and ROTC cadets, however, are eligible for the retirement system in effect when they entered the reserves, a federal military academy, or a delayed-entry program, such as ROTC.

Excluding the requirements for retirements based on physical disabilities, the three formulas now in effect are as follows:

- **Final Pay.** For retirees who entered military service before 8 September 1980, monthly checks are based on retired grade and number of years served on active duty. Beginning at half basic pay after 20 years' service, 2.5 percent of basic pay is added for each additional year served. For example, after 30 years' active service, the retiree draws 75 percent basic pay. Annual cost-of-living adjustments (COLAs) are attempts to compensate for inflation.

- **High-3 Year Average.** For those who entered military service after 7 September 1980 and before 1 August 1986, the "high three" formula applies. Retired pay is based on the average basic pay for the 36 months with the highest earnings, rather than on basic pay at retirement. That yearly average is multiplied by 2.5 percent for each year on active duty to determine retired pay. Officers retiring under this formula will receive less retirement compensation than those who entered military service before 8 September 1980. These retirees are also entitled to annual COLAs.

- **CBS/REDUX.** Those who enter military service after 31 July 1986 have two choice to be made when reaching 15 years Total Active Federal Military Service: (1) High-3 Year Average retirement as described above or (2) Military Retirement Reform Act of 1986 (REDUX as amended by the FY00 National Defense Authorization Act), plus a $30,000 Career Status Bonus (CSB). Because the REDUX multiplier increases the longer the service and because of annual cost of living adjustments and a catch-up increase at age 62—in addition to the $30,000 CSB, the service member with this choice must be extremely careful calculating the relative monetary merits of selecting either the High-3 Year Average retirement plan or REDUX/CSB.

RETIREMENT FOR PHYSICAL DISABILITY

The Career Compensation Act established a very important departure in remuneration following separation from active service as a result of physical disability. No member is retired for physical disability if the disability is less than 30 percent, unless the member has at least 20 years' service.

The first stage in any proceeding for separation for physical reasons is a finding by the service that members, by reason of a disability, are not qualified to perform their duties. If members are kept on duty, there are, of course, no separation proceedings. But if a finding is made that the members *cannot* be retained in service, the proceedings enter a second stage. If the disability resulted from "intentional misconduct" or "willful neglect" or was incurred during unauthorized absence, the government gives the members nothing, but merely separates them.

If the disability was *not* due to misconduct or neglect, the next question is: Is the disability 30 percent or more under the VA standard rating? If the disability is less than 30 percent, and the member has less than 20 years' service, no retirement is given. Instead, the servicemember is given *severance pay,* which is two months' basic active-duty pay for each year of active service, to a maximum of two full years' active pay.

Types of Disability Retirement. Two types of disability retirement are possible. If the disability is obviously permanent, retirement is final. But if the Personnel Evaluation Board has any question about the permanency of the disability, the servicemember goes on a temporary disability.

Persons who have completed 20 years' active service are entitled to retirement even if their disability is less than 30 percent.

If you are facing retirement for disability, you should study all methods of compensation—including VA compensation—weighing the income-tax factor, if any, before making a decision.

Disability Claims. Regardless of whether or not a member is retired for disability from the Air Force, a claim should be filed with the VA at the time of retirement through the military personnel facility. Compensation awarded by the VA is tax exempt, but has required the waiver of an equal amount of Air Force retired pay. Over the decade, the 2004 National Defense Authorization Act will phase out the VA disability offset to military retirees. However, concurrent retirement disability payments will be for 20-year retirees who have a VA-rated, service-connected disability of 50 percent or higher. Disability retirees with less that 20 years of service or retirees who have combined their military and civil service times to qualify for a civil service retirement are ineligible. Furthermore, the 2004 act also broadened the Combat Related Special Compensation benefit to include all combat- or operations-related disabilities that have been service-connected by the VA at 10 percent or higher.

VA disability compensation is paid based upon the percent of disability and ranges from approximately $100 to over $2,000 monthly. These rates are subject to change annually according to the law providing cost-of-living adjustments. If you are an eligible veteran who suffers certain specific severe disabilities, you may be paid up to approximately $4,000 a month, but this is determined on an individual basis. If your service-connected disabilities are rated 30 percent or more, you are entitled to additional allowances for dependents. If VA compensation is reduced or discontinued at some later date, Air Force retired pay will be adjusted accordingly.

STATUTORY AGE RETIREMENT

Unless retired or separated earlier, commissioned officers will be retired on the first day of the month following the month in which they become 62 years of age. The president may defer the retirement of an officer serving in a position that carries a grade above major general.

MANDATORY RETIREMENT

Unless provided otherwise by some provision of law, mandatory retirement for lieutenant colonels is 28 years of active service; colonels and brigadier generals, 30 years; and major generals, 35 years.

RETIRED GRADE, RANK, AND STATUS

Commissioned officers shall be retired in the highest grade in which they served on active duty satisfactorily for not less than six months, as determined by the secretary of the Air Force. To be eligible for voluntary retirement in a grade above major or below lieutenant general, commissioned officers must have served on active duty in that grade for not less than three years.

Officers whose length of service in the highest grade they held while on active duty does not meet the service-in-grade requirements specified will be retired in the next lower grade in which they served on active duty satisfactorily for not less than six months. Upon retirement, officers who are serving in or have served in a position of importance and responsibility designated by the president to carry the grade of general or lieutenant general may, at the discretion of the president, be retired, by and with the consent of the Senate, in the highest grade held by them while serving on active duty. Exceptions to the above have been made to facilitate the reduction in force, such as after the end of the Cold War and to reduce force strength through Palace Chase and the Limited Active Duty Service Commitment Waiver Program.

Increases of Retired Pay. Retired pay is increased in accord with rises in the Consumer Price Index. Increases, however, have been altered by the Congress.

MISCELLANEOUS

Medical Care. For retiree medical benefits, see chapter 22.

Government Employment of Officers after Retirement. In 1964, Congress authorized the federal government to employ retired regular officers on a basis of compensation making it feasible for the retired regular officer to accept such employment. It is now possible for the retired regular officer to receive the full pay of a civilian government job, plus the officer's full retirement pay. Retired military officers may not be hired by the Department of Defense for at least six months after their retirement.

Residence and Travel Abroad. Permission to travel and reside in a foreign country is not required of retired Air Force personnel, except for personnel who occupied "sensitive" positions or acquired "sensitive" information before retirement. Officers restricted because of access to "sensitive" counterintelligence information should correspond with Headquarters, Air Force Office of Special Investigations.

Officers' requests for retirement at foreign service stations, if otherwise appropriate, normally will be approved by the Department of the Air Force. Such approval will not be given if it becomes necessary to return them to the United States for hospitalization or other purposes of the government, and they will not be returned to an overseas station solely for the purpose of retirement there. The officers may, however, obtain authority for foreign residence or travel, after retirement, as indicated above.

Travel to Home. Officers of the Regular Air Force are presumed to have no established home. They may select and proceed to a home at government expense, so far as authorized, at any place they intend to establish a bona fide home at any time within one year after retirement.

Travel of Retired Personnel by Military Transport. An important privilege for specified retired personnel is space-available (space-A) transportation. Space-A means space unassigned after all space requirement travel assignments have been made and space that would otherwise be unused if not authorized and assigned to the use indicated. There is a nominal charge to cover meals and service.

Applications for space-available travel are to be submitted to the appropriate terminal authority, who acts on them on a first-come, first-served basis. Retirees have the lowest priority for space-A seats. Return transportation cannot be ensured; return by commercial transportation may be necessary at personal expense.

Retired Officer Status. An Air Force officer placed on the retired list is still an officer of the United States.

Change in Status after Retirement. In the absence of fraud, the retirement of an officer under a particular statute exhausts the power of the president and the secretary of the Air Force, and the record of executive action cannot be revoked or modified so as to make retirement relate to another statute, even though the case were one to which more than one statute properly applied at the time retirement was accomplished. Further, the statutes relating to retirement apply only to officers on the active list, and there is no authority for the restoration of a retired officer to the active list for the purpose of being again retired.

RETIREMENT OF AIR NATIONAL GUARD AND AIR FORCE RESERVE OFFICERS

Retirement for Physical Disability. The laws governing retirement for physical disability apply equally to all officers on active military duty whether of the Regular Air Force or of the Air Reserve Forces.

Retirement for Age and Length of Service. Chapter 67, Title 10, U.S. Code, establishes retirement opportunities for AF Reserve and Air National Guard officers who attain age 60 and who satisfy stated requirements of service or service credits described in the law as "points."

Officers of the Air National Guard and AF Reserve should have their own records of service carefully checked and verified establishing their retirement credits.

Retirement pay does not reduce other retirement benefits, such as that which may accrue from Social Security legislation or civil service retirement pay, nor should it serve to reduce retirement pay earned by participating in retirement programs of corporations or other employers.

MILITARY OFFICERS ASSOCIATION OF AMERICA

The purpose of the Military Officers Association (MOAA) is to aid all personnel of the various services and components. This nonprofit, veterans' association is dedicated to maintaining a strong national defense and to preserving the earned entitlements of members of the uniformed services, their families, and survivors. Regardless of years in service, all military officers should belong to this association. Membership is open to active-duty and retired officers and to those who have held a warrant or commission in the Army, Marine Corps, Navy, Air Force, Coast Guard, and Public Health Service, as well as to their surviving spouses. MOAA, 201 N. Washington Street, Alexandria, VA 22314-2539; 800-234-6622, *http://www.moaa.org.*

25

Benefits after Separation

During military service, all servicemembers accrue certain rights and privileges under various public laws that will be available to them after discharge, release from active duty, or retirement. The administration and payment of these benefits are the responsibility of the Department of Veterans Affairs (VA). Entitlement to benefits varies with length, time, and type of service, as well as disabilities incurred in service. In all cases in which veterans desire to apply for one or more of these statutory benefits, they should obtain all necessary information from the nearest VA office or consulting the Department of Veterans Affairs web site at *www.va.gov.*

Federal Benefits for Veterans and Dependents, a publication of the VA Office of Public Affairs, is another excellent source of information. It is available through *www.va.gov.* To order the handbook, write to the Superintendent of Documents, U.S. Government Printing Office, Washington, D.C. 20402 and ask for GPO stock number 051-000-00227-0. The remainder of this chapter is extracted from this publication.

Eligibility for most VA benefits is based on discharge from active military service under other-than-dishonorable conditions for a minimum period specified by law. Honorable and general discharges qualify a veteran for most VA benefits; dishonorable and some bad-conduct discharges issued by general courts-martial bar VA benefits. Veterans with similar service are entitled to the same VA benefits. Certain VA benefits and medical care require wartime service.

All veterans must safeguard their service discharge forms; they document service dates and type of discharge and are necessary for filing claims.

HOME LOAN GUARANTIES

VA guarantees loans made to veterans and unremarried surviving spouses for the purchase or refinancing of homes, condominiums, and manufactured homes. VA guarantees part of the total loan, permitting the veteran to obtain a mortgage with a competitive interest rate, even without a down payment if the lender agrees. VA requires a down payment for the purchase of a manufactured home. VA also requires a down payment for a home or condominium if the purchase price exceeds the reasonable value of the property or the loan has a graduated payment feature. With a VA guaranty, the lender is protected against loss up to the amount of the guaranty if the borrower fails to repay the loan. A VA loan guaranty can be used to do the following:

- Buy a home.
- Buy a residential condominium.
- Build a home.
- Repair, alter, or improve a home.
- Refinance an existing home loan.
- Buy a manufactured home with or without a lot.
- Buy and improve a manufactured home lot.
- Install a solar heating or cooling system or other weatherization improvements.
- Purchase and improve a home simultaneously with energy-efficient improvements.
- Refinance a VA loan to reduce the interest rate.
- Refinance a manufactured home loan to acquire a lot.

Eligibility. Applicants must have a good credit rating, have an income sufficient to support mortgage payments, and agree to live on the property. To obtain a VA certificate of eligibility, complete VA Form 26-1880, *Request for Determination of Eligibility and Available Loan Guaranty Entitlement,* and submit it along with required supporting documents to the nearest VA regional office.

DISABILITY COMPENSATION

Monetary benefits, called disability compensation, are paid to veterans who are disabled by injury or disease incurred or aggravated during active military service. Monetary benefits are related to the residual effects of the injury or disease. The amounts of the benefits, which are not subject to federal or state income tax, are set by Congress.

The payment of military retirement pay, disability severance pay, and separation incentive payments known as SSB and VSI (Special Separation Benefits and Voluntary Separation Incentives) affect the amount of VA compensation payable. Since 2004, concurrent receipt of retired pay and disability pay for disabled retirees with 50 percent or more disability is allowed. Compensation for the severely disabled is payable for those with 60 percent or higher disability.

Allowances for Family Members. Veterans whose service-connected disabilities are rated at 30 percent or more are entitled to additional allowances for family members.

EDUCATION AND TRAINING

Eligibility and benefits of the various types of the GI Bill and the Veterans' Educational Assistance Program are complicated. For the most up-to-date information, consult *www.gibill.va.gov.*

Montgomery GI Bill (Active Duty).

Eligibility. The Montgomery GI Bill (Active Duty) is a program of education benefits for individuals who entered active duty for the first time after 30 June 1985. The Montgomery GI Bill is generally used by enlisted members. It is available, however, for officers who received their commissions through Officer Training School or AFROTC (but did not receive ROTC scholarships). Active duty for benefit purposes includes full-time National Guard duty performed after 29 November 1989. An honorable discharge is required. To receive the maximum benefit over a period of up to 36 months for a full-time student, the participant must serve continuously on active duty for three years.

An individual also may qualify for the full benefit by initially serving two continuous years on active duty, followed by four years of Selected Reserve service, beginning within one year of release from active duty. Individuals who initially serve a continuous period of at least three years of active duty, even though they were initially obligated to serve less, will be paid the maximum benefit.

For the most part, benefits end 10 years from the date of the veteran's last discharge or release from active duty. VA can extend this 10-year period under certain circumstances.

Participation Requirements. Participation in the Montgomery GI Bill requires that servicemembers have their military pay reduced by $100 a month for the first 12 months of active duty. This money is not refundable. If an individual decides not to participate in this program, this decision cannot be changed at a later date, except in special circumstances. An exception is made for servicemembers who are involuntarily separated from active duty with an honorable discharge after 2 February 1991. A second exception is made for those who voluntarily separate from active duty after 4 December 1991. If the servicemember decides to participate before separation, military pay will be reduced before separation, and education or training may take place following separation.

Vietnam Era GI Bill and VEAP Conversions. Also eligible for Montgomery GI Bill benefits are those individuals who had remaining entitlement under the Vietnam Era GI Bill on 31 December 1989, served on active duty without a break sometime between 19 October 1984 and 1 July 1985, and continued to serve on active duty to 1 July 1988, or to 1 July 1987, followed by four years in the Selected Reserve. Individuals who were eligible for the post-Vietnam Era Veterans' Educational Assistance Program (VEAP) must elect to receive benefits under the Montgomery GI Bill and apply for a refund of the contributions to VEAP.

Discharges and Separations. For the Montgomery GI Bill program, the discharge must be honorable. Discharges designated "under honorable conditions" and "general" do not establish eligibility. A discharge for one of the following reasons may result in a reduction of the required length of active duty: convenience of the government, disability, hardship, a medical condition existing before service, force reductions, or physical or mental conditions that prevent satisfactory performance of duty.

Education and Training Available. The following are available under the Montgomery GI Bill:

- Courses at colleges and universities leading to associate, bachelor, or graduate degrees, and accredited independent study. Cooperative training programs are available to individuals not on active duty.
- Courses leading to a certificate or diploma from business, technical, or vocational schools.
- Apprenticeship or on-the-job training programs for individuals not on active duty.
- Correspondence courses, under certain conditions.
- Flight training. Before beginning training, the veteran must have a private pilot license and meet the physical requirements for a commercial license. Benefits also may be received for solo flying hours up to the minimum required by the FAA for the rating or certification being pursued.
- Tutorial assistance benefits if individual is enrolled in school half-time or more. Remedial, deficiency, and refresher training also may be available.

Montgomery GI Bill (Selected Reserve).

Eligibility. The Montgomery GI Bill (Selected Reserve) is a program of education benefits for members of the reserve. To be eligible for the program, a reservist must meet the following criteria:

- Have a six-year obligation to serve in the Selected Reserve signed after 30 June 1985 or, if an officer, agree to serve six years in addition to the original obligation.
- Complete Initial Active Duty for Training (IADT).
- Meet the requirements for a high school diploma or equivalency certificate before completing IADT.
- Remain in good standing in a Selected Reserve unit.

Education and Training Available. Reservists may seek an undergraduate degree or graduate training or take technical courses at colleges and universities. Those who have a six-year commitment beginning after 30 September 1990, may take courses leading to a certificate or diploma from business, technical, or vocational schools; cooperative training; apprenticeship or on-the-job training; correspondence courses; independent study programs; flight training; tutorial assistance; and remedial, refresher, and deficiency training.

Work-Study. Reservists training at the three-quarter or full-time rate are eligible for the work-study program. Terms of participation are the same as under the Montgomery GI Bill (Active Duty) program, except that reservists can also work at a military facility if the work is related to Selected Reserve education.

Period of Eligibility. If a reservist stays in the Selected Reserve, benefits end 10 years from the date the reservist became eligible for the program. VA can extend this 10-year period under certain circumstances.

BENEFITS FOR SURVIVORS

Consult AFPAM 36-3028, *Benefits and Entitlements for Family Members of Retired Air Force Deceased*, which is available at *http://www.e-publishing .af.mil*, for the most up-to-date information.

Dependency and Indemnity Compensation. Dependency and Indemnity Compensation (DIC) payments may be authorized for surviving spouses, unmarried children under 18, helpless children, those between 18 and 23 if attending a VA-approved school, and low-income parents of service personnel or veterans who died from a disease or injury incurred or aggravated while on active duty or active duty for training; an injury incurred or aggravated in line of duty while on inactive-duty training; or a disability compensable by VA. Death cannot be the result of willful misconduct.

DIC payments also may be authorized for surviving spouses, unmarried children under 18, helpless children, and those between 18 and 23 if attending a VA-approved school, of veterans who were totally service-connected disabled at time of death but whose death was not the result of the service-connected disability, if the veteran was continuously rated totally disabled for a period of 10 or more years immediately preceding death or the veteran was so rated for a period of not less than five years from the date of discharge from military service. Payments under this provision are subject to offset by the amount received from judicial proceedings brought on account of the veteran's death. When death occurred after service, the veteran's discharge must have been under conditions other than dishonorable.

Remarriage makes a spouse ineligible for survivor benefits unless the remarriage is made void or is annulled by a court. A surviving spouse also may be ineligible if, after the death of the veteran, the spouse lived with another and was held out openly to the public to be a spouse.

Death Pension. Surviving spouses and unmarried children of deceased veterans with wartime service may be eligible for a non-service-connected pension based on need. Children must be under age 18, or up to age 23 if attending a VA-approved school. Pension is not payable to those with estates large enough to provide maintenance. The veteran must have been discharged under conditions other than dishonorable and must have had 90 days or more of active military service, at least one day of which was during a period of war, or a service-connected disability justifying discharge for disability. If the veteran died in service not in line of duty, benefits may be payable if the veteran had completed at least two years of honorable service. Children who became permanently incapable of self-support because of a disability before reaching age 18 may be eligible for a pension as long as the condition exists, unless the child marries or the child's income exceeds the applicable limit. A surviving spouse who is a patient in a nursing home, is in need of the regular aid and attendance of another person, or is permanently housebound may be entitled to higher income limitations or additional benefits.

Dependents' Education. Education assistance benefits are available to spouses and children of the following:

- Veterans who died or are permanently and totally disabled as the result of a disability arising from active service in the armed forces.
- Veterans who died from any cause while rated permanently and totally disabled from service-connected disability.
- Servicemembers currently missing in action or captured in line of duty by a hostile force.
- Servicemembers presently detained or interned in line of duty by a foreign government or power.

Benefits may be awarded for pursuit of associate, bachelor, or graduate degrees at colleges and universities—including independent study, cooperative training, and study abroad programs. Courses leading to a certificate or diploma from business, technical, or vocational schools may be taken. Benefits may be awarded for apprenticeships, on-the-job training programs, and farm cooperative courses. Benefits for correspondence courses under certain conditions are available to spouses only. Secondary-school programs may be pursued if the individual is not a high school graduate. An individual with a deficiency in a subject may receive tutorial assistance benefits if enrolled half-time or more. Remedial deficiency and refresher training also may be available.

Educational Loans. Loans are available to spouses who qualify for educational assistance benefits. Spouses who have passed their 10-year period of eligibility may be eligible for an educational loan. During the first two years after the end of their eligibility period, they may borrow up to $2,500 per academic year to continue a full-time course leading to a college degree or to a professional or vocational objective that requires at least six months to complete. VA may waive the six-month requirement. The loan program is based on financial need.

Home Loan Guaranties. A GI loan guaranty to acquire a home may be available to an unremarried spouse of a veteran or servicemember who died as a result of service-connected disabilities, or to a spouse of a servicemember who has been officially listed as missing in action or as a prisoner of war for more than 90 days. Spouses of those listed as a POW or MIA are limited to one loan.

Montgomery GI Bill (Active Duty) Death Benefit. VA will pay a special Montgomery GI Bill death benefit to a designated survivor if the servicemember's death is in service or is service-connected and within one year after discharge or release. The deceased must have been a participant in the Montgomery GI Bill program. The death benefit also will be paid if the service-member would have been eligible to participate but for the high school diploma requirement and the length-of-service requirement. The amount paid will be equal to the participant's actual military pay reduction less any education benefits paid.

INSURANCE
Service-Disabled Veterans' Insurance (SDVI). This program was first issued in April 1951 and continues to be issued today. It is restricted to veterans who have service-connected disabilities at the time they retire or separate from active duty. The insurance is issued to these individuals at standard premium rates regardless of the severity of the service-connected disability. The insurance is offered in many plans, including unlimited five-year term.

Servicemembers' Group Life Insurance (SGLI). Servicemembers on active duty today and most categories of reservists are covered by Servicemembers' Group Life Insurance. SGLI is a group insurance purchased from a commercial company and administered by the Office of Servicemembers' Group Life Insurance. The program is supervised by the VA. The insurance is term insurance and has no cash value, with the maximum amount of coverage fixed at $400,000. Premiums for active-duty members with full coverage are $29 per month for the full $400,000. There is also a 120-day period of free coverage following separation from active duty. This can be extended to one year if disabled at retirement.

Veterans' Group Life Insurance (VGLI). Upon leaving active duty, and after the period of free SGLI, members are eligible to obtain a like amount of SGLI coverage in a five-year term plan known as Veterans' Group Life Insurance. This insurance has no cash value. VGLI is designed to provide low-cost coverage. Monthly premiums are based upon age and are much higher than SGLI. At the end of the five-year term, individuals may renew or convert their coverage to any permanent plan of insurance with any of a number of participating commercial insurance companies at standard premium rates regardless of health or military status.

ADDITIONAL VA PROGRAMS
In addition to the benefits mentioned above, there are numerous other VA benefits and programs for veterans and their dependents. Other disability benefits include specially adapted homes and automobiles. There are a variety of pensions, few of which apply to officers or their dependents. There are also vocational rehabilitation and life insurance programs. Health-care benefits include hospital, nursing home, and domiciliary care; outpatient medical, pharmacy, and dental treatment; alcohol and drug dependence treatment; and services for the blind. And there are burial benefits, including national cemeteries, headstones, and flags.

Complete, current information on VA benefits and programs is available in *Federal Benefits for Veterans and Dependents,* as cited at the beginning of this chapter. Also consult *Veteran's Guide to Benefits* (Stackpole Books).

STATE BENEFITS

Some states offer benefits to veterans that are independent of federal VA benefits. These benefits differ from state to state. Often eligibility is dependent on the state being the place of residency or home of record at the time the officer entered military service. For information, consult your state veterans office.

PART VI

Personal Affairs

26

Legal Documents
and Assistance

All officers of the U.S. Air Force may expect sudden changes of station or in their personal status. Personnel affected by such movements may anticipate months of separation from their families, during which time they may be unable to properly attend to their personal affairs and welfare.

Efficiency of job performance is directly related to servicemembers' peace of mind and mental stability. Servicemembers do not want to expose their families to distress, want, or insecurity. Consequently, officers should arrange their personal affairs so that their families will be adequately protected and provided for and to prevent legal entanglement or embarrassment that could be caused by their absence.

The time to prepare for the sudden separation caused by military transfer is now, while personal matters are moving along in a routine manner, rather than during that turbulent and busy period immediately preceding departure upon a change of station or temporary duty. It is imperative that military personnel keep their personal affairs properly arranged to provide the maximum protection and security for their families, and ensure that their dependents have ample knowledge of and receive all rights and benefits to which they are entitled. Because individual preparations are determined by the needs of the individuals concerned, it is impossible to prescribe an exact set of preparations applicable to all Air Force officers. The status of some may require only simple adjustments, while others may require complicated and minutely detailed arrangements. To help officers properly arrange their personal affairs, this chapter sets forth in detail the varied subjects that Air Force personnel should consider to provide for the welfare, protection, and security of their families at all times.

The Air Force is acutely conscious of the importance to its members of sound guidance in providing assistance in the solution of personal problems. For this reason, each base has a personal affairs staff. Air Force officers who need advice on personal matters should go first to their personal affairs or legal

270

office, state their problems candidly and completely, and ask for guidance. It will be extended willingly, authoritatively, and without cost.

ALLOTMENTS OF PAY AND DEDUCTIONS

Allotments of pay may be authorized by all military personnel on active duty, wherever serving, to the following people and organizations:

- Individuals or banks for the support of dependents or to savings or checking accounts.
- Life insurance companies for the payment of premiums on life insurance.
- Federal savings and loan associations.
- Lending institutions holding loans insured by the Federal Housing Administration or the Housing and Home Finance Agency.
- Air Force Aid Society and American Red Cross for payment of loans made by these organizations to military personnel.

Officers may allot so much of their basic pay, monthly subsistence allowance, and quarters allowance as will leave sufficient balance equal to or greater than the amount of Social Security and income tax to be withheld according to current Internal Revenue Service regulations.

In exceptional cases, where persons in active service have not made adequate provision for the support of certain dependents, the secretary of the Air Force may act in their behalf to make allotments for the well-being and protection of their dependents. Such allotments may be terminated at the request of the person whose pay is charged.

FAMILY CARE PLAN

Single-parent servicemembers and dual-service parents are required to plan the financial, legal, and medical care for their families in the duty absence of the parents. Unit first sergeants help complete AF Form 357, *Family Care Certification.*

LEGAL ASSISTANCE PROGRAM

If members of the armed forces have problems of such a nature that the services of an attorney are desirable or necessary, they may go to the nearest legal assistance office. The legal assistance office will counsel, advise, carry on necessary correspondence, negotiate, and draw up any legal papers necessary. Assistance includes separation and divorce agreements; child support, custody, and alimony payments; adoption; naturalization and citizenships; contracts for home purchase; and claims against the government. Legal assistance officers cannot represent servicemembers or their families in criminal matters under civilian law.

Wills of Air Force Personnel. All servicemembers should give consideration to the making of a will. Whether a will is necessary or desirable and the form it should take depend on the desires and circumstances of the individual, and the laws of the place of execution and of the probable place of probate.

State laws govern the execution and probate of wills, and the requirements in these respects vary considerably among states.

When people die without having made a will, they are said to have died "intestate." In such event, the estate is administered and distributed according to the statute of "descent and distribution" of the state of legal domicile or, in the case of real property, the state or states in which such real property is located. This law, in effect, creates a will for the individual, which is administered by an administrator appointed by the court, and the estate is distributed to the family members in the manner prescribed by the applicable state's statutes.

If the manner of distribution so prescribed by law does not meet your desires or needs, you can direct a distribution of your estate according to your wishes by making a will. Officers with children should seriously consider a revocable living trust, rather than a will.

Review of a Will. An executed will should be reviewed from time to time, especially when such events as marriage, birth of children, divorce, or death of a named beneficiary occur. Changes of status such as these often affect the provisions of a will. A will is not effective until death and can be replaced by a new will or changed by a codicil at any time that the testator feels it is necessary. Unless the will is extremely complicated, the use of codicils should be avoided. If the will is replaced by a new will, all copies of the previous will should be destroyed. Whenever circumstances change, officers should review their wills with the aid of legal counsel.

Safekeeping. Military personnel, because of their transient status, should not keep the original copy of the will in their possession. After completion, the original copy of the will should be mailed to the named executor or chief beneficiary for safekeeping or placed in some other secure place where it will be available in the event of death. It is advisable, for reference purposes, to keep a copy of the will, with a notation as to the location of the original will. The principal beneficiary should be advised of the location of the original.

Emergency Will. If an emergency necessitates the immediate execution of a will, officers should write out their desires as to the distribution of possessions and have them attested by three competent witnesses. Such a handwritten will should state the full name, grade, Social Security number, and permanent address of the officer, the exact desires as to the distribution of possessions, the name and address of the person desired to be the executor, and the date, place, and circumstances of execution. Such a will should definitely be replaced as soon as possible by one prepared with the aid of legal counsel.

Power of Attorney. A power of attorney is a legal instrument by which you may designate another person to act on your behalf in legal or personal matters. The one executing the power of attorney is usually referred to as the principal, and the one to whom the authority is given is usually referred to as the attorney-in-fact or simply as the attorney for the principal. You may grant the authority of a power of attorney to a member of your family or to any other person of legal age; however, when appointing your attorney-in-fact, you should select somebody in whom you have complete trust. The authority given in a power of attorney, unlike that of a will, becomes invalid upon the death of the principal.

The power of attorney can be made very general and unlimited in scope, or it can be restricted to certain specific functions, depending on the needs and desires of the principal. A power of attorney may or may not be honored, depending on its acceptance by the individual to whom it may be presented for a transaction in the principal's name. Because the principal is held responsible for the actions of an attorney-in-fact performed within the limits of the power of attorney, it is advisable not to execute power of attorney until a specific need or use for it exists. As a rule, a restricted power of attorney will accomplish the specific needs of the individual.

Preparation and Legal Counsel. The requirements as to preparation of the form and content of a legally effective power of attorney vary considerably under the laws of the various states. For this reason, and to properly fulfill the needs and desires of the principal, each power of attorney should be individually prepared under the guidance of legal counsel with due regard to the laws of the state of execution and of the probable place of exercise of the powers granted. Legal counsel should be consulted for the preparation of a power of attorney when the need for such instrument exists.

Estates. A person accumulates various types of possessions during a lifetime, which become known collectively as an estate. This estate may consist of real estate, which is land and any buildings on it; personalty, which includes all items of personal property, such as clothes, household furnishings, automobiles, money, stocks, bonds, jewelry, and, in general, any property that is not real estate; or a combination of both real estate and personalty.

Importance of Joint Tenancy. Air Force personnel, in their arrangements of personal matters for the protection of their families, should consider the importance and advantages of arranging title to most of their property by joint tenancy. In this way, officers will enable the joint tenants to use and control the property during their lifetime, and in the event of their death, to obtain full title as survivor without the property being subject to administration through the courts. Property owned in joint tenancy cannot be disposed of by a will if the joint tenants survive. The solution to the officers' obligation to provide for the care, welfare, and comfort of their families in the event of prolonged absence or death can be more effectively accomplished through the establishment of title to property by joint tenancy than by a power of attorney and a will. The rights of control of property by the joint tenant are full and absolute when title is kept in joint tenancy, and upon the death of the officer, the property will pass automatically into full possession of the joint tenant without judicial proceedings. Personal property held in joint tenancy may, however, make it subject to tax because the Soldiers' and Sailors' Civil Relief Act does not protect dependents.

Sound appraisement on the part of the owner concerning the capabilities and integrity of the contemplated joint owner should be exercised, and, in general, it is not advisable to establish joint property title with a person of short acquaintance.

Except as limited by state statutes, titles by joint tenancy with right of survivorship can be granted for various types of property. Deeds establishing ownership of real estate, and bills of sale for personal property, such as automobiles and household goods, can be held in joint tenancy with right of survivorship. Joint bank accounts can be opened, and stocks and bonds can be issued to joint owners, with the right of survivorship.

U.S. savings bonds can be issued to joint owners with right of survivorship if the purchaser so requests. A savings bond already issued to a single owner (without a designated beneficiary) is part of the estate but can be reissued during the owner's lifetime to joint owners upon proper application to the Treasury Department. Bonds issued to a single owner with a designated beneficiary can be cashed only by the owner during the owner's lifetime, and on death of the owner do not become part of the estate but go directly to the named beneficiary. Such bonds cannot be reissued without the consent of the beneficiary. A bond held in joint ownership can be cashed by either joint owner with or without the consent of the other joint tenant.

Legal Assistance. Legal advice should be obtained before anybody creates a joint tenancy title on property. Gift, inheritance, or other taxes may often affect the enactment of joint tenancy titles. Competent legal assistance can explain the advantages and disadvantages of holding the various kinds of property in joint tenancy and can also facilitate the proper establishment of such an estate with due regard to all applicable laws.

Safe-Deposit Boxes. Many banks maintain safe-deposit boxes and rent them for a yearly fee that varies with the size of the box. When available, a safe-deposit box in a conveniently located reputable bank is usually the best place to keep valuable papers, such as stocks, bonds, deeds to property, house insurance policies, receipts, and a copy of one's will. As the box will be sealed on the renter's death, do not keep the original will or life insurance policies in a safe-deposit box.

Automobiles. The determination as to the proper owner of an automobile is made not by possession, but by the certificate of title or other evidence of ownership from the state in which the automobile is registered. If the title of the automobile is in the name of one person, the automobile, in the event of the death of the owner, would become part of the estate, subject to that person's will, if executed, or the laws of "descent and distribution" of the appropriate state. The actual determination as to disposition of the automobile, pending the result of probate, would rest with the state authorities. Subject to statutory limitations of the state of registration, title to an automobile may be held jointly by a husband and a wife. Under such title, in the event of death of one, the automobile would become the property of the survivor. This method is usually the most effective for providing for the use of and title to the automobile for the spouse in the case of prolonged absence or death of the officer. It has its disadvantages, however, in the statutory limitations mentioned above and in the fact that difficulties are sometimes encountered in effecting transfer of the automobile without the presence and signatures of both joint owners, and in the spouse's being subject to personal property taxes in some states.

Changing of Title. Because state laws govern the transfer of title to an automobile, extreme care should be exercised that all provisions of law relative to such transfer are met. If you want to transfer title to an automobile from yourself to your spouse and you jointly, you should check with the bureau of motor vehicles in the state in which the automobile is registered, requesting the exact procedure necessary to accomplish the transfer.

Importance of Insurance. In many cases, an automobile is the most valuable single item of property owned by a young officer. It is, therefore, essential to protect this property with adequate insurance. The insurance policy should cover the owner, spouse, and all other persons who may have occasion to drive the vehicle. Lack of adequate insurance protection may result in extreme financial, legal, and personal difficulties.

Most states have enacted compulsory insurance laws, and strict compliance with these laws is obligatory. Although a few states do not have compulsory insurance laws, it is foolish not to carry automobile insurance. Officers should not be deceived into a false state of security by possessing only the amount of insurance required by law. In some states, compulsory insurance provides only minimum protection rather than adequate insurance protection.

Soldiers' and Sailors' Civil Relief Act. The purpose of this act is to relieve members of the armed forces from worry over the inability to meet their civil obligations by providing adequate representation for the servicemember during an absence and postponement of certain civil proceedings and transactions until release from such military service. There is nothing in the act that relieves one from the actual payment of the debts or other obligations, but if the servicemember is unable to pay premiums on commercial insurance policies, to pay taxes, or to perform other obligations with reference to right and claims to lands of the United States, certain relief may be afforded by this act. If there is legal action based on a servicemember's breach of obligation, the relief afforded under this act is within the discretion of the court and depends upon whether the ability of the servicemember to discharge the obligations or to prosecute the action or defense is materially affected by reason of military service.

Insurance. The payment of premiums on commercial life insurance may be protected under Article IV of this act.

Other Protections. In addition to the protection of commercial life insurance, the Soldiers' and Sailors' Civil Relief Act provides arrangements for adequate legal representation and stays of execution for servicemembers on the following legal matters:

- Eviction for nonpayment of rent.
- Court proceedings arising from mortgages, leases, liens, and other contractual obligations.
- Payment of taxes may be deferred in some cases. Officers are not required to pay local taxes in the state where they are stationed unless, by some act of the officers, they become legal residents, provided the officers maintain legal residence in another state and discharge their liability in that state.

Importance of Legal Assistance. This summary of the Soldiers' and Sailors' Civil Relief Act has mentioned only the major points contained in the act. It is very important, therefore, that any officers who are suddenly presented with a tax bill or threatened with legal action of any kind while away from their state of domicile immediately report the matter to their legal assistance officer, who can then study the case and possibly avert court action through implementation of some of the points of the Soldiers' and Sailors' Civil Relief Act. Too often, people delay in notifying the legal assistance officer of their legal difficulties until the case has already reached the litigation stage, with the result that the legal assistance officer is unable to help. The importance of prompt notification and use of base legal assistance facilities in any legal entanglement cannot be overemphasized.

Joint Bank Accounts. A joint bank account is one in which two persons have full authority to perform the functions of depositing and withdrawing funds from the same account. Such an account may be either a savings account or a checking account and is considered to be the joint property of the persons concerned. It is possible in most states to maintain joint accounts, and most banks have a specially prepared contract form setting out the legal status of such accounts in accordance with the state laws that govern the operations of the bank. Such a contract and the accompanying passbook usually contain a phrase somewhat as follows: "John Doe and Mary Doe, jointly or either, with rights of survivorship and not as tenants in common."

The chief advantage of a joint account is that the funds are readily available to either or both of the parties at any time. This situation is especially important to Air Force personnel because by maintaining their accounts in such a status, they enable their spouses to obtain the funds even though the servicemember is absent. If officers carry bank accounts in their names only, their spouses may be deprived of the use of the money at a time when it is most urgently needed. Another great advantage is that in the event of death of one of the parties, the survivor automatically becomes sole owner of the money in the account, usually without having the funds frozen while the will of the deceased is being probated. Thus, the spouse or other family members will have the money available at a time when it is urgently needed.

Allotments to Joint Bank Accounts. Allotments to a bank for deposit in a savings or checking account must be made to the credit of one person. It is permissible, however, to make an allotment to a bank even though the one to whom the allotment is credited is a party in a joint account. Proper arrangements for acceptance and depositing of the allotment must be made with the bank concerned before initiation of such an allotment.

Credit Unions. The Air Force assists the establishment of credit union facilities on Air Force installations as cooperative organizations to encourage systematic savings and create a source of credit for Air Force personnel and their families. A credit union is usually found on any good-sized base.

PERSONAL AFFAIRS RECORD

It is very important that you keep an up-to-date record of your personal affairs and property. Both you and your family will probably have many occasions to refer to such a record during your military service.

Fill in your record carefully and completely and then make as many copies of your record as you will need for your family or for other persons whom you wish to trust with such information. Be sure you consider each item and make the record as complete and accurate as possible.

Remember, keep your records up-to-date, as changes or additions occur, by amending the original record or preparing a completely new record, and send copies to whomever you give copies of the original record.

Start now to get the necessary information and to prepare your record, and do not stop until it is complete.

FAMILY SUPPORT CENTER PROGRAMS

At each Air Force base, an organization exists to aid Air Force personnel and their families in solving personal problems. The focus of operations is known as the Family Support Center. The Air Force's Family Support Center home page can be accessed at *http://www.airforceonesource.com*; user ID is "airforce" and password is "ready." The Family Support Center's One Source help line is 800-707-5784 from within the U.S., 800-7075-7844 from outside the U.S. only, and 800-375-5971 for Spanish. The activities of this program include providing assistance to Air Force families in respect to such matters as these:

- Information/referral center, where airmen or officers can get information or specialized assistance.
- Relocation assistance, for help when moving to another base.
- Support during family separations, mobilization, and deployment.
- Personal financial management programs, including Air Force Aid.
- Spouse employment programs, which offer information about job opportunities and programs on how to develop job-hunting skills.
- Heart Link program, an Air Force-wide standardized spouse orientation, is a one-day class held quarterly to acclimatize military spouses with Air Force life. Its target group is military spouses with five years or less of military affiliation.
- Family life education programs, such as on parenting, stress management, building self-esteem.

- Special-needs programs, such as single parents' groups.
- Family skills, which offer programs on communication and enhancing a family's quality of life.
- Private and professional assistance for personal crisis issues, marital, child-related, and so forth.
- Transition assistance and relocation assistance for those separating from the Air Force.

AIR FORCE AID SOCIETY

Mission. The Air Force Aid Society (AFAS) is the emergency relief organization for the U.S. Air Force. Its mission is to improve the morale and welfare of Air Force personnel and their dependents by providing financial assistance in times of emergency. The AFAS augments the relief available to the servicemember through the American Red Cross; it is not intended that the AFAS will compete with or replace the work of the Red Cross because the congressional charter of the Red Cross makes it the primary relief organization for the armed forces.

Eligibility. The following classes of individuals are eligible for assistance:
- USAF personnel on active duty or retired from active duty for length of service or disability, and their dependents.
- Dependents of recently deceased USAF personnel who died while on active duty or after they were retired from active duty for length of service or disability.
- AF Reserve and Air National Guard personnel on full-time active duty with the USAF for at least 90 days, and their dependents. (Does not include tours of active duty for training or attendance at service academies or the armed forces preparatory schools.)

In addition, Army, Navy, and Marine personnel and their dependents may receive assistance through the Air Force Aid Society when an Army Emergency Relief or Navy Relief Services office is not readily accessible and it is not feasible to refer the applicant to the Red Cross.

Eligible dependents are the spouse and minor children of Air Force personnel. Parents who are wholly dependent upon the servicemember may be considered eligible dependents. The existence of an allotment to a relative other than the spouse or child of an officer is acceptable as reasonable evidence of an officer's acceptance of responsibility to support the relative. The existence of a voluntary allotment in an amount constituting substantial support, regular maintenance as a member of an officer's household, or other reliable indication of true dependency will be accepted as evidence that an officer's dependent is eligible for AFAS assistance.

Assistance. AFAS assistance is rendered in the form of non-interest-bearing loans or cash grants or combinations of both. Assistance may be obtained by those entitled to it by contacting the Aid Society officer at any Air Force installation. Persons eligible for assistance who are not connected with or living at or near an Air Force base should make application for assistance from the AFAS through their local chapter of the American Red Cross.

The Air Force Aid Society is a charitable organization. It receives no government funds that can be used for relief purposes. The income of the AFAS comes from gifts and contributions, royalties from books and songs given to the Aid Society, legacies, and interest on the invested capital. The limited resources of the Aid Society and the very large number of persons eligible under its charter for assistance make it mandatory for assistance to be limited to cases of emergency only and also make it essential that Aid Society assistance be restricted to those cases that do not rightfully belong to some other welfare organization.

AMERICAN RED CROSS

Consistent with the congressional charter of the American Red Cross, the Red Cross has been charged with the primary responsibility of a broad program of volunteer aid to military personnel and their families. The Air Force Aid Society coordinates its functions with the American Red Cross in such a manner as to avoid duplication of effort in providing for the welfare of military personnel and their dependents. The American Red Cross carries out its responsibilities through personnel assigned to military establishments and through the home service program of local Red Cross chapters.

AIR FORCE CHAPLAINS
Religious Services.

Worship Services. Chaplains conduct worship services as are required for the religious practice of the members of each faith. Air Force personnel are afforded every opportunity to attend their individual religious services. Chapels at most bases also offer religious instruction, such as Sunday school and catechism classes.

Marriage. The chaplain is authorized, but not required, to perform the marriage rite, provided that all local laws are met and proper legal permission is obtained in each case. Persons contemplating marriage are urged to confer with a chaplain of their faith to ensure that proper arrangements are made.

Funerals. The commander or his representative will assist in making funeral arrangements, and a chaplain will conduct appropriate burial services at the interment of members of the military service, active and retired, and for their family members, when requested. If the family of a servicemember who dies in the United States requests transportation of the body to a home burial ground instead of permitting burial in a local or national cemetery, the family will normally be expected to provide a clergyman for the burial services because the chaplain's other duties preclude absence for an extended period.

Conferences and Retreats. Chaplains, assisted by civilian religious leaders, are authorized to conduct religious conferences and retreats for Air Force personnel. For the purpose of attending such conferences and retreats, Air

Force personnel may be placed on temporary duty. These may be conducted at either military or civilian locations.

PERSONAL AFFAIRS OFFICER

Casualty Assistance. The personal affairs officer assists and advises the dependents of deceased servicemembers of the various benefits and privileges to which they are entitled. Such advice includes information regarding six months' death gratuity, dependents' compensation, arrears in pay, personal effects, family allowance, burial flag, settlement of government life insurance, and burial allowance. The personal affairs officer is also in a position to refer the dependents to related agencies in regard to civil service preference, Social Security benefits, states' benefits, transportation of dependents and household goods, and issuance of grave markers.

Other Assistance. Personal affairs officers advise military personnel and their dependents as to their rights in securing benefits from the government and as to sources of information and procedures, but are strictly forbidden by law from acting as an agent or attorney for such persons other than in the discharge of their official duties. In their capacity as advisor to military personnel and their dependents, personal affairs officers maintain liaison with the American Red Cross director, the Air Force Aid Society officer, and other agencies, so they may bring to the attention of these organizations servicemembers and their families who are in financial need or in need of other assistance.

SCHOLARSHIPS FOR DEPENDENTS OF AIR FORCE PERSONNEL

Air Force Aid Society General Arnold Grant Program. Those eligible for this program are children (including stepchildren and legally adopted children) of an Air Force member in any of the following categories:

- Active member of the Air Force.
- Retired because of length of active-duty service, disability, or attainment of age 60 (reserve component).
- Deceased while on active duty.

Additionally, the applicant must be a U.S. citizen enrolled and in good standing at or accepted for admission to an approved educational institution on a full-time basis.

Applicants or interested persons who desire additional information should contact their local Family Support Center.

Air Force Clubs' and Spouses Clubs' Scholarships. Air Force Clubs and many servicemembers spouses' clubs grant small annual scholarships on a competitive basis.

APPOINTMENT TO THE FEDERAL SERVICE ACADEMIES

The president is authorized to appoint a limited number of cadets from the United States at large to be selected from sons and daughters of members of the armed services who were killed or died in service as the result of wounds, injuries, or disease received or aggravated in active service. All such appointees must be otherwise qualified and will be selected in order of merit as established by competitive examination.

Sons and daughters of persons who have been awarded the Medal of Honor, if otherwise qualified, may be appointed by the president as cadets from the United States at large to the federal service academies.

IN-SERVICE HOUSING LOANS
If officers have been on extended active duty for at least two years, they may finance the purchase of a home by an FHA loan. The law provides a system of mortgage insurance that enables the officers to more easily build or purchase homes.

PAY, ALLOWANCES, AND ALLOTMENTS OF PERSONNEL REPORTED MISSING
Pay and Allowances. All personnel who are on active duty and who are officially determined to be absent in a status of missing are entitled, for the period they are officially carried or determined to be in such status, to have credited to their accounts the same pay and allowances entitled at the beginning of such period of absence or to which they may become entitled thereafter. Such entitlement shall terminate upon the date of receipt by the Department of the Air Force of evidence that the servicemember is dead or upon the date of death prescribed or determined. Such entitlement, however, shall not terminate upon expiration of term of service during absence, and in case of death during absence shall not terminate earlier than the dates stated herein. No pay and allowances accrue to such missing persons for any period during which they may be officially determined absent from their posts of duty without authority, and they shall be indebted to the government for any payments from amounts credited to their account for such period of absence.

Allotments. Allotments instituted before the absence of a missing person who is entitled to accrued pay and allowances will continue to be paid regularly for a period of 12 months from the date of absence. In the absence of an allotment for support for dependents or payment of insurance premiums, or if an existing allotment is insufficient for its purposes, the secretary of the Air Force can direct that adequate allotments be instituted. Information listed on DD Form 93 (*Record of Emergency Data*) will be used as a guide in such determinations. The total of all allotments, however, may not exceed the total pay and allowances to which the missing person is entitled.

When the 12-month period from date of commencement of absence is about to expire in the case of a missing person, the secretary of the Air Force shall cause a full review of the case to be made.

27

Financial Security
for Your Family

Few newly commissioned Air Force officers think about their retirement, and fewer still about the aftermath of their own death. Consequently, some do not give serious attention to the need for estate planning. Yet all officers should study the financial needs of their families and make provisions to meet them.

Unmarried officers should also begin financial planning, systematic savings, and probably insurance programs. One of the most important aspects of building an estate is time; the earlier begun, the more that can accumulate. Estate planning should be approached systematically. Officers should assess their responsibilities (or potential future responsibilities), determine the long-term needs of their families, understand benefits due them as active-duty and retired officers, take out insurance to make up the difference between the needs of their families and their current assets, and begin systematic financial investment programs. For more information, consult Stackpole Books' *Armed Forces Guide to Personal Financial Planning*; AFPAM 36-3028, *Benefits and Entitlements for Family Members of Retired Air Force Deceased*; and the Department of Veterans Affairs' *Federal Benefits for Veterans and Dependents*.

LONG-TERM RESPONSIBILITIES
Every Air Force family's needs vary, and every family's needs change over time. It is important to consider the long-term needs of the officer's spouse and children should the officer die. Is the spouse prepared to earn an adequate income? Do the children have special needs? What do the officer and spouse believe are their responsibilities for their children's education, and what level of comfort is desired for the survivors? Will the officer's or the spouse's parents or other relatives require support? The servicemember should also consider the family's needs should the spouse die: What is required to carry on as a single parent? Other factors to consider are inflation, when the family's financial needs will

peak, and how assets will change over time and after retirement. Each Air Force family should reassess its long-term needs every few years or when a significant event, such as the birth of a child, makes a significant change.

GOVERNMENT BENEFITS

Government benefits vary depending on the officer's status: active duty less than 20 years, active duty over 20 years, retired, retired with disability, or eligible for Social Security. Benefits also vary depending on the ages of the surviving spouse and children. Every officer has the moral obligation to know what survivor benefits are available for family members—and provide for shortfalls between anticipated needs and government benefits. For additional details, consult AFPAM 36-3028, *Benefits and Entitlements for Family Members of Retired Air Force Deceased.*

Death Gratuity. Death gratuity is a tax-free, lump-sum payment of $12,000 made by the Air Force to the eligible beneficiary of a member who dies on active duty or within 120 days after retirement or separation. Usually paid within 48 hours of death, its purpose is to help the survivors in their readjustment and to aid their meeting immediate expenses incurred. Death gratuity is paid to survivors in the following order: spouse, children, parents, siblings. Death gratuity is not paid to any other person when there are no survivors as listed. A will is not a legal designation for death gratuity, since the death gratuity is not money or a debt due the member and cannot be part of the estate.

Unpaid Pay and Allowances. Upon death of an active-duty or retired member, any pay and allowances due, but not paid to the member, are paid to the designated beneficiary. Unpaid pay and allowances may include unpaid basic or retired pay, payment for accrued leave (not to exceed 60 days), amounts due for travel, per diem, and transportation of dependents and shipment of household goods. The decedent's pay record is completely audited by the Defense Finance and Accounting Service, and a check for any amount due is issued to the designated beneficiary.

Burial Benefits. For members who die on active duty, the mortuary affairs officer will assist the survivors in making funeral arrangements. The Air Force will provide services and benefits that will cover, within reason, most funeral expenses. A small lump sum is paid by the Social Security Administration.

Normally, no burial benefits are provided by the Air Force when a retiree dies. The only exception is if the retired member was a patient in a U.S. military hospital while on active duty and continued to be a patient, physically in the hospital, until the date of death. Survivors of retirees in this category will be assisted by the mortuary officer at the nearest Air Force base.

The following burial benefits are provided by other government agencies in the case of a retired member's death:

- A lump sum is paid by the Social Security Administration.
- The VA pays a modest burial allowance if the retiree died in a VA hospital or was drawing compensation from the VA. Also, if burial is in

a private cemetery, a plot allowance is payable, but only if the burial allowance is paid. The allowance is greater if death is determined to have been from service-connected causes rather than service-connected.

Dependency and Indemnity Compensation. The Survivors Dependency and Indemnity Compensation Act of 1974 provides for compensation to survivors for the loss of a servicemember whose death is attributable to military service. All service-connected deaths that occur in peace or wartime in the line of duty qualify the eligible survivors for the Dependency and Indemnity Compensation (DIC). Retired officers' survivors may qualify also, provided the VA rules the death to have been from service-connected causes. The higher the pay grade of the deceased member, the higher the compensation payable to the member's survivors. Once established, however, the DIC rate is fixed. Rate increases are only by separate congressional action. DIC payments are not authorized to the survivors of a retired officer whose death is not service-connected. (A small pension may be paid to the widow or widower, as discussed later, provided her or his income is below a stated minimum.) This gap must receive consideration in developing a total family security plan.

Compensations may be increased for widows and widowers with children under 18 or with a child over 18 who is incapable of self-support. An additional sum may be awarded for each child between 18 and 23 who attends a VA-approved school. All such compensations are exempt from federal income tax. The officer's surviving children will receive compensations if the spouse dies. Dependent parents likewise qualify for compensations. Your finance officer or any VA office can assist you in computing the various possible compensations and pensions for your particular family situation.

Survivor Benefit Plan (SBP). The Survivor Benefit Plan allows members of the uniformed services to elect to receive a reduced retirement pay in order to provide annuities for their survivors, for another person with an insurable interest in the servicemember, or under certain conditions, for an ex-spouse. Under SBP, the federal government pays a substantial portion of the overall cost. Participation in the SBP is open to all future retirees, including members of the reserve forces when they attain age 60 and become entitled to retired or retainer pay.

Under SBP, future retirees may elect to leave up to 55 percent of their retired pay to their selected annuitants. Participation in SBP is automatic at the 55 percent rate for those still on active duty who have a spouse or children and who have a minimum of 20 years' service at the time of their death. Before retirement, the member may elect a reduced coverage or the minimum base amount, or may decline to participate. However, the spouse must concur in the election of reduced or no coverage.

Costs for spouse-only coverage under SBP are 2.5 percent of the minimum base amount, plus 10 percent of the annuity from $513 to $1,097 or plus 6.5 percent of the annuity of $1,098 or over. Threshold amounts are revised from time to time. Note that the cost is based upon the total retired pay used to compute the SBP annuity and not upon the amount of the annuity. Extension of the coverage to a child or children costs about .05 percent of the annuity amount a month. Children-only SBP is based on the age of the youngest child and on the age of the retiree, as well as the base amount.

There are a number of points about the SBP that deserve careful consideration. Most decisions are irrevocable, but deductions under the plan cease during any month in which there is no eligible beneficiary. Further, the coverage may be switched to a new spouse if the retiree remarries. An important advantage of SBP is that the amount of coverage is tied to the Consumer Price Index (CPI). Whenever retired pay is adjusted on the basis of the CPI, the amount selected by the retiree as an annuity base, the deduction from retired pay covering the adjusted base, and the annuity payable to selected beneficiaries will be adjusted accordingly. The survivor receives 55 percent of the base amount of retired pay until the survivor begins to draw Social Security, at which time the amount drops to 35 percent of the base amount of retired pay, which continues for the life of the survivor. After being intensively lobbied, the Congress has approved that this inequity will be removed over the next few years. Subsequently, survivors will receive both their Social Security and their full retirement annuities. Furthermore, Congress has approved a measure that, effective 1 October 2008, will end the SBP premium deduction when the retiree has paid the SBP premium for 360 months and has reached 70 years of age.

The plan also provides that if a retiree dies of a service-connected cause, as a result of which survivors are entitled to DIC payments (see "Dependency and Indemnity Compensation" above), the SBP payment will be reduced so that the total of the two payments—DIC and SBP—will be equal to the full amount otherwise payable under SBP. Thus, the total income to the survivors from SBP, DIC, and Social Security can equal or be slightly higher than the SBP income alone, depending upon the extent of the offset for Social Security. On the other hand, since SBP (as well as Social Security) is tied to the Consumer Price Index, the retired member also is assured, unless Congress again alters the program, that the spending power provided through SBP will remain relatively constant regardless of the effects of inflation.

It is apparent that participation in SBP has definite advantages and, perhaps, disadvantages that call for study, obtaining advice, and care in deciding if coverage is desired and in selecting the amount. SBP is not necessarily a panacea for all military retirees, but it deserves careful consideration as a benefit accruing to you as a result of military service, which is available for use in planning your estate.

SOCIAL SECURITY

Military personnel accrue Social Security benefits for active service as an important element of their overall security program. Participation is mandatory. Under the Social Security program, your base pay is taxed at a prescribed rate. The maximum taxable earnings are increased as average wage levels rise. At the same time, the benefits payable also increase. The amount of the benefit received from Social Security will depend upon the average monthly earnings and the number of years of credit that have been accrued. The benefit of most general interest is the monthly income that an officer and eligible members of the officer's family attain when the officer reaches age 65. Congress has recently increased the retirement age for certain year groups; further changes, perhaps even radical ones, should be anticipated.

Payments are provided for disabled officers and for their spouses and children. Monthly income is provided for an officer's widow or widower with children under 18 years of age, for children alone, for the widow or widower at age 60, or for dependent parents. These important benefits, then, supplement other insurance-type security programs. Application for benefits may be made at any Social Security office.

Note: It is important that you ensure that the Social Security Administration has credited you with the correct contributions. This may be accomplished by requesting the status of your account at approximately three-year intervals. Postcard-type forms are available at any Social Security office to use for this request.

Pension for Dependents of Retired Personnel and Veterans Whose Death Was Not Service-Connected. A modest survivor pension may be payable to dependents of veterans or retired personnel when retirement was for a reason other than physical disability or death occurred for a reason other than a service-connected cause. But the spouse and children of the veteran or retired individual are the only ones eligible.

The following payments are not considered income as to death pension payments:

- Government life insurance proceeds and, in some cases, commercial life insurance proceeds.
- The death gratuity.
- Donations from public or private relief or welfare organizations.
- Payments of VA pension, compensation, and dependency compensation.
- Survivor Benefit Plan.
- Lump-sum Social Security death payments.
- Payments to a person under public or private retirement annuity, endowment, or similar plans or programs equal to that person's contributions.
- Proceeds of a fire insurance policy.
- Amounts equal to amounts paid by a spouse or a child of a deceased veteran for just debts, the expenses of the last illness, and the expenses of burial that are not reimbursed by the VA.

For pension and other benefit rates, consult your personal affairs office.

INSURANCE

There are many variations of insurance, some inexpensive, some very expensive. Never lose sight of the basic fact that the primary object of life insurance is to provide for the well-being of your survivors after your death; this includes having tax-free cash assets to meet pressing financial obligations without having to liquidate savings. Everything else is incidental; in other words, insurance is not an investment program. See to it that your insurance program gives your family a reasonable chance for an acceptable standard of living after you have died.

Timing. In general, the time to take out insurance policies is at the earliest age you can afford them. All types of policies involve increased premiums with increased age. Remember that insurance is paid off in dollars that are subject to inflation; in other words, the purchasing power of insurance dollars may become less and less with passing years. Therefore, along with your insurance program and throughout your active service, you should follow a sound investment program in mutual funds, common stocks, and so on.

Educational Policies. Educational policies are designed to produce a given amount of money for the education of your children. Such a policy matures and is payable to you at a stipulated age of your child or is payable to your child at the time of your death. These are worthwhile policies, but they are relatively expensive.

Ordinary Life Insurance. This form of life insurance is often called whole, or straight, life insurance. Although it does have a cash surrender value that you can use in circumstances of acute financial stress, its main characteristic is that it provides a high level of financial security for your family at a low cost. You may use the proceeds of such a policy to serve the purposes of educational and endowment policies when protection is no longer needed.

After years of advocating term insurance, many financial advisors are again stressing the importance of whole-life insurance.

Term Life Insurance. You will hear that term insurance is far less expensive than whole-life insurance. So it is, for a limited period. However, term policies must be renewed *at the increased age of the applicant.* Thus your so-called inexpensive term life insurance will eventually become prohibitive in price. Moreover, upon retirement or later, you may become uninsurable because of physical disability or age. If, however, your need for insurance or for additional insurance is temporary, term insurance may best meet this special need. Term insurance provides the most coverage for the money when an officer is young. If you save systematically, the need for life insurance will decrease as term premiums increase with your age. But you will always need some life insurance even if you accumulate a large estate, because life insurance will provide cash for your survivors.

Servicemembers' Group Life Insurance (SGLI). Congress approved in 1965 a group life insurance program for all members of the armed forces. This program now authorizes $400,000 life insurance to any active-duty or reserve component servicemember. The benefits of this insurance will be paid to the beneficiary named by the servicemember (spouse, children, parents, next of kin, or executor), with minimum limitation as to place or manner of death.

The SGLI program costs the servicemember a small monthly premium, which is deducted from monthly pay and additional costs met by the government. This monthly premium is automatically deducted from your pay unless you decline in writing to have coverage or wish to have a lesser amount of coverage. The insurance is valid until 120 days after termination of active duty; within that 120 days, you may convert the insurance into a commercial life insurance policy without physical examination if desired. Although coverage under this program is optional, its advantages to Air Force members are so obvious and considerable that it should not be necessary to urge it upon you. In no other way can you obtain so much life insurance so inexpensively.

Mutual Insurance Associations for Servicemembers. There are mutual associations of officers of the military services. Eligible officers may assume with confidence that these organizations are carefully administered and that the services provided are tailored to fit military requirements.

Air Force Association Life Insurance. This plan provides term insurance at low rates, convertible to commercial insurance without physical examination on separation from the service. Write to AFA Insurance Division, 1501 Lee Highway, Arlington, VA 22209-1198; call 800-727-3337; or visit *http://www.afa.org.*

The Armed Forces Benefit Association. This nonprofit service organization offers group life and health insurance with its attendant low cost to supplement an officer's permanent program. Rates are very low because it is group insurance. At death, the life insurance may be paid in a lump sum or part in lump sum, part in installments, all in installments, or as an annuity.

In addition to life and health insurance, AFBA offers the Five Star Bank, a credit card, a mutual fund, and long-term care insurance.

Membership is open to regular officers and to reserve officers on extended active duty. Although this insurance is limited to active officers, there are provisions for conversion to other forms of insurance with the John Hancock Mutual Life Insurance Company, one of the underwriters of the program. Contact The Armed Forces Benefit Association, 909 N. Washington St., Alexandria, VA 22314-1556; telephone 800-776-2322; or visit *http://www.afba.com.*

Armed Forces Insurance. This group offers insurance against losses to personal and household effects, regardless of station or duty and at actual cost to members. Coverage is worldwide. Premium rates are very low. Settlements are prompt and fair to all concerned. Automobile insurance is also offered. Eligibility for membership includes any commissioned officer of the regular services or of the reserve components on active duty, except that a reserve member must have signified, by contract, an intent to remain on active duty for a period not less than three years. The spouse of a deceased member is permitted to continue the insurance in his or her name until remarriage or death. For information, visit *http://www.afi.org* or call 800-255-6792.

The Army and Air Force Mutual Aid Association. Write to 102 Sheridan Ave., Fort Myer, VA 22211; call 800-522-5221; or visit *http://www.aafmaa.com.*

This association services officers and enlisted personnel of the Army and Air Force.

United Services Automobile Association. This association was founded to provide automobile insurance at cost for officers and warrant officers of the armed services. USAA coverage has been expanded to include a variety of life insurance instruments, household goods and personal effects insurance, and home owner's and renter's insurance. All programs are arranged to meet the specific conditions of officers, such as the need for coverage in many foreign countries.

Policies may be obtained by active and retired officers; advanced ROTC, OTS, and academy cadets; those in certain precommissioning programs; officers of National Guard and reserve components when ordered to extended active federal duty; selected enlisted servicemembers; and the spouses of such deceased officers so long as their status is not changed by remarriage.

The automobile coverage is broad and similar in scope to policies offered by commercial companies. Its policies cover throughout the United States and in many foreign countries. Shipment coverage is provided upon request.

The association also offers insurance on personal effects and household goods. There is no adjustment of premium because of relocation of goods. Coverage is worldwide. For information: call 800-531-4440, or visit *http:// www.usaa.com.*

INVESTMENTS

Life insurance is used to make up the difference between a family's needs and the financial benefits available from the government. But investments are the real basis of financial security and independence. Furthermore, you do not have to die to enjoy their fruits.

To devise an investment strategy, you should evaluate the financial obligations and needs of your family. The objective should be to arrange your spending habits so that you not only live within your income, but also save systematically. From your income, you must first meet your financial obligations, and then you should save a fixed amount monthly. If anything is left, it is discretionary money, which can also be saved, or which can be spent on nonessentials. The priority order is first obligations, then savings, and only then nonessentials. Financial discipline, like any other discipline, pays dividends. Systematic savings in well-chosen investment instruments, plus time, result in financial security and independence. Because time is so important, you should begin a systematic investment plan now. Time forfeited can never be regained.

There are a variety of investment instruments: the military's tax-deferred Thrift Savings Plan (*http://www.tsp.gov*), bank savings accounts, government savings bonds, treasury notes and bills, certificates of deposit, annuities, municipal bonds, individual stocks, and mutual funds. Some of these instruments offer fixed rates of return, and others variable rates of return—or loss. Some are conservative and secure; others are risky. The greatest potential for high return comes from risky instruments. For the average investor, this means individual stocks or mutual funds whose objective is growth, not income.

Unless you have the skills, interest, and time to be your own financial expert, you need to select an investment instrument and/or an investment advisor. Conventional wisdom identifies mutual funds as the instrument of choice for those who cannot personally manage their investments, but who want their investments to be constantly and professionally managed. There are hundreds of funds to choose from, focusing on differing needs and inclinations of investors: growth or income or both, high or low risk, and so on. Selecting a fund can be a daunting task. Conventional wisdom recommends no-load or low-load funds—those without brokerage fees. However, for the novice investor, especially one unwilling to do a good deal of research before selecting a fund, professional advice may be of more value than saving the load fees. But do not let the task of selecting long-term investment instruments stop you from beginning saving now; use the military's Thrift Savings Plan or a bank or a credit union savings account until you have made your long-term financial investment plan.

Thrift Savings Plan. The Thrift Savings Plan for Uniformed Services is designed to help provide sufficient retirement income to members of the uniformed services. It has the same types of savings and tax benefits as "401(k)" plans. Each TSP participant selects any of five TSP investment funds. Contributions are made by allotment. Information on the Thrift Savings Plan is available online at *http://www.tsp.gov,* or from your military personnel flight, from family support center financial counselors, or from the Air Force Personnel Center, DSN 665-5000.

Professional Help. There are many professional financial planners who can assist officers in meeting the obligation to provide for the financial security of their families. Some financial investment and planning institutions cater to officers and senior NCOs. That they are in business to make money does not negate their usefulness as advisors. If you feel unprepared to do your own estate planning, a perfectly realistic feeling for the majority of officers, then consult the professionals. Ask several senior officers to recommend estate-planning professionals, or consult *Armed Forces Guide to Personal Financial Planning,* published by Stackpole Books.

Precious metals and stones, fine arts, antiques, and other collectibles are best left to the experts or mere gamblers. If you acquire these, you should like to live with them, because they may very well turn out to have been poor investments.

Credit Cards. Credit cards are convenient. Use them as a convenience only. Misuse of credit cards can cause financial disaster. Paying interest on a credit card loan is not wise. Pay off your monthly credit card balance in full; only carry over debt in an emergency. And even then, pay off the loan—which is given at a very high interest rate—the following month.

Except in unusual circumstances, an Air Force officer's income is sufficient to meet financial obligations, maintain a reasonable lifestyle, systematically invest, and indulge in an occasional luxury. Each officer must recognize the moral obligation and responsibility to provide family financial security. Government benefits paid to survivors of deceased officers are inadequate to meet the needs of most Air Force families. Insurance can cover the gap between government benefits and family needs, but only systematic investment can build real financial security and independence.

28

Overseas Assignment

One of the benefits of service in the Air Force is travel. During the Cold War especially, but not as prevalent today, most Air Force families look back on their overseas assignments as highlights of their careers. For those who take advantage of living abroad, there are numerous life-enriching opportunities. Living abroad broadens perspective—on culture, on values, on history, and even on the United States. There are opportunities for friendships, entertainment, recreation, and sightseeing that are not available in the United States or that are restricted to those with the financial wherewithal to travel privately. For all the advantages, however, there is also some trepidation. This natural response to the unknown can be alleviated to a degree by asking questions and by planning. The Air Force, and especially other Air Force families, can provide the answers.

Air Force officers expect to spend some of their careers at overseas stations. Depending on where the officers are assigned, they may go alone to an overseas assignment, leaving their families behind in the United States for some months, the period varying with different overseas stations. This separation of officers and their families may be the result of military hostilities, unstable politico-military situations, or limited housing available at overseas bases. On arrival in the overseas area, officers allowed to bring dependents sign up on a priority list for family housing. This list is governed by the length of the period of separation that has occurred. In some overseas areas, officers are permitted to obtain for themselves private rental housing, but this housing must be approved by the overseas command before it can be used as a basis for dependent travel. Other overseas assignments are designated unaccompanied; families cannot join their sponsors.

ACTION BEFORE DEPARTURE

When alerted for an overseas move, officers are counseled on travel procedures and tour elections. When dependent travel is authorized, an advance application for concurrent travel should be submitted if the officers intend to move their families overseas.

Official orders of the Department of the Air Force assigning officers to an overseas command prescribe the timing, the method of transportation, and other essential information about the journey. Officers must set their official and personal houses in order so that no unfinished official or personal business will arise before or after departure.

At every step, officers must bear in mind that their spouses, if not authorized to travel concurrently, will have need for certain documents in connection with later movement to the overseas area. Officers must therefore ensure that their spouses have all necessary documents, such as titles to automobiles, copies of officers' orders, passports, insurance policies, inventories of household goods, children's school records, birth certificates, and the like. Officers must also ensure that their spouses have sufficient money (an allotment may be needed) to cover family needs during the period of separation, including the period of movement overseas.

Receipt of Passport Authorization. After the officer's application for dependent travel is approved by the overseas commander, a letter authorizing the family members to apply for a no-fee passport is furnished to them. Upon receipt of passport authorization, family members should make application for a no-fee passport through the military personnel flight at the nearest military base, preferably an Air Force base. When making application, family members must present these documents:

- A birth certificate for each member of the family going overseas.
- Two identical photographs not smaller than 2 inches by 2 inches and taken full face and without a hat.
- Proof of American citizenship, if not native born.

Immunizations Required. All family members going overseas at government expense are required to receive certain immunizations before leaving the United States. Immunization requirements may change without notice; current information may be obtained from the nearest armed forces medical facility.

Shipment of Household Goods. Specific recommendations concerning items of household goods to be shipped to a particular foreign country are best obtained from the officer's sponsor at the overseas location. The transportation officer will arrange for storage of all or any portion of the family's household goods in commercial facilities located in the general vicinity of the base. Decisions must therefore be made as to what, if any, items of household goods should be left in storage in the United States. Other household goods will be shipped to the overseas base. Some commands limit the weight and nature of household goods that can be shipped.

ACTIONS ON RECEIPT OF PORT CALL

When the family has received its port call—that is, information as to the exact time for reporting to the aerial port of embarkation—final decisions must be made on the following points:

- The exact time for household goods to be picked up by the commercial carriers for delivery to the overseas base of assignment or the commercial storage facility.
- What will be shipped as unaccompanied baggage. Unaccompanied baggage is limited by weight. This baggage may include clothes, kitchen utensils, light housekeeping items, and collapsible items, such as cribs and playpens, when necessary for the care of an infant. It may be expected that the unaccompanied baggage will arrive in the overseas area several weeks after the arrival of the family members.
- What to do about the automobile. If the servicemember's orders authorized the shipment of a privately owned vehicle, the officer must see that the car is delivered to the port of shipment.

Movement of POV. The privately owned vehicle turned in for shipment will move to a seaport in the area to which the family is traveling. The automobile will be about one month in transit. It will arrive at a port, where it must be picked up by the officer or the officer's agent. The officer will be notified by the port authorities of the arrival of the automobile.

Shipment of Pets to Overseas Areas. Certain pets may be shipped at the owner's risk and at no expense to the government. The United Kingdom, which does not have rabies, restricts the importation of pets.

Exchange Facilities Overseas. Air Force personnel preparing for overseas assignments should *not* assume that they must take with them all things needed for a three-year tour. The exchanges overseas are excellent. They are prepared to meet every conceivable need, from clothing to washing machines, stereos, and automobiles. Virtually everything needed by an Air Force family can be obtained in the exchanges. The exchanges are complete in themselves, because overseas exchanges are allowed to stock and sell items denied to exchanges in the United States. Moreover, the local economies of such countries as Germany, Italy, Japan, and England offer many supplementary sources from which family needs can be met.

Commissaries Overseas. Military commissaries overseas meet all normal food needs. Food prices in the overseas commissaries are comparable to those in military facilities in the United States. Military families who buy food at the local markets do so merely because they prefer that option.

Medical Care Overseas. The family need not be concerned regarding adequate medical care overseas for adults or children, including prenatal treatment. Excellent clinics are available in most areas. Optical and dental services are available for family members in the military facilities.

Schools Overseas. Elementary, middle, and high school facilities are provided in all established commands. Standards are closely supervised. Considering the intangible values to be derived by travel and life overseas for a few years, most parents feel that their children benefit by the experience. In the unusual case where schools are not provided under military control, parents should learn about facilities used by American citizens in the areas or explore the possibilities of home schooling. Unless there are very unusual circumstances, there is no strong reason for Air Force families to be separated merely because of the school situation of their children.

Movement of Dependent Students to and from Overseas Areas. Student dependents of military personnel stationed outside the continental United States are authorized transportation on a space-available basis to the port of embarkation in the United States to attend school in the United States, and between the United States and an overseas port to spend their summer vacations with their families. Only one round-trip a year is authorized and normally will be taken during the summer vacation period. Dependents who pass the age of 21 years while engaged in full-time undergraduate study will be authorized the same transportation privilege.

Postal Service. The Army—Air Force Postal Service provides mail service overseas for Air Force and Army personnel. Postal rates are identical to those in the continental United States.

Merchandise Subject to U.S. Customs. Service overseas provides an opportunity for the purchase of merchandise made in foreign countries. Items are often sold for prices lower than the cost of similar items in the United States. The officer and spouse who make a real study of these possibilities and purchase wisely may acquire unusual possessions they will cherish throughout their lives.

All such purchases should be made with due regard to U.S. and host country customs regulations. The laws and regulations governing the entry of merchandise purchased abroad into the United States are quite liberal. The entry or attempt at entry of merchandise purchased abroad without the required customs declaration is an evasion of the law. It is smuggling, and it is subject to severe penalties. Find out what can be brought into the United States openly and legally. For articles of personal use and enjoyment in a household, the quantity authorized for free entry should be sufficient. Taking certain items, especially antiquities, out of some countries is a crime. Learn the laws.

Housing in Overseas Areas. Each foreign country presents the Air Force officer and family with new and sometimes challenging living conditions. Conditions vary widely among countries. Therefore, each foreign station must be studied separately; generalizations are worthless and misleading. Officers and their families who are on orders to a foreign country should learn about the local conditions, such as housing, cost of living, currency, operation of appliances, furniture, clothes, and pets.

Will your electrical equipment work on the current (voltage and cycle) in the overseas area? A 220-volt system can be reduced to 110 volts by use of a transformer available at the overseas exchange or a thrift shop.

As an observation applicable to life in almost all overseas areas, it is possible to say this: You will find the situation not at all difficult, nor nearly as different as you might have thought. So, relax. You are not going to the moon, but rather, in most cases, to highly civilized and industrialized countries whose cultures were ancient when the United States was a wilderness.

Housing available to officers overseas varies considerably among areas. Government quarters are, however, generally adequate, and some are excellent. Although the standard of government quarters in any overseas area approximates that of quarters on bases in the United States, there are exceptions.

Private housing is an entirely different proposition. The price of private housing is often very high. The cost of utilities is also higher than in the United States. On the other hand, officers who are authorized to find housing on the local economy may receive a station allowance that partly compensates for the increased costs encountered. The amount of the COLA (cost-of-living allowance) varies with overseas stations.

Travel and Recreation Opportunities in Overseas Areas. One of the great attractions of life overseas is the opportunity provided to travel in foreign countries and to take advantage of the recreational facilities available. By using the facilities of the various U.S. military installations sprinkled over Europe, it is possible to visit a vast number of interesting places at a reasonable cost. In the Far East, distances become a problem; nonetheless, it is possible for officers to make arrangements to visit countries other than the one in which they are stationed. In Europe and in Japan, facilities for sports of all kinds are not only available, but also close at hand. Where the overseas station is somewhat isolated, such as in Korea, arrangements have been made to accommodate sports enthusiasts of all types.

TOURS OF DUTY

The Air Force seeks to ensure equitable distribution of overseas assignments to its personnel. Although the policy is on a "first to return, first to go" basis, specific requirements must influence actual selections, and lengths of tours may change with the military situation.

LEARNING THE LANGUAGE

Learning the language of your host country is personally beneficial, and could prove beneficial to the United States as well. Off-duty classes, mixing with the nationals, and studying the local culture and government are methods that can be used to learn the language. Even if the language is a difficult one, you and your family should learn at least the phrases of courtesy and of the social amenities. They will carry you a long way.

CULTURAL DIFFERENCES

Some of the most exciting, and at times most confusing and even exasperating, experiences of living overseas are based on cultural differences. Living overseas requires constant observation—similar to prudent behavior anywhere or anytime you do not know what to expect and what is expected of you.

Before venturing afield, acquaint yourself with cultural differences that have the potential to offend the sensitivities of your host nation. Be particular about religion, appropriate clothing and public behavior for men and women, use of tobacco and alcohol, and social customs regarding eating and being introduced to host nationals. Be aware that the freedoms you are accustomed to as an American may be restricted or may not even exist—freedoms regarding religious observation, public speech (including written materials), and gender equality. You must always remember that all Americans abroad are unofficial ambassadors of the United States; this fact is all the more important for employees of the U.S. government: you and your family members.

Appendix A

Initial Active-Duty
and Follow-On Assignments

Reporting to your initial active-duty assignment, the first unit after commissioning, can be somewhat traumatic. Actually, as officers move from assignment to assignment, they always experience some uneasiness: Will I like the location, the work, my fellow workers, my boss? And will they like me? Will I be up to what is required of me? Chances are that the answers to all these questions will be yes. Except under the most unusual circumstances, professional success, fulfillment, and happiness are under your control.

Some of the uneasiness about your first active-duty assignment, or any follow-on assignment, can be dispelled by being prepared. The more you know about your assignment, the more comfortable you will be. Try to find out as much as possible from your commissioning source. In any case, each new assignment will involve recurring tasks. You'll learn to do them in your sleep—and sponsors, checklists, and all the personnel at the in-processing section of your military personnel flight (MPF) will help you make it smooth.

INITIAL ASSIGNMENT

Notification of Assignment. The Air Force Personnel Center (AFPC) will send you a notification of assignment letter, or extended active-duty order. It will give you your duty unit, generally a specialty course in one of Air Education and Training Command's schools. As most officers begin their service as officer students, transition to active duty is eased somewhat. The letter will tell you when and where to report. Read and understand this letter. For follow-on assignments, officers receive permanent-change-of-station (PCS) orders.

Sponsorship. Officers going to school are not assigned sponsors. If you are one of the few officers with a direct-duty assignment—and for all follow-on assignments—you will have a sponsor who will ease your PCS in many ways.

Shipping Household Goods. If you have more household goods than you can carry in your automobile, contact the traffic management office (TMO) at the nearest Air Force base (see appendix C). If you're going to school, you will probably live in the bachelor officer quarters (BOQ), so you will want to store your household goods at government expense. Question the TMO on this. Don't exceed your weight limit: 10,000 pounds for single second lieutenants and 12,000 pounds for married lieutenants.

Travel. Most officers will drive their own automobiles to their first assignments. The government reimburses a set amount per mile for the official distance from your home of record to your initial base and a daily rate called per diem for lodging and food up to the number of travel days authorized in your orders. If you will not be driving, talk with the TMO about commercial travel, such as by air.

Paperwork and Documents. You will need to have ready access to certain documents during your Air Force career. Bring them with you when you report for your first duty assignment. You will not need all of them, but it is better to have them if required than to have to hunt them down later. Carry those documents that you will not need immediate access to in a small fireproof metal box. Of course, it is always a good practice to have photocopies of your most important personal documents. The threat of identity theft dictates that you always safeguard your personal documents, especially your credit card, bank account, and Social Security card numbers. After reaching your PCS assignment, you should consider renting a safe-deposit box in a local bank. In an age of identity theft, it is crucial that you safeguard documents such as these. The following documents should be included:

- Any remaining copies of travel orders and amendments
- Transportation request (TR)
- Household goods shipping documents
- Driver's license
- Car registration and title
- Car insurance policies
- Personal property insurance policies
- Checkbook
- Credit cards
- Immunization records
- Official copies of birth certificates for all family members
- Naturalization papers, if applicable
- Passports
- Copy of will
- Social Security card
- Official college transcripts
- Marriage certificate
- Divorce or death certificates terminating any previous marriages
- Certified true copies of adoption papers for any adopted children
- Children's school records

Uniforms. When going to your first assignment, at the minimum take one dress uniform (coat and trousers or skirt) and at least two service uniforms (shirt and trousers or skirt) for the season of the year (coat if necessary); have all accessories, including hat and shoes. You can buy additional uniforms and uniform items at your first base.

Expenses. Take enough money (cash, checks, credit card) to handle your travel expenses and at least the first two weeks at your new base; after two weeks, you should get paid.

Actions on Arrival. Report during the time window indicated on your orders. If no times are indicated, you have until midnight of your report-not-later-than date (RNLTD), although you are well advised to report between 0900 and 1500. The security police at the gate will give you a temporary pass if necessary, and direct you to your unit during duty hours or to the 24-hour arrival point during nonduty hours (generally the base billeting office). In any case, you'll want to take care of your billeting, especially if you have a family with you. If you are single or unaccompanied, you will probably be billeted in the visiting officer quarters (VOQ) or bachelor officer quarters (BOQ), or if you are accompanied by your family, in the temporary lodging facility (TLF). In any case, the billeting office will help you. (If you have a sponsor, billeting arrangements should already have been made.) If you arrive after duty hours, call your sponsor if you have one, or call your unit first thing in the morning. You may be expected to in-process immediately, or you may be expected to report to your unit first. If this is your first assignment, you'll probably be at an Air Education and Training Command base, where there will be more than ample instructions. In either case (unit or in-processing), you'll be expected to be in uniform; remember the importance of a good first impression.

In-Processing. All bases have well-organized, easy-to-follow in-processing. If you're at a school, you'll be led through the process. Otherwise, you'll have to in-process with your unit's orderly room and/or your military personnel flight (MPF), accounting and finance office, various briefings, and unit processing. It all begins at the MPF. For your first assignment take all the documents listed above (just leave them locked in your car); you may not need them all, but it's better to come prepared.

Permanent Housing. If your first assignment is an Air Force Education and Training Command school and if you're single or unaccompanied, you will almost certainly be billeted on base. But if you have a direct-duty assignment, or a follow-on assignment, and you're accompanied, housing may be more of a problem. You could be housed on base. If quarters are not available, the base housing referral office will help with leads, advice, and perhaps some restrictions. Your unit or school will recognize that you will not really be settled and ready to devote all your efforts to the job until you have housing, especially if you're accompanied. Be assured that they will help you get settled. The base Family Services Center can provide loaned household items: bedding, cooking and eating utensils, and baby needs.

Starting to Work. As a newly commissioned officer arriving on active duty for a first tour, you will find that no one expects you to be expert in performing your duties or in knowing about the Air Force. You will also find, however, that seniors and contemporaries will expect you to go about bettering your technical capabilities and expanding your knowledge. Practically everyone on the base, from the airman to the commander and even civilian personnel, will be ready to assist you in any way they can. As a new officer, you should neither bluff nor be too proud to seek information and assistance. Simply proceed to learn your job and your way around. Always remember: The only stupid question is the one not asked.

CHANGE OF STATION
When you, as an officer already assigned on active duty, receive orders reassigning you to a different base, you must perform certain tasks before you leave. Although the most important of these duties relates to securing release from responsibility for unit property and funds, you must also take care of certain personal responsibilities when departing a station. For example, you must turn in equipment drawn from the base supply officer. Generally, you can clear the base from one central location. If you have outstanding debts or bills in the local civilian community, you should either pay these obligations or make satisfactory arrangements with your creditors.

ASSUMPTION OF NEW DUTIES
Many of the rapidly occurring changes in the lives and careers of Air Force officers involve physical movement from one base to another; quite often, the change confronting an Air Force officer is in the nature of the assumption of a new duty. Command is a very infrequent duty assignment. By far the majority of the officers of the Air Force are engaged in duties, most frequently staff assignments, that do not involve exercising command over units of the Air Force.

Assuming a Staff Position. Staff work is extremely important; commanders could not function without their staffs. Every officer must be determined to perform every assignment in an outstanding manner.

Upon reporting for duty on staff assignments, officers should report to the executive officer of the staff agency to which assigned and thereafter to the chiefs of subbranches or sections as directed by the exec. (Your sponsor should direct you in this and accompany you on your orientation.) Usually, a well-administered headquarters will have published a manual for staff officers that sets forth the organization and the particular staff procedures desired by the commander of the headquarters. On joining a staff, you should find one of these manuals and study it with care.

Another step is to become acquainted with the other members of the staff, especially with those members of staff sections closely allied to your own.

Having mastered the organization and the procedures and having become acquainted with the members of the staff to which you are assigned, you should get acquainted with officers in staffs senior and junior to your own. For example, as an officer assigned to the operations section of a group headquarters, you should become acquainted with the operations personnel in the wing headquarters and also in each of the squadron headquarters within your own group. These personal relationships often go far in mitigating misunderstanding among staffs of various levels.

As a staff officer, you must constantly bear in mind that you are not a commander and do not have the power of command. Occasionally, however, you may act for the commander in matters of considerable importance. In doing so, you must strictly adhere to the policies of the commander. Never use your commander's name, rank, title, or position to affect actions that are, in fact, your own preferences. Do not pretend to represent your commander when, in fact, you are actually representing yourself. On the other hand, you certainly should not evade your own responsibilities by seeking to discover the views of the commander in every specific instance. You must act within the scope of the commander's authority and policies, and you must act as if you bear the sole responsibility for your actions. Consider these questions whenever you have to make decisions for or in other ways act for your commander: (1) Would I be willing to undertake the execution of the decision I recommend were I a subordinate element commander receiving orders of this staff? (2) Would I be willing to accept the full responsibility for the effects of this decision were I the chief of this staff?

Assuming a Command Position. See chapter 4.

Appendix B

Professional Reading Guide

Professional competence demands that all Air Force officers study air and space power, service doctrine, employment concepts, and the Air Force contribution to joint and combined operations. In 1996, then chief of staff of the Air Force, General Ronald Fogleman, created the first CSAF Professional Reading List. Since that time, the list has been changed frequently. Consequently, in this appendix you will find the 2000 Air University Professional Reading Guide. It provides the foundation for developing professional expertise.

All officers should read *Air and Space Power Journal,* as well as books selected from the lists below.

2000 AIR UNIVERSITY PROFESSIONAL READING GUIDE
The books listed in the Air University Professional Reading Guide, which is no longer published, are divided into three categories. *Warfare Studies* builds a foundation of knowledge about war and deals with particular types and periods of warfare. It includes historical and analytical readings, as well as firsthand accounts. *Command and Leadership* examines the challenges of military leadership and management and includes the biographies and autobiographies of some whose measure of success is now a matter of public record. *National Security Affairs and Strategy* deals with the theory and practice of creating and implementing military strategies and policies. Included in this category are studies of air warfare, from its infancy through its maturation in Desert Storm.

WARFARE STUDIES
General Military History, Strategy, and Doctrine
Brodie, Bernard, and Fawn M. Brodie. *From Crossbow to H-bomb.* Bloomington, IN: Indiana University Press, 1973. 320 pp. A historical survey of science and technology in warfare.

Builder, Carl H. *The Icarus Syndrome.* New Brunswick, NJ: Transaction Publishers, 1993. 299 pp. A provocative and critical look at the role of air power theory in the development of the U.S. Air Force.

Clausewitz, Carl von. *On War.* Edited and translated by Peter Paret and Michael Howard. Princeton: Princeton University Press, 1984 (1976). 732 pp. The military classic on the nature and art of waging war.

Douhet, Guilio. *The Command of the Air.* Translated by Dino Ferrari. Washington, DC: Office of Air Force History, 1983 (1942). 394 pp. The first and most passionate exposition of a comprehensive air warfare theory.

Freedman, Lawrence. *War.* New York: Oxford University Press, 1994. 385 pp. Excellent anthology of articles on all aspects of war.

Hallion, Richard P. *Strike from the Sky: The History of Battlefield Air Attack, 1911–1945.* Washington, DC: Smithsonian Institute Press, 1989. 323 pp. Comprehensive look at the development of tactical airpower.

Headquarters, Training and Doctrine Command. *FM 100-5: Operations.* Washington, DC: Government Printing Office, June 1993. 99 pp. The U.S. Army doctrine for combat operations.

Howard, Michael E. *War in European History.* New York: Oxford University Press, 1976. 165 pp. Short but brilliant study that links society, politics, economics, and technology to explain the changes in war on that continent.

Liddell Hart, Sir Basil H. *Strategy: The Indirect Approach.* London: Praeger Publishers, 1954. 420 pp. The author explains through historical examples his concept of the indirect approach.

McNeill, William H. *The Pursuit of Power: Technology, Armed Force, and Society Since A.D. 1000.* Chicago: University of Chicago Press, 1982. 405 pp. Postulates that the West's rise to military dominance has roots in the military and economic diversity that characterized Europe's situation after the fall of Rome.

Meilinger, Phillip S. *10 Propositions Regarding Air Power.* Washington, DC: Air Force History and Museums Program, 1995. 86 pp. Provocative propositions to instill an appreciation for airpower.

Millett, Allan R., and Peter Mazlowski. *For the Common Defense: A Military History of the United States of America.* New York: Free Press, 1984. 621 pp. A balanced, thorough one-volume examination of American military policy from the colonial period to the Reagan era.

Millis, Walter. *Arms and Men: A Study in American Military History.* New Brunswick, NJ: Rutgers University Press, 1981 (1956). 382 pp. Though concerned with American military policy, Millis's real contribution is his discussion of revolutions in warfare and how they contributed to the appearance of total war.

Naval Doctrine Command. *NDP 1: Naval Warfare.* Washington, DC: Government Printing Office, 1994. 76 pp. The Navy's first official statement of its doctrine.

Preston, Richard A., Sidney F. Wise, and Alex Roland. *Men in Arms: A History of Warfare and Its Interrelationships with Western Society.* Fort Worth:

Holt, Rhinehart and Winston, 1991. 458 pp. Sets military history in the broad spectrum of social, economic, political, and technological change in world history.

Strachan, Hew. *European Armies and the Conduct of War.* Boston: Allen and Unwin, 1983. 224 pp. Modern European military history analyzed by examining the principal military theorists and practitioners.

Sun Tzu. *The Art of War.* Translated by T. R. Phillips. New York: Delta, 1988. 82 pp. This short treatise lays down the basic and timeless principles dealing with strategy, tactics, communications, supply, intelligence, etc.

United States Air Force. *AFM 1-1, Volumes I and II: Basic Aerospace Doctrine of the United States Air Force.* Washington, DC: Government Printing Office, March 1992. Vol. I: 20 pp. Vol. II: 308 pp. Volume I contains the definitive statement of U.S. Air Force basic doctrine. Volume II contains a set of background essays explaining and supporting Air Force basic doctrine.

United States Marine Corps. *FMFM 1: Warfighting.* Washington, DC: Government Printing Office, March 6, 1989. 88 pp. The concepts and values that underpin Marine Corps doctrine.

Warden, John A., III. *The Air Campaign: Planning for Combat.* Washington, DC: Pergamon-Brassey's, 1989. 160 pp. A new look at the theory of air warfare that links the theory to practical application at the operational level of war.

Weigley, Russell F. *The American Way of War.* Bloomington, IN: Indiana University Press, 1977 (1973). 584 pp. Analyzes the historical roots of American military strategy.

Period-Specific Studies

Atkinson, Rick. *Crusade: The Untold Story of the Persian Gulf War.* New York: Houghton Mifflin Company, 1993. 575 pp. Balanced journalistic account of Operation Desert Storm.

Baucom, Donald K. *The Origins of SDI, 1944–1983.* Lawrence, KS: University Press of Kansas, 1992. 276 pp. An insider's account of the development of the Strategic Defense Initiative Program through the post–Cold War era.

Clodfelter, Mark. *The Limits of Airpower: The American Bombing of Vietnam.* New York: The Free Press, 1989. 297 pp. An excellent study of the use and misuse of airpower.

Futrell, Robert F. *The United States Air Force in Korea, 1950–1953.* Washington, DC: Office of Air Force History, 1983 (1961). 823 pp. Official history and analysis of air power in Korea.

Greer, Thomas H. *The Development of Air Doctrine in the Army Air Arm, 1917–1941.* Washington, DC: Office of Air Force History, 1985. 154 pp. The evolution of air doctrine between the world wars.

Herring, George C. *America's Longest War: The United States and Vietnam, 1950–1975.* New York: Knopf, 1986. 316 pp. Review of the politico-military issues of the Vietnam War.

Mann, Edward C., III. *Thunder and Lightning: Desert Storm and the Air Power Debates.* Montgomery, AL. Air University Press, 1995. 220 pp. Volume II on the Operation Desert Storm air campaign.

Morrow, Robert. *The Great War in the Air.* Washington, DC: Smithsonian Institution Press, 1993. 300 pp. The best overall book available on airpower in World War I.

Murray, Williamson. *Strategy for Defeat: The Luftwaffe, 1933–1945.* Montgomery, AL: Air University Press, 1983. 365 pp. Well-balanced analysis of the Luftwaffe in World War II.

Overy, R. J. *The Air War, 1939–1945.* Chelsea, MI: Scarborough House, 1981. 263 pp. Excellent one-volume work on the role of air forces in World War II.

Perret, Geoffrey. *Winged Victory: The Army Air Forces in World War II.* New York: Random House, Inc., 1993. 549 pp. The best treatment of the Air Force's World War II experience.

Reynolds, Richard T. *Heart of the Storm.* Montgomery, AL. Air University Press, 1995. 147 pp. Volume I on the genesis of the air campaign against Iraq.

Spector, Ronald H. *Eagle Against the Sun: The American War with Japan.* New York: Free Press, 1985. 589 pp. The best single-volume history of the Pacific War.

Stokesbury, James L. *A Short History of World War.* New York: William Morrow & Company, 1981. 348 pp. Stokesbury's survey is the best brief account of the war.

Weinberg, Gerhardt L. *A World at Arms: A Global History of World War II.* New York: Cambridge University Press, 1994. 1,178 pp. The latest comprehensive look at World War II.

Topic-Specific Studies

Freedman, Lawrence. *The Evolution of Nuclear Strategy.* New York: St. Martin's Press, 1989. 522 pp. Examination of the theories and theorists of the nuclear age.

Hough, Harold. *Satellite Surveillance.* Port Townsend, WA: Loompanics Unlimited, 1991. 196 pp. Explores spaceborne imagery and details uses and abuses of satellite technology.

Joint Chiefs of Staff. *Joint Publication 30: Doctrine for Joint Operations.* Washington, DC: Government Printing Office, September 9, 1993. 203 pp. The fundamental principles and concepts for joint and multinational operations.

Laquer, Walter. Guerrilla: *A Historical and Critical Study.* Boston: Little, Brown, 1976. 462 pp. A comparative study of guerrilla and terrorist theory.

Levine, Alan J. *The Missile and Space Race.* Westport, CT: Praeger Publishers, 1994. 247 pp. Comprehensive look at the U.S.-Soviet space and missile program development.

Mason, R. A. *Air Power: A Centennial Appraisal.* Washington, DC: Brassey's, 1994. 320 pp. Comprehensive look at airpower in theory and practice.

Pagonis, William G. *Moving Mountains: Lessons in Leadership and Logistics from the Gulf War.* Boston, MA: Harvard Business School Press, 1992. 248 pp. Reviews leadership, management, and logistics in the Gulf War.

Van Creveld, Martin L. *Supplying War: Logistics from Wallenstein to Patton.* Cambridge, MA: Cambridge University Press, 1977. 284 pp. Examines the practical art of moving and supplying armies.

Command and Leadership

Frisbee, John L. *Makers of the United States Air Force.* Washington, DC: Pergamon-Brassey's International Defense Publishers, 1989. 347 pp. A must-read on those who helped develop the USAF.

Gardner, John. *On Leadership.* New York: Free Press, 1990. 220 pp. A searching examination of leadership as it is practiced, or malpracticed, in America today.

Hackett, John Winthrop. *The Profession of Arms.* London: Times Publishing Co., 1963. 68 pp. Traces the development, meaning, and implications of our military traditions.

Keegan, John. *The Face of Battle.* Harmondsworth: Penguin, 1978 (1976). 364 pp. Classic work that examines the battles at Agincourt (1415), Waterloo (1815), and the Somme (1916).

Puryear, Edgar F. *Nineteen Stars: A Study in Military Character and Leadership.* Novato, CA: Presidio Press, 1981 (1971). 437 pp. This purely leadership-oriented work highlights the careers of four outstanding Army officers.

Toner, James H. *True Faith and Allegiance: The Burden of Military Ethics.* Lexington, KY: The University Press of Kentucky, 1995. 202 pp. An officer's ethical foundation is based on true faith and allegiance and the knowledge to do the right thing.

National Security Affairs and Strategy

Brodie, Bernard. *Strategy in the Missile Age.* Princeton, NJ: Princeton University Press, 1965. 423 pp. One of this era's wisest thinkers reviews the relationship between military policy, strategy, and nuclear weapons.

Builder, Carl H. *The Mask of War.* Baltimore, MD: The Johns Hopkins University Press, 1989. 242 pp. A provocative study arguing that institutional personalities determine how the services approach strategy and planning.

Huntington, Samuel P. *The Soldier and the State: The Theory and Politics of Civil-Military Relations.* Cambridge: Belknap Press of Harvard University,

1957. 534 pp. Classic realist exposition on American civil-military relations.

Paret, Peter, ed. *Makers of Modern Strategy: From Machiavelli to the Nuclear Age.* Princeton, NJ: Princeton University Press, 1986. 941 pp. Twenty-eight essays tracing the evolution of military thought. An essential book on the subject of strategy.

Schelling, T. C. *The Strategy of Conflict.* Cambridge, MA: Harvard University Press, 1960. 272 pp. One of the earliest and best books on modern strategy. Ideas are extremely relevant for a post–Cold War environment.

Wright, Q. *A Study of War.* Chicago: University of Chicago Press, 1965. 365 pp. The classic account of why wars occur, with a masterful blend of history and international relations.

Appendix C

Major Active-Duty USAF Installations

Altus AFB, Okla. 73523-5000; 120 mi. SW of Oklahoma City. Phone: 580-482-8100; DSN 866-1110. Majcom: AETC. Host: 97th Air Mobility Wing. Mission: trains aircrew members for C-5, C-17, and KC-135 aircraft. History: activated January 1943; inactivated May 1945; reactivated January 1953. Area: 7,746 acres. Runways: 13,440 ft., 9,000-ft. parallel runway, and 3,515-ft. assault strip. Altitude: 1,381 ft. Personnel: permanent party military, 2,220; DOD civilians, 2,384. Housing: single family, 726; visiting, VOQ/VAQ, 315; TLF, 30. Clinic.

Andersen AFB, Guam, APO AP 96543-5000; 2 mi. N of Yigo. Phone: (cmcl, from CONUS) 671-366-1110; DSN 315-366-1110. Majcom: PACAF. Host: 36th Wing. Mission: Pacific center for power projection, regional cooperation, and multinational training; serves as a logistic support and staging base for aircraft operating in the Pacific and Indian Oceans. Major tenants: Det. 5, 22nd Space Operations Sq. (AFSPC); 613th Contingency Response Gp. (AMC); 734th Air Mobility Sq. (AMC); Helicopter Combat Support Sq. 5 (US Navy). History: activated 1945. Named for Gen. James Roy Andersen, who was chief of staff, Hq. AAF, Pacific Ocean Areas, and lost at sea in February 1945. Area: 20,270 acres. Runways: 11,182 ft. and 10,555 ft. Altitude: 612 ft. Personnel: permanent party military, 2,108; DOD civilians, 1,561. Housing: single family, officer, 236, enlisted, 1,153; unaccompanied, UOQ, 74, UAQ/UEQ, 1,018; visiting, VOQ, 23, VAQ/VEQ, 519, TLF, 232. Clinic.

Andrews AFB, Md. 20762-5000; 10 mi. SE of Washington, D.C. Phone: 301-981-1110; DSN 858-1110. Host: 316th Wing. Mission: provides contingency response capability critical to national security. This capability includes emergency reaction rotary-wing airlift for the National Capital Region, combat-ready airmen for air and space expeditionary forces, and a secure installation and robust infrastructure to support base organizations. Major tenants: Hq. AFOSI; Air National Guard Readiness Center; 89th AW (AMC); 113th Wing (ANG), F-16; 459th ARW (AFRC), KC-135; Naval Air Facility; Marine Aircraft Gp. 49, Det. A; Air Force Review Boards Agency. History: activated May 1943. Named for Lt. Gen. Frank M. Andrews, military air pioneer and WWII commander of the European Theater, killed in aircraft accident 3 May 1943 in Iceland. Area: 6,853 acres. Runways: 9,755 ft. and 9,300 ft. Altitude: 281 ft. Personnel:

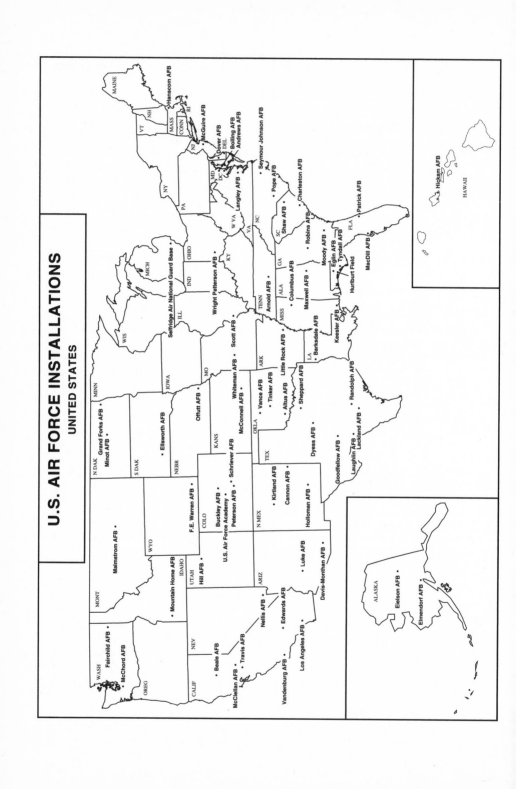

U.S. AIR FORCE INSTALLATIONS
UNITED STATES

permanent party military 5,502; DOD civilians, 3,247. Housing: single family, officer, 138 (including 96 govt.-leased), enlisted, 1,342 (including 318 govt.-leased); visiting, VOQ, 64, VAQ/VEQ, 35, TLF, 20. Hospital.

Arnold AFB, Tenn. 37389; approx. 7 mi. SE of Manchester. Phone: 931-454-1110; DSN 340-1110. Majcom: AFMC. Host: Arnold Engineering Development Center. Mission: supports acquisition and sustainment of aerospace systems by conducting flight simulation research, development, and evaluation testing for DOD, other government agencies, and commercial aerospace firms with the world's largest complex of wind tunnels, jet and rocket engine test cells, space simulation chambers, and hyperballistic ranges. History: base dedicated 25 June 1951. Named for Gen. of the Army H.H. "Hap" Arnold, wartime Chief of the Army Air Forces. Area: 39,081 acres. Runway: 6,000 ft. Altitude: 1,100 ft. Personnel: permanent party military, 79; DOD civilians, 255. Housing: single family, officer, 19, enlisted, 21; visiting, 40. Medical aid station and small VA clinic.

Aviano AB, Italy, APO AE 09604; adjacent to Aviano, 50 mi. N of Venice. Phone: (cmcl, from CONUS) 011-39-0434-30-1110/1113; DSN 314-632-1110. Majcom: USAFE. Host: 31st Fighter Wing. Mission: maintains two LANTIRN-equipped F-16 fighter squadrons, the 510th and the 555th, and 603rd Air Control Sq. Major tenants: Hq. 401st Air Expeditionary Wing (USAFE). Geographically Separated Units (GSUs): Det. 2, 401st AEW Pristina (Kosovo) Serbia; Det. 1, 401st AEW, Sarajevo, Bosnia; 774th Expeditionary Air Base Gp., Istres AB, France; 31st RED HORSE Flt. and 31st Munitions Sq., Camp Darby, Italy; 31st Munitions Support Sq., Ghedi AB, Italy; 99th Ex. Recon. Sq., RAF Akrotiri, Cyprus; 496th Air Base Sq., Moron AB, Spain. History: one of the oldest Italian air bases, dating to 1911. USAF began operations 1954. Area: 1,331 acres. Runway: 8,596 ft. Altitude: 413 ft. Personnel: permanent party military, 3,500; DOD civilians, 260. Housing: 681 govt.-leased (189 officer, 592 enlisted); unaccompanied, UAQ/UEQ, 812; visiting, 74, DV, 6. Clinic (contracted with local hospital).

Barksdale AFB, La. 71110-5000; in Bossier City. Phone: 318-456-1110; DSN 781-1110. Majcom: ACC. Host: 2nd Bomb Wing. Mission: B-52H operations and training. Major tenants: 8th Air Force (ACC); 917th Wing (AFRC), A-10, B-52H; 8th Air Force Museum. History: activated 2 Feb. 1933. Named for Lt. Eugene H. Barksdale, WWI airman killed in an August 1926 crash. Area: 22,000 acres (18,000 acres reserved for recreation). Runway: 11,756 ft. Altitude: 166 ft. Personnel: permanent party military, 7,442; DOD civilians, 1,122. Housing: single family, officer, 135, enlisted, 594; unaccompanied, 876; visiting, VOQ, 118, VAQ, 102, TLF, 24. Superclinic.

Beale AFB, Calif. 95903-5000; 13 mi. E of Marysville. Phone: 530-634-3000; DSN 368-1110. Majcom: ACC. Host: 9th Reconnaissance Wing. Mission: U-2, KC-135, and Global Hawk missions. Major tenants: 940th ARW (AFRC), KC-135; 7th Space Warning Sq. (AFSPC), PAVE PAWS; 548th Intelligence Gp. (ACC). History: originally US Army's Camp Beale; transferred to Air Force in 1948; became Air Force base in April 1951. Named for Brig. Gen. E.F. Beale, Indian agent in California prior to Civil War. Area: 22,944 acres. Runway: 12,000 ft. Altitude: 113 ft. Personnel: permanent party military, 3,742; DOD civilians, 718. Housing: single family, officer, 159, enlisted, 1,294; unaccompanied, 545; visiting, VOQ, 53, VAQ/VEQ, 125, TLF, 46. Clinic.

Bolling AFB, D.C. 20032-5000; 3 mi. S of US Capitol. Phone: 703-545-6700; DSN 227-0101. Host: 11th Wing, which includes the USAF Band and USAF Honor Guard. Mission: Provides support responsibilities for Hq. USAF and 40,000 USAF

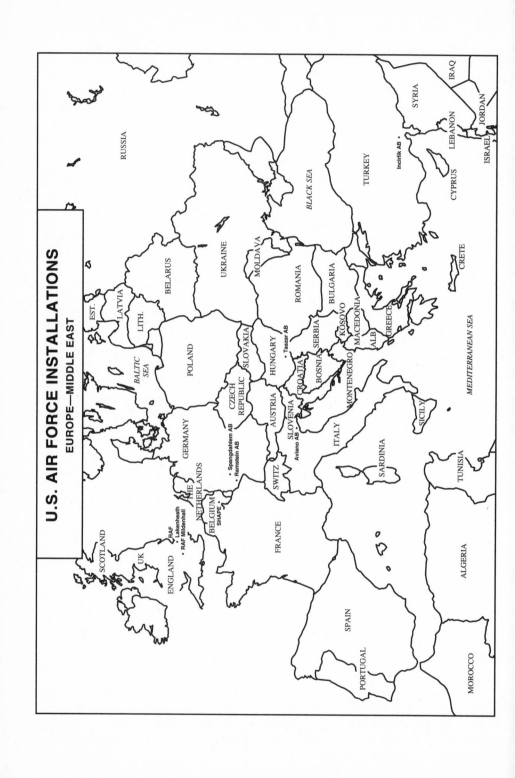

U.S. AIR FORCE INSTALLATIONS
EUROPE—MIDDLE EAST

members worldwide. Major tenants: Air Force Chief of Chaplains; Air Force District of Washington; Air Force Surgeon General; Air Force Medical Operations Agency; Defense Intelligence Agency; Air Force Legal Operations Agency; 497th Intelligence Gp. (ACC). History: activated October 1917. Named for Col. Raynal C. Bolling, first high-ranking Army Air Service officer killed in WWI. Area: 607 acres. Runway: Helipad only. Altitude: 20 ft. Personnel: permanent party military, 1,566; DOD civilians, 848. Housing: single family, officer, 361, enlisted, 860; unaccompanied, UAQ/UEQ, 262; visiting, VOQ, 80, VAQ/VEQ, 87, TLF, 100. Clinic.

Buckley AFB, Colo. 80011-9524; 8 mi. E of Denver. Phone: 720-847-9011 DSN 847-9011. Majcom: AFSPC. Host: 460th Space Wing. Mission: provides to combatant commanders superior global surveilllance, worldwide missile warning, homeland defense, and expeditionary forces. Focal point for transition to Space Based Infrared System. Major tenants: 140th Wing (ANG); Aerospace Data Facility; Navy/Marine Reserve Center; Army Aviation Support Facility. History: activated 1 April 1942 as a gunnery training facility. Named for 1st Lt. John H. Buckley, a WW I flier, killed 17 Sept. 1918. ANG assumed control from US Navy in 1959. Became active duty Air Force base 2 Oct. 2000. Area: 3,832 acres. Runway: 11,000 ft. Altitude: 5,663 ft. Personnel: permanent party military, 3,626; DOD civilians, 3,337. Housing: two dorms and 351 units under construction. Clinic.

Cannon AFB, N.M. 88103-5000; 7 mi. W of Clovis. Phone: 505-784-1110; DSN 681-1110. Majcom: ACC. Host: 27th FW. Mission: F-16 operations. History: activated August 1942. Named for Gen. John K. Cannon, WWII commander of all Allied air forces in the Mediterranean Theater and former commander, Tactical Air Command. Area: 3,789 acres, excluding range. Runways: 10,000 ft. and 8,200 ft. Altitude: 4,295 ft. Personnel: permanent party military, 3,471; DOD civilians, 622. Housing: single family, officer, 143, enlisted, 1,501; unaccompanied, 835; visiting, 57, TLF, 36. Ambulatory care clinic.

Charleston AFB, S.C. 29404-5000; 10 mi. from downtown Charleston. Phone: 843-963-2100; DSN 673-8400. Majcom: AMC. Host: 437th AW. Mission: C-17 operations. Major tenant: 315th AW (AFRC assoc.), C-17. History: activated October 1942; inactivated March 1946; reactivated August 1953. Area: 6,033 acres (including auxiliary airfield). Runway: 9,000 ft.; joint-use airfield. Altitude: 46 ft. Personnel: permanent party military, 4,169; DOD civilians, 1,450. Housing: single family, officer, 148, enlisted, 1,178; unaccompanied, UAQ/UEQ, 587; visiting, VOQ, 156, VAQ/VEQ, 40, TLF, 40. Clinic.

Columbus AFB, Miss. 39710-1000; 7.5 mi. NW of Columbus. Phone: 662-434-7322; DSN 742-1110. Majcom: AETC. Host: 14th Flying Training Wing. Mission: Specialized Undergraduate Pilot Training (T-1, T-6, T-37, T-38). History: activated 1942 for pilot training. Area: 5,325 acres. Runways: 12,000 ft., 8,000 ft., and 6,300 ft. Altitude: 219 ft. Personnel: permanent party military, 1,165; DOD civilians, 570. Housing: single family, 517; unaccompanied, UOQ, 234, UAQ/UEQ, 166; visiting, 73, DV, 4, TLF, 20. Clinic.

Davis-Monthan AFB, Ariz. 85707-5000; within Tucson. Phone: 520-228-1110; DSN 228-1110. Majcom: ACC. Host: 355th Wing. Mission: A-10 combat crew training; OA-10 and FAC HC-130 training and operations; EC-130H; HH-60 Pavehawk; and CSAR operations. Major tenants: 12th Air Force (ACC); Aerospace Maintenance and Regeneration Center (AFMC), DOD's single location for regeneration, maintenance, parts reclamation, preservation, storage, and disposal of excess DOD and government

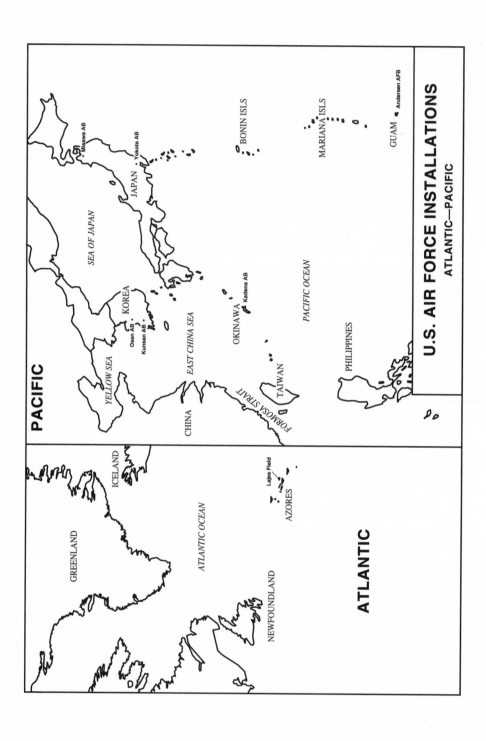

U.S. AIR FORCE INSTALLATIONS
ATLANTIC—PACIFIC

PACIFIC

SEA OF JAPAN

YELLOW SEA

KOREA

Osan AB

Kunsan AB

CHINA

EAST CHINA SEA

JAPAN

Misawa AB

Yokota AB

OKINAWA

Kadena AB

TAIWAN

FORMOSA STRAIT

PACIFIC OCEAN

BONIN ISLS

MARIANA ISLS

GUAM

Andersen AFB

PHILIPPINES

ATLANTIC

GREENLAND

ICELAND

ATLANTIC OCEAN

NEWFOUNDLAND

AZORES

Lajes Field

aerospace vehicles; 943rd Rescue Gp. (AFRC), HH-60; 55th ECG (ACC); 563rd RQG (AFSOC); US Customs and Border Protection. History: activated 1927. Named for two local aviators: 2nd Lt. Samuel H. Davis, killed 28 Dec. 1921, and 2nd Lt. Oscar Monthan, killed 27 March, 1924. Area: 10,633 acres. Runway: 13,643 ft. Altitude: 2,404 ft. Personnel: permanent party military, 6,900; DOD civilians, 1,970. Housing: single family, officer, 125, enlisted, 1,129; unaccompanied, 756; visiting, VOQ, 20, VAQ/VEQ, 61, DV, 165, TLF, 50. Clinic.

Dover AFB, Del. 19902-7209; 6 mi. SE of Dover. Phone: 302-677-3000; DSN 445-3000. Majcom: AMC. Host: 436th AW. Mission: C-5 operations; operates largest DOD aerial port facility; houses military's East Coast mortuary. Major tenant: 512th AW (AFRC assoc.). History: activated December 1941; inactivated 1946; reactivated February 1951. Area: 3,400 acres. Runways: 12,900 ft. and 9,600 ft. Altitude: 28 ft. Personnel: permanent party military, 3,300; DOD civilians, 1,100. Housing: single family, officer, 62, enlisted, 599; unaccompanied, UAQ/UEQ, 507; visiting, VQ, 251, TLF, 0. Clinic.

Dyess AFB, Tex. 79607-1980; WSW border of Abilene. Phone: 325-696-1110; DSN 461-1110. Majcom: ACC. Host: 7th BW. Mission: B-1 operations. Major tenant: 317th Airlift Gp. (AMC), C-130. History: activated April 1942; deactivated December 1945; reactivated as Abilene AFB September 1955. In December 1956, renamed for Lt. Col. William E. Dyess, WWII fighter pilot who escaped from a Japanese prison camp, killed in P-38 crash in December 1943. Area: 6,342 acres (including off-base sites). Runway: 13,500 ft. Altitude: 1,789 ft. Personnel: permanent party military, 5,354; DOD civilians, 346. Housing: single family, officer, 153, enlisted, 258; unaccompanied, 808; visiting, 147, TLF, 39. Clinic.

Edwards AFB, Calif. 93524; adjacent to Rosamond. Phone: 661-227-1110; DSN 527-1110. Majcom: AFMC. Host: 95th Air Base Wing. Mission: The Air Force Flight Test Center is AFMC's center of excellence for conducting and supporting research, development, test, and evaluation of aerospace systems from concept to combat. It operates the US Air Force Test Pilot School and is home to NASA's Dryden Research Center and considerable test activity conducted by America's commercial aerospace industry. Major tenants: AFRL's Propulsion Directorate (AFMC); Dryden Flight Research Center (NASA); Air Force Operational Test and Evaluation Center, Det. 5; 31st Test and Evaluation Squadron (ACC); Marine Aircraft Group 46, Det. Bravo. History: activities began in September 1933 when the Muroc Bombing and Gunnery Range was established. In 1942, it was designated Muroc Army Air Base. Renamed in 1949 for Capt. Glen W. Edwards, killed 5 June 1948 in crash of a YB-49 "Flying Wing." Area: 301,000 acres. Runways: 21, from 4,000 to 39,000 ft. Altitude: 2,302 ft. Personnel: permanent party military, 2,665; DOD civilians, 3,360. Housing: Family housing is limited due to downsizing and ongoing construction through FY07. After project is complete: officer, 194; enlisted, 603; unaccompanied, UOQ, 80; UEQ; 670. Medical and dental clinics.

Eglin AFB, Fla. 32542; 2 mi. SW of the twin cities of Niceville and Valparaiso; 7 mi. NE of Fort Walton Beach. Phone: 850-882-1110; DSN 872-1110. Majcom: AFMC. Host: 96th ABW. Mission: supporting the Eglin Air Armament Center and associate units with traditional military services as well as civil engineering, personnel, logistics, communications, computer, medical, security, and all other host services. Major tenants: AFRL's Munitions Directorate (AFMC); 33rd FW (ACC), F-15; 53rd Wing (ACC); 919th Special Operations Wing (AFRC) at Duke Field, MC-130; Air Force Armament

Museum; Army 6th Ranger Training Battalion; Naval School Explosive Ordnance Disposal. History: activated 1935. Named for Lt. Col. Frederick I. Eglin, WWI flier killed in aircraft accident 1 Jan. 1937. Area: 463,452 acres. Eglin is the nation's largest Air Force base in terms of acreage, covering an area roughly two-thirds the size of Rhode Island. Runways: 12,000 ft. and 10,000 ft. Altitude: 85 ft. Personnel: permanent party military, 7,127; DOD civilians, 3,884 (excluding Hurlburt Field). Housing: single family, officer, 285, enlisted, 1,767; unaccompanied, UAQ/UEQ, 933; visiting, VOQ, 169, VAQ/VEQ, 156, TLF, 87. Hospital.

Eielson AFB, Alaska 99702-5000; 26 mi. SE of Fairbanks. Phone: 907-377-1110; DSN 317-377-1110. Majcom: PACAF. Host: 354th FW. Mission: F-16C/D and A/OA-10 operations. Major tenants: Arctic Survival School (AETC); 168th Air Refueling Wing (ANG), KC-135; 353rd Combat Training Sq. History: activated October 1944. Named for Carl Ben Eielson, Arctic aviation pioneer who died in an Arctic rescue mission in November 1929. Area: 19,790 acres (including 16 remote sites, 63,195 acres). Runway: 14,500 ft. Altitude: 534 ft. Personnel: permanent party military, 2,953; DOD civilians, 641. Housing: single family, officer, 181, enlisted, 1,243; unaccompanied, UOQ, 8, UAQ, 522, UEQ, 16; visiting, VOQ, 206, VAQ/VEQ, 328, TLF, 40. Outpatient clinic.

Ellsworth AFB, S.D. 57706-5000; 12 mi. ENE of Rapid City. Phone: 605-385-5056; DSN 675-5056. Majcom: ACC. Host: 28th BW. Mission: B-1 operations. Major tenants: Det. 21, Belle Fourche Electronic Scoring Site; Det. 8, 372nd Training Sq. (AETC); Det. 226, AFOSI. History: activated January 1942 as Rapid City AAB; renamed June 13, 1953 for Brig. Gen. Richard E. Ellsworth, killed 18 March 1953 in RB-36 crash. Area: 5,411 acres. Runway: 13,500 ft. Altitude: 3,276 ft. Personnel: permanent party military, 3,550; DOD civilians, 421. Housing: single family, officer, 307, enlisted, 1,729, unaccompanied, 728; visiting, 80, TLF, 29. Clinic.

Elmendorf AFB, Alaska 99506-5000; bordering Anchorage. Phone: 907-552-1110; DSN 317-552-1110. Majcom: PACAF. Host: 3rd Wing. Mission: C-12, C-130, E-3B Airborne Warning and Control System, F-15C, and F-15E operations. Hub for air traffic to and from Far East. Major tenants: Alaskan Command; 11th Air Force (PACAF); Alaskan NORAD Region. History: activated July 1940. Named for Capt. Hugh Elmendorf, killed 13 Jan. 1933. Area: 13,100 acres. Runways: 10,000 ft. and 7,500 ft. Altitude: 213 ft. Personnel: permanent party military, 6,485; DOD civilians, 891. Housing: single family, officer, 112, enlisted, 1,910; unaccompanied, UAQ/UEQ, 850; visiting, VOQ, 178, VAQ/VEQ, 195, TLF, 86. Hospital.

Fairchild AFB, Wash. 99011-9588; 10 mi. WSW of Spokane. Phone: 509-247-1110; DSN 657-1110. Majcom: AMC. Host: 92nd Air Refueling Wing. Mission: KC-135R operations. Major tenants: 336th Training Gp. (USAF Survival School, AETC); 141st ARW (ANG). History: activated January 1942. Named for Gen. Muir S. Fairchild, USAF vice chief of staff at his death in 1950. Area: 5,823 acres; 530,205 acres used for survival school. Runway: 13,901 ft. Altitude: 2,426 ft. Personnel: permanent party military, 2,494; DOD civilians, 700. Housing: single family, officer, 167, enlisted, 889; unaccompanied, VOQ, 126, VAQ, 200, TLF, 43. Clinic.

F. E. Warren AFB, Wyo. 82005-5000; adjacent to Cheyenne. Phone: 307-773-1110; DSN 481-1110. Majcom: AFSPC. Host: 90th SW. Mission: Minuteman III ICBMs; UH-1N. Major tenants: 20th Air Force (AFSPC); Air Force ICBM Museum. History: activated as Ft. D.A. Russell 4 July 1867; under Army jurisdiction until 1949, when reassigned to USAF; renamed in 1930 for Francis Emory Warren, Wyoming Senator and first state governor. Area: 5,866 acres. Missile site area covering more than 12,600 sq. mi. in Wyoming, Colorado, and Nebraska. Runway: none. Altitude: 6,142 ft. Personnel: permanent party military, 3,182; DOD civilians, 974. Housing: single family, officer, 156, enlisted, 675; unaccompanied, officer, 12, enlisted, 767; visiting, 30, TLF, 39. Clinic.

Goodfellow AFB, Tex. 76908-4410; SE of San Angelo. Phone: 325-654-3231; DSN 477-3231. Majcom: AETC. Host: 17th Training Wing. Mission: trains intelligence, fire protection, and special instruments personnel for US military and DOD and international agencies. Major tenants: 344th Military Intelligence Battalion (Army); Center for Information Dominance det. (Navy); USMC det.; NCO Academy. History: activated January 1941. Named for Lt. John J. Goodfellow Jr., WWI observation airplane pilot killed in combat 14 Sept. 1918. Area: 1,136 acres. Runway: none. Altitude: 1,900 ft. Personnel: permanent party military, 1,550; DOD civilians, 851. Housing: single family, officer, 2, enlisted, 296; unaccompanied, UOQ, 144, UAQ/UEQ, 236; visiting, VOQ, 114, VAQ/VEQ, 321, TLF, 31. Clinic.

Grand Forks AFB, N.D. 58205-5000; 16 mi. W of Grand Forks. Phone: 701-747-3000; DSN 362-3000. Majcom: AMC. Host: 319th ARW. Mission: KC-135R operations. History: activated 1956. Named after town of Grand Forks, whose citizens bought the property for the Air Force. Area: 5,418 acres. Runway: 12,351 ft. Altitude: 911 ft. Personnel: permanent party military, 2,318; DOD civilians, 415. Housing: single family, officer, 111, enlisted, 770; unaccompanied, UAQ/UEQ, 377; visiting; VOQ, 5, VAQ/VEQ, 2, TLF, 27. Hospital.

Hanscom AFB, Mass. 01731-5000; 17 mi. NW of Boston. Phone: 781-377-1110; DSN 478-1110. Majcom: AFMC. Host: 66th ABW. Mission: Electronic Systems Center manages development and acquisition of command and control systems. Major tenants: AFRL's Space Vehicles Directorate-Hanscom; AFRL's Sensors Directorate-Hanscom. History: activated 1941. Named for Laurence G. Hanscom, a pre-WWII advocate of private aviation, killed in a lightplane accident in 1941. Area: 846 acres. Runway: no flying mission; transient USAF aircraft use runways of Laurence G. Hanscom Field, state-operated airfield adjoining the base. Altitude: 133 ft. Personnel: permanent party military, 1,769; DOD civilians, 2,316. Housing: single family, officer, 314, enlisted, 470; unaccompanied, UAQ/UEQ, 122; visiting, 148, TLF, 47. Clinic.

Hickam AFB, Hawaii 96853-5000; 9 mi. W of Honolulu. Phone: 808-449-7110 (Oahu military operator); DSN 315-449-7110. Majcom: PACAF. Host: 15th AW (C-17, C-37, C-40). Mission: provides base and logistical support for 140 associate and tenant units in Hawaii and other Pacific region locations; airlift for commander, PACOM, and commander, PACAF; and maintenance and refueling support for aircraft transiting between the US mainland and the western Pacific. Major tenants: PACAF; 13th AF; 154th Wing (ANG), C-17, C-130, F-15, KC-135R; Joint POW/MIA Accounting Command. History: activated September 1938. Named for Lt. Col. Horace M. Hickam, aviation pioneer killed in crash 5 Nov. 1934. Area: 2,761 acres. Runways: Four joint-use runways shared with Honolulu Arpt.: 12,357 ft., 12,000 ft., 9,000 ft., and 6,952 ft. Altitude: 13 ft. Personnel: permanent party military, 4,174; DOD civilians, 1,273. Housing: single family, officer, 585, enlisted, 698; unaccompanied, UAQ/UEQ, 765; visiting, VOQ, 155, VAQ/VEQ, 68, TLF, 40. Clinic.

Hill AFB, Utah 84056-5990; 25 mi. N. of Salt Lake City. Phone: 801-777-1110; DSN 777-1110. Majcom: AFMC. Host: 75th ABW. Mission: Ogden Air Logistics Center provides worldwide engineering and logistics management for F-16s; maintains the

A-10, C-130, and F-16; handles logistics management and maintenance for Minuteman ICBMs; provides sustainment and logistics support for space and C3I programs; overhauls and repairs landing gear for all USAF (and 70 percent of DOD) aircraft; leading provider of rocket motors, small missiles, air munitions and guided bombs, photonics imaging and reconnaissance equipment, simulators and training devices, avionics, hydraulics and pneudraulics instruments, and software. Major tenants: 388th FW (ACC); 419th FW (AFRC), F-16; Hill Aerospace Museum; Defense Enterprise Computing Center (DISA); Defense Distribution Depot Hill Utah; Defense Logistics Agency; 372nd Recruiting Gp. (USAF). History: activated 1940. Named for Maj. Ployer P. Hill, killed 30 Oct. 1935 while test flying the first B-17. Area: 6,797 acres; manages 962,076 acres (Utah Test and Training Range). Runway: 13,500 ft. Altitude: 4,789 ft. Personnel: permanent party military, 4,700; DOD civilians, 13,000. Housing: single family, officer, 109, enlisted, 909; unaccompanied, UAQ/UEQ, 774; visiting, VOQ, 13, VAQ/VEQ, 147, TLF, 61. Clinic.

Holloman AFB, N.M. 88310; 8 mi. SW of Alamogordo. Phone: 505-572-1110; DSN 572-1110. Majcom: ACC. Host: 49th FW. Mission: F-117A operations; Basic Expeditionary Airfield Resources (BEAR Base Assets) and two air transportable clinics. Major tenants: 46th Test Gp. (AFMC); 4th Space Control Sq. (AFSPC); German Air Force Flying Training Center. History: activated 1941. Named for Col. George Holloman, guided-missile pioneer. Area: 58,000 acres. Runways: 12,000 ft., 10,500 ft., and 8,000 ft. Altitude: 4,350 ft. Personnel: permanent party military, 3,383; DOD civilians, 835. Housing: single family, officer, 190, enlisted, 1,223; unaccompanied, 945; visiting, 192, TLF, 49. Clinic.

Hurlburt Field, Fla. 32544-5000; 5 mi. W of Fort Walton Beach. Phone: 850-884-7464; DSN 579-7464. Majcom: AFSOC. Host: 1st Special Operations Wing. Mission: specialized airpower, equipped with AC-130H/U, MC-130/H/W, MC-130P (located at Eglin), MH-53J/M, U-28A, UH-1N. Major tenants: AFSOC; 823rd RED HORSE Sq.; USAF Combat Weather Center; USAF Special Operations School; Joint Special Operations University; 505th Command and Control Wing (ACC); 605th Training Sq.; 25th Information Operations Sq.; 18th Flight Test Sq.; 720th Special Tactics Gp.; Det. 3, 334th Training Sq. History: activated 1943. Named for Lt. Donald W. Hurlburt, WWII pilot killed 1 Oct. 1943. Area: 6,600 acres. Runway: 6,900 ft. Altitude: 38 ft. Personnel: permanent party military, 8,000; DOD civilians, 700. Housing: single family, officer, 52, enlisted, 628; unaccompanied, UAQ/UEQ, 1,231; visiting, VOQ, 163, VAQ/VEQ, 51, TLF, 24. Clinic.

Incirlik AB, Turkey, APO AE 09824; 6 mi. E of Adana. Phone: (cmcl, from CONUS) 011-90-322-316-6060; DSN (from CONUS) 676-6060. Majcom: USAFE. Host: 39th ABW. Mission: provides full spectrum, forward operating base support to expeditionary forces while developing the professional talents of our airmen. History: activated May 1954. Present unit began operations March 1966. Incirlik, in Turkish, means fig orchard. Area: 3,400 acres. Runway: 10,000 ft. Altitude: 240 ft. Personnel: permanent party military, 1,500; DOD civilians, 65. Housing: single family, 750; unaccompanied, UOQ, 105, UEQ, 756; visiting, VOQ, 91, VAQ/VEQ, 192, DV, 18, TLF, 80. Clinic.

Kadena AB, Japan, APO AP 96368-5000; 15 mi. N of Naha. Phone: (cmcl, from CONUS) 011-81-6117-34-1110; DSN 315- 634-1110. Majcom: PACAF. Host: 18th Wing. Mission: E-3, F-15C/D, KC-135R, and HH-60 operations. Major tenants: 353rd Special Operations Gp. (AFSOC); 390th Intelligence Sq.; 82nd Reconnaissance Sq.

(ACC); 733rd Air Mobility Support Sq. (AMC). History: occupied by US forces in April 1945. Named for city of Kadena, Okinawa. Area: 11,210 acres. Runway: 12,100 ft. Altitude: 146 ft. Personnel: permanent party military, 7,200; DOD civilians, 466. Housing: single family, officer, 1,495 enlisted, 5,296; unaccompanied, UOQ, 35, UAQ/UEQ, 1,629; visiting, VOQ, 226, VAQ/VEQ, 222, TLF, 122. Clinic.

Keesler AFB, Miss. 39534-5000; located in Biloxi. Phone: 228-377-1110; DSN 597-1110. Majcom: AETC. Host: 81st TRW. Mission: conducts Air Force, joint service, and international training for basic electronics, communications electronic systems, communications computer systems, air traffic control, airfield management, command post, air weapons control, weather, precision measurement, education and training, financial management and comptroller, information management, manpower and personnel, and medical, dental, and nursing specialties. Major tenants: 2nd Air Force (AETC); 45th Airlift Sq. (AETC), C-21; 403rd Wing (AFRC), C-130, WC-130. History: activated 12 June 1941. Named for 2nd Lt. Samuel R. Keesler Jr., a native of Mississippi and WWI aerial observer killed in action Oct. 9, 1918. Area: 3,554 acres, excluding off-base housing. Runway: 6,600 ft. Altitude: 33 ft. Personnel: permanent party military, 4,445; DOD civilians, 1,945. Housing: 606 existing for officer and enlisted; post-Katrina construction ongoing; visiting, 1,306, TLF, 79. Keesler Medical Center.

Kirtland AFB, N.M. 87117-5606; SE quadrant of Albuquerque. Phone: 505-846-1110; DSN 246-1110. Majcom: AFMC. Host: 377th ABW. Mission: provide world-class nuclear surety, expeditionary forces, and support to base operations. Major tenants: 498th Armament Systems Wing (AFMC); GSU 498th Missile Sustainment Gp.; 58th SOW (AETC), HC-130, MC-130, HH-60, MH-53,UH-1, CV-22. Missile Defense Agency's Airborne Laser Program Of.ce; Air Force Distributed Mission Operations Center; Air Force Nuclear Weapons and Counterproliferation Agency; Det. 1, 342nd TRS, Air Force Pararescue and Combat Rescue Officer School; Air Force Of.ce of Aerospace Studies; Air Force Operational Test and Evaluation Center; Air Force Research Laboratory Space Vehicles and Directed Energy Directorates (AFMC); 150th FW (ANG), F-16; Defense Threat Reduction Agency; Nuclear Weapons Center (AFMC); Nuclear Weapons Directorate (AFMC); Sandia National Laboratories; National Nuclear Security Administration (DOE); Det. 12, Space and Missile Systems Center (AFSPC); Defense Nuclear Weapons School; Air Force Inspection Agency; Air Force Safety Center. History: activated January 1941. Named for Col. Roy C. Kirtland, aviation pioneer who died 2 May 1941. Area: 52,678 acres. Runways: two, each 13,000 ft.; 10,000 ft.; and 6,000 ft. Altitude: 5,352 ft. Personnel: permanent party military, 3,784; DOD civilians, 1,974. Housing: single family, officer, 187, enlisted, 891; unaccompanied, UAQ/UEQ, 828; visiting, VOQ, 181, VAQ/VEQ, 216, DV, 38, TLF, 39. Air Force-VA joint medical center.

Kunsan AB, South Korea, APO AP 96264-5000; 8 mi. SW of Kunsan City. Phone: (cmcl, from CONUS) 011-82-63-470-1110; DSN 782-1110. Majcom: PACAF. Host: 8th FW. Mission: F-16C/D operations; home of the "Wolf Pack" and the first active overseas F-16 wing (September 1981). Major tenants: US Army's Charlie and Delta Batteries, 2nd Battalion, 1st Air Defense Artillery; US Army Contracting Command Korea. History: built by the Japanese in 1938. Area: 2,157 acres. Runway: 9,000 ft. Altitude: 29 ft. Personnel: permanent party military, 2,550; DOD civilians, 25. Housing: unaccompanied, UOQ, 245, UAQ/UEQ, 2,475; visiting, VOQ, 26, VAQ/VEQ, 60. Clinic.

Lackland AFB, Tex. 78236-5000; 8 mi. SW of downtown San Antonio. Phone: 210-671-1110; DSN 473-1110. Majcom: AETC. Host: 37th TRW. Mission: One of the largest USAF training wings. Provides basic military training for civilian recruits entering Air Force, ANG, and AFRC; conducts courses in ground combat (base support) functions, English language training for international and US military students, and specialized maintenance and security training in Spanish to military forces and government agencies from 26 Latin American nations. Major tenants: Air Intelligence Agency; 433rd AW (AFRC); 149th FW (ANG); 67th Network Warfare Wing (ACC); National Security Agency/Central Security Service Texas; 59th Medical Wing; Air Force Security Forces Center; Force Protection Battlelab; Cryptologic Systems Gp. History: activated 1941. Named for Brig. Gen. Frank D. Lackland, early commandant of Kelly Field .ying school, who died in 1943. Area: 9,572 acres. Runway: 11,550 ft. Altitude: 691 ft. Personnel: permanent party military, 18,480; DOD civilians, 5,197. Housing: single family, officer, 151, enlisted, 1,060; unaccompanied, enlisted, 1,243; visiting, 2,760, TLF, 96. Wilford Hall Medical Center.

Lajes Field, Azores, Portugal, APO AE 09720-5000; Terceira Island, 900 mi. W of Portugal. Phone: (cmcl, from CONUS) 011-351-295-57-1110; DSN from US 535-1110, from Europe 312-535-1110. Majcom: USAFE. Host: 65th ABW. Mission: provides support to US and allied aircraft and personnel transiting the Atlantic, through US military and host-nation coordination. Major tenants: 65th ABW; 729th AMS (AMC). History: US operations began at Lajes Field 1943. Area: 1,192 acres. Runway: 10,865 ft. Altitude: 180 ft. Personnel: permanent party military, 835; DOD civilians, 197. Housing: single family, officer, 74, enlisted, 368; unaccompanied, UOQ, 10, UAQ/UEQ, 240; visiting, 242, TLF, 30. Clinic.

Langley AFB, Va. 23665-5000; 3 mi. N of Hampton. Phone: 757-764-1110; DSN 574-1110. Majcom: ACC. Host: 1st FW. Mission: F-15 and F-22A air dominance operations. Major tenants: Air Combat Command; Air Force Rescue Coordination Center; Aerospace C2ISR Center; USAF Heritage of America Band; 480th Intelligence Wg. (ACC); Air and Space Expeditionary Force Center (ACC). History: activated 30 Dec. 1916. Langley is the first military base in the US purchased and built specifically for military aviation. Named for aviation pioneer and scientist Samuel Pierpont Langley, who died in 1906. Area: 2,900 acres. Runway: 10,000 ft. Altitude: 11 ft. Personnel: permanent party military, 8,861; DOD civilians, 2,016. Housing: single family, officer, 328, enlisted, 1,053; unaccompanied, 1,053; visiting, VOQ, 78, VAQ/VEQ, 153, TLF, 60. Hospital.

Laughlin AFB, Tex. 78843-5000; 6 mi. E of Del Rio. Phone: 830-298-3511; DSN 732-1110. Majcom: AETC. Host: 47th FTW. Mission: SUPT (T-1, T-6, T-38). History: activated July 1942. Named for 1st Lt. Jack Thomas Laughlin, Del Rio native, B-17 pilot, killed 29 Jan. 1942. Area: 5,343 acres. Runways: 8,852 ft., 8,316 ft., and 6,236 ft. Altitude: 1,081 ft. Personnel: permanent party military, 883; DOD civilians, 879. Housing: single family, officer, 298, enlisted, 218; unaccompanied, UOQ, 320, UEQ, 264; visiting, VQ, 90, DV, 6, TLF, 20. Clinic.

Little Rock AFB, Ark. 72099-4940; 17 mi. NE of Little Rock (Jacksonville). Phone: 501-987-1110; DSN 731-1110. Majcom: AETC. Host: 314th AW. Mission: largest C-130 training base in the world; trains crew members from all services and 31 nations. Major tenants: 463rd Airlift Gp. (AMC), C-130; 189th AW (ANG), C-130; US Air Force Mobility Weapons School (ACC); Hq. Ark. ANG. History: activated Oct. 9, 1955. Area: 6,600 acres. Runway: 12,000 ft. Altitude: 310 ft. Personnel: permanent party military, 6,000; DOD civilians, 500. Housing: single family, officer, 185, enlisted, 1,286; unaccompanied, 840; visiting, VOQ, 102, VAQ/VEQ, 52. Clinic, no emergency room.

Los Angeles AFB, Calif. 90245-4657; in El Segundo, 3 mi. SE of Los Angeles Arpt.; base housing and support facilities 18 mi. S of the main base, in San Pedro. Phone: 310-653-1110; DSN 633-1110. Majcom: AFSPC. Host: Space and Missile Systems Center. Mission: responsible for research, development, acquisition, on-orbit testing, and sustainment of military space and missile systems. History: activated as Air Research and Development Command's Western Development Division 1 July 1954. Area: 57 acres at Los Angeles AFB and 156 acres at Ft. MacArthur Military Family Housing Annex. Runway: none. Altitude: 95 ft. Personnel: permanent party military, 1,352; DOD civilians, 1,068. Housing: 644 units, TLF, 57. Clinic.

Luke AFB, Ariz. 85309-5000; 20 mi. WNW of downtown Phoenix. Phone: 623-856-1110; DSN 896-1110. Majcom: AETC. Host: 56th FW. Mission: F-16 operations; conducts USAF and allied F-16 pilot and crew chief training. Major tenant: 944th FW (AFRC), F-16. History: activated 1941. Named for 2nd Lt. Frank Luke Jr., observation balloon-busting ace of WWI and first American aviator to receive the Medal of Honor, killed in action 29 Sept. 1918. Luke is the largest fighter training base in the world. Area: 4,200 acres, plus 1.9 million-acre Barry M. Goldwater Range. Runways: 10,000 ft. and 9,910 ft. Altitude: 1,090 ft. Personnel: permanent party military, 5,600; DOD civilians, 1,400. Housing: single family, 724; unaccompanied, UAQ/UEQ, 730; visiting, 186, TLF, 84. Clinic.

MacDill AFB, Fla. 33621-5000; on the Interbay Peninsula in southern Tampa. Phone: 813-828-1110; DSN 968-1110. Majcom: AMC. Host: 6th AMW. Mission: KC-135 operations; provides worldwide air refueling and combatant commander support. Major tenants: SOCOM; CENTCOM; Joint Communications Support Element; NOAA Aircraft Operations Center. History: activated April 15, 1941. Named for Col. Leslie MacDill, killed in aircraft accident 8 Nov. 1938. Area: 5,767 acres. Runways: 11,420 ft. and 7,167 ft. Altitude: 6 ft. Personnel: permanent party military, 4,182; DOD civilians, 1,271. Housing: single family, officer, 45, enlisted, 629; unaccompanied, UAQ/UEQ, 610; visiting, VOQ, 112, VAQ/VEQ, 130, TLF, 5. Clinic.

Malmstrom AFB, Mont. 59402-5000; 1.5 mi. E of Great Falls. Phone: 406-731-1110; DSN 632-1110. Majcom: AFSPC. Host: 341st SW. Mission: Minuteman III ICBM operations, UH-1N. Major tenant: 819th RED HORSE Sq. (ACC). History: activated 15 Dec. 1942. Named for Col. Einar A. Malmstrom, WWII fighter commander killed in air accident 21 Aug. 1954. Site of SAC's first Minuteman wing. Area: 3,716 acres, plus about 23,500 sq. mi. for missile sites. Runway: closed. Altitude: 3,460 ft. Personnel: permanent party military, 3,600; DOD civilians, 400. Housing: single family, officer, 210, enlisted, 974; unaccompanied, UAQ/UEQ, 834; visiting, 53, TLF, 30. Clinic.

Maxwell AFB, Ala. 36112-5000; 1 mi. WNW of Montgomery. Phone: 334-953-1110; DSN 493-1110. Majcom: AETC. Host: 42nd ABW. Mission: Air University conducts professional military, graduate, and professional continuing education for precommissioned and commissioned officers, enlisted personnel, and civilians. Major tenants: Air University; Air War College; Air Command and Staff College; Air University Library; College of Aerospace Doctrine, Research, and Education; School of Advanced Air and Space Studies; Air Force Officer Accession and Training Schools; Ira C. Eaker College for Professional Development; College for Enlisted Professional Military Education; Community College of the Air Force; Air Force Institute for Advanced Distributed Learning; Squadron Officer College; Civil Air Patrol; 908th AW (AFRC), C-130; Air Force Historical Research Agency; Air Force Doctrine Center; 754th Electronic Systems Gp.; USAF Counterproliferation Center. History: activated 1918. Named for 2nd Lt. William C. Maxwell, killed in air accident 12 Aug. 1920. Area: 3,028 acres (includes Gunter Annex). Runway: 8,000 ft. Altitude: 172 ft. Personnel: permanent party military, 2,463; DOD civilians, 3,888. Housing: single family, officer, 364, enlisted, 377; unaccompanied, UAQ/UEQ, 211; visiting, 2,246, TLF, 30. Clinic.

McChord AFB, Wash. 98438-1109; 8 mi. S of Tacoma. Phone: 253-982-1110; DSN 382-1110. Majcom: AMC. Host: 62nd AW. Mission: C-17 operations. Base is adjacent to Ft. Lewis, its primary customer for strategic airlift worldwide. Major tenant: 446th AW (AFRC assoc.). History: activated 5 May 1938. Named for Col. William C. McChord, killed 18 Aug. 1937. Area: 4,639 acres. Runway: 10,100 ft. Altitude: 323 ft. Personnel: permanent party military, 4,007; DOD civilians, 1,123. Housing: single family, officer, 113, enlisted, 867; unaccompanied, UOQ, 2, UAQ/UEQ, 729; visiting, VOQ, 68, VAQ/VEQ, 230, TLF, 20. Dispensary. Madigan Army Medical Center is located 4 mi. SE.

McConnell AFB, Kan. 67221-5000; SE corner of Wichita. Phone: 316-759-6100; DSN 734-1110. Majcom: AMC. Host: 22nd ARW. Mission: KC-135 operations. Major tenants: 184th ARW (ANG); 931st Air Refueling Gp. (AFRC assoc.). History: activated June 5, 1951. Named for the three McConnell brothers, WWII B-24 pilots from Wichita—Lt. Col. Edwin M. McConnell (died 1 Sept. 1997), Capt. Fred J. McConnell (died in a private airplane crash 25 Oct. 1945), and 2nd Lt. Thomas L. McConnell (killed 10 July 1943). Area: 3,533 acres. Runways: two, 12,000 ft. each. Altitude: 1,371 ft. Personnel: permanent party military, 2,940; DOD civilians, 403. Housing: single family, officer, 83, enlisted, 506; unaccompanied, UAQ/UEQ, 615; visiting, VOQ, 42, VAQ/VEQ, 44, TLF, 45. Clinic.

McGuire AFB, N.J. 08641-5000; 18 mi. SE of Trenton. Phone: 609-754-1100; DSN 650-1100. Majcom: AMC. Host: 305th AMW. Mission: C-17 and KC-10 operations. Major tenants: 21st Expeditionary Mobility Task Force (AMC); Air Force Expeditionary Center, Ft. Dix, N.J.; N.J. Civil Air Patrol; 108th ARW (ANG), KC-135; 514th AMW (AFRC assoc.). History: adjoins Army's Ft. Dix. Formerly Ft. Dix AAB; activated as Air Force base 1949. Named for Maj. Thomas B. McGuire Jr., P-38 pilot, second leading US ace of WWII, Medal of Honor recipient, killed in action Jan. 7, 1945. Area: 3,598 acres. Runways: 10,001 ft. and 7,129 ft. Altitude: 133 ft. Personnel: permanent party military, 5,184, DOD civilians, 1,313. Housing: single family, officer, 275, enlisted, 2,089; unaccompanied, UAQ/UEQ, 767; visiting, VOQ, 40, VAQ/VEQ, 444, TLF, 30. Clinic.

Minot AFB, N.D. 58705-5000; 13 mi. N of Minot. Phone: 701-723-1110; DSN 453-1110. Majcom: ACC. Host: 5th BW. Mission: B-52 operations. Major tenant: 91st SW (AFSPC), Minuteman III, UH-1N. History: activated January 1957. Named after the city of Minot, whose citizens donated $50,000 toward purchase of the land for USAF. Area: 4,732 acres, plus additional 330 acres for missile sites spread over 8,500 sq. miles. Runway: 13,200 ft. Altitude: 1,668 ft. Personnel: permanent party military, 4,951; DOD civilians, 518. Housing: single family, officer, 324, enlisted, 1,521; unaccompanied, 813; visiting, 51, TLF, 15. Clinic.

Misawa AB, Japan, APO AP 96319-5000; within Misawa city limits. Phone: (cmcl, from CONUS) 011-81-176-53-5181 ext. 226-3075; DSN 315- 226-5181. Majcom: PACAF. Host: 35th FW. Mission: F-16C/D operations. Major tenants: 301st Intelligence Sq. (ACC); Naval Air Facility; Naval Security Gp. Activity; 750th Military Intelligence Det. (Army); Co. E, US Marine Support Battalion; Northern Air Defense Force (JASDF). History: occupied by US forces September 1945. Area: 3,865 acres. Runway: 10,000 ft. Altitude: 119 ft. Personnel: permanent party military, 4,564; DOD civilians, 122. Housing: single family, officer, 298, enlisted, 1,810; unaccompanied, UOQ, 40, UAQ/UEQ, 951; visiting, VOQ, 82, VAQ/VEQ, 44, TLF, 40. Hospital.

Moody AFB, Ga. 31699-5000; 10 mi. NNE of Valdosta. Phone: 229-257-1110; DSN 460-1110. Majcom: ACC. Host: 23rd Wing. Mission: HC-130, HH-60, pararescue, and force protection operations. Major tenants: 479th Flying Training Gp. (AETC). History: activated June 1941. Named for Maj. George P. Moody, killed May 5, 1941. Area: 6,050 acres. Runways: 9,300 ft. and 8,000 ft. Altitude: 235 ft. Personnel: permanent party military, 4,278; DOD civilians, 375. Housing: single family, officer, 32, enlisted, 271; unaccompanied, 714; visiting, VOQ, 37, VAQ/VEQ, 19, TLF, 32. Clinic.

Mountain Home AFB, Idaho 83648-5000; 50 mi. SE of Boise. Phone: 208-828-6800; DSN 728-6800. Majcom: ACC. Host: 366th FW. Mission: F-15C/D, F-15E, and F-16CJ/D operations. Major tenants: Air Warfare Battlelab; 266th Range Sq. History: activated August 1943. Area: 9,112 acres. Runway: 13,500 ft. Altitude: 3,000 ft. Personnel: permanent party military, 4,465; DOD civilians, 460. Housing: single family, officer, 175, enlisted, 1,170; unaccompanied, 883; visiting, VOQ, 43, VAQ/VEQ, 54, TLF, 15. Hospital.

Nellis AFB, Nev. 89191-5000; 8 mi. NE of Las Vegas. Phone: 702-652-1110; DSN 682-1110. Majcom: ACC. Host: 99th ABW. Mission: USAF Warfare Center manages advanced pilot training and tactics development and integrates test and evaluation programs. Its 98th Range Wing oversees a 15,000 sq.-mile Nellis Range Complex and two emergency airfields. 57th Wing, A-10A, F-15C/D/E, F-16C/D, HH-60G, Predator MQ-1/9 UAV. 57th Wing missions include Red Flag exercises (414th Combat Training Sq.); graduate-level pilot training (USAF Weapons School); support for Army exercises (549th Combat Training Sq.); training for international personnel in joint firepower procedures and techniques (Hq. USAF Air Ground Operations School); and USAF Air Demonstration Sq. (Thunderbirds). 53rd Wing, at 17 locations nationwide, serves as focal point for combat air forces in electronic warfare, armament and avionics, chemical defense, reconnaissance, and aircrew training devices, and operational testing and evaluation of proposed new equipment and systems. 505th Command and Control Wing builds the predominant air and space command and control ability for combined joint warfighters through training, testing, exercising, and experimentation. Major tenants: Aerospace Integration Center; Triservice Reserve Center; 58th and 67th Intelligence Gp. (ACC); 58th and 66th RQS (AFSOC); 820th RED HORSE Sq. (ACC); and 896th Munitions Sq. (AFMC). History: activated July 1941 as Las Vegas AAF with Army Air Corps Flexible Gunnery School; closed 1947; reopened 1948. Named for 1st Lt. William H. Nellis, WWII P-47 fighter pilot, killed 27 Dec. 1944. Area: Main base is 14,000 acres. NRC occupies 3 million acres of restricted air-land use and an additional 7,000 sq.-mile military operating area shared with civilian aircraft. Runways: 10,119 ft. and 10,051 ft. Altitude: 1,868 ft. Personnel: permanent party military, 8,251; DOD civilians, 2,808. Housing: single family, officer, 88, enlisted, 1,190; unaccompanied, 1,190; visiting, VOQ, 340, VAQ/VEQ, 354, TLF, 60. Air Force-VA joint hospital.

Offutt AFB, Neb. 68113-5000; 8 mi. S of Omaha. Phone: 402-294-1110; DSN 271-1110. Majcom: ACC. Host: 55th Wing. Mission: provides worldwide reconnaissance, intelligence, information warfare, treaty verification, and command and control to warfighting commanders and national leadership. Major tenants: STRATCOM; Joint Intelligence Center (STRATCOM); Air Force Weather Agency; National Airborne Operations Center (JCS); USAF Heartland of America Band. History: activated 1896 as Army's Ft. Crook. Landing field named for 1st Lt. Jarvis J. Offutt, WWI pilot who died 13 Aug. 1918. Area: 4,039 acres. Runway: 11,700 ft. Altitude: 1,048 ft. Personnel: permanent party military, 7,748; DOD civilians, 2,052. Housing: single family, officer, 344, enlisted, 2,256; unaccompanied, 793; visiting, 171, TLF, 60. Clinic.

Osan AB, South Korea, APO AP 96278-5000; 38 mi. S of Seoul. Phone: (cmcl, from CONUS) 011-82-31-661-1110; DSN 315-784-1110. Majcom: PACAF. Host: 51st FW. Mission: A/OA-10, C-12, and F-16C/D operations. Major tenants: 7th Air Force (PACAF); 5th RS (ACC); 31st SOS (AFSOC); 33rd Rescue Sq. (PACAF); 303rd Intelligence Sq. (AIA); 731st Air Mobility Sq. (AMC); Charlie and Delta Batteries, 1st Battalion, 43rd Air Defense Artillery (Army). History: originally designated K-55; runway opened December 1952. Renamed Osan AB in 1956 for nearby town that was the scene of first fighting between US and North Korean forces in July 1950. Area: 1,674 acres. Runway: 9,000 ft. Altitude: 38 ft. Personnel: permanent party military, 5,656; DOD civilians, 106. Housing: single family, officer, 242, enlisted, 80; unaccompanied, UOQ, 390, UAQ/UEQ, 4,681; visiting, VOQ, 57, VAQ/VEQ, 20, DV, 350, TLF, 15. Hospital.

Patrick AFB, Fla. 32925-3237; 2 mi. S of Cocoa Beach. Phone: 321-494-1110; DSN 854-1110. Majcom: AFSPC. Host: 45th SW. Mission: supports DOD, NASA, Navy (Trident), and other government agency and commercial missile and space programs. Host responsibilities include Cape Canaveral AFS and tracking stations on Antigua and Ascension islands. Major tenants: Defense Equal Opportunity Management Institute; Air Force Technical Applications Center; 920th Rescue Wing (AFRC), HC-130, HH-60; 2nd Brigade, 87th Division (Army); Naval Ordnance Test Unit (Navy); Joint Task Force for Joint STARS at Melbourne, Fla. History: activated 1940. Named for Maj. Gen. Mason M. Patrick, Chief of AEF's Air Service in WWI and Chief of the Air Service/Air Corps, 1921-27. Area: 2,341 acres. Runway: 9,000 ft. Altitude: 9 ft. Personnel: permanent party military, 4,000; DOD civilians, 1,768. Housing: single family, enlisted, 524; unaccompanied, UAQ/UEQ, 204; visiting, VOQ, 96, VAQ/VEQ, 163, TLF, 51. Clinic.

Peterson AFB, Colo. 80914-5000; at eastern edge of Colorado Springs. Phone: 719-556-7321; DSN 834-7321. Majcom: AFSPC. Host: 21st SW. Mission: provides missile warning and space control; detects, tracks, and catalogs objects in space. Major tenants: NORAD; AFSPC; NORTHCOM; US Army Space and Missile Defense Command/Army Forces Strategic Command; 302nd AW (AFRC), C-130. History: activated 1942. Named for 1st Lt. Edward J. Peterson, killed 8 Aug. 1942. Area: 1,277 acres. Runway: shared with city. Altitude: 6,200 ft. Personnel: permanent party military, 4,889; DOD civilians, 2,256. Housing: single family, officer, 103, enlisted, 384; unaccompanied, UAQ/UEQ, 704; visiting, VOQ, 100, VAQ/VEQ, 54, TLF, 68. Clinic.

Pope AFB, N.C. 28308-2391; 12 mi. NNW of Fayetteville. Phone: 910-394-1110; DSN 424-1110. Majcom: AMC. Host: 43rd AW. Mission: C-130 operations. Adjoins Army's Ft. Bragg and provides intratheater combat airlift and close air support for airborne forces and other personnel, equipment, and supplies. Major tenants: 23rd Fighter Gp. (ACC), A/OA-10; 18th Air Support Operations Gp. (ACC); 440th AW (AFRC); 21st and 24th STSs (AFSOC); USAF Combat Control School. History: activated 1919. Named after 1st Lt. Harley H. Pope, WWI pilot, killed 7 Jan. 1919. Area: 2,198 acres.

Runway: 7,500 ft. Altitude: 218 ft. Personnel: permanent party military, 5,805; DOD civilians, 4,848. Housing: single family, officer, 84, enlisted, 543; unaccompanied, UAQ/UEQ, 668; visiting, VOQ, 8, VAQ/VEQ, 159, TLF, 22. Clinic.

RAF Lakenheath, UK, APO AE 09461-5000; 70 mi. NE of London; 25 mi. NE of Cambridge. Phone: (cmcl, from CONUS) 011-44-1638-52-3000; DSN 226-1110. Majcom: USAFE. Host: 48th FW (USAFE). Mission: F-15C/D and F-15E operations. History: activated 1941. US forces arrived August 1948; the 48th FW arrived January 1960. Named after nearby village. Area: 2,290 acres. Runway: 9,000 ft. Altitude: 32 ft. Personnel: permanent party military, 4,800; DOD civilians, 260; Housing: single family, officer, 196, enlisted, 1,869; unaccompanied, UAQ/UEQ, 984; visiting, VOQ, 88, VAQ/VEQ, 48, TLF, 33. Regional medical center.

RAF Mildenhall, UK, APO AE 09459-5000; 20 mi. NE of Cambridge. Phone: (cmcl, from CONUS) 011-44-1638-54-3000; DSN 238-3000. Majcom: USAFE. Host: 100th ARW. Mission: KC-135R operations. Major tenants: 352nd SOG (AFSOC), MC-130, MH-53; 95th RS (ACC); 488th Intelligence Sq. (ACC); Naval Air Facility. History: activated 1934; US presence began July 1950. Named after nearby town. Area: 1,144 acres. Runway: 9,227 ft. Altitude: 33 ft. Personnel: permanent party military, 3,900; DOD civilians, 440. Housing: single family, officer, 64, enlisted, 137; unaccompanied, UAQ/UEQ, 783; visiting, 328, TLF, 36.

Ramstein AB, Germany, APO AE 09094-0385; adjacent to the city of Ramstein, 10 mi. W of Kaiserslautern. Phone: (cmcl, from CONUS) 011-49-6371-47-1110; DSN 314-480-1110. Majcom: USAFE. Host: 86th AW. Mission: C-20, C-21, C-40, and C-130E operations; provides expeditionary airlift for first-in base opening capabilities; 86th AW commander also serves as commander of the Kaiserslautern Military Community; also at Ramstein is the 435th Air Base Wing and the 38th Combat Support Wing. The 435th ABW provides expeditionary combat support and quality of life services for the Kaiserslautern community; the 38th CSW provides mission support to geographically separated units delivering American and European alliance combat support. Major tenant: USAFE. History: activated and US presence began 1953. Area: 3,212 acres. Runways: 10,498 ft. and 8,015 ft. Altitude: 782 ft. Personnel: permanent party military, 14,761; DOD civilians, 6,698. Housing: single family, officer, 473, enlisted, 4,588; unaccompanied, UOQ, 32, UAQ/UEQ, 1,795; visiting, 547, TLF, 70. Clinic.

Randolph AFB, Tex. 78150-5000; 17 mi. NE of San Antonio. Phone: 210-652-1110; DSN 487-1110. Majcom: AETC. Host: 12th FTW. Mission: conducts T-1, T-6, and T-38 instructor pilot training and combat systems officer training in the T-43. Major tenants: AETC; 19th Air Force; Air Force Personnel Center; Air Force Manpower Agency; Air Force Recruiting Service. History: dedicated June 1930. Named for Capt. William M. Randolph, killed 17 Feb. 1928. Area: 5,044 acres. Runways: two, 8,350 ft. each. Altitude: 761 ft. Personnel: permanent party military, 3,800; DOD civilians, 4,325. Housing: single family, officer, 218, enlisted, 441; unaccompanied, UOQ, 200, UEQ, 168; visiting, VOQ, 381, VAQ/VEQ, 169, TLF, 30. Clinic.

Robins AFB, Ga. 31098; 15 mi. SSE of Macon at Warner Robins. Phone: 478-926-1110; DSN 468-1001. Majcom: AFMC. Host: 78th ABW. Mission: Warner Robins Air Logistics Center provides worldwide logistics management for the C-5, C-17, C-130, E-8, F-15, U-2, and various special operations forces aircraft and helicopters. Provide combat-ready weapon systems, equipment, services, and support personnel for the Air Force. Deliver best-value sustainment and contingency response for US and allied warfighters through world-class cradle-to-grave management, maintenance, and combat support. Major tenants: Air Force Reserve Command; 116th Air Control Wing (ACC), E-8; 19th ARG (AMC), KC-135; 5th Combat Communications Gp. (ACC); 367th Air Force Recruiting Gp.; Defense Information Systems Agency. History: activated March 1942. Named for Brig. Gen. Augustine Warner Robins, an early chief of the Materiel Division of the Army Air Corps, who died June 16, 1940. Area: 8,700 acres. Runway: 12,000 ft. Altitude: 294 ft. Personnel: permanent party military, 5,369; DOD civilians, 12,605. Housing: single family, officer, 108, enlisted, 675; unaccompanied, UAQ/UEQ, 672; visiting, VOQ, 134, VAQ/VEQ, 157, TLF, 50. Clinic.

Schriever AFB, Colo. 80912-2101; 10 mi. E of Colorado Springs. Phone: 719-567-1110; DSN 560-1110. Majcom: AFSPC. Host: 50th SW. Mission: Provide space combat capability through command, control, operations, and support of more than 170 communication, navigation, warning, surveillance, and weather satellite weapon systems and conduct of expeditionary operations. Major tenants: Joint National Integration Center; Space Battlelab; 310th Space Gp. (AFRC); Space Innovation and Development Center. History: designated as Falcon AFB June 1988. Renamed in June 1998 for Gen. Bernard A. Schriever. Area: 3,840 acres. Runway: none. Altitude: 6,267 ft. Personnel: permanent party military, 1,710; DOD civilians, 645. Housing: none. Medical and dental clinic.

Scott AFB, Ill. 62225-5000; 6 mi. ENE of Belleville. Phone: 618-256-1110; DSN 576-1110. Majcom: AMC. Host: 375th AW. Mission: C-21 operations. Major tenants: TRANSCOM; AMC; Military Surface Deployment and Distribution Command;18th Air Force; Air Force Communications Agency; Defense Information Technology Contracting Office; 126th ARW (ANG), KC-135; 932nd AW (AFRC), C-9, C-40. History: activated 14 June 1917. Named for Cpl. Frank S. Scott, the first enlisted man to die in an aircraft accident, killed 28 Sept. 1912. Area: 3,230 acres. Runways: 10,000 ft. and 8,000 ft. (joint-use airfield). Altitude: 453 ft. Personnel: permanent party military, 5,884; DOD civilians, 3,156. Housing: single family, officer, 298, enlisted, 1,122; unaccompanied, UAQ/UEQ, 564; visiting, VOQ, 222, VAQ/VEQ, 173, TLF, 60. Clinic.

Seymour Johnson AFB, N.C. 27531; within city limits of Goldsboro. Phone: 919-722-1110; DSN 722-1110. Majcom: ACC. Host: 4th FW. Mission: F-15E operations and training. Major tenant: 916th ARW (AFRC), KC-135R. History: activated 12 June 1942. Named for Navy Lt. Seymour A. Johnson, Goldsboro native, killed 5 March 1941. Area: 3,558 acres. Runway: 11,758 ft. Altitude: 110 ft. Personnel: permanent party military, 6,066; DOD civilians, 1,108. Housing: single family, officer, 150, enlisted, 1,117; unaccompanied, 794; visiting, VOQ, 63, VAQ/VEQ, 40, DV, 10, TLF, 49. Clinic.

Shaw AFB, S.C. 29152-5000; 8 mi. WNW of Sumter. Phone: 803-895-1110; DSN 965-1110. Majcom: ACC. Host: 20th FW. Mission: F-16CJ operations. Major tenants: 9th Air Force (ACC); CENTCOM Air Forces. History: activated 30 Aug. 1941. Named for 1st Lt. Ervin D. Shaw, one of the first Americans to see air action in WWI, killed in France 9 July 1918. Area: 121,930 acres. Runways: 10,000 ft. and 8,000 ft. Altitude: 242 ft. Personnel: permanent party military, 6,208; DOD civilians, 1,751. Housing: single family, officer, 160, enlisted, 1,362; unaccompanied, 1,112; visiting, VQ, 97, TLF, 19. Hospital (no emergency room).

Sheppard AFB, Tex. 76311-5000; 5 mi. N of Wichita Falls. Phone: 940-676-1110; DSN 736-2511. Majcom: AETC. Host: 82nd TRW. Mission: largest of AETC's four technical training centers. Conducts resident training in aircraft maintenance, aircraft avionics, aerospace propulsion, fuels, ammo and munitions, armament, aerospace ground equipment, life support, civil engineering, communications, and various medical and dental specialties; provides instruction in a wide range of specialties at more than 40 USAF installations worldwide. Major tenant: 80th FTW (AETC), conducts T-37 and T-38 UPT, instructor pilot training in the Euro-NATO Joint Jet Pilot Training program, and Introduction to Fighter Fundamentals course with AT-38 aircraft. History: activated 14 June 1941. Named for US Sen. Morris E. Sheppard, who died 9 April 1941. Area: 6,158 acres. Runways: 13,100 ft., 10,000 ft., 7,000 ft., and 6,000 ft. Altitude: 1,019 ft. Personnel: permanent party military, 3,419; DOD civilians, 1,440. Housing: single family, officer, 200, enlisted, 967; unaccompanied, UOQ, 196, UAQ/UEQ, 396; visiting, 1,278, TLF, 73. Clinic.

Spangdahlem AB, Germany, APO AE 09126-5000; 20 mi. NE of Trier; 9 mi. E of Bitburg. Phone: (cmcl, from CONUS) 011-49-6565-61-1110; DSN 452-1110. Majcom: USAFE. Host: 52nd FW. Mission: A/OA-10A and HARM-equipped F-16CJ operations; air control squadron operations with logistics responsibilities at dozens of GSUs. History: built by the French in 1951 and turned over to US in 1952. Named after nearby town. Area: 1,616 acres. Runway: 10,000 ft. Altitude: 1,196 ft. Personnel: permanent party military, 5,472; DOD civilians, 218. Housing: single family, officer, 73, enlisted, 114; unaccompanied, UAQ/UEQ, 792; visiting, 102, TLF, 54. Hospital.

Tinker AFB, Okla. 73145-3010; 8 mi. SE of Oklahoma City. Phone: 405-732-1110; DSN 884-1110. Majcom: AFMC. Host: 72nd ABW. Mission: Oklahoma City Air Logistics Center manages and repairs the engines that power cruise missiles and a variety of Air Force and Navy aircraft. The center also accomplishes aircraft modi.cations and repairs and maintains bombers, refuelers, and reconnaissance aircraft, including the B-1, B-2, B-52, C/KC-135, E-3 AWACS, and E-6 Mercury. Major tenants: 552nd Air Control Wing (ACC), E-3; Navy Strategic Communications Wing One, E-6; 507th ARW (AFRC), KC-135; 513th Air Control Gp. (AFRC assoc.), E-3; Defense Information Systems Agency; Defense Distribution Center Oklahoma (DLA); 3rd Combat Communications Gp. (ACC); 38th Engineering Installation Gp. (AFMC). History: activated March 1942. Named for Maj. Gen. Clarence L. Tinker, who went down at sea 7 June 1942 while leading a group of LB-30 bombers against Japan. Area: 5,033 acres. Runways: 11,100 ft. and 10,000 ft. Altitude: 1,291 ft. Personnel: permanent party military, 6,113; DOD civilians, 13,547. Housing: single family, officer, 107, enlisted, 587; unaccompanied, UAQ/UEQ, 1,222; visiting, VOQ, 109, VAQ/VEQ, 50, TLF, 40. Clinic.

Travis AFB, Calif. 94535-5000; 50 mi. NE of San Francisco at Fairfield. Phone: 707-424-1110; DSN 837-1110. Majcom: AMC. Host: 60th AMW. Mission: C-5, C-17, and KC-10 operations. Major tenants: 615th Contingency Response Wing (AMC); 15th Expeditionary Mobility Task Force (AMC); 349th AMW (AFRC assoc.); USAF Band of the Golden West; Air Museum. History: activated 17 May 1943. Named for Brig. Gen. Robert F. Travis, killed 5 Aug. 1950. Area: 6,383 acres. Runways: two, approx. 11,000 ft. each. Altitude: 62 ft. Personnel: permanent party military, 8,443; DOD civilians, 3,511. Housing: single family, officer, 148, enlisted, 1,057; unaccompanied, UAQ/UEQ, 873; visiting, VQ, 340, TLF, 46. David Grant Medical Center.

Tyndall AFB, Fla. 32403-5000; 12 mi. E of Panama City. Phone: 850-283-1113; DSN 523-1113. Majcom: AETC. Host: 325th FW. Mission: F-15 and F-22 operations; trains USAF F-15 and F-22 pilots. Major tenants: 1st Air Force (ANG); Southeast Air Defense Sector (ANG); 53rd Weapons Evaluation Gp. (ACC); Air Force Civil Engineer Support Agency. History: activated 7 Dec. 1941. Named for 1st Lt. Frank B. Tyndall, WWI fighter pilot killed 15 July 1930. Area: 29,102 acres. Runways: 10,000 ft., 9,000 ft., and 7,000 ft. Altitude: 18 ft. Personnel: permanent party military, 3,421; DOD civilians, 565. Housing: single family, officer, 111, enlisted, 737; unaccompanied, UAQ/UEQ, 448; visiting, 648, TLF, 52. Clinic.

US Air Force Academy, Colo. 80840-5025; N of Colorado Springs. Phone: 719-333-1110; DSN 333-1110. Host: USAFA. Mission: inspires and develops outstanding young men and women to become Air Force officers with knowledge, character, and discipline. History: established 1 April 1954. Moved to permanent location August 1958. Area: 18,500 acres. Runways: 4,500 ft., 3,500 ft., and 2,300 ft. Altitude: 7,200 ft. Personnel: permanent party military, 1,973; DOD civilians, 2,000. Housing: single family, officer, 231, enlisted, 978; unaccompanied, 130; visiting, 90, TLF, 30. Hospital.

Vance AFB, Okla. 73705-5000; 3 mi. SSW of Enid. Phone: 580-213-5000; DSN 448-7110. Majcom:AETC. Host: 71st FTW. Mission: provides Joint SUPT in T-1, T-6, and T-38 aircraft. History: activated November 1941. Named for Lt. Col. Leon R. Vance Jr., Enid native, 1939 West Point graduate, and Medal of Honor recipient, killed 26 July 1944. Area: 2,000 acres. Runways: 9,200 ft., 9,200 ft., and 5,001 ft. Altitude: 1,307 ft. Personnel: permanent party military, 1,200; DOD civilians, 142. Housing: single family, 229; unaccompanied, UOQ, 200, UAQ/UEQ, 109; visiting, 62, TLF, 10. Clinic.

Vandenberg AFB, Calif. 93437-5000; 8 mi. NNW of Lompoc. Phone: 805-606-1110; DSN 276-1110. Majcom: AFSPC. Host: 30th SW. Mission: conducts polar-orbiting space launches and supports R&D tests and launch range operations for DOD, USAF, and NASA space, ballistic missile, and aeronautical systems and commercial space launches; provides test support for DOD space and ICBM systems; furnishes facilities and essential services to more than 36 aerospace contractors. Major tenants: 14th Air Force (AFSPC); 381st Training Gp. (AETC); 576th Flight Test Sq. (Space Warfare Center). History: originally Army's Camp Cooke. Activated October 1941; taken over by USAF 7 June 1957. Renamed for Gen. Hoyt S. Vandenberg, USAF's second Chief of Staff. Area: 98,400 acres. Runway: 15,000 ft. Altitude: 367 ft. Personnel: permanent party military, 3,400; DOD civilians, 1,400. Housing: single family, officer, 403, enlisted,1,566; unaccompanied, dorm rooms, 670, UOQ, 43, UAQ/UEQ, 59; visiting, VOQ, 111, VAQ/VEQ, 124, DV, 18, TLF, 26. Clinic.

Whiteman AFB, Mo. 65305-5000; 2 mi. S of Knob Noster. Phone: 660-687-1110; DSN 975-1110. Majcom: ACC. Host: 509th BW. Mission: B-2 operations. Major tenants: 442nd FW (AFRC), A/OA-10; 1st Battalion, 135th Aviation Regiment (ARNG); Mobile Inshore Undersea Warfare Unit 114 (Navy Reserve). History: activated 1942. Named for 2nd Lt. George A. Whiteman, first pilot to die in aerial combat during the attack on Pearl Harbor. Area: 4,993 acres. Runway: 12,400 ft. Altitude: 871 ft. Personnel: permanent party military, 5,480; DOD civilians, 707. Housing: single family, officer, 116, enlisted, 968; unaccompanied, 674; visiting, VOQ, 52, VAQ/VEQ, 35, TLF, 31. Clinic.

Wright-Patterson AFB, Ohio 45433; 10 mi. ENE of Dayton. Phone: 937-257-1110; DSN 787-1110. Majcom: AFMC. Host: 88th ABW. Mission: Aeronautical Systems Center develops, acquires, modernizes, and sustains aerospace systems. Major tenants: Air Force Materiel Command; Development and Fielding Systems Gp.; Air Force Research Laboratory (AFMC); Air Force Security Assistance Center (AFMC); 445th AW (AFRC), C-141 (converting to C-5); Air Force Institute of Technology (AETC); National Air and Space Intelligence Center; National Museum of the US Air Force. History: originally separate, Wright Field and Patterson Field were merged and redesignated Wright-Patterson AFB 13 Jan. 1948. Named for aviation pioneers Orville and Wilbur Wright and for 1st Lt. Frank S. Patterson, killed 19 June 1918. The Wright brothers did much of their early flying on Huffman Prairie, now in Area C of the present base. The prairie is part of the Dayton Aviation Heritage National Historical Park. Site of US Air Force Marathon, held annually on Saturday nearest 18 Sept. Area: 8,357 acres. Runway: 12,600 ft. Altitude: 824 ft. Personnel: permanent party military, 5,863; DOD civilians, 10,954. Housing: single family, officer, 182, enlisted, 294; unaccompanied, UAQ/UEQ, 408; privatized housing, oficers, 566, enlisted, 970; visiting, 414, TLF, 41. Wright-Patterson Medical Center.

Yokota AB, Japan, APO AP 96328-5000; approx. 28 mi. W of downtown Tokyo. Phone: (cmcl, from CONUS) 011-81-311-755-1110; DSN 315-225-1110. Majcom: PACAF. Host: 374th AW. Mission: C-21, C-130, and UH-1N operations. Primary aerial port in Japan. Major tenants: US Forces, Japan; 5th Air Force (PACAF); 730th AMS (AMC); Det. 1, Air Force Band of the Paci.c-Asia; American Forces Network Tokyo; DFAS-Japan. History: opened as Tama AAF by the Japanese in 1939. Area: 1,750 acres. Runway: 11,000 ft. Altitude: 457 ft. Personnel: permanent party military, 3,414; DOD civilians, 199. Housing: single family, officer, 683, enlisted, 1,956; unaccompanied, UOQ, 184, UAQ/UEQ, 896; visiting, VOQ, 202, VAQ/VEQ, 23, TLF, 189. Hospital.

Appendix D

Selected
Air Force Publications

The Air Force instructions, manuals, pamphlets, handbooks, and catalogs listed below should be of interest to Air Force officers in general. All officers should identify those additional publications related to their specialties and become familiar with their contents. A complete list of Air Force publications is available at *http://www.e-publishing.af.mil/mastercatalog/mastersearch.asp?org=AF.*

AIR FORCE INSTRUCTIONS (AFI)

AFI 10-248	*Fitness Program*
AFI 31-401	*Information Security Program Management*
AFI 31-501	*Personnel Security Program Management*
AFI 34-202	*Protecting Nonappropriated Funds Assets*
AFI 34-1201	*Protocol*
AFI 36-810	*Substance Abuse Prevention and Control*
AFI 36-2101	*Classifying Military Personnel*
AFI 36-2107	*Active Duty Service Commitments*
AFI 36-2110	*Assignments*
AFI 36-2116	*Extended Active Duty for Reserve Component Officers*
AFI 36-2301	*Professional Military Education*
AFI 36-2302	*Professional Development* (Advanced Academic Degrees and Professional Continuing Education)
AFI 36-2406	*Officer and Enlisted Evaluation Systems*
AFI 36-2501	*Officer Promotions and Selective Continuation*
AFI 36-2504	*Officer Promotions Continuation and Selective Early Removal in the Reserve of the Air Force*
AFI 36-2608	*Military Personnel Records Systems*
AFI 36-2610	*Appointing Regular Air Force Officers and Obtaining Conditional Reserve Status*
AFI 36-2611	*Officer Professional Development*

AFI 36-2640V1	*Total Force Development (Active-Duty Officers)*
AFI 36-2706	*Military Equal Opportunity Program*
AFI 36-2803	*The Air Force Awards and Decorations Program*
AFI 36-2903	*Dress and Personal Appearance of Air Force Personnel*
AFI 36-2906	*Personal Financial Responsibility*
AFI 36-2907	*Unfavorable Information File (UIF) Program*
AFI 36-2908	*Family Care Plans*
AFI 36-2909	*Professional and Unprofessional Relationships*
AFI 36-2910	*Line of Duty (Misconduct) Determination*
AFI 36-3003	*Military Leave Program*
AFI 36-3005	*Federal Housing Administration Insured Home Loans for Servicemembers*
AFI 36-3006	*Survivor Benefit Plan and Supplemental Survivor Benefit Plan (SSBP)* (Active, Guard, Reserve, and Retired)
AFI 36-3203	*Service Retirements*
AFI 36-3206	*Discharge Procedures for Commissioned Officers*
AFI 36-3207	*Separating Commissioned Officers*
AFI 36-3401	*Air Force Mentoring*
AFI 38-101	*Air Force Organization*
AFI 40-101	*Health Promotion Program*
AFI 40-102	*Tobacco Use in the Air Force*
AFI 40-104	*Nutrition Education*
AFI 41-115	*Authorized Health Care and Health Care Benefits in the Military Health Services System*
AFI 44-120	*Drug Abuse Testing Program*
AFI 44-121	*Alcohol and Drug Abuse Prevention and Treatment Program*
AFI 51-201	*Administration of Military Justice*
AFI 51-202	*Nonjudicial Punishment*
AFI 51-401	*Training and Reporting to Ensure Compliance with the Law of Armed Conflict*
AFI 51-902	*Political Activities by Members of the U.S. Air Force*
AFI 51-903	*Dissident and Protest Activities*
AFI 51-904	*Complaints of Wrongs Under Article 138, Uniform Code of Military Justice*
AFI 90-301	*Inspector General Complaints*
AFI 91-202	*U.S. Air Force Mishap Prevention Program*
AFI 91-204	*Safety Investigations and Reports*
AFI 91-301	*Air Force Occupational and Environmental Safety, Fire Protection, and Health (AFOSH) Program*

AIR FORCE MANUALS
AFMAN 10-100   *Airman's Manual*
AFMAN 33-326   *Preparing Official Communications*
AFMAN 36-2203   *Drill and Ceremonies*

AIR FORCE PAMPHLETS (AFPAM)
AFPAM 34-1202   *Guide to Protocol*
AFPAM 36-2506   *You and Your Promotions: The Air Force Officer Promotion Program*
AFPAM 36-2607   *Applicant's Guide to the Air Force Board for Correction of Military Records*
AFPAM 36-2705   *Discrimination and Sexual Harassment*
AFPAM 36-3027   *Benefits and Entitlements for Family Members of Air Force Deceased*
AFPAM 36-3028   *Benefits and Entitlements for Family Members of Retired Air Force Deceased*
AFPAM 38-102   *Headquarters United States Air Force Organization and Functions (Chartbook)*
AFPAM 169-10   *Law of Armed Conflict, Geneva Conventions, and Code of Conduct*

AIR FORCE POLICY DIRECTIVES
AFPD 36-27   *Social Actions*
AFPD 36-29   *Military Standards*
AFPD 36-30   *Military Entitlements*
AFPD 51-4   *Compliance with the Law of Armed Conflict*

AIR FORCE HANDBOOKS
AFH 33-337   *The Tongue and Quill* (Guide to Air Force Communications)

AIR FORCE CATALOG
AFCAT 36-2223   *USAF Formal Schools*

Appendix E

USAF Acronyms and Abbreviations

A1C	airman first class
AA&E	arms, ammunition, and explosives
AAF	Army Air Force
AAFES	Army and Air Force Exchange Service
AB	airman basic; air base
ABC	Aerospace Basic Course
ABU	Airman Battle Uniform
ACC	Air Combat Command
ACE	Allied Command Europe
ACSC	Air Command and Staff College
AD	active duty
ADAPT	alcohol and drug abuse prevention and treatment
ADAPTPM	ADAPT program manager
ADC	Area Defense Counsel; Air Defense Command
ADSC	Active Duty Service Commitment
AECP	Airman Education and Commissioning Program
AEF	air and space expeditionary force; American Expeditionary Force (WWI)
AETC	Air Education and Training Command
AEW	aerospace expeditionary wing
AFAS	Air Force Aid Society
AFBCMR	Air Force Board for Correction of Military Records
AFCFM	Air Force career field manager
AFEM	Armed Forces Expeditionary Medal
AFGCM	Air Force Good Conduct Medal
AFHRA	Air Force Historical Research Agency
AFIA	Air Force Inspection Agency
AFIADL	Air Force Institute for Advanced Distributed Learning

AFIT	Air Force Institute of Technology
AFLSA	Air Force Longevity Service Award
AFMC	Air Force Materiel Command
AFMIA	Air Force Manpower and Innovation Agency
AFOEA	Air Force Organizational Excellence Award
AFOMS	Air Force Occupational Measurement Squadron
AFOR	Air Force Overseas Ribbon
AFOSI	Air Force Office of Special Investigations
AFOUA	Air Force Outstanding Unit Award
AFPC	Air Force Personnel Center
AFR	Air Force Reserve
AFRC	Air Force Reserve Command
AFRH	Armed Forces Retirement Home
AFROTC	Air Force Reserve Officer Training Corps
AFS	Air Force specialty
AFSC	Air Force specialty code
AFSM	Armed Forces Service Medal
AFSNCOA	Air Force Senior NCO Academy
AFSOC	Air Force Special Operations Command
AFSPC	Air Force Space Command
AFTR	Air Force Training Ribbon
AGR	active guard or reserve
ALS	airman leadership school
AMC	Air Mobility Command
Amn	airman
ANG	Air National Guard
AOR	area of responsibility
APOD	aerial port of debarkation
APOE	aerial port of embarkation
APZ	above the promotion zone
ARC	American Red Cross; Air Reserve Component
ASCP	Airman Scholarship and Commissioning Program
AT	antiterrorism
ATC	Air Traffic Controller
ATM	automated teller machine
AWACS	Airborne Warning and Control System
AWC	Air War College
AWOL	absent without official leave
BAH	basic allowance for housing
BAS	basic allowance for subsistence
BDU	battle dress uniform
BMT	basic military training
BOP	base of preference
BOQ	bachelor officers' quarters

BPZ	below the promotion zone
BX	base exchange
C³	command, control, and communications
C³I	command, control, and communications, and intelligence
C⁴	command, control, and communications, and computer systems
CAA	career assistance advisor
CAF	Combat Air Forces
CAFSC	control Air Force specialty code
CAP	Civil Air Patrol
CAREERS	Career Airman Reenlistment Reservation System
CASF	composite air strike force
CB	chemical-biological
CCAF	Community College of the Air Force
CCMS	command chief master sergeant
CCRC	common core readiness criteria
CCT	combat controller
CDC	career development course
CENTAF	U.S. Air Force Central Command
CEPME	College for Enlisted Professional Military Education
CFC	Combined Federal Campaign
CFETP	career field education and training plan
CHAMPUS	Civilian Health and Medical Program of the Uniformed Services (former name for Tricare)
CI	compliance inspection; counterintelligence
CIA	Central Intelligence Agency
CINC	commander in chief
CJCS	Chairman, Joint Chiefs of Staff
CMC	Commandant of the Marine Corps
CMSAF	Chief Master Sergeant of the Air Force
CMSgt	chief master sergeant
COLA	cost-of-living adjustment
COMPUSEC	computer security
COMSEC	communications security
CONUS	continental United States
CPR	cardiopulmonary resuscitation
CRO	change of rating official
CSA	Chief of Staff, U.S. Army
CSAF	Chief of Staff, U.S. Air Force
CSS	commander support staff; combat service support
CTO	commercial travel office
DANTES	Defense Activity for Nontraditional Education Support
DCS	deputy chief of staff
DFAS	Defense Finance and Accounting Service

DIEMS	date initially entered military service
DLA	Defense Logistics Agency
DOB	date of birth
DOD	Department of Defense
DOPMA	Defense Officer Personnel Management Act
DOR	date of rank
DOS	date of separation
DOT	Department of Transportation
DRU	direct reporting unit
DTRA	Defense Threat Reduction Agency
DUI	driving under the influence
DV	distinguished visitors
EAD	extended active duty; entrance on active duty
EES	Enlisted Evaluation System
EFMP	Exceptional Family Member Program
EFT	electronic funds transfer
E-mail	electronic mail
ELA	educational leave of absence
EML	environmental and morale leave
EMSEC	emissions security
EOT	equal opportunity and treatment
EPA	Environmental Protection Agency
EPR	enlisted performance report
ETS	expiration of term of service
EXORD	execution order
FAC	functional account code
FAP	Family Advocacy Program
FBI	Federal Bureau of Investigation
FICA	Federal Insurance Contributions Act
FITW	Federal income tax withholding
FOA	field operating agency
FOIA	Freedom of Information Act
FOUO	for official use only
FPCON	force protection condition
FSA	family separation allowance
FSA-R	FSA reassignment
FSA-T	FSA temporary
FSC	family support center
FSH	family separation, basic allowance for housing
FSO	financial services office
FSSA	family subsistence supplemental allowance
FTA	first-term airmen
FVAP	Federal Voting Assistance Program
FWA	fraud, waste, and abuse

FY	fiscal year
GCE	ground crew ensemble
GCM	general court-martial
GHQ	general headquarters
HAZMAT	hazardous material
HUMINT	human intelligence
ICBM	intercontinental ballistic missile
IG	Inspector General
IMA	individual mobilization augmentee
IO	information operations
IPZ	in the promotion zone
IRA	individual retirement account
IRR	individual ready reserve
ISP	Internet service provider
ISR	intelligence, surveillance, reconnaissance
IW	information warfare
JCS	Joint Chiefs of Staff
JFACC	joint forces air component commander
JFTR	Joint Federal Travel Regulation
JOPS	Joint Operational Planning System
JTF	joint task force
JTR	Joint Travel Regulations
JUMPS	Joint Uniform Military Pay System
JV	Joint Vision
LD/HD	low density/high density
LES	leave and earnings statement
LOA	letter of admonishment
LOAC	law of armed conflict
LOC	letter of counseling; line of communication
LOD	line of duty
LOE	letter of evaluation
LOR	letter of reprimand
LOW	law of war
MAAG	Military Assistance Advisory Group
MAC	Military Airlift Command
MAJCOM	major command
MAF	mobility air forces
MALT	monetary allowance in lieu of transportation
MCM	Manual for Courts-Martial
MDS	Manpower Data System
MEO	military equal opportunity; most effective organization
MFR	memorandum for record
MGIB	Montgomery GI Bill
MilPDS	Military Personnel Data System

MOPP	mission-oriented protective posture
MPF	military personnel flight
MR	memorandum for record
MRE	meal, ready-to-eat
MSgt	master sergeant
MSO	military service obligation
MTF	military treatment facility; medical treatment facility
MTP	master training plan
MTW	major theater war
MWR	morale, welfare, and recreation
NAF	numbered Air Force; non-appropriated fund
NATO	North Atlantic Treaty Organization
NBC	nuclear, biological, and chemical
NBCC	nuclear, biological, chemical, and conventional
NCO	noncommissioned officer
NCOA	noncommissioned officer academy
NDSM	National Defense Service Medal
NOTAM	Notice to Airmen
NSI	nuclear surety inspection
OBAD	operating budget authority document
OJT	on-the-job training
OPLAN	operations plan
OPORD	operations order
OPR	office of primary responsibility; officer performance report
OPSEC	operations security
ORI	operational readiness inspection
ORM	operational risk management
OSD	Office of the Secretary of Defense
OSHA	occupational safety and health administration
OSI	Office of Special Investigations
OTS	Officer Training School
PACAF	Pacific Air Forces
PACOM	Pacific Command
PC	personal computer
PCA	permanent change of assignment
PCM	primary care manager
PCS	permanent change of station
PDA	personal digital assistant
PDS	permanent duty station; personnel data system
PECD	promotion eligibility cutoff date
PERSTEMPO	personnel tempo
PES	promotion eligibility status
PFE	promotion fitness examination

PFW	performance feedback worksheet
PIN	personal identification number
PJ	pararescue
P.L.	public law
PME	professional military education
POV	privately owned vehicle
POW	prisoner of war
PRP	Personnel Reliability Program
PSN	promotion sequence number
PT	physical training
PTDY	permissive TDY
QRP	Qualified Recycling Program; Quality Retraining Program
QT	qualification training
RAC	risk assessment code
RHIP	rank has its privileges
RIC	record of individual counseling
RMS	resource management system
RNLTD	report not later than date
ROE	rules of engagement
ROTC	Reserve Officer Training Corps
SAC	Strategic Air Command
SAF	Secretary of the Air Force
SAM	surface-to-air missile
SAV	staff assistance visit
SBP	survivor benefit plan
SCG	security classification guide
SCM	summary court-martial
SDI	special duty identifier
SEA	senior enlisted advisor
SECAF	Secretary of the Air Force
SECDEF	Secretary of Defense
SEI	special experience identifier
SelRes	selected reserve
SG	surgeon general
SGLI	servicemembers' group life insurance
SII	special interest item
SJA	staff judge advocate
SLA	special leave accrual
SMSgt	senior master sergeant
SNCO	senior noncommissioned officer
SOAR	Scholarships for Outstanding Airmen to ROTC
SOF	special operations force
SOP	standing operating procedure

SPCM	special court-martial
SrA	senior airman
SRB	selective reenlistment bonus
SRID	senior rater identification
SROE	standing rules of engagement
SRP	Selective Reenlistment Program
SSgt	staff sergeant
STEP	Stripes for Exceptional Performers
TAC	Tactical Air Command
TAFMS	total active federal military service
TDP	TRICARE Dental Program
TDY	temporary duty
TFW	tactical fighter wing
TIG	time in grade
TIS	time in service
TJAG	The Judge Advocate General
TMO	traffic/transportation management office
TO	technical order
TOS	time on station
TRW	tactical reconnaissance wing
TSCO	Top Secret control officer
TSgt	technical sergeant
TSP	Thrift Savings Plan
UCMJ	Uniform Code of Military Justice
UETM	unit education and training manager
UFPM	unit fitness program manager
UIF	unfavorable information file
UMD	unit manning document
UN	United Nations
UOCAVA	Uniformed and Overseas Citizens Absentee Voting Act
UPMR	unit personnel management roster
USAAF	U.S. Army Air Forces
USAF	United States Air Force
USAFA	United States Air Force Academy
USAFE	U.S. Air Forces in Europe
USAFR	U.S. Air Force Reserves
U.S.C.	United States Code
USEUCOM	U.S. European Command
UTM	unit training manager
VA	Veterans Affairs
VAO	voting assistance officer
VCJCS	Vice Chairman, Joint Chief of Staff
VEAP	Veterans Education Assistance Program
VIP	very important person

WAPS	Weighted Airman Promotion System
WASP	Women Airforce Service Pilots
WMD	weapons of mass destruction
WOC	wing operations center
WR	war reserve
WWI	World War I
WWII	World War II

Appendix F

USAF Fitness Charts

DETERMINING FITNESS SCORE
Fitness level is determined by adding aerobic fitness, body composition, push-up, and crunch component points.

FITNESS LEVEL	TOTAL SCORE
Excellent	≥ 90
Good	75–89.9
Marginal	70–74.9
Poor	< 70

    Members must complete *all* components unless medically exempted. If a member is medically exempted from any component, the total score is calculated as follows:

$$\frac{\text{Total component points achieved}}{\text{Total possible points}} \times 100$$

COMPONENT	POSSIBLE POINTS
Aerobic	50
Body Comp	30
Push-ups	10
Crunches	10

DETERMINING BODY COMPOSITION
To measure abdominal circumference, locate the upper hip bone and the top of the right iliac crest. Place a measuring tape in a horizontal plane around the abdomen at the level of the iliac crest. Before reading the tape measure, ensure that the tape is snug, but does not compress the skin, and is parallel to the floor. The measurement is made at the end of a normal expiration.

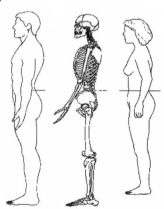

MEN UNDER 25

AEROBIC FITNESS

BODY COMPOSITION

1.5-Mile Run Time (min.)	Bike Test (VO₂)	Component Points	Abdominal Circumference (inches)	Component Points
≤ 9:36	≥ 54	50.00	< 32.50	30.00
9:37–9:48	53	47.50	32.50	28.75
9:49–10:12	51–52	45.00	33.00	27.50
10:13–10:36	49–50	43.50	33.50	26.25
10:37–11:06	47–48	42.00	34.00	25.00
11:07–11:36	45–46	40.50	34.50	23.75
11:37–12:12	43–44	39.00	35.00	22.50
12:13–12:54	41–42	37.50	35.50	22.35
12:55–13:36	39–40	36.00	36.00	22.20
13:37–14:24	37–38	34.00	36.50	22.05
14:25–14:54	36	32.00	37.00	21.90
14:55–15:18	35	30.00	37.50	21.75
15:19–15:48	34	27.00	38.00	21.60
15:49–16:24	33	24.00	38.50	21.45
16:25–16:54	32	21.00	39.00	21.30
16:55–17:36	31	18.00	39.50	21.25
17:37–18:12	30	15.00	40.00	21.00
18:13–18:54	29	12.00	40.50	18.00
18:55–19:42	28	9.00	41.00	15.00
19:43–20:36	27	6.00	41.50	12.00
20:37–21:30	26	3.00	42.00	9.00
> 21:30	< 26	0.00	42.50	6.00
			43.00	3.00
			> 43.00	0.00

MUSCLE FITNESS

1 minute Push-up (# reps)	Component Points	1 minute Crunch (# reps)	Component Points
≥ 62	10.00	≥ 55	10.00
61	9.75	53–54	9.50
60	9.50	52	9.00
59	9.25	50–51	8.75
57–58	9.00	48–49	8.50
52–56	8.75	46–47	8.25
49–51	8.50	44–45	8.00
45–48	8.25	42–43	7.75
41–44	8.00	40–41	7.50
37–40	7.75	38–39	7.40
33–36	7.50	36–37	7.30
30–32	7.40	35	7.20
27–29	7.30	33–34	7.10
24–26	7.20	32	7.00
21–23	7.10	30–31	6.00
19–20	7.00	28–29	4.00
17–18	6.00	27	2.00
15–16	5.00	< 27	0.00
14	4.00		
12–13	3.00		
10–11	2.00		
8–9	1.00		
< 8	0.00		

MEN 25–29

AEROBIC FITNESS

1.5-Mile Run Time (min.)	Bike Test (VO2)	Component Points
≤ 9:36	≥ 54	50.00
9:37–9:48	53	47.50
9:49–10:12	51–52	45.00
10:13–10:36	49–50	43.50
10:37–11:06	47–48	42.00
11:07–11:36	45–46	40.50
11:37–12:12	43–44	39.00
12:13–12:54	41–42	37.50
12:55–13:36	39–40	36.00
13:37–14:24	37–38	34.00
14:25–14:54	36	32.00
14:55–15:18	35	30.00
15:19–15:48	34	27.00
15:49–16:24	33	24.00
16:25–16:54	32	21.00
16:55–17:36	31	18.00
17:37–18:12	30	15.00
18:13–18:54	29	12.00
18:55–19:42	28	9.00
19:43–20:36	27	6.00
20:37–21:30	26	3.00
> 21:30	< 26	0.00

BODY COMPOSITION

Abdominal Circumference (inches)	Component Points
< 32.50	30.00
32.50	28.75
33.00	27.50
33.50	26.25
34.00	25.00
34.50	23.75
35.00	22.50
35.50	22.35
36.00	22.20
36.50	22.05
37.00	21.90
37.50	21.75
38.00	21.60
38.50	21.45
39.00	21.30
39.50	21.25
40.00	21.00
40.50	18.00
41.00	15.00
41.50	12.00
42.00	9.00
42.50	6.00
43.00	3.00
> 43.00	0.00

MUSCLE FITNESS

1 minute Push-up (# reps)	Component Points	1 minute Crunch (# reps)	Component Points
≥ 57	10.00	≥ 53	10.00
56	9.75	51–52	9.50
55	9.50	50	9.00
54	9.25	48–49	8.75
52–53	9.00	46–47	8.50
48–51	8.75	44–45	8.25
45–47	8.50	42–43	8.00
41–44	8.25	40–41	7.75
37–40	8.00	38–39	7.50
34–36	7.75	36–37	7.40
30–33	7.50	34–35	7.30
27–29	7.40	33	7.20
25–26	7.30	31–32	7.10
23–24	7.20	30	7.00
20–22	7.10	28–29	6.00
17–19	7.00	27	4.00
15–16	6.00	25–26	2.00
13–14	5.00	< 25	0.00
11–12	4.00		
10	3.00		
9	2.00		
7–8	1.00		
< 7	0.00		

MEN 30–34

AEROBIC FITNESS

1.5-Mile Run Time (min.)	Bike Test (VO₂)	Component Points
≤ 9:48	≥ 53	50.00
9:49–10:12	51–52	47.50
10:13–10:24	50	45.00
10:25–10:54	48–49	43.50
10:55–11:24	46–47	42.00
11:25–11:54	44–45	40.50
11:55–12:30	42–43	39.00
12:31–12:54	41	37.50
12:55–13:36	39–40	36.00
13:37–14:24	37–38	34.00
14:25–14:54	36	32.00
14:55–15:18	35	30.00
15:19–15:48	34	27.00
15:49–16:24	33	24.00
16:25–16:54	32	21.00
16:55–17:36	31	18.00
17:37–18:12	30	15.00
18:13–18:54	29	12.00
18:55–19:42	28	9.00
19:43–20:36	27	6.00
20:37–21:30	26	3.00
> 21:30	< 26	0.00

BODY COMPOSITION

Abdominal Circumference (inches)	Component Points
< 32.50	30.00
32.50	28.75
33.00	27.50
33.50	26.25
34.00	25.00
34.50	23.75
35.00	22.50
35.50	22.35
36.00	22.20
36.50	22.05
37.00	21.90
37.50	21.75
38.00	21.60
38.50	21.45
39.00	21.30
39.50	21.25
40.00	21.00
40.50	18.00
41.00	15.00
41.50	12.00
42.00	9.00
42.50	6.00
43.00	3.00
> 43.00	0.00

MUSCLE FITNESS

1 minute Push-up (# reps)	Component Points	1 minute Crunch (# reps)	Component Points
≥ 52	10.00	≥ 51	10.00
50–51	9.75	49–50	9.50
49	9.50	48	9.00
48	9.25	46–47	8.75
46–47	9.00	44–45	8.50
43–45	8.75	42–43	8.25
40–42	8.50	40–41	8.00
36–39	8.25	38–39	7.75
33–35	8.00	36–37	7.50
30–32	7.75	34–35	7.40
27–29	7.50	33	7.30
24–26	7.40	31–32	7.20
22–23	7.30	30	7.10
20–21	7.20	28–29	7.00
17–19	7.10	26–27	6.00
15–16	7.00	25	4.00
13–14	6.00	23–24	2.00
12	5.00	< 23	0.00
10–11	4.00		
8–9	3.00		
7	2.00		
5–6	1.00		
< 5	0.00		

MEN 35–39

AEROBIC FITNESS

1.5-Mile Run Time (min.)	Bike Test (VO2)	Component Points
≤ 9:48	≥ 53	50.00
9:49–10:12	51–52	47.50
10:13–10:24	50	45.00
10:25–10:54	48–49	43.50
10:55–11:24	46–47	42.00
11:25–11:54	44–45	40.50
11:55–12:30	42–43	39.00
12:31–12:54	41	37.50
12:55–13:36	39–40	36.00
13:37–14:24	37–38	34.00
14:25–14:54	36	32.00
14:55–15:18	35	30.00
15:19–15:48	34	27.00
15:49–16:24	33	24.00
16:25–16:54	32	21.00
16:55–17:36	31	18.00
17:37–18:12	30	15.00
18:13–18:54	29	12.00
18:55–19:42	28	9.00
19:43–20:36	27	6.00
20:37–21:30	26	3.00
> 21:30	< 26	0.00

BODY COMPOSITION

Abdominal Circumference (inches)	Component Points
< 32.50	30.00
32.50	28.75
33.00	27.50
33.50	26.25
34.00	25.00
34.50	23.75
35.00	22.50
35.50	22.35
36.00	22.20
36.50	22.05
37.00	21.90
37.50	21.75
38.00	21.60
38.50	21.45
39.00	21.30
39.50	21.25
40.00	21.00
40.50	18.00
41.00	15.00
41.50	12.00
42.00	9.00
42.50	6.00
43.00	3.00
> 43.00	0.00

MUSCLE FITNESS

1 minute Push-up (# reps)	Component Points	1 minute Crunch (# reps)	Component Points
≥ 46	10.00	≥ 49	10.00
45	9.75	47–48	9.50
44	9.50	46	9.00
42–43	9.25	44–45	8.75
41	9.00	42–43	8.50
38–40	8.75	40–41	8.25
35–37	8.50	38–39	8.00
32–34	8.25	36–37	7.75
30–31	8.00	34–35	7.50
27–29	7.75	32–33	7.40
24–26	7.50	30–31	7.30
21–23	7.40	29	7.20
19–20	7.30	27–28	7.10
17–18	7.20	25–26	7.00
15–16	7.10	23–24	6.00
13–14	7.00	22	4.00
11–12	6.00	20–21	2.00
9–10	5.00	< 20	0.00
8	4.00		
6–7	3.00		
5	2.00		
3–4	1.00		
< 3	0.00		

MEN 40–44

AEROBIC FITNESS

1.5-Mile Run Time (min.)	Bike Test (VO₂)	Component Points
≤ 10:24	≥ 50	50.00
10:25–10:36	49	47.50
10:37–10:54	48	45.00
10:55–11:24	46–47	43.50
11:25–11:54	44–45	42.00
11:55–12:30	42–43	40.50
12:31–13:12	40–41	39.00
13:13–13:36	39	37.50
13:37–14:24	37–38	36.00
14:25–15:18	35–36	34.00
15:19–15:48	34	32.00
15:49–16:24	33	30.00
16:25–16:54	32	27.00
16:55–17:36	31	24.00
17:37–18:12	30	21.00
18:13–18:54	29	18.00
18:55–19:42	28	15.00
19:43–20:36	27	12.00
20:37–21:30	26	9.00
21:31–22:30	25	6.00
22:31–23:36	24	3.00
> 23:36	< 24	0.00

BODY COMPOSITION

Abdominal Circumference (inches)	Component Points
< 32.50	30.00
32.50	28.75
33.00	27.50
33.50	26.25
34.00	25.00
34.50	23.75
35.00	22.50
35.50	22.35
36.00	22.20
36.50	22.05
37.00	21.90
37.50	21.75
38.00	21.60
38.50	21.45
39.00	21.30
39.50	21.25
40.00	21.00
40.50	18.00
41.00	15.00
41.50	12.00
42.00	9.00
42.50	6.00
43.00	3.00
> 43.00	0.00

MUSCLE FITNESS

1 minute Push-up (# reps)	Component Points	1 minute Crunch (# reps)	Component Points
≥ 40	10.00	≥ 47	10.00
39	9.75	45–46	9.50
38	9.50	43–44	9.00
37	9.25	41–42	8.75
36	9.00	39–40	8.50
33–35	8.75	37–38	8.25
31–32	8.50	35–36	8.00
28–30	8.25	33–34	7.75
26–27	8.00	31–32	7.50
23–25	7.75	29–30	7.40
21–22	7.50	27–28	7.30
18–20	7.40	26	7.20
16–17	7.30	24–25	7.10
14–15	7.20	22–23	7.00
12–13	7.10	20–21	6.00
10–11	7.00	19	4.00
8–9	6.00	17–18	2.00
7	5.00	< 17	0.00
6	4.00		
4–5	3.00		
3	2.00		
1–2	1.00		
< 1	0.00		

MEN 45–49

AEROBIC FITNESS

1.5-Mile Run Time (min.)	Bike Test (VO₂)	Component Points
≤ 10:24	≥ 50	50.00
10:25–10:36	49	47.50
10:37–10:54	48	45.00
10:55–11:24	46–47	43.50
11:25–11:54	44–45	42.00
11:55–12:30	42–43	40.50
12:31–13:12	40–41	39.00
13:13–13:36	39	37.50
13:37–14:24	37–38	36.00
14:25–15:18	35–36	34.00
15:19–15:48	34	32.00
15:49–16:24	33	30.00
16:25–16:54	32	27.00
16:55–17:36	31	24.00
17:37–18:12	30	21.00
18:13–18:54	29	18.00
18:55–19:42	28	15.00
19:43–20:36	27	12.00
20:37–21:30	26	9.00
21:31–22:30	25	6.00
22:31–23:36	24	3.00
> 23:36	< 24	0.00

BODY COMPOSITION

Abdominal Circumference (inches)	Component Points
< 32.50	30.00
32.50	28.75
33.00	27.50
33.50	26.25
34.00	25.00
34.50	23.75
35.00	22.50
35.50	22.35
36.00	22.20
36.50	22.05
37.00	21.90
37.50	21.75
38.00	21.60
38.50	21.45
39.00	21.30
39.50	21.25
40.00	21.00
40.50	18.00
41.00	15.00
41.50	12.00
42.00	9.00
42.50	6.00
43.00	3.00
> 43.00	0.00

MUSCLE FITNESS

1 minute Push-up (# reps)	Component Points	1 minute Crunch (# reps)	Component Points
≥ 40	10.00	≥ 45	10.00
39	9.75	43–44	9.50
37–38	9.50	41–42	9.00
35–36	9.25	39–40	8.75
33–34	9.00	37–38	8.50
30–32	8.75	35–36	8.25
27–29	8.50	33–34	8.00
25–26	8.25	31–32	7.75
22–24	8.00	29–30	7.50
20–21	7.75	27–28	7.40
18–19	7.50	25–26	7.30
16–17	7.40	24	7.20
14–15	7.30	22–23	7.10
12–13	7.20	20–21	7.00
10–11	7.10	18–19	6.00
9	7.00	17	4.00
7–8	6.00	15–16	2.00
6	5.00	< 15	0.00
5	4.00		
4	3.00		
2–3	2.00		
1	1.00		
0	0.00		

MEN 50–54

AEROBIC FITNESS

1.5-Mile Run Time (min.)	Bike Test (VO2)	Component Points
≤ 11:06	≥ 47	50.00
11:07–11:24	46	47.50
11:25–11:36	45	45.00
11:37–12:12	43–44	43.50
12:13–12:54	41–42	42.00
12:55–13:36	39–40	40.50
13:37–14:24	37–38	39.00
14:25–15:18	35–36	37.50
15:19–15:48	34	36.00
15:49–16:54	32–33	34.00
16:55–17:36	31	32.00
17:37–18:12	30	30.00
18:13–18:54	29	27.00
18:55–19:42	28	24.00
19:43–20:36	27	21.00
20:37–21:30	26	18.00
21:31–22:30	25	15.00
22:31–23:36	24	12.00
23:37–24:48	23	9.00
24:49–26:06	22	6.00
26:07–27:36	21	3.00
> 27:36	< 21	0.00

BODY COMPOSITION

Abdominal Circumference (inches)	Component Points
< 32.50	30.00
32.50	28.75
33.00	27.50
33.50	26.25
34.00	25.00
34.50	23.75
35.00	22.50
35.50	22.35
36.00	22.20
36.50	22.05
37.00	21.90
37.50	21.75
38.00	21.60
38.50	21.45
39.00	21.30
39.50	21.25
40.00	21.00
40.50	18.00
41.00	15.00
41.50	12.00
42.00	9.00
42.50	6.00
43.00	3.00
> 43.00	0.00

MUSCLE FITNESS

1 minute Push-up (# reps)	Component Points	1 minute Crunch (# reps)	Component Points
≥ 39	10.00	≥ 43	10.00
37–38	9.75	41–42	9.50
35–36	9.50	39–40	9.00
32–34	9.25	37–38	8.75
30–31	9.00	35–36	8.50
27–29	8.75	32–34	8.25
25–26	8.50	30–31	8.00
22–24	8.25	28–29	7.75
20–21	8.00	26–27	7.50
17–19	7.75	24–25	7.40
15–16	7.50	22–23	7.30
13–14	7.40	21	7.20
12	7.30	19–20	7.10
10–11	7.20	17–18	7.00
9	7.10	15–16	6.00
7–8	7.00	14	4.00
6	6.00	12–13	2.00
5	5.00	< 12	0.00
4	4.00		
3	3.00		
2	2.00		
1	1.00		
0	0.00		

MEN 55+

AEROBIC FITNESS

1.5-Mile Run Time (min.)	Bike Test (VO2)	Component Points
≤ 11:06	≥ 47	50.00
11:07–11:24	46	47.50
11:25–11:36	45	45.00
11:37–12:12	43–44	43.50
12:13–12:54	41–42	42.00
12:55–13:36	39–40	40.50
13:37–14:24	37–38	39.00
14:25–15:18	35–36	37.50
15:19–15:48	34	36.00
15:49–16:54	32–33	34.00
16:55–17:36	31	32.00
17:37–18:12	30	30.00
18:13–18:54	29	27.00
18:55–19:42	28	24.00
19:43–20:36	27	21.00
20:37–21:30	26	18.00
21:31–22:30	25	15.00
22:31–23:36	24	12.00
23:37–24:48	23	9.00
24:49–26:06	22	6.00
26:07–27:36	21	3.00
> 27:36	< 21	0.00

BODY COMPOSITION

Abdominal Circumference (inches)	Component Points
< 32.50	30.00
32.50	28.75
33.00	27.50
33.50	26.25
34.00	25.00
34.50	23.75
35.00	22.50
35.50	22.35
36.00	22.20
36.50	22.05
37.00	21.90
37.50	21.75
38.00	21.60
38.50	21.45
39.00	21.30
39.50	21.25
40.00	21.00
40.50	18.00
41.00	15.00
41.50	12.00
42.00	9.00
42.50	6.00
43.00	3.00
> 43.00	0.00

MUSCLE FITNESS

1 minute Push-up (# reps)	Component Points	1 minute Crunch (# reps)	Component Points
≥ 35	10.00	≥ 41	10.00
33–34	9.75	39–40	9.50
31–32	9.50	37–38	9.00
29–30	9.25	34–36	8.75
28	9.00	32–33	8.50
26–27	8.75	30–31	8.25
24–25	8.50	27–29	8.00
21–23	8.25	25–26	7.75
19–20	8.00	23–24	7.50
17–18	7.75	21–22	7.40
15–16	7.50	20	7.30
13–14	7.40	18–19	7.20
11–12	7.30	16–17	7.10
10	7.20	15	7.00
8–9	7.10	13–14	6.00
6–7	7.00	12	4.00
5	6.00	10–11	2.00
4	5.00	< 10	0.00
3	4.00		
2	3.00		
1	2.00		
0	0.00		

WOMEN UNDER 25

AEROBIC FITNESS

1.5-Mile Run Time (min.)	Bike Test (VO₂)	Component Points
≤ 11:06	≥ 47	50.00
11:07–11:36	45–46	47.50
11:37–11:54	44	45.00
11:55–12:30	42–43	43.50
12:31–13:12	40–41	42.00
13:13–14:00	38–39	40.50
14:01–14:54	36–37	39.00
14:55–15:18	35	37.50
15:19–15:48	34	36.00
15:49–16:24	33	34.00
16:25–16:54	32	32.00
16:55–17:36	31	30.00
17:37–18:12	30	27.00
18:13–18:54	29	24.00
18:55–19:42	28	21.00
19:43–20:36	27	18.00
20:37–21:30	26	15.00
21:31–22:30	25	12.00
22:31–23:36	24	9.00
23:37–24:48	23	6.00
24:49–26:06	22	3.00
> 26:06	< 22	0.00

BODY COMPOSITION

Abdominal Circumference (inches)	Component Points
< 29.50	30.00
29.50	28.75
30.00	27.50
30.50	26.25
31.00	25.00
31.50	23.75
32.00	22.50
32.50	22.30
33.00	22.00
33.50	21.80
34.00	21.50
34.50	21.30
35.00	21.00
35.50	18.00
36.00	15.00
36.50	12.00
37.00	9.00
37.50	6.00
38.00	3.00
> 38.00	0.00

MUSCLE FITNESS

1 minute Push-up (# reps)	Component Points	1 minute Crunch (# reps)	Component Points
≥ 42	10.00	≥ 51	10.00
41	9.75	50	9.50
40	9.50	49	9.00
38–39	9.25	46–48	8.75
37	9.00	44–45	8.50
34–36	8.75	42–43	8.25
31–33	8.50	40–41	8.00
27–30	8.25	37–39	7.75
24–26	8.00	35–36	7.50
21–23	7.75	33–34	7.40
18–20	7.50	30–32	7.30
16–17	7.40	28–29	7.20
14–15	7.30	26–27	7.10
12–13	7.20	24–25	7.00
10–11	7.10	22–23	6.00
9	7.00	20–21	4.00
8	6.00	18–19	2.00
7	5.00	< 18	0.00
6	4.00		
5	3.00		
4	2.00		
3	1.00		
< 3	0.00		

WOMEN 25–29

AEROBIC FITNESS

1.5-Mile Run Time (min.)	Bike Test (VO₂)	Component Points
≤ 11:24	≥ 46	50.00
11:25–11:36	45	47.50
11:37–11:54	44	45.00
11:55–12:30	42–43	43.50
12:31–13:12	40–41	42.00
13:13–14:00	38–39	40.50
14:01–14:54	36–37	39.00
14:55–15:18	35	37.50
15:19–15:48	34	36.00
15:49–16:24	33	34.00
16:25–16:54	32	32.00
16:55–17:36	31	30.00
17:37–18:12	30	27.00
18:13–18:54	29	24.00
18:55–19:42	28	21.00
19:43–20:36	27	18.00
20:37–21:30	26	15.00
21:31–22:30	25	12.00
22:31–23:36	24	9.00
23:37–24:48	23	6.00
24:49–26:06	22	3.00
> 26:06	21	0.00

BODY COMPOSITION

Abdominal Circumference (inches)	Component Points
< 29.50	30.00
29.50	28.75
30.00	27.50
30.50	26.25
31.00	25.00
31.50	23.75
32.00	22.50
32.50	22.30
33.00	22.00
33.50	21.80
34.00	21.50
34.50	21.30
35.00	21.00
35.50	18.00
36.00	15.00
36.50	12.00
37.00	9.00
37.50	6.00
38.00	3.00
> 38.00	0.00

MUSCLE FITNESS

1 minute Push-up (# reps)	Component Points	1 minute Crunch (# reps)	Component Points
≥ 41	10.00	≥ 47	10.00
40	9.75	46	9.50
38–39	9.50	45	9.00
36–37	9.25	42–44	8.75
35	9.00	40–41	8.50
31–34	8.75	38–39	8.25
28–30	8.50	36–37	8.00
25–27	8.25	34–35	7.75
22–24	8.00	31–33	7.50
19–21	7.75	29–30	7.40
16–18	7.50	27–28	7.30
14–15	7.40	25–26	7.20
13	7.30	23–24	7.10
11–12	7.20	21–22	7.00
10	7.10	19–20	6.00
8–9	7.00	17–18	4.00
7	6.00	15–16	2.00
6	5.00	< 15	0.00
5	4.00		
4	3.00		
3	2.00		
2	1.00		
< 2	0.00		

WOMEN 30–34

AEROBIC FITNESS

1.5-Mile Run Time (min.)	Bike Test (VO₂)	Component Points
≤ 11:54	≥ 44	50.00
11:55–12:30	42–43	47.50
12:31–12:54	41	45.00
12:55–13:12	40	43.50
13:13–13:36	39	42.00
13:37–14:24	37–38	40.50
14:25–14:54	36	39.00
14:55–15:18	35	37.50
15:19–15:48	34	36.00
15:49–16:24	33	34.00
16:25–16:54	32	32.00
16:55–17:36	31	30.00
17:37–18:12	30	27.00
18:13–18:54	29	24.00
18:55–19:42	28	21.00
19:43–20:36	27	18.00
20:37–21:30	26	15.00
21:31–22:30	25	12.00
22:31–23:36	24	9.00
23:37–24:48	23	6.00
24:49–26:06	22	3.00
> 26:06	< 22	0.00

BODY COMPOSITION

Abdominal Circumference (inches)	Component Points
< 29.50	30.00
29.50	28.75
30.00	27.50
30.50	26.25
31.00	25.00
31.50	23.75
32.00	22.50
32.50	22.30
33.00	22.00
33.50	21.80
34.00	21.50
34.50	21.30
35.00	21.00
35.50	18.00
36.00	15.00
36.50	12.00
37.00	9.00
37.50	6.00
38.00	3.00
> 38.00	0.00

MUSCLE FITNESS

1 minute Push-up (# reps)	Component Points	1 minute Crunch (# reps)	Component Points
≥ 40	10.00	≥ 42	10.00
39	9.75	41	9.50
37–38	9.50	40	9.00
35–36	9.25	37–39	8.75
33–34	9.00	35–36	8.50
29–32	8.75	33–34	8.25
26–28	8.50	31–32	8.00
23–25	8.25	29–30	7.75
20–22	8.00	27–28	7.50
17–19	7.75	25–26	7.40
14–16	7.50	23–24	7.30
12–13	7.40	22	7.20
11	7.30	20–21	7.10
10	7.20	18–19	7.00
9	7.10	16–17	6.00
7–8	7.00	13–15	4.00
6	6.00	11–12	2.00
5	5.00	< 11	0.00
4	4.00		
3	3.00		
2	2.00		
1	1.00		
0	0.00		

WOMEN 35–39

AEROBIC FITNESS

1.5-Mile Run Time (min.)	Bike Test (VO₂)	Component Points
≤ 11:54	≥ 44	50.00
11:55–12:30	42–43	47.50
12:31–12:54	41	45.00
12:55–13:12	40	43.50
13:13–13:36	39	42.00
13:37–14:24	37–38	40.50
14:25–14:54	36	39.00
14:55–15:18	35	37.50
15:19–15:48	34	36.00
15:49–16:24	33	34.00
16:25–16:54	32	32.00
16:55–17:36	31	30.00
17:37–18:12	30	27.00
18:13–18:54	29	24.00
18:55–19:42	28	21.00
19:43–20:36	27	18.00
20:37–21:30	26	15.00
21:31–22:30	25	12.00
22:31–23:36	24	9.00
23:37–24:48	23	6.00
24:49–26:06	22	3.00
> 26:06	< 22	0.00

BODY COMPOSITION

Abdominal Circumference (inches)	Component Points
< 29.50	30.00
29.50	28.75
30.00	27.50
30.50	26.25
31.00	25.00
31.50	23.75
32.00	22.50
32.50	22.30
33.00	22.00
33.50	21.80
34.00	21.50
34.50	21.30
35.00	21.00
35.50	18.00
36.00	15.00
36.50	12.00
37.00	9.00
37.50	6.00
38.00	3.00
> 38.00	0.00

MUSCLE FITNESS

1 minute Push-up (# reps)	Component Points	1 minute Crunch (# reps)	Component Points
≥ 30	10.00	≥ 40	10.00
29	9.75	38–39	9.50
28	9.50	37	9.00
27	9.25	35–36	8.75
26	9.00	33–34	8.50
23–25	8.75	31–32	8.25
21–22	8.50	29–30	8.00
19–20	8.25	27–28	7.75
17–18	8.00	25–26	7.50
15–16	7.75	23–24	7.40
13–14	7.50	21–22	7.30
11–12	7.40	20	7.20
10	7.30	18–19	7.10
9	7.20	16–17	7.00
8	7.10	14–15	6.00
6–7	7.00	12–13	4.00
4–5	6.00	9–11	2.00
3	4.00	< 9	0.00
1–2	2.00		
< 1	0.00		

WOMEN 40–44

AEROBIC FITNESS

1.5-Mile Run Time (min.)	Bike Test (VO₂)	Component Points
≤ 12:30	≥ 42	50.00
12:31–12:54	41	47.50
12:55–13:12	40	45.00
13:13–14:00	38–39	43.50
14:01–14:54	36–37	42.00
14:55–15:48	34–35	40.50
15:49–16:24	33	39.00
16:25–16:54	32	37.50
16:55–17:36	31	36.00
17:37–18:12	30	34.00
18:13–18:54	29	32.00
18:55–19:42	28	30.00
19:43–20:36	27	27.00
20:37–21:30	26	24.00
21:31–22:30	25	21.00
22:31–23:36	24	18.00
23:37–24:48	23	15.00
24:49–26:06	22	12.00
26:07–27:36	21	9.00
27:37–29:18	20	6.00
29:19–31:12	19	3.00
> 31:12	< 19	0.00

BODY COMPOSITION

Abdominal Circumference (inches)	Component Points
< 29.50	30.00
29.50	28.75
30.00	27.50
30.50	26.25
31.00	25.00
31.50	23.75
32.00	22.50
32.50	22.30
33.00	22.00
33.50	21.80
34.00	21.50
34.50	21.30
35.00	21.00
35.50	18.00
36.00	15.00
36.50	12.00
37.00	9.00
37.50	6.00
38.00	3.00
> 38.00	0.00

MUSCLE FITNESS

1 minute Push-up (# reps)	Component Points	1 minute Crunch (# reps)	Component Points
≥ 20	10.00	≥ 38	10.00
19	9.50	36–37	9.50
18	9.00	34–35	9.00
16–17	8.75	32–33	8.75
15	8.50	30–31	8.50
14	8.25	28–29	8.25
13	8.00	26–27	8.00
12	7.75	24–25	7.75
11	7.50	22–23	7.50
9–10	7.40	20–21	7.40
8	7.30	18–19	7.30
7	7.20	17	7.20
6	7.10	15–16	7.10
5	7.00	13–14	7.00
3–4	6.00	11–12	6.00
2	4.00	9–10	4.00
1	2.00	7–8	2.00
0	0.00	< 7	0.00

WOMEN 45–49

AEROBIC FITNESS

1.5-Mile Run Time (min.)	Bike Test (VO2)	Component Points
≤ 12:30	≥ 42	50.00
12:31–12:54	41	47.50
12:55–13:12	40	45.00
13:13–14:00	38–39	43.50
14:01–14:54	36–37	42.00
14:55–15:48	34–35	40.50
15:49–16:24	33	39.00
16:25–16:54	32	37.50
16:55–17:36	31	36.00
17:37–18:12	30	34.00
18:13–18:54	29	32.00
18:55–19:42	28	30.00
19:43–20:36	27	27.00
20:37–21:30	26	24.00
21:31–22:30	25	21.00
22:31–23:36	24	18.00
23:37–24:48	23	15.00
24:49–26:06	22	12.00
26:07–27:36	21	9.00
27:37–29:18	20	6.00
29:19–31:12	19	3.00
> 31:12	< 19	0.00

BODY COMPOSITION

Abdominal Circumference (inches)	Component Points
< 29.50	30.00
29.50	28.75
30.00	27.50
30.50	26.25
31.00	25.00
31.50	23.75
32.00	22.50
32.50	22.30
33.00	22.00
33.50	21.80
34.00	21.50
34.50	21.30
35.00	21.00
35.50	18.00
36.00	15.00
36.50	12.00
37.00	9.00
37.50	6.00
38.00	3.00
> 38.00	0.00

MUSCLE FITNESS

1 minute Push-up (# reps)	Component Points	1 minute Crunch (# reps)	Component Points
≥ 18	10.00	≥ 34	10.00
17	9.50	33	9.50
16	9.00	32	9.00
14–15	8.75	30–31	8.75
13	8.50	28–29	8.50
12	8.25	26–27	8.25
11	8.00	24–25	8.00
10	7.75	22–23	7.75
9	7.50	20–21	7.50
8	7.40	18–19	7.40
7	7.30	16–17	7.30
6	7.20	14–15	7.20
5	7.10	12–13	7.10
4	7.00	10–11	7.00
3	6.00	8–9	6.00
2	4.00	7	4.00
1	2.00	6	2.00
0	0.00	< 6	0.00

WOMEN 50–54

AEROBIC FITNESS

BODY COMPOSITION

1.5-Mile Run Time (min.)	Bike Test (VO2)	Component Points	Abdominal Circumference (inches)	Component Points
≤ 14:24	≥ 37	50.00	< 29.50	30.00
14:25–14:54	36	47.50	29.50	28.75
14:55–15:18	35	45.00	30.00	27.50
15:19–16:24	33–34	43.50	30.50	26.25
16:25–16:54	32	42.00	31.00	25.00
16:55–17:36	31	40.50	31.50	23.75
17:37–18:12	30	39.00	32.00	22.50
18:13–18:54	29	37.50	32.50	22.30
18:55–19:42	28	36.00	33.00	22.00
19:43–20:36	27	34.00	33.50	21.80
20:37–21:30	26	32.00	34.00	21.50
21:31–22:30	25	30.00	34.50	21.30
22:31–23:36	24	27.00	35.00	21.00
23:37–24:48	23	24.00	35.50	18.00
24:49–26:06	22	21.00	36.00	15.00
26:07–27:36	21	18.00	36.50	12.00
27:37–29:18	20	15.00	37.00	9.00
29:19–31:12	19	12.00	37.50	6.00
31:13–33:18	18	9.00	38.00	3.00
33:19–35:48	17	6.00	> 38.00	0.00
35:49–38:36	16	3.00		
> 38:36	< 16	0.00		

MUSCLE FITNESS

1 minute Push-up (# reps)	Component Points	1 minute Crunch (# reps)	Component Points
≥ 16	10.00	≥ 30	10.00
15	9.50	29	9.00
14	9.00	27–28	8.75
13	8.75	25–26	8.50
12	8.50	23–24	8.25
11	8.25	21–22	8.00
10	8.00	19–20	7.75
9	7.75	17–18	7.50
8	7.50	15–16	7.40
7	7.40	13–14	7.30
6	7.30	11–12	7.20
5	7.20	9–10	7.10
4	7.10	7–8	7.00
3	7.00	5–6	6.00
2	6.00	3–4	4.00
1	3.00	1–2	2.00
< 1	0.00	< 1	0.00

WOMEN 55+

AEROBIC FITNESS

1.5-Mile Run Time (min.)	Bike Test (VO2)	Component Points
≤ 14:24	≥ 37	50.00
14:25–14:54	36	47.50
14:55–15:18	35	45.00
15:19–16:24	33–34	43.50
16:25–16:54	32	42.00
16:55–17:36	31	40.50
17:37–18:12	30	39.00
18:13–18:54	29	37.50
18:55–19:42	28	36.00
19:43–20:36	27	34.00
20:37–21:30	26	32.00
21:31–22:30	25	30.00
22:31–23:36	24	27.00
23:37–24:48	23	24.00
24:49–26:06	22	21.00
26:07–27:36	21	18.00
27:37–29:18	20	15.00
29:19–31:12	19	12.00
31:13–33:18	18	9.00
33:19–35:48	17	6.00
35:49–38:36	16	3.00
> 38:36	< 16	0.00

BODY COMPOSITION

Abdominal Circumference (inches)	Component Points
< 29.50	30.00
29.50	28.75
30.00	27.50
30.50	26.25
31.00	25.00
31.50	23.75
32.00	22.50
32.50	22.30
33.00	22.00
33.50	21.80
34.00	21.50
34.50	21.30
35.00	21.00
35.50	18.00
36.00	15.00
36.50	12.00
37.00	9.00
37.50	6.00
38.00	3.00
> 38.00	0.00

MUSCLE FITNESS

1 minute Push-up (# reps)	Component Points	1 minute Crunch (# reps)	Component Points
≥ 14	10.00	≥ 27	10.00
13	9.50	26	9.50
12	9.00	25	9.00
10–11	8.50	23–24	8.75
9	8.00	21–22	8.50
7–8	7.50	19–20	8.25
6	7.40	18	8.00
5	7.30	16–17	7.75
4	7.20	14–15	7.50
3	7.10	12–13	7.40
2	7.00	10–11	7.30
1	6.00	8–9	7.20
< 1	0.00	6–7	7.10
		4–5	7.00
		3	6.00
		2	4.00
		1	2.00
		< 1	0.00

Index

Notes

Notes

Notes

Notes

Notes

Notes

Notes

STACKPOLE BOOKS

Military Professional Reference Library

Air Force Officer's Guide
Airman's Guide
Armed Forces Guide to Personal Financial Planning
Army Dictionary and Desk Reference
Army Officer's Guide
Career Progression Guide
Combat Leader's Field Guide
Combat Service Support Guide
Enlisted Soldier's Guide
Guide to Effective Military Writing
Guide to Military Installations
Guide to Military Operations Other Than War
Job Search: Marketing Your Military Experience
Military Money Guide
NCO Guide
Reservist's Money Guide
Servicemember's Legal Guide
Servicemember's Guide to a College Degree
Soldier's Study Guide
Today's Military Wife
Veteran's Guide to Benefits
Virtual Combat

Professional Reading Library

Fighting for the Future: Will America Triumph?
by Ralph Peters

Roots of Strategy, Books 1, 2, 3, and 4

Guardians of the Republic: History of the NCO
by Ernest F. Fisher

Vietnam Order of Battle
by Shelby L. Stanton

No Gun Ri
by Robert L. Bateman